MW01461357

Museum Teen Programs How-To Kit

Edited by Simona Zappas, Nisa Mackie,
and Dr. Yolanda J. Majors

With contributions by
Michelle Antonisse, Lauren Bína, Dr. Kendall
Crabbe, Jorge Espinosa, Araya Henry, Jo Higgins,
Lyra Hill, Marie Hofer, Amanda Hunt, Melissa
Katzin, Andreas Laszlo Konrath, Savannah Knoop,
Jeremy Kreusch, Stephen Kwok, Nisa Mackie,
Devin Malone, Mollie McKinley, Grace Needlman,
Nancy Nowacek, Sean J. Patrick Carney, Nohemi
Rodriguez, and Alex Chung Vargo

Walker Art Center, Minneapolis

How-To Kit

Museum Teen Programs How-To Kit

A

6–9
  A.1. *Foreword* by Mary Ceruti
10–13
  A.2. *Acknowledgments* by Simona Zappas
14–29
  A.3. *Introduction* by Simona Zappas, Nisa Mackie, Dr. Yolanda J. Majors, Dr. Kendall Crabbe & Amanda Hunt

1

Containers
1.1. Essays, Reflections & Advice
36–51
  1.1.1. *Walker Art Center Teen Arts Council Founding, History, and Timeline* by Simona Zappas
52–88
  1.1.2. *Teen Programs Fundamentals Table*
89–102
  1.1.3. *It's Not Sexy, but It's Crazy Cool: Age Diversity* by Nancy Nowacek
103–106
  1.1.4. *By Teens, for Tweens* by Marie Hofer
107–115
  1.1.5. *For Teens, by Teens: Public Event Planning* by Araya Henry
121–133
  1.1.6. *Planning for a Year of Programming* by Simona Zappas
134–156
  1.1.7. *Consensus + Conflict: A Reflective Facilitation Guide* by Grace Needlman

1.2. Resources
162–171
  1.2.1.1.–1.2.1.4. *Walker Art Center Teen Arts Council (WACTAC) 2022–2023 Onboarding Materials* by Simona Zappas
172–176
  1.2.2. *Snack Curators* by Jorge Espinosa
181–184
  1.2.3. *Breaking the Grid* by Jorge Espinosa
185–192
  1.2.4. *Respect Is… Activity* by Simona Zappas
193–201
  1.2.5. *Walker Art Center Teen Arts Council (WACTAC) "Go-Around Questions"* by Simona Zappas
202–207
  1.2.6. *Building Connection through Creative Icebreakers* by Nohemi Rodriguez
208–216
  1.2.7. *Two Activities for Taking Up Space* by Grace Needlman

2

Practice
2.1. Essays, Reflections & Advice
226–234
  2.1.1. *Museums as Youth Opportunity Spaces* by Dr. Yolanda J. Majors
235–243
  2.1.2. *Talk Time with Teens* by Michelle Antonisse
244–255
  2.1.3. *From Bellini to Basquiat: Equitable Education Practices in Encyclopedic Museums* by Melissa Katzin
256–288
  2.1.4. *Performer, Producer, Conduit: Artist Educators in Conversation* by Alex Chung Vargo & Devin Malone

Contents

with Sean J. Patrick Carney, Savannah Knoop, Andreas Laszlo Konrath, Stephen Kwok, and Mollie McKinley

2.2. Resources
290–307
2.2.1. *Gallery Conversation Lesson Plans* by Lauren Bína
308–311
2.2.2. *Art Chopped* by Sean J. Patrick Carney
312–314
2.2.3. *Sensorium Workshop* by Savannah Knoop
315–322
2.2.4. *Studio Systems* by Andreas Laszlo Konrath
323–326
2.2.5. *Bodies and Nature, Marble and Fruit Studio Prompt* by Mollie McKinley
327–329
2.2.6. *An Incomplete Dictionary of Art in Action* by Stephen Kwok
330–336
2.2.7. *Evaluation and Virtual Facilitation Tips Grab Bag* by Simona Zappas

3

Big Feelings
3.1. Essays, Reflections & Advice
346–367
3.1.1. *Positionality and Pedagogy* by Dr. Kendall Crabbe & Simona Zappas
368–381
3.1.2. *The Potential Impact of Walker Teen Programs for Youth* by Dr. Yolanda J. Majors
382–395
3.1.3. *Setting Boundaries and Making Pivots* by Simona Zappas
396–410
3.1.4. *Heartbreakers & Troublemakers: How to Navigate, Embrace, and Ultimately Survive Disruption* by Jo Higgins

411–428
3.1.5. *Museum as Home Base: Creating a Stable Foundation for Youth Changemakers* by Nisa Mackie & Simona Zappas
429–433
3.1.6.1. *Ritual within Teen Creative Agency: A Brief Overview* by Lyra Hill
434–441
3.1.6.2. *Rituals and Belonging, Values, and Care: Some Thoughts on Agency and Collaboration* by Jeremy Kreusch
442–448
3.1.7. *Strategies for Engaging Colleagues* by Amanda Hunt & Simona Zappas

3.2. Resources
450–456
3.2.1. *The WACTAC Guide to Tough Conversations* by Simona Zappas
461–487
3.2.2. *Intergenerational Tools for Constructive Conversation* by Nancy Nowacek

B

489
B.1. Walker Art Center Board of Trustees
490–495
B.2. Walker Art Center Staff, February 2023
496
B.3. Colophon

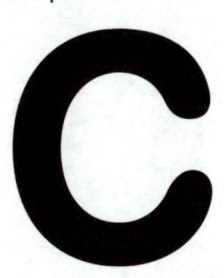

C

497–510
C.1. Photo Essay Captions

Contents

Foreword

Mary Ceruti
Executive Director, Walker Art Center

In 1999 the Walker Art Center's teen programs staff put out a ten-page booklet titled *A Teen Programs How-To Kit: Some Directions, Suggestions, Examples, and Stories to Get You Started. Some Assembly Required*. The booklet shared the lessons learned from the first years of the Walker Art Center Teen Arts Council. Now, almost twenty-five years later, we are excited to share a new Museum Teen Programs How-To Kit that celebrates the work of museums, facilitators, and youth from across the country and aims to deepen the conversation and practices that support youth in carving out spaces for themselves within arts institutions that will hopefully stick with them for life.

If you're reading this publication, you likely need little convincing of the power of museum teen programs, but this quote from a Walker Teen Arts Council (WACTAC) participant in the 1999 *How-To Kit* sums it up beautifully:

> What I've taken from it is a new perspective as far as things that are going on, like some of the artists I'd never heard of before until I came here. I think it's a really cool place, and my mind, as far as creativity, has expanded since I've been here. And in such a short time, I'm a little more open to things I haven't seen before, and I think the Walker has shown that to me.[1]

The work done in teen programs today elicits the same sort of reaction from participants but has a renewed sense of urgency in the heightened political and social stratifications and complexities young people must traverse daily. Open-mindedness and creativity can be essential skills for navigating the challenges our world brings us. These are the exact skills used by museum teen programs staff to facilitate youth in building their own. The 1999 *How-To Kit* also shares: "Engage people who can work well with teenagers and have good negotiating and organizational skills. Know how to identify such people."[2] What this publication aims to do is to take this instruction a step further by helping peers identify their approaches to look for and offer recognition to their processes and thoughts with the intention of instilling that sense of open-mindedness and creativity for more young people.

It's hard not to consider that some of these young people may pursue museum work in their futures. That they will come equipped with thoughtful perspectives ready to be lent to the challenges of the day. This vision creates a strong sense of optimism for the future of museums and their ability to welcome audiences and foster their creativity—all of which I look forward to reading in the next Museum Teen Programs How-To Kit.

    Thank you,
    Mary Ceruti

1. Christi Atkinson, *A Teen Programs How-To Kit: Some Directions, Suggestions, Examples, and Stories to Get You Started. Some Assembly Required* (Minneapolis: Walker Art Center, 1999), 5.
2. Atkinson, *Teen Programs How-To Kit*, 6.

Acknowledgements

Simona Zappas

Thank you, my coauthors, Nisa Mackie and Dr. Yolanda J. Majors. Nisa, you have been an incredible mentor and friend through the years. Yolanda, you brought so much thought to the Walker Art Center and shared it beautifully. An additional thank-you to Dr. Majors's team at the Hurston Institute of Learning and Development (HILD) for their observations and contributions. A round of applause to Dr. Kendall Crabbe, whose expertise in Youth Participatory Action Research, art education, and teen programs in art museums helped shape this book. Thank you to Amanda Hunt, Head of Public Engagement, Learning, and Impact (PELI), who picked it up, polished it off, and made it feel like new when joining the Walker team and bringing this project across the finish line.

Many thanks to incredible teachers Lauren Bína and Annie Flynn, who cofacilitated the Walker Art Center Teen Arts Council (WACTAC) over the years. Thank you to the Walker's PELI department team members over the past five years. You each left an imprint on this publication in its many iterations over the years. Many thanks to the broader community and incredible staff at the Walker, and special thanks to those who gifted their time to visit and collaborate with WACTAC cohorts. A special thank-you to the Walker design team members, Kate Arford and Jake Yuzna, for their work in getting this book made. Thanks to the designer, Ian Babineau, for making it gorgeous. Thank you to the Walker leadership, especially Mary Ceruti and Henriette Huldisch, for their staunch support of Walker Teen Programs. Thank you to the Walker's spectacular development and finance teams, who stewarded the resources that ensured this project could be completed.

Profound thanks to the Peer Learning Community on Museum Teen Programs members who met over 2021; I am so grateful for the friendship, support, and ideation that came from sharing about our weird jobs. Thank you to Eli Burke, Adrianna Benavides, Grace Needlman, Jorge Espinosa, Rayna Mathis, Michelle Antonisse, Melissa Katzin, Marie Hofer, Alex Chung Vargo, Araya Henry, Nohemi Rodriguez, Devin Malone, and Jo Higgins. A huge thank-you to the contributors to this publication—you have shown immense patience with all my emails. Thanks to the many artists who have contributed to Walker Teen Programs and inspired young people (and staff!), with special recognition to Nancy Nowacek, Bereket Weddall, and Jordan Weber.

With support from our partners, the Walker Art Center's teen programs have helped create space to bring teen voices to the museum since 1994. The Walker remains a leader in innovative youth programming and prioritizes creating meaningful and relevant arts experiences for teens today. Most recently, teen programs have received generous support from Walker trustee Ann Hatch, who has been a champion of arts learning for teens; the Hearst Foundations, a longtime supporter of the Walker and advocate of the importance of arts within society; and the Institute of Museum and Library Services (IMLS), whose Museums for America grants help transform community engagement and education programs across the country and made this publication possible.

A big thank-you to the teen program participants across all the programs featured in this publication. This publication may be by and for educators, but you are the muses.

On a personal note, I would like to thank my family—my parents, Nick and Patricia, for supporting me from teen program participant to leader (and beyond); my sisters, Alivia and Marika, and their partners, Will and Trevor; my niece, Ione; my aunts, Lorie, Karen, and Maria; and in memory of my grandparents Mack and Geri. Thank you to my dearest friends Martha, Som, Anna Memphis, and Matt. Finally, thank you to my incredible partner,

Nathan; you scaffolded this.

    XO,
    Simona Zappas

Introduction

Simona Zappas, Nisa Mackie, Dr. Yolanda J. Majors, Dr. Kendall Crabbe, Amanda Hunt

This publication is for the practitioners, educators, facilitators, and administrative staff contributing to museum teen programs. In teen programs the phrases "by teens for teens," "teen-led," and "teen voice" are everywhere. All these phrases point to the overall aim of the work—supporting teens to take up space within arts institutions; however, these phrases cover up the role, work, and layered skill sets of the adult practitioners who support youth voices and leadership in art museums. Furthermore, museum teen programs—including both educators and youth—must be understood in the current sociopolitical context. In the wake of the murders of George Floyd, Breonna Taylor, Tony McDade, and countless others, with the COVID-19 pandemic amplifying existing inequities, museums have been "called on to establish antiracist practices, take action in support of the Black Lives Matter movement, and authentically engage audiences representative of their diverse communities."[1]

According to a 2021 report by the Ford Foundation, less than 20 percent of leadership positions in art museums are held by people of color and underrepresented populations.[2] In stark contrast, most museum teen programs actively recruit and serve a racially, ethnically, socioeconomically, and educationally diverse cohort of teens.[3] A study on teen programs in art museums, *Room to Rise*, reports that "more than 50 percent of Whitney respondents

1. Priya Frank and Theresa Sotto, "Preface," in *From Small Wins to Sweeping Change: Working Together to Foster Equity, Inclusion, and Antiracism in Museums* (Lanham, MD: American Alliance of Museums, 2022), xi.
2. Kendall Crabbe, "Intergenerational Counternarratives of Creative Agency: Reimagining Inclusive Practices through Youth Participatory Action Research" (PhD diss., University of Arizona, 2022), ProQuest (19891), 16.
3. Danielle Linzer and Mary Ellen Munley, *Room to Rise: The Lasting Impact of Intensive Teen Programs in Art Museums* (New York: Whitney Museum of American Art, 2015), 29.

and more than 79 percent of MOCA respondents identified as nonwhite, with many coming from environments where they had little to no access to cultural institutions like museums prior to their participation."[4] Scores of teen programs target young people—and youth of color, specifically—as a way to grow and diversify art museum attendance. "Yet few studies recognize the inherent asymmetry of the power dynamics in museums between white and BIPOC communities, or between adults and youth. To decolonize museum education and teen programs in particular, we must challenge the inclusivity discourse and decenter whiteness and adultism in museum education."[5]

As museums reckon with their problematic histories and challenging present, Priya Frank and Theresa Sotto assert that museums were not built to be inclusive, "yet, many museums' missions and the people who bring these missions to life have egalitarian aims."[6] With this tension, what can museum teen programmers do to address racist practices in art museums? How can we move beyond Diversity, Equity, and Inclusion (DEAI) initiatives to radically reimagine our collective work with young people in art museums?

This publication aims to support and name the praxis of museum teen programs practitioners, which manages to be both broad and specific. It also serves as a reflective space to engage in critical dialogue and consciousness-raising in teen-centric programs. In this publication, you will find instructional writing and narratives from practitioners working in museums ranging in size, location, and collecting practices. The writing offers perspectives around shared challenges that are nuanced by institutions,

---

4. Linzer and Munley, *Room to Rise*, 29.
5. Kendall Crabbe, Oona Husok, and Amelia M. Kraehe, "Youth Creative Agency toward Art Museum Futurity: Re-imagining Inclusive Practices through Youth Participatory Action Research," *Journal of Museum Education* 47, no. 1 (2022): 59–70.
6. Frank and Sotto, *From Small Wins*, xi.

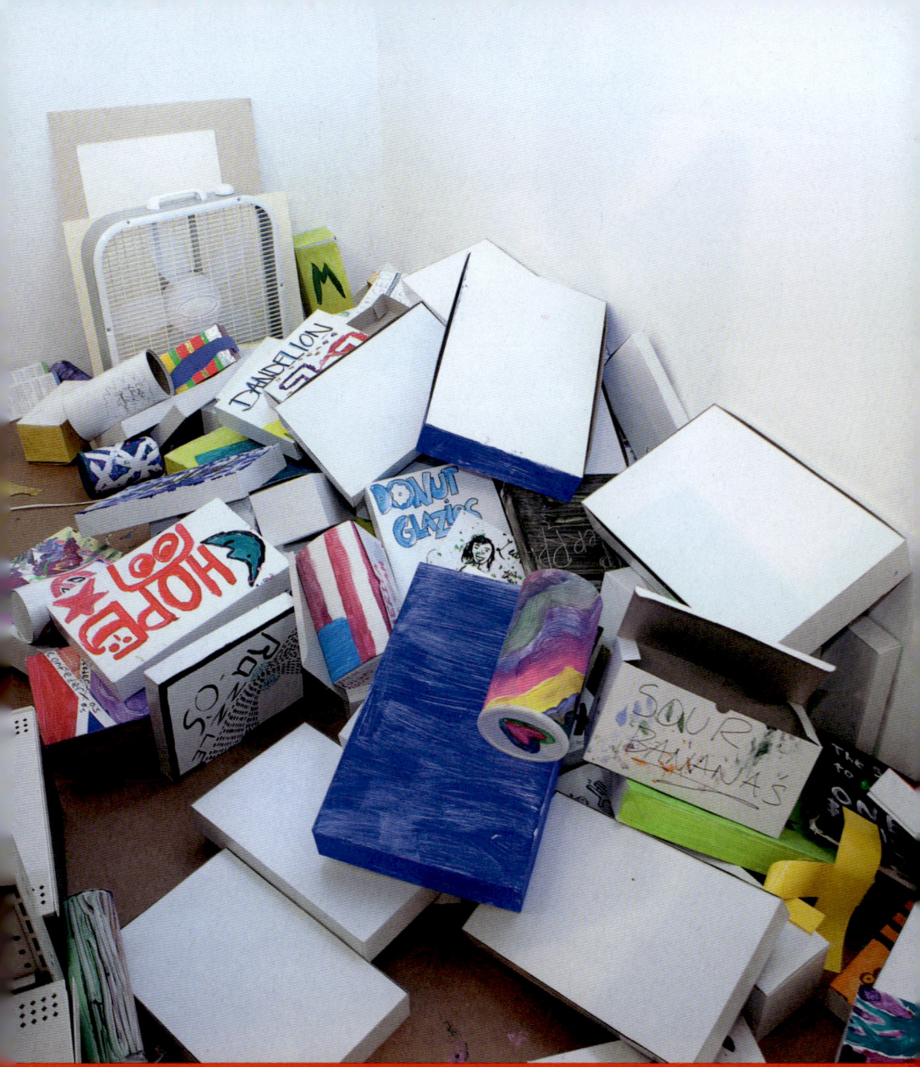
DANDELION
DONUT
HOPE
SOUR
BANANAS

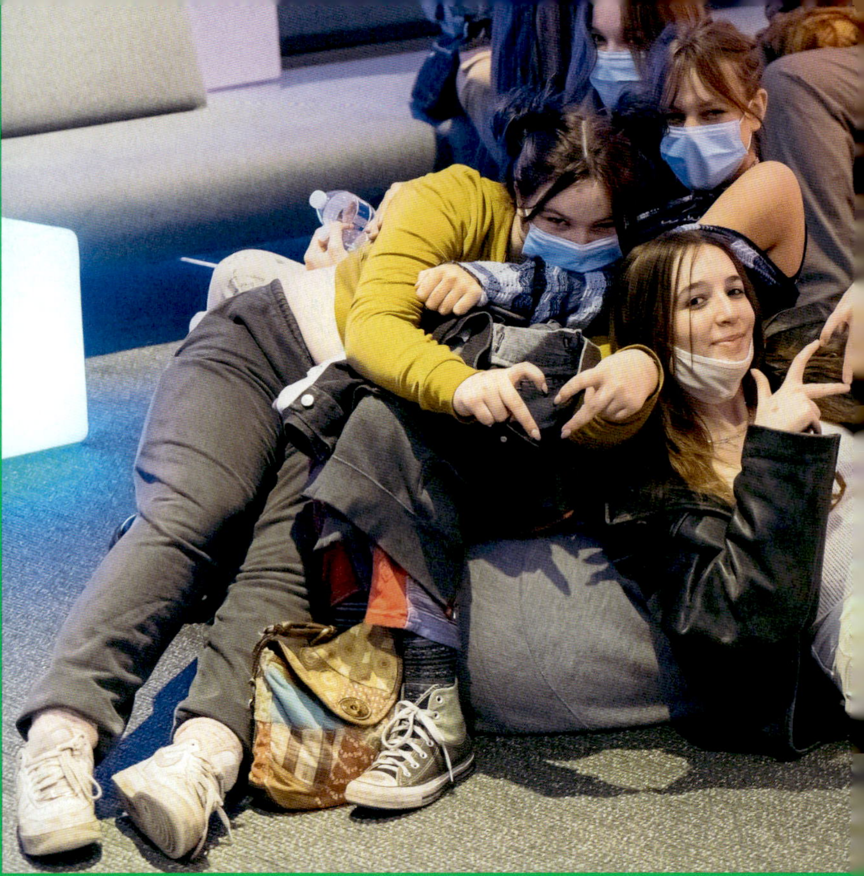

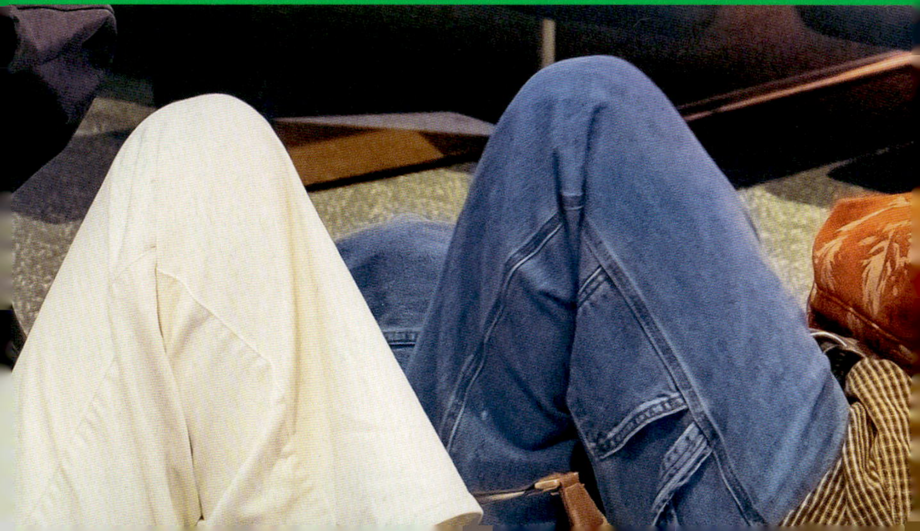

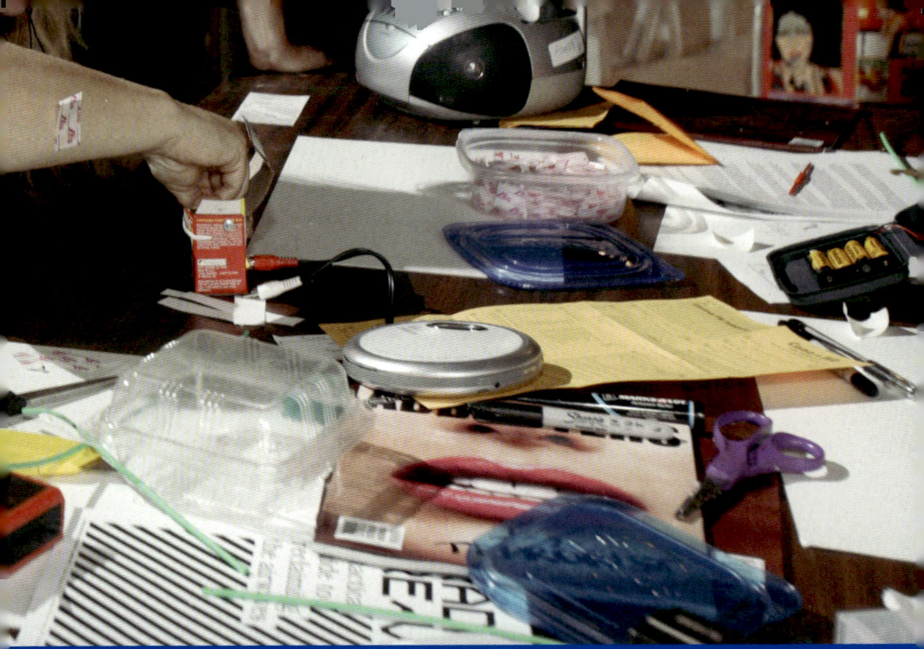

youth, and practitioners themselves. The publication offers resources like lesson formats, planning documents, and activities that can be applied immediately, and reflective writing that can serve as a companion while navigating the many big feelings and challenges that intersect this important work. The publication is divided into three sections:

> Containers
> Writing and tools on the containers that define programming. This section covers plans, payment, paperwork, and what makes museum teen programs unique.
>
> Practice
> An exploration of what teens gain from museum teen programs, from the practitioners' perspectives. This section examines how we facilitate teen programs, use tools, leverage and apply museum collections to enhance learning.
>
> Big Feelings
> A deep dive into the emotional weight, risks, and relationships developed in museum teen programs, analysis of how we engage with colleagues and teens, and frank conversation on how the identities of practitioners and teens play into it all.

We suggest using this publication as a triage resource, a trusted mentor, or perhaps an introduction. Triage usages are for when you need an icebreaker for youth coming in this afternoon—refer to our resource sections for games and thoughtful activities. A trusted mentor, for when you are facing conflict, like when a young person shares sensitive information or teens want to speak out against a policy at your museum—see our reflective writing in the Big Feelings section. Perhaps you do not work at a museum, or you do, but you rarely interact with youth; we still hope this publication can serve as inspiration for how to carve out space for collaborative and critical skill building within institutional spaces.

This is not intended to be a complete resource, nor does it assume that the tools and perspectives offered will apply to all institutions or practitioners. The publication does, however, intend to celebrate the work of museum teen program practitioners. We combine skill sets from language arts classes, creative youth development, youth work, art history, theater, counseling, organizing—and we could keep going—to facilitate the cognitive and emotional growth of diverse teens in the space of the museum, which can be fraught with class, race, and age biases that manifest in both blatant and coded ways. We hope this publication celebrates teen programs while recognizing them as a professional and critical aspect of museum work that can and should inform future practices in museum education.

As museums strive to address issues of race and equity, museum teen programs offer a model of shared decision-making, celebrated identities, and collaborative learning fueled by a drive to ask questions and examine the why behind institutional decisions. Teen programs are a space where new futures for museums are imagined and played out. While we hope this text can serve as inspiration for cultural workers, it is aimed to be an actionable applied resource mainly for museum teen program practitioners. This text is also meant to be a companion to navigate the big feelings involved in museum teen programs—those of the teens, who are part and parcel with adolescence, and those of the facilitators, who, from their own identities, workplace navigations, and care for the teens, are going to have big feelings themselves. For whatever rupture or big feeling comes up, this publication is a tool to feel connected to the network of folks who have seen something (sort of) similar. For educators, by educators, we hope it helps.

This publication follows the inspirational footsteps of *Room to Rise: The Lasting Impact of Intensive Teen Programs in Museums*,[7] a landmark study from the Whitney Museum of American Art, the Walker Art Center, the Museum of Contemporary Art, Los Angeles, and the Contemporary Art Museum, Houston. *Room to Rise* made a powerful argument for how museum teen programs support long-term development, achievement, and connection for teen participants well into adulthood. The years around the publication saw growth in the field of teen programs in museums; however, scholarship, resources, time, and professional development focused specifically on museum teen programs remain limited.[8] This publication is a step to move those resources forward and serves as a tool kit on how to critically reimagine the successes celebrated by *Room to Rise*. Specifically, we hope to engage educators in reflecting on their positionality, curricular choices, and roles within the power dynamics of museum teen programs.

The idea for this publication began sometime in 2019. During her tenure as the Head of Public Engagement, Learning, and Impact at the Walker Art Center, Nisa Mackie saw an opportunity to revamp the curriculum for the Walker Art Center's long-running Teen Arts Council (WACTAC) to empower young people to feel and act on a sense of ownership over institutions, develop an investment in them, and demonstrate an understanding of what it means to navigate them. To ensure that future WACTAC cohorts would feel equipped to speak back to the Walker Art Center about issues that matter to them, Nisa decided to train Walker Teen Programs staff in Youth Participatory Action Research (YPAR). YPAR guides teens in utilizing institutions and community spaces to research their questions and ultimately produce their own findings.[9] Nisa contracted Dr. Yolanda J. Majors of the Hurston Institute for

7. Linzer and Munley, *Room to Rise*.
8. Crabbe, Husok, and Kraehe, "Youth Creative Agency."

Learning and Development to lead the YPAR training. Concurrent to this, in 2018, Simona Zappas stepped into the role of Youth Programs Coordinator at the Walker. In stepping into the role, Simona could find few instructional resources on how to do the work of running a museum teen program, despite the nearly thirty-year existence of this work in the museum field.[10]

The gaps in the field led Simona into a two-year-long extended research of museum teen programs, WACTAC archival history, and overlapping theories and practices to help inform the work. Simona spoke with colleagues around the country to understand their work. In 2019, Simona was introduced to Kendall Crabbe, then a PhD candidate at the University of Arizona in the Department of Art and Visual Culture Education. Kendall and Simona began meeting, brainstorming, and presenting on the intersections of YPAR, art education, and teen council programs in art museums. As researchers and educators, Kendall and Simona connected over their shared finding that museums educators lacked concrete resources and training on how to engage relevant pedagogies, like YPAR, in an art museum setting.

In the same year, Dr. Majors's contract was extended to include an evaluative study of WACTAC and an extended mentorship with Simona. Dr. Majors's evaluation, mentorship, and collaboration with Walker staff led to the production of Arts Platforming Action (APA) research, an original curriculum specifically for museum teen programs that borrows from YPAR in that youth produce an original project; however, it adds elements specific to museum teen programs—namely, the engagement

---

9. Julio Cammarota and Michelle Fine, "Youth Participatory Action Research: A Pedagogy for Transformational Resistance," in *Revolutionizing Education: Youth Participatory Action Research in Motion*, eds. Julio Cammarota and Michelle Fine (New York: Taylor & Francis, 2008), 1–11.
10. Crabbe, Husok, and Kraehe, "Youth Creative Agency."

with works of art to develop and practice critical literacy skills. Following the advent of APA, Walker Teen Programs won a Museums for America grant from the Institute of Museum and Library Services that supported the creation of an eight-month virtual peer-learning community (PLC) for museum teen program practitioners, comprising the following members:

> Grace Needlman (formerly at Museum of Contemporary Art, Chicago)
> Jorge Espinosa (Museum of Contemporary Art, Los Angeles)
> Eli Burke (formerly at Museum of Contemporary Art, Tucson)
> Rayna Mathis (formerly at Seattle Art Museum)
> Michelle Antonisse (Museum of Contemporary Art, Los Angeles)
> Melissa Katzin (High Museum of Art)
> Marie Hofer (Crystal Bridges Museum of American Art)
> Alex Vargo (Dia Art Foundation)
> Araya Henry (Whitney Museum of American Art)
> Adrianna Benavides (Contemporary Arts Museum, Houston)
> Nohemi Rodriguez (Institute of Contemporary Art, Boston)
> Devin Malone (formerly at Dia Art Foundation)
> Jo Higgins (formerly at Museum of Contemporary Art, Sydney)

The PLC participants were invited to contribute to this publication and offer their perspectives, advice, and questions. The contributions in this text span far—geographically, theoretically, conceptually, and, most of all, emotionally. As a learning community, the group listed above determined some of the biggest challenge areas in museum teen programs (given here in no particular order):

Understanding intragroup power dynamics: How are the teens affected by the ways they interact with one another, the museum staff and spaces, and the practitioners?
Connecting instructional policies, trust, and a desire for social justice: How do we navigate the frequent challenge of a contrast between what museums do and what teens see as just and equitable?
Introducing external constituents to the group: How do we maintain the safe space developed in teen programs and bring in visitors, such as museum staff or artists, who, despite best intentions, might break the boundaries of the space?
Balancing the need to create a "product" with an understanding of its importance to teens and the institution: How do we respond to one entity expecting a produced event or project when the other might not see its need?
Mediating conflict and emotion when discussing difficult topics: How do we ensure safe exploration of opposing viewpoints, and cultivate a space where teens can question potentially triggering topics without causing harm?
Knowing when teens have "learned" something: How do we measure and understand what teens gain from our programs?

To write the introduction to this publication, Nisa Mackie, Dr. Yolanda J. Majors, and Simona Zappas sat down for a wide-spanning conversation on the drive to create this publication, the intentions behind it, and overall reflections on the work of museum teen programs. In the conversation, Dr. Majors summed up both the unique space of teen programs and the drive and design of the publication:

> One of the gaps that we are identifying as existing within [museum] teen programs exists in most spaces of learning, whether they are in

school or at a school. [The gap is] whether it's a space that offers the opportunity to engage around [issues] and to make some meaning around decoding them in some way. And if that action is taking place, there's going to be a set of challenges, and often those challenges reside in the fact that we're all coming from different social and cultural histories. Through those histories, we each have a certain set of tools we can apply to the circumstances presented by the space. When we think about spaces like the art museum, it's an opportunity space. It's an opportunity to engage in something with tools, a vision, and a shared goal.

[To that end, we must consider] what are the requirements of doing it collectively? What do each of us contribute from our historical and social tools and backgrounds to the broader group and to the broader purpose? [We should also consider how] the kinds of beliefs that we have about what counts as a tool, the values we place on them, and the ways that we use them can sometimes have competing forms. So, how we negotiate and navigate that becomes one of the first and biggest challenges and this is all done while trying to figure out the meaning of the context we're in with the opportunity space, like a museum.

The second challenge requires that [teen programmers] consider what is local [to the culture] within the museum. And a part of the challenge is sometimes we can see what's local and other times we have blinders on to it. So, how do we overcome the challenge of seeing and listening?

And then the third challenge is how do we create scalable things that have transfer and are still meaningful and continuous for all of us who invest in them. This is particularly prescient in the changing times we are in. We don't think about work that is driven by engagement or a wanting to engage and improve people's lives and help them in terms of one-offs. We want to approach it in terms of longevity and wanting to have an impact. So, one of the challenges is how to do that within our limitations.

Nisa Mackie built on Dr. Yolanda J. Majors's observations to add her own thoughts on how the context of the museum affects museum staff's perception, and, in turn, how that affects how museum staff empower youth within the museum:

Oftentimes museum staff conceptualize the places in which they work as incredibly pluralist spaces because they are open to the public. However, they are constituted by a particular distribution of power. Whether it is the power of the institution to decide what gets exhibited or the power of the individuals that work at the institution to contextualize, write about, and interpret works of art in specific ways. And so, to speak to some of the challenges of seeing and hearing we aim to tackle are self-created.

The work we have done collectively in developing this book engages with learning around the sociocultural and sociopolitical constructs navigated by youth on a day-to-day basis, whether it is the museum, school, or elsewhere. And so, it is a complex kind of contextual type of awareness building that we're trying to create for these young learners. Within that there are these tools, skill sets, and literacies that need to be developed in order for youth to be empowered to engage those spaces and engage with one another in those spaces.

We have talked a lot about the conflict between institutional perspectives and lived experiences and perspectives. The way the present-day museum is constituted provides space for the rupture between these two perspectives. Because of the types of young people that we engage, the rupture will always emerge. Learning to anticipate and prepare and not panic when it comes time for that rupture as young people come to know the museum was a major discovery from our work. In museum teen programs, each year, it's only a matter of time until the group comes to that rupture, and the question for staff is if they have tools to support that as a positive learning experience, where young people can feel self-determined. If it isn't done properly, the consequences can be rather dire because this is potentially the first institution and institutional perspective that teens come up against where there is the opportunity to, either individually or collectively, butt up against in an impactful way.

The intention behind approaches in this publication is to help navigate that inevitable rupture before, during, and after it happens. We hope that even if the outcome of the rupture is not what the teens want, they still come out on the other side with the critical-thinking skills to move from the reaction that follows a rupture into a thoughtful, action-based response. We hope to build trust between young people and arts institutions and a sense of ownership and care so that they feel long-term investment and connection to arts institutions and their peers.

The goals of our work go in both directions—not only are we aiming to develop skills for practitioners supporting youth, but we also hope that this publication models ways for educators to critically reflect on their role in this work to authentically support youth voices in institutional spaces. More specifically, we are interested in the strategies and curricular approaches that ignite and foster youth voices beyond lip service to expanding the impact of youth action beyond the sanctioned space of teen programs.

1

Containers

Introduction

In this section, you will find pieces focused on the who, what, where, and how of museum teen programs. These pieces center the core structural elements of programs like key activities, intergenerational collaboration, and plans for the year. Consider this the foundation upon which you build.

   With works by
Simona Zappas, Nancy Nowacek, Marie Hofer, Araya Henry, Jorge Espinosa, Grace Needlman, and Nohemi Rodriguez

Essays, Reflections & Advice

Simona Zappas

1.1.1.

Walker Art Center Teen Arts Council Founding, History, and Timeline

Bio

Simona Zappas (she/her) is the Youth Programs Manager at the Walker Art Center. In her work she designs and facilitates informal learning opportunities for youth. She collaborates with curatorial staff to bring a learning lens to museum public engagement with a social practice bent on programmatic strategy. Before this, she was the director of WFNU Frogtown, a low-power radio station in Saint Paul. Simona holds a BA with honors from Macalester College and a master of education from the University of Minnesota. Simona sits on the Saint Paul Neighborhood Network board and volunteers at Planned Parenthood as an abortion doula.

Essay
Founding

The origin story of the Walker Art Center Teen Arts Council (WACTAC) is challenging to unravel. Some records are spotty, and many claim the title of founder. The Walker began several programs for

MODERN
PAINTERS

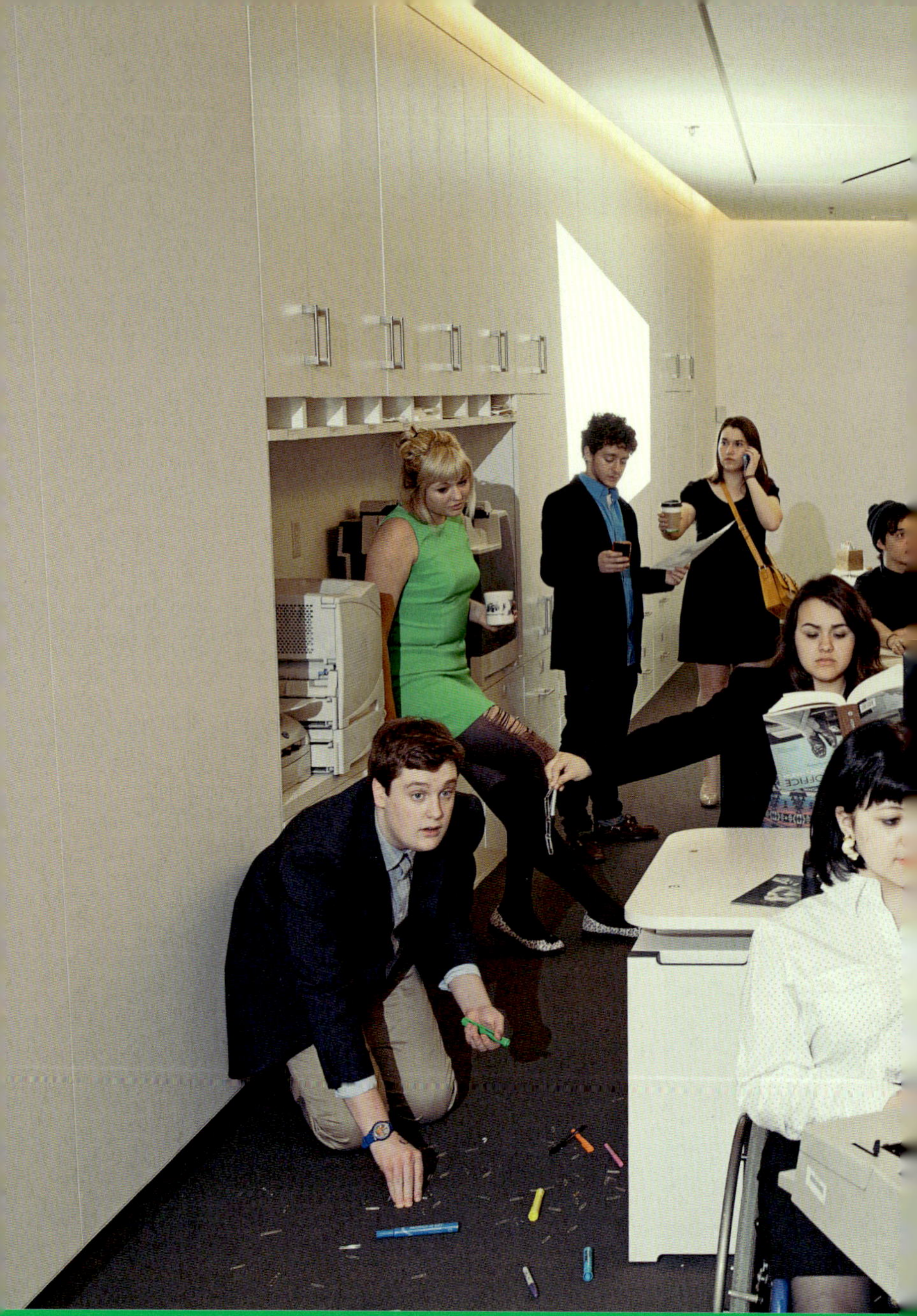

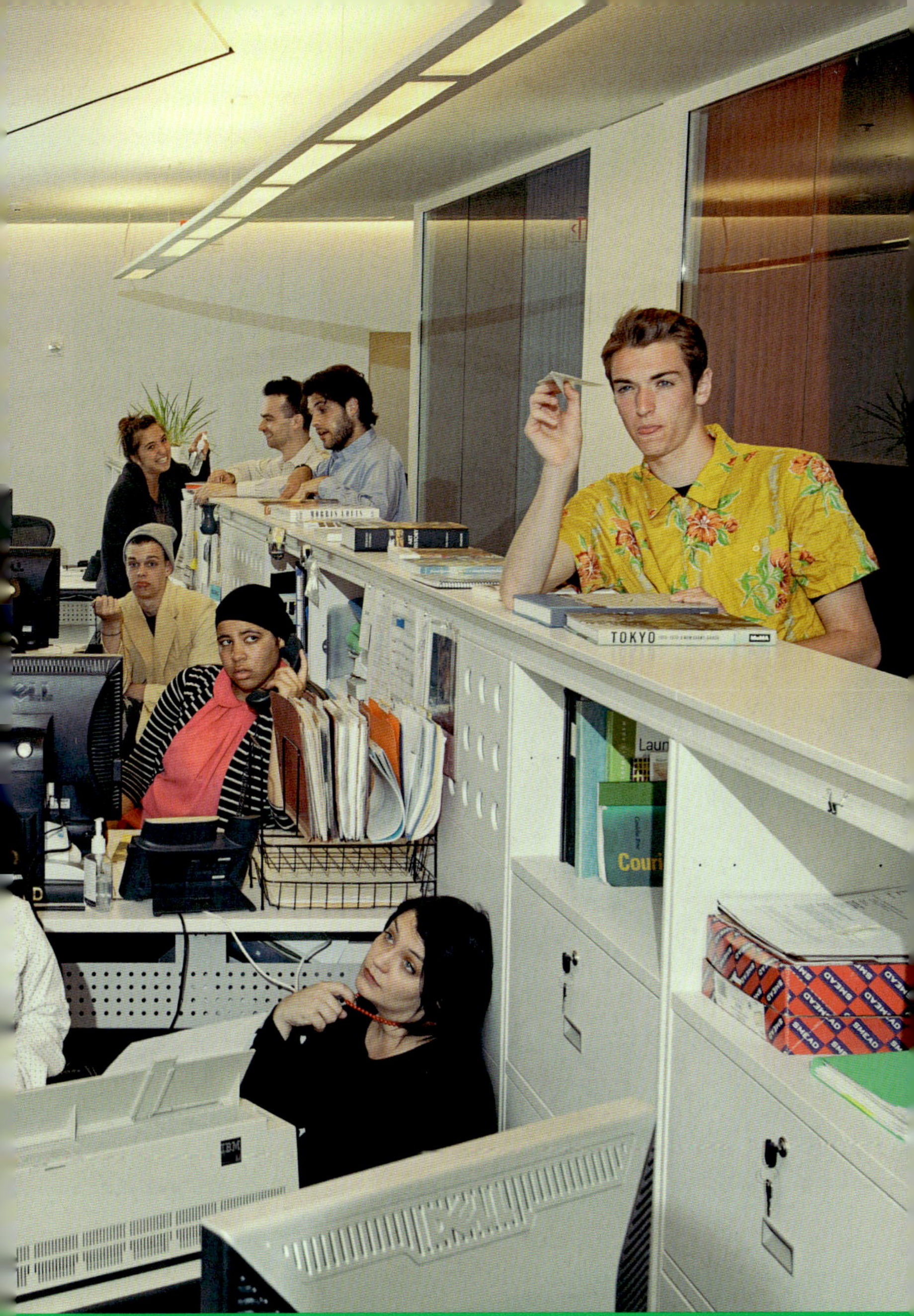
TOKYO

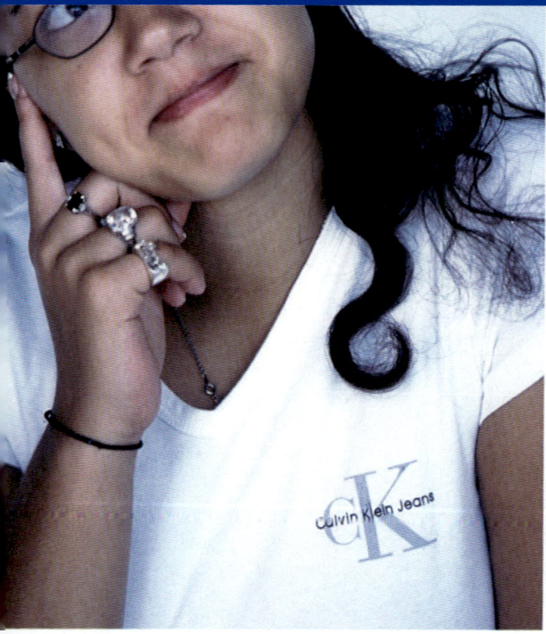
cK
Calvin Klein Jeans

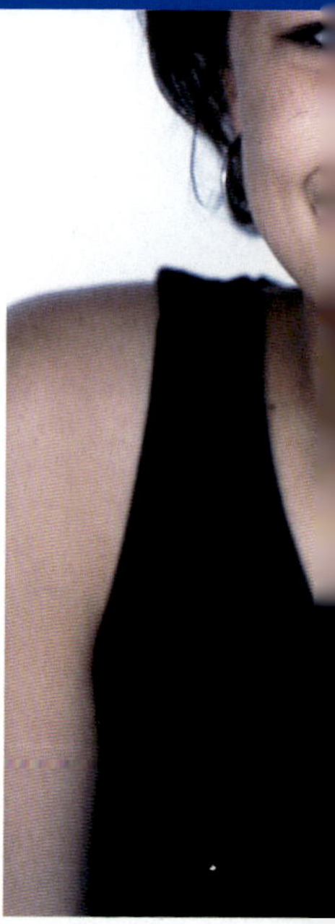

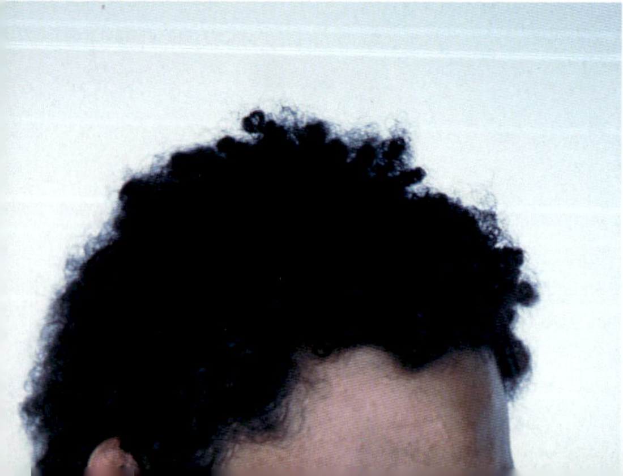

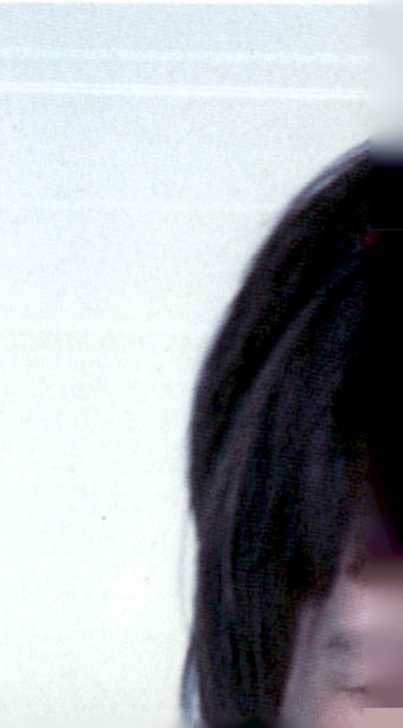

teens simultaneously, but most importantly, starting a program like WACTAC is iterative and can be a slow process. Working in a large cultural institution affords many contributors, phases, and hands to build something special.

In 1994 the Walker pursued a major $1.5 million grant from the Lila Wallace Foundation to fund a cross-institution initiative titled "New Definitions and New Audiences." The initiative aimed to reposition the Walker for increased relevance with low-income families, people of color, and teens after identifying a severe lack of attendance from these social groups. Much of the work to engage teens came from the marketing department's "Campaign to Target Youth," which fell under the umbrella of the grant and included focus groups comprising educators, teens, and out-of-school-program workers.

Throughout the 1990s the Walker prototyped several programs to increase attendance and interest from the Twin Cities teen population. There was never a plan to create a "signature" program, only to determine best practices and grow teen attendance. It should be noted that the program was not run perfectly at this time, though clearly full of excitement and ideation. Interoffice memos show over- and underspent budgets, a lack of clarity over job titles and responsibilities, and a constant flux of programming.

The Walker's initial teen programs included targeting specific high schools, a think tank to ideate on teen programs, and extended workshops with artists. Notably, the Walker hired three artists: Seitu Jones, Ernest Whiteman, and Sue Kolita. The artists worked as community program coordinators to build strong relationships with specific communities through art-making programs at local high schools. Staff aimed to have an artist-led workshop for teens as part of each permanent collection show at the Walker; these workshops included artists like Carrie Mae Weems and Helen De Michiel, but curricula, recruitment, and the teen selection processes are unclear. During this period, the Walker also trained teens to lead tours of the Minneapolis Sculpture Garden and hoped to hire a teen intern to work in each department.

In November 1994 the Walker hired Michelle Coffey as their first (then titled) adolescent coordinator to manage these programs. The Walker's marketing department weighed in on teen programs by hosting focus groups and, with the (then titled) Education and Community Program Department, a think tank aimed at designing programming for teens. The Adolescent Think Tank, and the start of Walker Teen Programs, is described beautifully in the 1999 *How-To Kit*:[1]

> Six years ago, we started out in a slow and episodic manner. We began with something called the Adolescent Think Tank, a city-wide alliance between educators, teenagers, and staff from local and national cultural institutions. The group met monthly to identify and develop programming that would interest and intellectually nourish adolescents. Ideas sparked by these discussions shaped the Walker's earliest teen programs. This allowed us to gain some experience and figure out what we were doing right and what we were doing wrong.[2]

It is a bit unclear how the jump from the think tank and all other programs led to the WACTAC model. The original *How-To Kit* shares two key tenets of teen programming determined by the think tank. Teens want a say in designing the projects they do, and the social aspect of a program is key to its success. Teens seek out opportunities to meet peers with different backgrounds and shared interests. It is clear that the think tank birthed an appealing

1. In 1999, the Walker produced a 10-page booklet that was shared with museums across the country as a response to the high interest in the Teen Arts Council model.
2. Christi Atkinson, *A Teen Programs How-To Kit: Some Directions, Suggestions, Examples, and Stories to Get You Started. Some Assembly Required* (Minneapolis: Walker Art Center, 1999).

model and pulled out key values and structures still used in WACTAC today, like empowering teens with actual responsibilities and say, a weekly meeting, and a diverse council.

Things seemed to come together rather quickly because mentions of WACTAC appeared in museum records as early as December 1996. In February 1996 staff submitted a course change document to the Lila Wallace Foundation. The course change lays out the addition of WACTAC, renames the position of "adolescent coordinator" to "teen coordinator," increases the position to full-time, and states that they plan to reallocate funds from marketing's "Campaign to Target Youth" to fund the position's salary and basic program costs, such as snacks and T-shirts. The course change also states a goal to pursue other grants to fund the position into fiscal year 1997–1998.

As WACTAC came together, the teen programs team expanded to include a consultant with experience running programming for youth and a teenage intern (potentially an original WACTAC or think tank member). Along with the teen coordinator, they determined the program's structures, values, and language. One of their key contributions was the structure of a roughly fifteen-member council focused on providing feedback on existing programs and interpretive materials and generating new ideas for the institution. Little changed with the program through the end of the decade beyond the addition of projects that included an annual zine and a building-wide, large-scale event with art-making and performances designed by the WACTAC members titled Student Open House. By 1999 it was clear that the program had hit a stride and was receiving national attention from hopeful copycats, leading to the publication of the *How-To Kit* that shared best practices and lessons learned, which serves as a marker of the end of the program's nascent period.

1.1.1.

History and Timeline

The timeline is pieced together from archival materials, photos, website archives, and videos without a certain promise of accuracy.

1994–1999: Unprecedented Access

The Walker's efforts to connect with teens began as a marketing initiative to better appeal to low-income families, teens, and people of color through a more culturally expansive and relevant repositioning of the museum. This initiative was funded by a five-year $1.5 million institution-wide Lila Wallace Foundation grant. Teen focus groups and think tanks birthed the idea of a council of teens situated in the museum with an actual say in the Walker's decisions and access to resources. The council migrated to the Education and Community Programs Department and began solidifying into a formal program: the Walker Art Center Teen Arts Council, or WACTAC. Several other short-term teen programs, like tour guides and programs at South High in Minneapolis, ran concurrent with the formation of WACTAC, but WACTAC prevailed as the signature teen program. It is essential to point out that many people contributed to the program's formation, and many individuals claimed its founding. There was great institutional support and excitement over the program at this time. Teens received unprecedented access to work with internationally regarded artists and support to stage their off-site exhibition of teen-made works, *Hot Art Injection*. WACTAC received national attention from the museum field, which led staff to produce the *How-To Kit* in 1999 to share best practices learned from the first years of programming.

1994

Lila Wallace "New Definitions, New Audiences" grant—March 1, 1994, to February 28, 1999

Listening Project, Seitu Jones and Helen De Michiel—June 9, 1994

Adolescent coordinator position created—November 1994

1995
Dawoud Bey teen photography workshop; Carrie Mae Weems teen workshop—1995
First rollout of WACTAC by teen intern and teen consultant—Spring 1995

1996
Listening Project with Helen De Michiel shown in galleries—November 1996
Teen Tour Guides program with South High School—Fall 1996
Lila Wallace grant course change to officially create WACTAC and reallocate grant monies to target youth from the marketing department to Education and Community Programs—February 26, 1996

1997
First *Hot Art Injection* exhibition—June 6, 1997
7,000 Oaks tree-planting ceremony—October 4, 1997

1998
Writers Reading: The Guerrilla Girls—February 5, 1998

1999
Second *Hot Art Injection* exhibition—May 15, 1999
Glenn Ligon meets with WACTAC—November 11, 1999

2000–2009: Internet and Identity
In the early 2000s we saw WACTAC and its facilitators present a very casual, teenage attitude through events and web-based platforms as the program continued to define its identity within the institution. WACTAC continued to work with prominent artists over the decade and hosted numerous events and parties, including the Un-Prom, more off-site exhi-

bitions, and student open houses. WACTAC's promotion of its identity comes up most in the language that staff used to describe programming in online marketing materials. This decade was undoubtedly an exciting time for the internet and a chance to explore how best to use its potential. WACTAC staff took full advantage of this by creating a separate teen website and writing personal blogs on the Walker's website to chronicle events and forgo the buttoned-up tone expected from the public-facing voice of a museum, as shown by this example copy posted on the Walker's website for a calendar posting in July 2002 for Made from Scratch: An Opening Night Party for *One Planet under a Groove: Hip Hop and Contemporary Art*:

> WACTAC threw the opening party, and, boy, do they know how to throw a party. Peanut Butter Wolf blessed the audience with a live set, breakers were breaking, and ciphers broke out all through the galleries. Later in the night, a young man overcame his trailer-park upbringing, stage fright, and melanin-deficiency to finally realize his dream of becoming the best freestyler in the city, destroying his bitter rivals and learning a few lessons about life, and love, in the process. Oh wait, that was sucky-ass *8 Mile*... Hmmm... I don't think I remember what went on at the party.[3]

While WACTAC has always carried a playfulness and youthful energy that comes with the territory of the audience, the casualness of this era seems intentional, as if there was an apparent effort to define the program against the traditional professionalism of a large institution and embrace an identity characterized by the rebellion associated with adolescence.

3. Walker Art Center, "Made from Scratch: An Opening Night Party for *One Planet under a Groove: Hip Hop and Contemporary Art*," online calendar, July 1, 2002, https://walkerart.org/calendar/2002/made-from-scratch-an-opening-night-party-for.

2002
Robin Rhode WACTAC residency—2002 to 2003
Nikki S. Lee, Snapshot: A Talk with the Walker Art Center Teen Arts Council—2002
Made from Scratch, an opening-night party for *One Planet under a Groove*—July 1, 2002
WACTAC Artist Talk with Franco Mondini Ruiz—September 24, 2002
Student Open House with Ursula Rucker—October 1, 2002

2003
Whatever: Battle of the Underage—August 8, 2003

2006
OPEN-ENDED (the art of engagement), Spencer Nakasako residency, "What Does Freedom Mean to You?" film project and video jukebox—March 25, 2006
Open mic night with Ise Lyfe and DJ Trinidad, co-presented by WACTAC—March 30, 2006
Walker Un-Prom: Not Yo Mama's Formal—May 25, 2006
Radio Revolt with Allora Calzadilla—July 16, 2006

2007
Kara Walker Postcard Project—February 26, 2007
Fourth *Hot Art Injection* exhibition—July 1, 2007
Artist Talk: David Choe, presented by WACTAC, and Banners over Broadway project with Juxtaposition Arts—May 25, 2007
Total Chaos: The Art and Aesthetics of Hip-Hop, presented by WACTAC—June 14, 2007

2008
Artist Talk: Chris Johanson and Jo Jackson, presented by WACTAC—May 1, 2008

2009
13 Most Beautiful Young Artists screening—March 26, 2009

Don't Sleep on It event—2009
Artist Talk: Ty Evans—June 21, 2009
Student Open House: Bust Magazine—October 10, 2009
Student Open House: School of Rock—October 29, 2009

2010–2015: Celebration of Past & Alumni
From 2010 to 2015, WACTAC continued to follow a path of defining its own identity separate from the Walker with increased distance. We started to see a drop in the number of events combined with consistency in programming; at this point, WACTAC had set event outcomes for each year: TAC Labs (drop-in teen-designed workshops), a Student Open House / Teen Takeover (a building-wide party by teens for teens), and an annual zine. This period focused on program alums; the blogging shifted into promotional event posts and was replaced by social media pages, like Twitter, Facebook, Instagram, and Tumblr, to keep alums connected and updated on program activities. Alums were celebrated with the off-site exhibition *Still? 20 Years of WACTAC* and in the groundbreaking *Room to Rise*[4] publication in 2015, which touted the long-term success of teen arts council alums at the Walker and other partner institutions.

2010
Pirate Press Zine Workshop—April 8, 2010
Residency with Peter Haakon Thompson—June 26, 2010
PixelVisions: Music Video Workshop—2010
Open Exposure: Eyedea and Abilities concert—July 11, 2020
Student Open House: Street Level—October 14, 2010

4. Danielle Linzer and Mary Ellen Munley, *Room to Rise: The Lasting Impact of Intensive Teen Programs in Art Museums* (New York: Whitney Museum of American Art, 2015).

2011
WACTAC Task Party—February 17, 2011
WAC ATTACK: Music Looping with Dosh—March 3, 2011
Student Open House: Get Scrappy—October 27, 2011
Student Open House: Friend Request Dance—May 14, 2011

2012
Bad Art: A Night of Bad Art at the Walker Art Center—April 19, 2012
Student Open House: Identity Crisis—November 15, 2012

2013
Teen Art Lounge with Abraham Cruzvillegas—March 21, 2013
Teen Takeover: Where Art Thou—April 25, 2013
Teen Art Lounge with Surprise Artist—May 16, 2013
Jay Heikes: WACTAC interview—July 31, 2013
Student Open House: It's Happening!—November 14, 2013

2014
Teen Art Lounge: Make and Meet—January 16, 2014
Teen Takeover: Double Take—April 17, 2014

2015–Present: Institutional Critique
The self-determination that WACTAC sought over the years reached a new point as the group aimed to be a space defined by youth voice and social justice organizing. A critical moment was a 2015 visit from the artist collective the Guerrilla Girls. The WACTAC members disagreed with perspectives shared by the artists and took it upon themselves to speak out against them publicly. WACTAC organized a panel discussion in response to programming featuring the Guerrilla Girls and published a zine criticizing the artists and the Walker's funding sources. Following this major project, the program

1.1.1.

continued to focus externally and have an activism lens to their work as they pursued a long-term project with the Kulture Klub Collaborative, an arts program for highly mobile teens. It was clear that the participants in the program joined seeking opportunities to create action in the museum, but it is not every year that the Walker hosts artists who elicit such a strong response. Staff began to develop a flexible curriculum to support the teens in pursuing a similar project each year. Rather than continue the path of defining WACTAC against the institution, program staff worked to identify and leverage institutional resources that could be used to support youth in articulating their perspectives. The social-justice-informed curriculum supports the development of inquiry skills to spark action.

2015
Teen Takeover: Pop Culture Shock—April 23, 2015
Student Open House: The Time Is Now!—November 12, 2015
Still? 20 Years of WACTAC exhibition (opening-night celebration)—December 27, 2015

2016
Guerrilla Girls and WACTAC discussion, Twin Cities Takeover—January 21, 2016
Seitu Jones and Ta-coumba Aiken visit WACTAC—September 22, 2016
TAC Lab: Teens Take Charge—October 27, 2016
TAC Lab at Big Bash Open House Party—December 1, 2016

2017
Teen Takeover with Kulture Klub Collective—April 2017

2018
TAC Lab for *I Am You, You Are Too* exhibition in-gallery booklet launch—March 15, 2018
Teen Takeover—May 25, 2018

Shadows at the Crossroads meeting with WACTAC, Seitu Jones, and Ta-coumba Aiken—September 2018
Teen Takeover—November 11, 2018

2019
Teen Takeover—May 25, 2019
Teen Takeover—November 16, 2019

2020
Virtual Teen Takeover: Unmuted Mic, open mic event—July 16, 2020
Virtual Teen Takeover: Come Be a Visionary—October 30, 2020

2021
Virtual Teen Takeover: Bloom—April 23, 2021
Teen Takeover Fall 2021, first in-person Teen Takeover following COVID-19 pandemic—November 12, 2021
Teen Takeover: Summerween—May 27, 2021

☺

Teen Programs Fundamentals

Table
This table offers an "at a glance" overview of key structural elements of teen programs, such as size, payment amount, and staff support at a handful of teen programs in midsize to large museums across the United States. The table shows that, even with similarities, there is no one-size-fits-all approach to supporting teens in museums.

Walker Art Center
Program Structure
The Walker Art Center Teen Arts Council (WACTAC) runs September to June and meets every Thursday from 4:30 pm to 6:30 pm at the Walker, or virtually over Zoom. WACTAC meets in either the Walker's classroom space or a conference room in the main office block. WACTAC consists of roughly a dozen 10th–12th graders coming from the metro area. The group size varies each year but is never less than 10 and never more than 13. We break for school holidays and plan winter and spring breaks to coordi-

nate with the Minneapolis Public Schools calendar.

Payment

Participants receive a $100 prepaid debit card at the start of each month to recognize their participation, with the expectation that they will attend each meeting. Payment is a challenge, because there isn't a perfect solution for both accounting responsibility and ease of use for teens. Cash payments are difficult in terms of accounting, but checks can present a barrier as not every teen has a bank account.

Recruitment/Outreach

Program staff spend the year meeting with school counselors, art teachers, and staff at other youth-serving organizations to build trust, rapport, and a knowledge of the program. This builds a foundation so that when mass mailings and emails to announce recruitment go out, there is a supportive network to confidently refer youth. WACTAC staff work with the Walker's marketing department to fold messaging into email blasts, the institution's Instagram account, and press releases; @walkerteens is an Instagram account run by the WACTAC members and has the most success connecting with teens because it is promoted and written in their voice.

Interviews/Applications

The WACTAC application process usually takes up the majority of the summer. Youth can participate in WACTAC for only one year (to reduce repetition and cliques), so there are roughly 12 spots to fill. Staff look for a diversity of geography, identities, and personality types that can create a balanced group where youth can learn from each other. There is no "ideal" WACTAC applicant, but we look for teens who ask questions, demonstrate room to grow, with no duplication of program learning (aka, room in their schedules!), and an interest in thinking about how to apply art for change. Applicants fill out an online survey that collects basic contact information and a few narrative questions on interest in the program and art. Usually, the program receives 70–90 applications. Staff work together to select 40 applicants who will move on to a group interview designed and led by an artist. A final 20 will be selected for a one-on-one interview. The interview process is always in flux because there is a lot of room to improve to ensure the process doesn't favor more extroverted youth and isn't too anxiety inducing.

Events

Over the year, WACTAC plans two Teen Takeover events, in the spring and fall. The teens entirely plan Teen Takeover with administrative support from staff and a structure to follow that gives teens control over selecting performers, food, art-making activities, theme, and decorations. The museum stays open late on a Friday, and staff check IDs at the door to ensure all visitors are in high school. WACTAC designs the marketing strategy and deliverables. The events are a bonding experience for the WACTAC members and a fun on-ramp for the audiences.

Typical Meeting

WACTAC meets at the Walker or virtually, on Thursday evenings, 4:30 pm–6:30 pm. Participants get snacks, bus tokens, and/or parking vouchers. Meetings kick off with open announcements and a silly check-in question before launching into the content. There's always an assortment of fidgets and art-making materials on the table. A portion of every meeting is spent discussing work in the galleries that connect to the rest of the day's material or to scaffold larger projects. Meeting content varies, from staff visitors to brainstorming, event planning, artist visits, or work time on a collaborative project.

Transportation

As a matter of safety for staff and youth, Walker staff does not provide rides to WACTAC members or pay for rideshares or taxis. Staff encourage members to create carpools with each other. Participants are given free parking vouchers and bus tokens.

Evaluation
WACTAC members fill out three surveys a year that collect data on how they view and interpret their own learning. The surveys were designed by an external firm and are conducted virtually over Google Forms. These forms are mainly quantitative, reviewing teens' analysis of their own skill development against learning goals determined in program curricula and reported to grant funders. Additionally, the staff does one-on-one midyear interviews with the teens to hear more about what they'd like to see and to connect them with more specific resources. Each major project has a dedicated evaluation section. The teens design their own evaluative tools for major projects after a presentation on community-based evaluation from program staff.

Staff
WACTAC is always led by two staff members who divide up facilitation based on skill areas and interests. Instructional design is collaborative. Staff meet regularly to discuss scaffolding and group dynamics. Having two staff members allows the Walker to provide one-on-one support to youth, greater classroom-management strategies, and flexiblity if there is an absence.

Youth
WACTAC youth come from all over the Twin Cities metro area and are in grades 10–12. To find a good fit for WACTAC, the staff look for youth who are curious about broadening their perception of art and exhibit a growth mindset. Staff learn more about their existing extracurriculars to ensure they have time to participate.

Social Media
At this publication's release, WACTAC holds an

Instagram and a TikTok account that are entirely driven by the youth. This was determined after conversations and trust-building with marketing staff. These accounts are distinct from the Walker and the teens lead a conversation each year on how they want the accounts to be run, determining the unique affordances of the platforms, and what the content is for each. The rule is that anything they post should be considered OK for a teacher to see. Should anyone break the rule, everyone loses access.

Absences

WACTAC members have six excused absences over the year. An excused absence is one that the WACTAC facilitators have had a heads-up on—ideally 24 hours, but within a few hours is OK. The teens are allowed to have three unexcused absences over the year. After each unexcused absence, the teens will hear from the facilitators to check-in on time management and safety. With each absence, the teens are encouraged to talk about their time management and accountability. The absence policy is enforced because the program moves fast, and the teens determine the content—staff wants the teens there so they can shape it. After three absences, their place in the program is up for discussion. In practice, the absence policy is always a bit more lax than initially communicated. Teens are busy, and a lot of life happens during the program year. What is important is that teens are learning time management and accountability skills, show interest in the program, and realistically can fit it into their schedules. Staff uses the application process to find out if teens have other extracurriculars, jobs, or family responsibilities that will require more planning to attend. If the reasoning behind teens' struggling to come is transportation or a family matter, staff encourages facilitators to practice appropriate boundaries in helping them manage it.

Food

Snacks are essential! Teens are hungry, and sharing

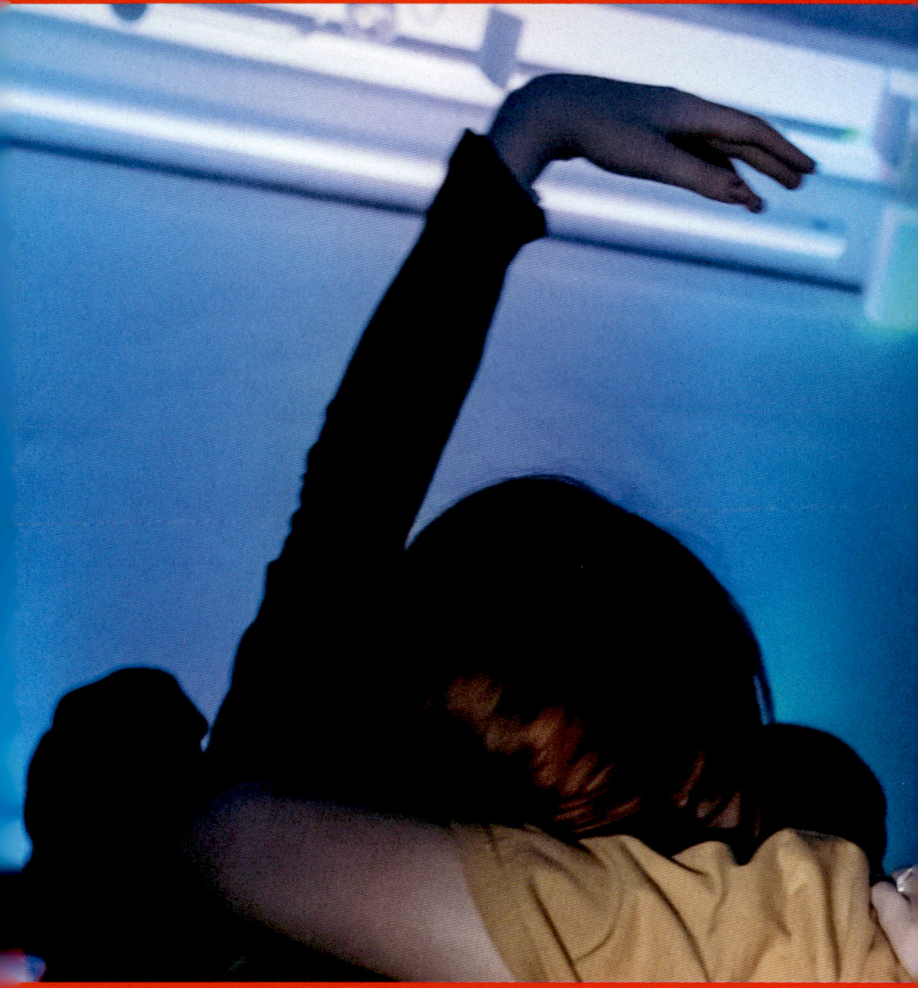

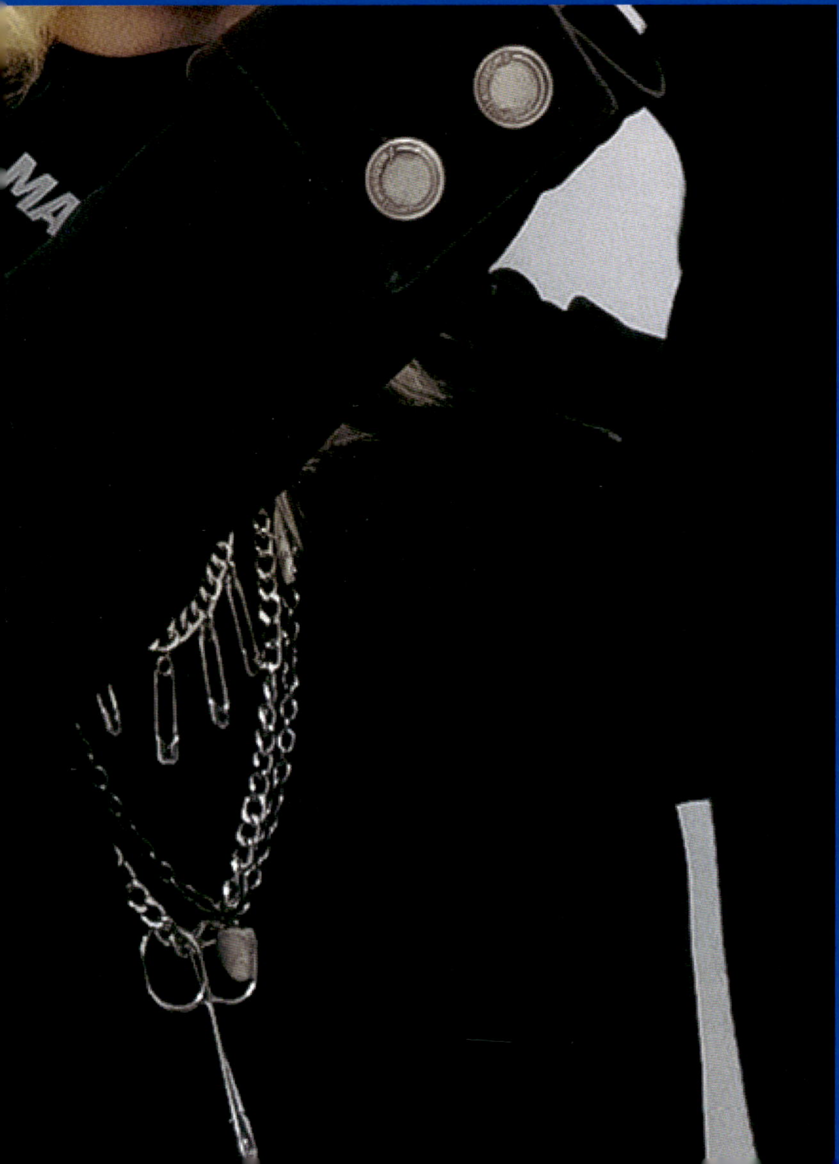

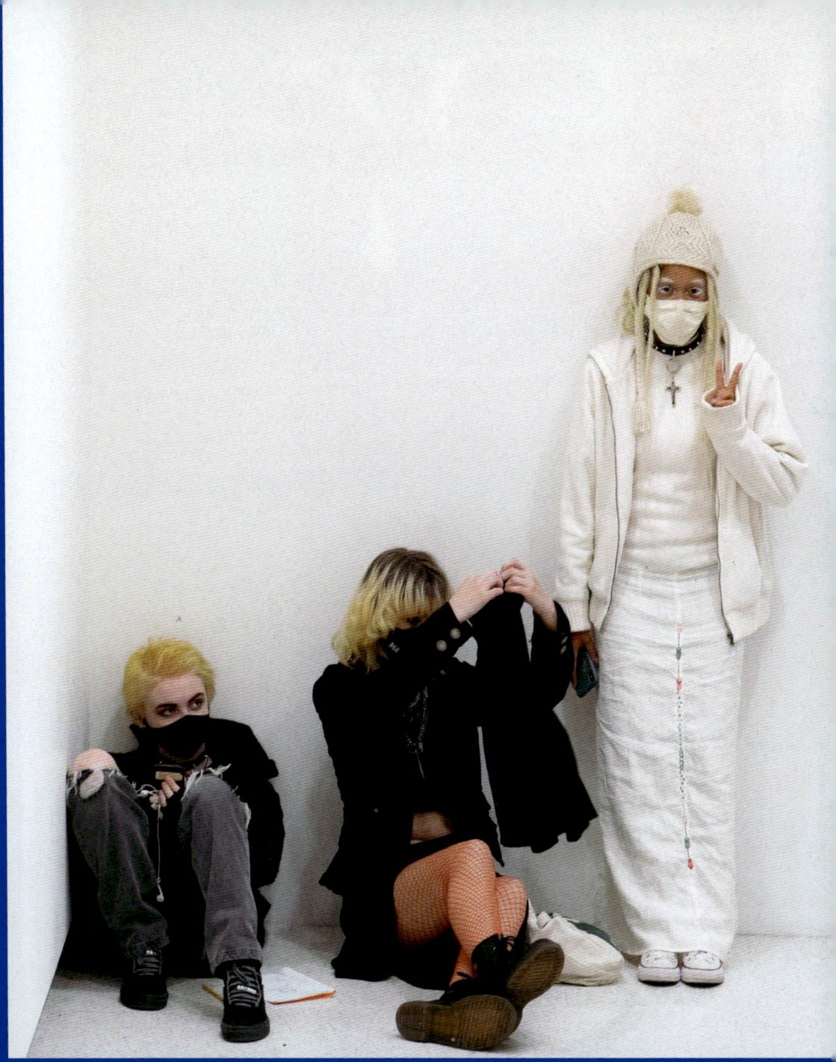

food creates bonding and conversation. WACTAC members can make snack demands, but typically WACTAC snacks are bulk chips and cookies from Costco. Staff collects any information on allergies or dietary practices before purchasing snacks.

General Contact
teenprograms@walkerart.org

Funding
Private donor, Museum and Library Services grants, solicitation of local corporate sponsors

Budget
$100,000 for teen programs as a whole. A typical WACTAC year costs about $13,000 between costs for part-time staff support, teen stipends, parking and bus tokens, food, tickets, and supplies. A typical Teen Takeover event costs $8,000 between staff time, food, materials, and performer fees. The rest of the budget covers alternative teen programs, artists' fees, travel, and research.

Location
The Walker prides itself on being an interdisciplinary institution, so the program is challenged with incorporating content and context across multiple media. Minneapolis is a midsize city with one of the highest opportunity gaps in the nation. It has significant suburban sprawl, and the Walker sits just outside Downtown Minneapolis in a busy intersection leading into freeways. The Walker is near parks and a wealthy neighborhood, but the scale of the campus can make it feel like a bit of an island. It is on several bus routes that connect to the rest of the city.

Alumni Opportunities
Every year, alumni are invited to the annual holiday party. The first half of the event is soda and fries with the current WACTAC members, and the second half is cocktails and mingling with alums. Alums

can participate in annual ticket giveaways.

⌿

Museum of Contemporary Art, Los Angeles
Program Structure

The MOCA teen program brings a diverse group of 15–18 high school juniors and seniors behind the scenes to learn about the museum, contemporary art, artists, and other creative careers. This paid internship runs from September to May. The program meets every Thursday from 4:30 pm to 6:30 pm and occasionally on weekends for longer sessions.

Payment

MOCA pays the minimum wage ($15 / hour) and covers public transportation to and from our meetings, or parking if students drive.

Recruitment / Outreach

Managers share information about the program with over 100 teachers from the school program at MOCA. Staff also attend a few yearly vocational fairs organized by downtown schools to promote the program. Specific information about the program and how to apply can be found on the museum's website, mocateens.org (a website created and managed by the MOCA Teens), and on social media.

Interviews / Applications

Applications for the MOCA teen program, which combines biographical and essay questions, are available on MOCA's and MOCA Teens' websites starting in mid to late April; the due date is late June. Every year the program receives around 90 applications. The program managers select a group of 30 applicants for a remote group interview, designed in collaboration with the second-year MOCA Teens (Juniors accepted for a second cycle). After the group interview, fewer applicants are selected for individual interviews. The number of available spots depends on the number of returning teens, but generally there are 12 to 16 open spots each year.

Events

Each year, the teen interns collaborate with one to two working artists in a workshop format. They create public engagement around these workshops through family programming, social media, or other online sharing methods (such as their website). The teens also assist in additional Education Department family programming. In mid-April, the teens host Teen Night, virtually or in person. At this event, fellow teenagers have an exclusive experience of the museum and enjoy art, activities, and entertainment curated by the MOCA Teens.

Typical Meeting

MOCA holds two-hour meetings, generally from 4:30 pm to 6:30 pm on Thursdays. When in person, teens share snacks (brought every week by a designated snack curator). Staff review the meeting's agenda before the teens share anything worth visiting, reading, or seeing. Meetings often include grounding or breathing meditation and space to debrief past activities, collaborations, or events. Sometimes, other MOCA employees or artists will join to share their experiences in the art world. Meetings often have short art-making activities and open-ended conversations about artworks using Visual Thinking Strategies.

Transportation

The museum provides Metro Cards to each teen taking public transport and parking validations for each student who drives to the museum.

Evaluation

Each teen has a midyear check-in with both managers, to talk about appreciations and growing edges. These areas for improvement are often based on engagement—for example, whether the staff hears the student's voice enough. The space is also open for feedback about the program and encourages each teen to take the initiative to ask for the changes they would like to see.

Staff
The MOCA teen program has two comanagers, each managing another space at the museum (Family or School Programs). Historically, these two managers represent different demographics and hold distinct organizational and/or teaching styles. Having two managers model effective collaboration and compromise allows leadership to be tempered. In addition to the managers, additional staff from the museum come into the program space for interview sessions, and one to two artists run collaborative multisession workshops with the teens.

Youth
MOCA Teen participants are juniors and seniors in high schools all over Los Angeles. The program seeks diversity in access and exposure to art, specifically contemporary art. In the application process, managers seek teens who are open to changing their opinions, are interested in contemporary art practices, and listen to their peers actively.

Social Media
There is a public Instagram account for MOCA Teens, @mocateens. Teens drive the account, but the process of posting and collaborating to create content is scaffolded through workshops and group conversations led by managers.

Absences
If a teen participant cannot attend a meeting due to school or family obligations, they must notify managers at least one week before that meeting. Unexcused absences, or more than two excused absences, will require a meeting with the program

managers. Two unexcused absences may result in elimination from the program.

Food
When in person, the program has a weekly snack curator, who is given a $20 bill the week before they are set to curate the snack. They must provide snacks for the whole group with that money and give the managers any change and accurate receipts.

General Contact
education@moca.org

Funding
The funding is stitched together from several grants and funders, including Los Angeles County Arts Commission, the Wallace Foundation, Good Works Foundation, and the MOCA Projects Council. From 2012 to 2015, the program was generously supported by Louis Vuitton. In 2022 the MOCA teen program is presented by Mary and David Martin's MADWORKSHOP.

Budget
The budget oscillates yearly, depending on funding, between $60,000 and $100,000.

Location
Weekly meetings generally occur at the museum's Grand Avenue, in the boardroom. Since March 2020, most virtual meetings have taken place over Zoom.

◊

Dia Art Foundation
Program Structure
Dia Teens is a multisite, year-round teen engagement program that elevates the voices, ideas, and contributions of youth at Dia while emphasizing collective agency, critical thinking, and choice. Serving up to 30 high-school-aged youth in New York City

and the Hudson Valley, Dia Teens prioritizes students who can participate for at least one full year and may experience barriers to graduation and/or lack of access to arts opportunities. While students may participate for up to four years, artist educators are in residence with the program for one year to collaborate with participants and introduce a range of cultural producers, practices, and teaching and learning styles.

During the school year, the Hudson Valley cohort meets every other Saturday, 11 am–3 pm, and the New York City cohort meets every Wednesday, 4 pm–6 pm; during the summer, both cohorts meet at their respective sites for six weeks, Monday–Thursday, 11 am–3 pm.

Payment
Recognizing each participant's creative contributions to the program and Dia, all teens in good standing receive a stipend. Hudson Valley teens receive a stipend of $500 at the end of the fall, spring, and summer sessions. New York City teens receive a stipend of $500 at the end of the fall and spring semesters. In the summer, participants are compensated at $15 per hour, with a maximum of 25 hours per week, paid through the New York City Department of Youth and Community Development's Summer Internship Program.

Recruitment/Outreach
Recruitment for the Dia Beacon and Dia Chelsea cohorts takes place biannually in October and June, and the number of openings is determined by how many current youth are continuing with the program. Cohorts are capped at fifteen participants per site. Available spots in the Hudson Valley teen program are open to all high-school-aged youth who have completed at least their freshman year, with priority given to local residents. Program staff shares the application with visual arts teachers and guidance counselors at all high schools in the surround-

1.1.2.

ing counties, public libraries, partner organizations, and youth and family services providers. Returning participants share program information with their school via presentations to relevant classes and clubs, morning announcements, and posting flyers. As a partner with the New York City Department of Youth and Community Development's (DYCD) Learn and Earn program, the NYC teen program recruits from 17 site providers throughout the five boroughs. Program staff regularly present at DYCD and site-provider meetings. Students not affiliated with DYCD are also invited to apply.

Interviews/Applications

All teens interested in the Hudson Valley or New York City programs are invited to participate in an informal group interview. The group interview, cofacilitated by returning teens, is an opportunity for youth to meet current participants and the Dia Teens artist educator and participate in a collaborative activity that is reflective of the themes and processes being explored in the curriculum for the year. The interview is active and participatory, so teens can get a feel for what it might be like to participate in the program. Aside from allowing the program team and current participants to observe how teens interact, a nontraditional interview format allows teens to decide for themselves if Dia Teens is the program that best suits their creative and intellectual interests.

Events

With the support of the Dia Teens artist educator, participants collectively determine the arc of the program, deciding together whether or not they would like to share their work publicly and/or work collaboratively on a project or event. Some cohorts organize a culminating event to share their progress and accomplishments with friends, family, and the public, whereas others choose to conclude their time in the program with an intimate gathering of peers, such as a potluck lunch. Exchanges with other teen programs have also created opportunities to share work and ideas with peers across the country. In Spring 2021, the Hudson Valley and New York City cohorts of Dia Teens participated in a virtual session with the Museum of Contemporary Art Detroit's Teen Council. Following a generative exchange, Dia Teens were invited to contribute a collaborative artwork to the MOCAD Teen Council's annual exhibition.

   Typical Meeting
Sessions are facilitated by an artist educator with support from program staff and often begin with an opening ritual. Typically, sessions introduce a new theme, idea, or question that builds on previous experiences, and teens may investigate these through discussion, engaging directly with artists and artworks, small group exercises, active research, studio time, and experimental prompts. Throughout the session, teens, staff, and interns may individually and collaboratively document their time and work through photography, group collages, collected materials, and written responses. The artist educator often closes the session with a full group reflection or share out centered on the teens' creative output, lingering questions, and outstanding thoughts. Program staff tends to housekeeping items, such as providing snacks, managing the sign-in/out process, distributing and collecting official forms, and disbursing transit cards and fares.

   Transportation
Dia Teens covers all in-program transportation costs, including group train tickets, subway travel, and chartered buses for field trips and site visits. All New York City participants are also given multiride MetroCards at every session. Financial support is available for all Hudson Valley students traveling to the program via public transportation, including

train, bus, and ferry fares.

Evaluation

Evaluation of Dia Teens takes place regularly throughout the school year and summer intensive and seeks to capture the voices, experiences, and learning of teens and artist educators both within a single program year and throughout the program's evolution and multiyear engagement with young people. Teen participants typically fill out written surveys and participate in a range of other evaluative strategies that include peer-to-peer interviews, where participants are divided into pairs to ask each other questions about their experiences in the program without the interference or pressure of performing any particular outcome for program staff; video "confessionals," where teens individually respond to a set of questions in front of a camera; facilitated group conversations; and writing, drawing, and mapping-based prompts. Artist educators regularly engage in reflective conversations with program staff and the wider learning and engagement team and conclude their position with a written reflection that includes a letter to the incoming artist educator.

Staff

Dia's Learning and Engagement Department collaboratively manages and facilitates the program across sites with the director of learning and engagement. The Dia Beacon and Dia Chelsea programs are each supported by two administrative staff members and one artist educator. The artist educator is a part-time staff member who develops an original and emergent curriculum and facilitates all program sessions over one full year. Drawing from their creative practice, the artist educator is a mentor, collaborator, and instigator for the teens as they explore their artistic and intellectual interests. Administrative staff oversee the program's day-to-day operations, including communications, program production, recruitment, evaluation, and reporting. Additionally, administrative staff collaborate with and provide coaching for the artist educator weekly throughout the year and facilitate ongoing reflective processes for the entire team, including paid program interns. Separating the administrative, logistical, and managerial responsibilities from curriculum design and facilitation creates space for artist educators to have maximal agency and structured support throughout their research, writing, facilitation, and reflective processes.

Youth
The Hudson Valley teen program recruits youth from several surrounding counties, while the NYC program recruits youth from across the five boroughs, and most teens are participants in the NYC Department of Youth and Community Development's Learn and Earn program. Across both sites, some program participants identify as artists, whereas others do not. Participants from both cohorts of Dia Teens are creative, critical thinkers interested in engaging with contemporary art, working closely on collaborative projects, and participating in a supportive community of peers.

Social Media
Dia Teens' Instagram account (@diateens) is populated by youth from both programs, overseen by learning and engagement administrative staff, and independent from Dia Art Foundation's social media accounts. The Instagram account is a platform for sharing and documenting sessions, field trips, and projects and is the most direct and relevant means of communication for the Hudson Valley cohort.

Absences
Dia Teens is an intentional community of learners that may change drastically depending on who is in the room, and as a result, absences are deeply felt. Participants commit to attending all program

sessions and being fully present for themselves and each other. Teens are encouraged to be proactive and communicate absences in advance whenever possible. While exceptions are made in the case of emergencies, school obligations, or illness, repeated absences lead to an informal one-on-one conversation with the participant to better understand the situation. Continued absences may lead to a more formal conversation with program staff, and dismissals are typically only considered if the well-being and safety of the individual and/or the larger group are negatively impacted.

Food
Dia Teens provides snacks, beverages, and meals (depending on the schedule) for all sessions. Teens take turns selecting, preparing, and presenting the snacks and meals for their peers, which can sometimes include arranging the lunch setup, place cards with personal notes, and organizing potlucks. In the past, meals and snacks—both the preparation and experience of eating together—have become an important ritual for the group and a central aspect of the curriculum. In Summer 2021, youth took turns preparing fresh juices and tea for each other at the start of every session.

General Contact
beaconprogram@diaart.org
chelseaprogram@diaart.org

Funding
Learning and engagement at Dia receives baseline support through an anonymous endowment fund. Additional fundraising from foundations and individual donors supplements this funding and supports ongoing growth. Recent funders have included the Andrew W. Mellon Foundation, Annenberg Foundation, Concordia Foundation, the New York City Department of Cultural Affairs, and the New York State Council on the Arts.

Budget

Dia Teens, which is part of Dia's larger youth and young adults initiative, has a budget of approximately $115,000. This covers the full program in both Beacon and New York City, with the majority of funds covering artist educator pay; stipends for all participating youth; food and transportation for students, including lunches, snacks, public transportation aid, and field trip travel; and program materials.

Location

The Hudson Valley teen program takes place in the Learning Lab at Dia Beacon, a large studio space adjacent to the galleries with storage, sinks, bathrooms, and technology. Other Dia Beacon sites include the galleries, the staff conference room, the grounds, and nearby walkable destinations, including parks and Main Street. Typically, the Dia Beacon cohort travels to New York City via commuter rail up to ten times per year. The NYC teen program takes place in the library at Dia Chelsea, on a floor between the offices and gallery space. It is a large open room with storage, access to bathrooms, a full kitchen, and technology. Other New York City sites include the Chelsea exhibition and program space and offices, Dia's Soho sites, and cultural destinations throughout the city. During the renovation of Dia's Chelsea spaces, the NYC cohort met at Judson Memorial Church in the 2019–2020 school year. Typically, the Dia Chelsea cohort travels to Beacon via commuter rail up to ten times per year. Dia Teens at both sites takes place in flexible and shared program spaces that feature lectures, larger meetings, readings, symposiums, etc., with priority given to the teen program's recurring schedule.

Alumni Opportunities

Dia is developing an alumni program that addresses the creative, professional, and learning-based interests of youth and young adults who have participated in Dia Teens and internships and fellowships across all departments of the organization. Dia Teens includes apprenticeship positions for program alums with both the Beacon and NYC cohort, a role that includes collaboration with the artist educator, mentorship responsibilities, and administrative program support. Additionally, Dia Teens alums have interned with other programs within the Learning and Engagement Department and taken permanent positions as part of the visitor services team.

◫

High Museum of Art
Program Structure

The High Museum of Art's Teen Team is a group of 15 creative high school students who share a common interest in art and community engagement. The Teen Team offers participants the opportunity to engage with art, culture, and history; develop workplace and team-building skills; and learn about various professional options and career paths. The Teen Team gets behind-the-scenes access to the museum, assists in planning Teen Nights, events, and other public programming, and learns about the museum's exhibitions and collections. Teen Team members will work on a summer project during the summer intensive while learning about the museum's collections, careers, and programs. Throughout the school year, Teen Team members will continue to assist in developing and implementing programming for teens, youths, and families. While part of the Teen Team program, members meet with High Museum staff, arts professionals, and other teens. Teen Team is a year-round commitment and a paid position. Teen Team members must be rising juniors or seniors enrolled full-time in high school.

Payment

Teen Team members are part-time temporary employees of the museum and are paid biweekly at an hourly rate of $7.50. Their time in the program also includes the standard employee benefits of discounted parking, discounts at the museum shop and cafés, and access to special events and exhibitions.

Recruitment / Outreach

The current Teen Team posts on social media to market and help recruit for their programs. Our Education staff reaches out to school staff (counselors, teachers, administrators) via email or in-person visits throughout the year.

Interviews / Applications

Applications are online via the High's website and usually open in January or February (with the program beginning in June). Traditionally, applications are open for one month, with interviews held during most local schools' spring breaks. Decisions are sent out to all applicants by May 1. The application includes standard contact information, demographic and school information, yes / no questions about commitment and expectations of the program, and short-answer / essay questions. A small group of museum staff reviews applications. Usually, 35–40 teens are interviewed for 15 spots. Interviews are conducted by a panel of the Teen Team instructor, a Teen Team alumnus / alumna, and an Education staff member.

Events

During the school year, the Teen Team hosts monthly workshops for teens, free for teen visitors. These programs are individually themed around our permanent collection or special exhibitions and have multiple art-making activities and Teen Team–led tours. The High hosts a Teen Night twice a year, traditionally in August and March, which is a teen takeover, including art-making, tours, performances, and more. The Teen Team develops, markets, and implements all of its programming.

Typical Meeting

School-year sessions are held immediately before

their monthly workshop for an hour. These are facilitated by the Teen Team members, with the Teen Team instructor offering guidance. The Teen Team members discuss marketing strategies, prep for upcoming programs, and other immediate information. The Education staff provides snacks. During their eight-week summer intensive, the teens meet Tuesday through Friday from 9:30 am to 3:30 pm and participate in projects, meetings with staff, art-making activities, workshops, etc.

Transportation
Teens are given an unlimited public transportation pass during the summer intensive program. The High is directly across from a train station. Teen Team members are offered discounted employee parking year-round.

Evaluation
Each Teen Team member has informal check-in meetings with program staff throughout the summer and school year. Staff conduct a formal evaluation each year for all current and previous Teen Team members, which helps adapt the program to fit the needs of teens better. These surveys are sent out via Google Forms.

Staff
The Teen Team instructor is a paid teaching artist at the museum, usually changing every one to two summers based on program needs and schedule. The Teen Team instructor is often a working artist with teaching experience. They co-lead the program with the manager of family programs. During the summer, an alum is a paid Teen Team assistant.

Youth
Teen Team members are rising high school juniors or seniors interested in art. Teen Team members are interested in learning about art and the workings of a museum and serving as ambassadors for

the High. They also enjoy working with visitors of all ages. Teen Team members are expected to utilize their peer network, take initiative, and display professionalism and responsibility.

Social Media
Teen Team members run their own social media, @hmateens. In the past, they have had a Facebook, Tumblr, etc., but currently only utilize Instagram. During the summer intensive, they meet with the museum's marketing and communications team to learn about best practices. Education staff has access to the Instagram account. The Teen Team is not required to run their ideas / posts past staff.

Absences
Up to three absences are allowed during the summer intensive, with exceptions for illness. If they miss more than three days, the staff meets with the Teen Team member to discuss. We do not have a requirement during the school year but ask members to attend as many programs as possible.

Food
Snacks are provided and readily available for Teen Team members during all meetings, including the summer intensive. Education staff purchases snacks, usually trying to mix healthy (carrots and hummus) with fun (weird potato chip flavors).

General Contact
HMAteenprograms@high.org

Funding
The majority of funding comes from grants. Currently, the Teen Team is funded by the Molly Blank Foundation.

Budget
The budget changes each year but is usually $60,000–$90,000.

Lucy Lawless as "Xe
Dream girls
What a day for b
"**TV's Sexiest Sci-**
Lucy Lawless an

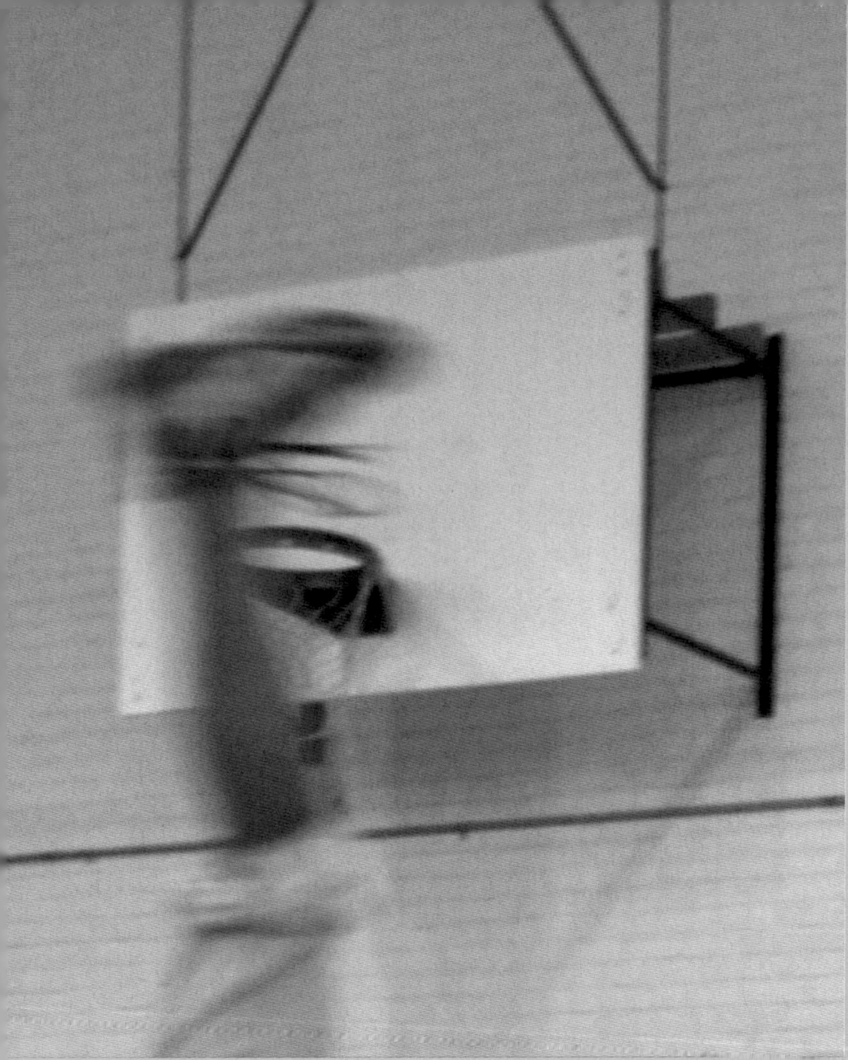

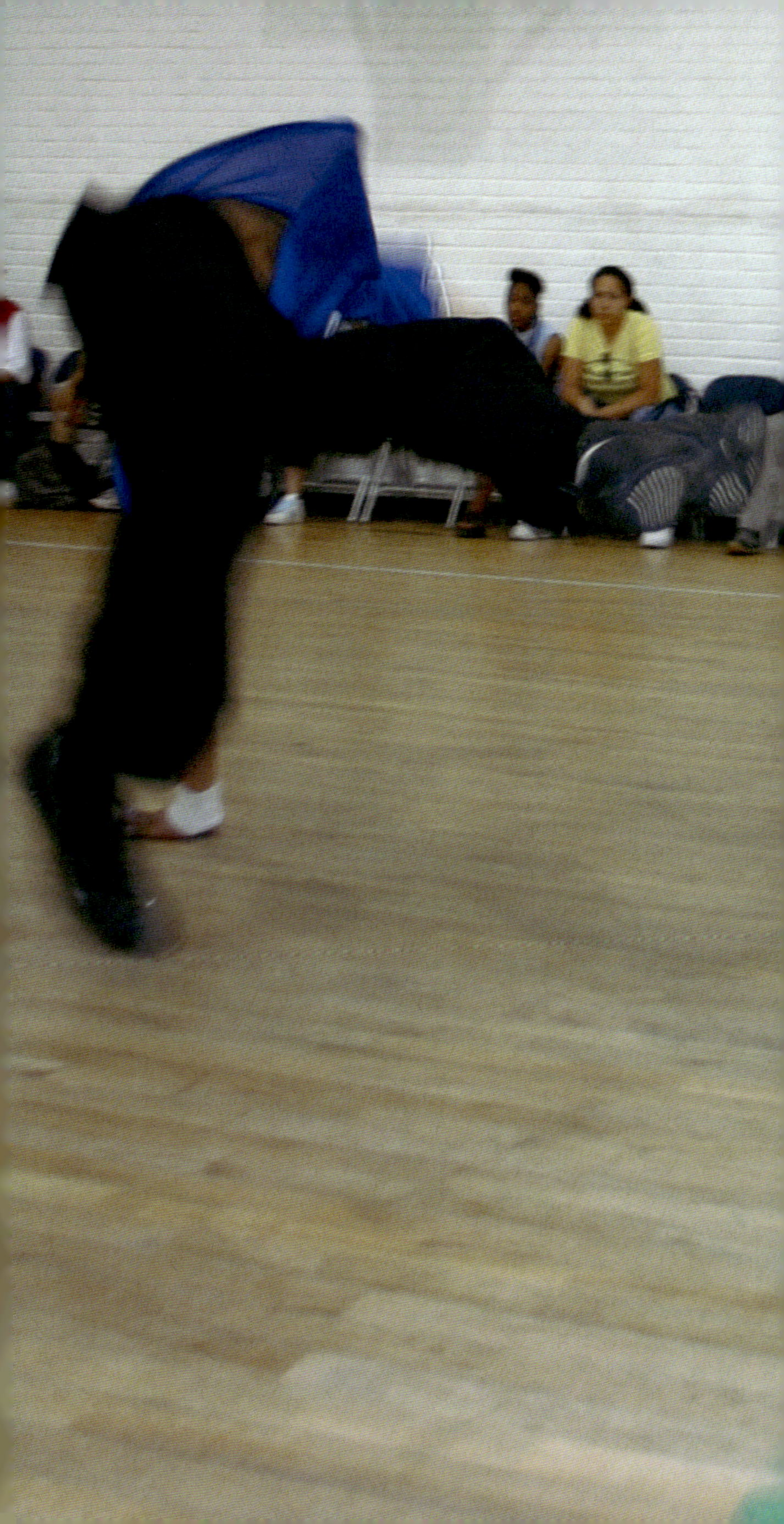

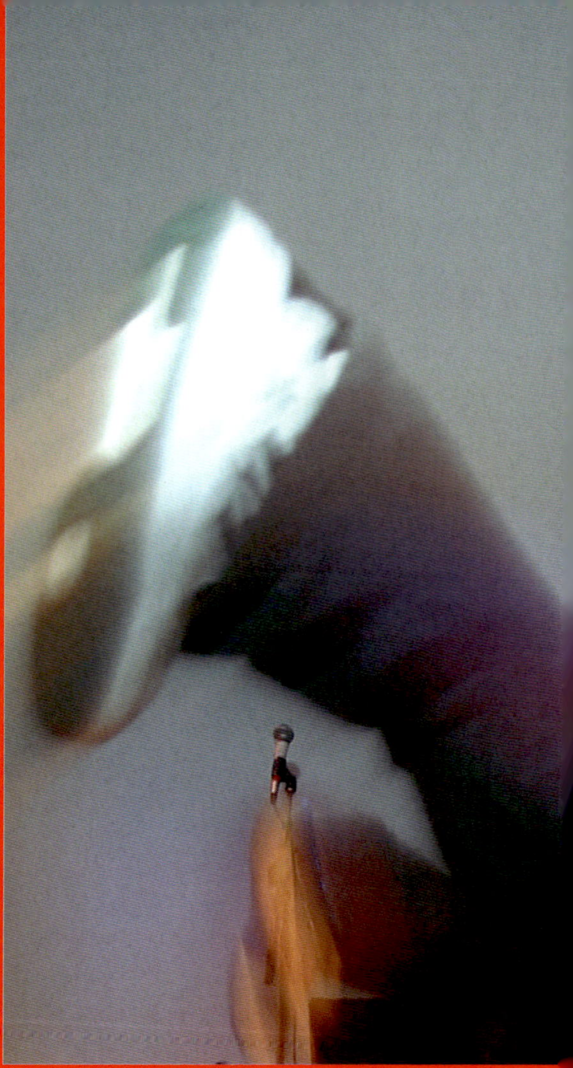

Location

All meetings and programs take place at the museum. The summer intensive is held in a workshop space where Teen Team members can decorate and rearrange as needed. Our monthly meetings and programs are held in our Education Center workshops and the museum's galleries.

Alumni Opportunities

Graduating Teen Team members are invited to work as summer camp workshop assistants, and those who stay local continue to work programs during the school year. Teen Team alums have become teaching artists, summer camp coordinators, curatorial assistants, and more. Each January, an alum meetup is held at the museum for previous and current members to network.

◫

Whitney Museum of American Art
Program Structure

The program brings New York City high school teens together with contemporary artists, providing opportunities to work collaboratively, discuss art critically, think creatively, and make art inspired by this exchange. Youth Insights currently offers two sections of a semester-long spring and fall program called Youth Insights Artists. Youth Insights Introductions, a special program for English language learners, and Youth Insights Arts Careers are offered during the summer. Graduates of YI Artists, YI Arts Careers, and YI Introductions are eligible to apply to the Youth Insights Leaders program, a yearlong paid after-school arts internship for 11th- and 12th-grade students. Leaders work closely with artists and educators to organize public programs and events for other teens from around NYC, learn to develop and facilitate interactive art-making and discussions, help lead Open Studio for Teens, and assist educators in the Whitney's Family and Community education programs. YI Leaders meets on Tuesday afternoons from 4 pm to 6:30 pm, with some additional Friday and Saturday sessions required. The program runs from late September through June, with some opportunities to work weekends in the summer in the Family Open Studio program. Students who begin the program in 11th grade can decide to continue in their 12th-grade year. YI Leaders work with Whitney educators to organize public programs and events for other teens from around the city, from artist talks to hands-on workshops. They also learn to develop and lead interactive tours of the Whitney's collection and exhibitions, assist educators in the Whitney's Family and Community programs, create special projects in response to the Whitney's collection and exhibitions, and participate in art-making workshops with artists.

Payment
YI Leaders are paid $14 an hour to attend meetings, assist in Open Studio programs, and lead Teen Events.

Recruitment / Outreach
Although the Youth Insights Leaders cohort begins at the start of the school year, other Youth Insights programs accept applications in the fall, spring, and summer. During each recruitment cycle, the staff shares information about all program areas, including the Youth Insights Leaders program. Recruitment and outreach are ongoing. The Youth Insights Leaders program comprises students who have previously participated in another Youth Insights program, and as such, recruitment is heavily based on this network. These students and their parents / guardians and recommending teachers receive emails about applying to the program. Information is also shared on the Whitney's website.

Interviews / Applications
Applications are open once a year from late July

until early September. In the application, students complete a section on basic information and a series of six reflection questions. These questions seek to understand why the applicant is applying, what they hope to gain from the experience, their definition of a leader, what they hope to contribute to the program, and their ideas for a Teen Event. Once the application closes, all applicants participate in a group interview with program staff and up to 5 fellow applicants. Interviews are informal and provide opportunities for students to share creative ideas for engaging with other teens. The number of students accepted depends on the number of openings in the program. A total of 14 teens can be enrolled in the program. YI Leaders help with YI Artist interviews throughout the school year.

Events

YI Leaders plan three to four events throughout the school year for other NYC teens. These events are often in collaboration with an artist whose work is on view at the Whitney. These events feature art-making, performances, music, giveaways, food, gallery activities such as tours or scavenger hunts, evaluation stations, and an entertainment feature related to the event or topic. For example, Halloween Teen Night may feature tarot card reading and/or face painting. In planning these events, YI Leaders will meet weekly to discuss event goals, key concepts in the artwork, and brainstorm ideas related to the exhibition. Throughout the planning process, YI Leaders will meet with show curators to discuss artists' work and highlight work they think will be most exciting for a teen audience. In addition, YI Leaders will be trained to lead an engaging tour and practice those tours. The featured artist will join for several meetings to brainstorm ideas, create a plan, and work through logistical details. In addition, YI Leaders create examples of art projects. In some instances, external teen program groups may join in the planning process for a collaborative teen event.

Typical Meeting

YI Leaders meet weekly on Tuesday afternoons from 4 pm to 6:30 pm, excluding school breaks and holidays. This amounts to approximately 50 meetings per school year. When students arrive, they are greeted by program staff as the music plays in the background. Each cohort adds their favorite music to a Spotify playlist. Snacks are set up for the entirety of the session, and students are welcome to pick up whatever snack they'd like at any point during the meeting. About 20 minutes in, the meeting begins. Program staff start the meeting with a fun check-in question that everyone can respond to, then jump into an icebreaker activity. Throughout the school year, a YI Leader signs up to take on the role of starting the meeting with a check-in question and leading an icebreaker activity of their choice. The content or focus of the day begins after the group has warmed up. This could be a teen exchange with another teen group, a gallery-based activity with program staff, an inquiry-based tour led by a curator, or an event-planning meeting with an artist.

Transportation

The program provides participants with multitrip MetroCards the week after and on the weekends after Open Studio programs.

Evaluation

Google Forms provide formal evaluations at the beginning and end of the school year. An informal evaluation is conducted at the midpoint of the programming year, between the fall and spring semesters. In addition, participants regularly engage in sharing feedback after every teen event planning cycle. These discussions include unpacking what went well and what could improve. Informal feedback is shared with program staff through group discussions and anonymous Post-it wall notes. These informal evaluation responses are recorded by program staff and saved for future discussions.

Staff
Youth Insights Leaders program staff consists of two full-time employees: the Coordinator of Teen Programs and the Assistant to Teen Programs. Several teen program interns help with program operations and logistics throughout the school year. On weekends, YI Leaders work with the family programs staff, which includes the Coordinator of Family Programs and the Assistant to Family Programs.

Youth
YI Leaders are 11th- and 12th-grade students in high school based in NYC. Leaders are previous participants in other YI programs, such as Artists, Arts Careers, and Introductions. These teens have an array of interests and are eager to learn about museum education, collaborative program planning, and working with artists and peers.

Social Media
Youth Insights does not have a social media presence controlled by teens. All social media is controlled by the Whitney Museum's Social Media Manager. Content for teen programs is shared only through organic posts, such as Instagram Stories.

Absences
The YI Leaders program strongly advises transparent and open communication around attendance. YI Leaders are encouraged to communicate with program staff before missing a meeting, being late, or helping find a replacement for their scheduled work day. YI Leaders are scheduled in advance to work on the Open Studio for Teens and Open Studios for Families programs. If a YI Leader cannot be present for their scheduled work day, they must communicate with fellow YI Leaders to find a replacement or switch their scheduled work day. If a YI Leader has an unexcused absence and has not communicated with program staff within 48 hours of the meeting,

program staff will send an email to check-in with the student. If a YI Leader has sustained more than two unexcused absences in a row, program staff will invite the student for an informal one-on-one meeting to discuss what may be going on and how the student can improve communication. If a YI Leader has sustained more than three unexcused absences in a row, program staff will meet with the student in a formal one-on-one meeting to discuss their status and detriment to the YI Leaders community. Very rarely are students dismissed from the program; however, it can be discussed if a YI Leader demonstrates they are no longer interested in attending the program.

Food

Snacks and beverages are provided at every meeting and Open Studio program. Most snacks are healthy, including whole grains, 100 percent juice, water, and fresh fruit. YI Leaders often get to choose the type of unhealthy snack option to be served during meetings, which is often Oreos. For teen events and nights, YI Leaders often get pizza as they work for hours as workshop instructors, tour guides, and more.

General Contact

youthinsights@whitney.org

Funding

Funding for Youth Insights comes from several sources, which include an endowment, individual donors, foundations, and government organizations. The complete list includes William Randolph Hearst Foundation; the Annenberg Foundation; GRoW @ Annenberg; Pinkerton Foundation; Nellie and Robert Gipson; the Keith Haring Foundation; the Milton and Sally Avery Arts Foundation; the Youth Insights Fund, supported by an anonymous donor, Lise and Michael Evans, Ellen and Andrew Celli, David Sigal, and the Yurman Family Foundation; public funds from the New York City Department of Cultural Affairs in partnership with the City Council; and the Whitney's Education Committee.

Budget
Youth Insights typically has an operating budget that ranges from $85,000 to $113,000, depending on the fiscal year. This budget covers all Youth Insights and Drop-In Teen Programming. The budget spans several operating expenses, such as meals, transportation, art supplies, honoraria, student pay, mailing, and consultant fees.

Location
The Whitney Museum is located in New York's Meatpacking District. The meeting and classroom spaces overlook the expansive Hudson River, offering views of New Jersey.

Alumni Opportunities
Youth Insights alumni often return as college/graduate school interns in departments across the museum. In addition, alums are invited to participate in college-readiness-related programs as presenters and mentors. Several of our alums join the museum as staff in the Visitor and Member Experience Department and Education Department.

☺

Nancy Nowacek

It's Not Sexy, but It's Crazy Cool: Age Diversity

Bio

Nancy Nowacek is a research-based and socially engaged artist. Her current research includes urban waterways, climate change, and intergenerational mental health. She cofounded the art collective Works on Water (worksonwater.org) to support and grow the community of artists committed to advocacy for urban ecologies. She is also one half of the Always Working Group (alwaysworkinggroup.art), a social practice collective that explores contemporary political issues through social forms. Nowacek holds an MFA in social practice from California College of the Arts, an MFA in visual communication from Virginia Commonwealth University, and a BFA in photography and design from the University of Michigan.

Essay

"The white wall…it was…nothing…and EVERYTHING!" gasps a member of the Walker Art Center Teen Arts Council (WACTAC). The wall in question is at one of the main entrances to the museum that visitors pass when entering through the parking ramp. They can hear the teens' praise for the wall in a satirical TikTok video subtly placed on the wall via QR code (QRc). The placard states:

> When you enter the museum, this is one of the first places you might see. Is every object in the Walker art? The walls? The doors? The chairs? How do you know which features are art? Is this wall one of the most viewed and ignored artworks in the museum? Your art journey begins now!

And so, it does. Four more meta-works by the 2020–2021 WACTAC cohort were strategically placed and installed midsummer 2021. Each confronted the viewer with an ontological question. QRc's activated WACTAC's thoughtful, unexpected, and joyfully creative reframings of the focal object or location.

I began with WACTAC in January 2020 as the Walker's Public Engagement, Learning, and Impact Department's artist-in-residence, with a plan to travel from New York to Minneapolis to meet with the teens in person once a month to mentor them through phases of project identification, research, and development. The culminating arc of the WACTAC program is a collaborative project designed and evaluated by the teens. Program staff gave them a scope, a budget, and past examples to support them in coming up with a central question to guide them through research and exploration that will be shared out through creative forms like a zine, TikTok videos, or a bingo board—to reference some past projects. I was there to respond to the teens' ideas and to help guide them through their creative project—rather than one of my own, as is more typically the case with artist-in-residence models in this context.

I worked with the 2019–2020 cohort first in person and then on Zoom during those first harried months of the pandemic lockdown. I continued working with the 2020–2021 cohort, an entirely new group of teens. Over the two years, I met with WACTAC twice in person and many more times over Zoom (with changing scenery of virtual backgrounds including Tom Selleck, waterfalls, and sandwiches). During that time, I supported and prompted the teens by cultivating their ideas (sort of sanctioned institutional critiques) and expanded my perception of the nuances of dynamic mentorship that occurs when working with young people.

Mentoring is caring improvisation. I found myself moving between observer, comic, and inventor—creating methods in the moment to help the group shape their ideas into a form. For example, in one session early on, the Idea Machine surfaced. Teens' conversations about their work sparked a method that started with brainstorming an inventory of resources and skills the teens had access to, possible social forms,[1] and desired audience responses. Each element was written on an index card, and decks for each category were accumulated. The group shuffled each deck and dealt the top card to create a project prompt, like "singing / jury duty / people laughing" and "party supplies / small boats / 'I did not know I liked art!'"

If not improvising, I found myself cheering the teens on. Cheerleaders get a bad rap, but the world today—powered by fearmongering, the rhetoric of winning and losing, and an *us vs. them* tribalism—is woefully lacking voices of support and encouragement. Moreover, neoliberalism[2] has turned every aspect of life into a competition and what is now known as hustle culture. Who has time to support others in this perpetual struggle, not just to get ahead, but to survive? I often wonder how the world might be if there was as much, if not way

---

1. "Social forms" are the grammars of social interactions, evolved by cultures to afford a measure of predictability to the inherent unpredictability of social encounters, and were first noted by sociologist Georg Simmel. For example, games and meals are social forms. Ted Purves introduced the concept of social forms at *Living as Form*, the 2011 Creative Time Summit.

more, championing and cheering as competition. And I think it is a role into which many more folks with privilege, platform, or power might want to consider moving—supporting the visions of those who lack equal privilege, platform, or access to power.

As a group of young people from all over the Twin Cities, with different backgrounds, cultures, and identities, the WACTAC teens model the world I want to live in. And they are smart as hell. I did not always understand their slang. Their interests and choices did not always make sense to me. But the invitation given to me was essentially an opportunity to show up and say YES, AND.[3]

The power of YES, AND can bridge differences of all sorts: ideas, interpretations, experiences, and backgrounds. Watching WACTAC work and adding to—rather than altering—their creative instincts expanded our shared imagination...and our respect for the humble potato.[4] The energy produced by the group was so powerful that I neglected to notice until the very end of two cycles that we—me, the teens, and the facilitators—had been engaged in an intergenerational exchange.[5]

Programs such as these are rarely framed as an intergenerational exchange or intergenerational contact,[6] because, most likely, it is not yet a cultural conversation. People do not often think about age diversity as a kind of diversity because, as the last

2. "Neoliberalism" generally refers to the governmental term of deregulation and an unraveling of the social safety net toward intensification in free-market capitalism. Their effects: the destruction of the welfare state and environmental protections, among others; but more importantly, the emergence of hustle culture, or a world in which all individuals are in competition with one another for economic survival. For a great reading on the effects of neoliberalism, please see George Monbiot, "Neoliberalism—the Ideology at the Root of All Our Problems," *Guardian*, April 1, 2016.
3. One of the main tenets in improv comedy: "Yes" accepts any reality suggested by a collaborator, then "and" moves the idea forward by introducing new information. See Tina Fey's rules in *Bossypants* (2011).
4. A group obsession with Claes Oldenburg's *Shoestring Potatoes Spilling from a Bag*, 1966.

form of "acceptable" bias, age is not yet considered a category of "other."

Extended family gatherings constitute intergenerational contact, but they may be one of the only contexts in which people of very different ages regularly interact with one another in the 2020s. Over the past fifty years, society has become a collection of siloed generations.[7] This condition is partly an effect of the ways institutions and services are structured, but it is also a dual function of "youth culture," first defined in the 1940s and mainstreamed in the 1960s, with ageism coined in 1969.[8] Ageism is a form of prejudice based on perceived age. The convergence of these two phenomena—the celebra-

5. "Intergenerational exchange" is often thought of as the passing down of economic resources or caregiving between adults and children in a biological family; however, I use it here to describe the social encounter between two different age cohorts. This purposeful comingling of different age cohorts is also referred to as intergenerational contact, but I use "exchange" to point to two-way communication and sharing.
6. Although the idea of generations is highly contestable, if not damaging (see the following footnote), I am explicitly using the term "intergenerational" to signify the idea of grouping cohorts by age and the monolithic stereotypes that occur from generational thinking.
7. Louis Menand, in "It's Time to Stop Talking about Generations," *New Yorker*, October 11, 2021, provides great insight into the origin of the contemporary idea of "generations": the point at which attending high school became the majority experience for teenagers instead of work (in the 1940s), leading to the codification of a "youth culture." The definition of youth culture expanded over the next twenty-five years as more and more late teens began attending college and were a recognizable and unique consumer base. The original meaning of "generation" was used in reproductive biology to describe parents and offspring. But in the mid-twentieth century, it became widely used as a tool to segment society by slippery thirty-year increments. Furthermore, these increments were ascribed monolithic traits based on the economic and/or political contexts of their youth: "the Silent Generation," "the Greatest Generation," "the Baby Boomers," and so on. Segmentation and stereotyping groups of people based on birth year create gross and untrue generalizations and, like all stereotypes, lead to discrimination. Moreover, "generations" as a social definition stratifies society, pitting one group against another, and weaponizes age, celebrating younger ages and attacking older ones.

tion of "youth" and the judgment of "the aged"—has slowly disappeared older people from mainstream culture. A contemporary example: the dismissive meme "OK, boomer."

Ageism goes both ways, and younger folks, like the WACTAC teens—aka Gen Z—are also targets of ageism. "Youngism," the form of ageism pointed at younger adults, is generationally based discrimination.[9] Contemporary young adults are described as "undisciplined, disrespectful, unfriendly, irresponsible, and lacking moral values."[10]

All forms of ageism affect those who suffer from it, including lack of social connection, loneliness, and lack of empathy. It also exacerbates stereotypes, misunderstandings, and conflict between generations. Where the value and benefits of diversity are sought, age diversity should be among them because bringing different ages into contact with one another can build compassion and mutual respect and improve the mental and emotional health of all involved.

When intergenerational encounters are framed as age diverse, they offer the opportunity to illuminate forms of power each group has or does not have and articulate differences in experiences brought by age, alongside the difference in experiences from race, culture, gender, and background. That is to say, age-diverse encounters pose an opportunity to welcome the often not-talked-about part of who

8. This first paragraph of *This Chair Rocks* (2016) reads: "When geriatrician Robert Butler coined the term 'ageism' in 1969—the same year 'sexism' made its debut—he defined it as a combination of prejudicial attitudes toward older people, old age, and aging itself; discriminatory practices against olders; and institutional practices and policies that perpetuate stereotypes about them. The media quickly adopted the term and added it to the Oxford English Dictionary. Almost half a century later, it has barely made inroads into public consciousness, not to mention provoke outcry."
9. Stéphane P. Francioli and Michael S. North, "Youngism: The Content, Causes, and Consequences of Prejudices toward Younger Adults," *Journal of Experimental Psychology* 150, no. 12 (2021).
10. Francioli and North, "Youngism," 2.

we are: the sum of our years. If the best learning environments are those that invite the totalities of each participant's identities to the table, so to speak, then one who has accrued life experiences from age should also be a part of that. Imagine age-diverse group introductions: name, pronouns, and a formative life experience / life lesson.

Creating space that acknowledges and leans into such differences requires particular considerations and supports. In addition to the common support of co-creating group norms, it is helpful to frame an age-diverse group as a community of practice conceptually or a group of people "who share a concern or a passion for something they do and learn how to do it better as they interact regularly."[11] Simply put, give the group a shared goal. There are other conditions that can foster "positive and mutually valuable" age-diverse encounters:[12]

> Specific moments for one-to-one interactions
> Interactions in which age-diverse pairs find themselves on equal footing (learning something new, for example)
> Opportunities to share personal information—significant life events, current feelings, etc.
> Specific definition of an age-diverse encounter

WACTAC meetings are scheduled after a long day at school (or work for me and the facilitators), and everyone needs a little time to snack and chill. For the record, snacking and chilling as a methodology[13] is underrated. I use the term "methodology"

11. Etienne Wenger-Trayner and Beverly Wenger-Trayner, "Introduction to Communities of Practice: A Brief Overview of the Concept and Its Uses," June 2015, available from authors at their website, https://www.wenger-trayner.com/introduction-to-communities-of-practice.
12. Contributions in this area of study include scholarly works by Abrams et al., 2006; Bousfield and Hutchison, 2010; Caspi, 1984; Clarke et al., 2003; Gaggioli et al., 2014; Harwood et al., 2005; McKeown, Clarke, and Repper, 2006; Newman, Faux, and Larimer, 1997; Pinquart and Forstmeier, 2012; Roodin et al., 2013; Schwartz and Simmons, 2001; Tam et al., 2006.

because it is the first step toward building a community and a collaborative space when used deliberately. It is the ease-in, warm-up, social space where inner states migrate outward. By sharing stresses, obsessions, weird dreams, and funny stories, the "brave space"[14] of the group emerges. Crinkling bags and shuffling chairs form the background for unfolding personalities: shy, observant, bold, reserved, and expectant. In snacking and chilling, we reveal ourselves and become a group banded together.

WACTAC facilitators seamlessly wove opportunities for sharing personal information into snacking and chilling. The icebreaker question for our final meeting in June of 2021 was "What is your favorite limb?" which turned into "What was your favorite childhood injury?" which turned into a funny, gasp-worthy set of stories that created a common ground for all of us, and a moment free of group goals or work. Snacking and chilling can also be thought of as Deep Hanging Out.

Deep Hanging Out[15] is a strategy and term I learned from the excellent organization Public Matters in Los Angeles. Deep Hanging Out is the sharing and learning that come from taskless time together. Though the teens and facilitators, who met every week over the entire school year, got regular deep hangout time, as an every-few-weeks artist-mentor dropping into weekly two-hour meetings with an agenda of three or four tasks, I needed

13. See page 172 for Jorge Espinosa's piece 1.2.2. Snack Curators on creating practices around snacking.
14. "Brave space" is defined by Brian Arao and Kristi Clemens, "From Safe Spaces to Brave Spaces: A New Way to Frame Dialogue around Diversity and Social Justice," in *The Art of Effective Facilitation: Reflections from Social Justice Educators*, ed. Lisa M. Landreman (Sterling, VA: Stylus Publishing, 2013), 135–51.
15. "Deep Hanging Out" was coined by anthropologist Renato Rosaldo, but popularized by James Clifford in *Routes: Travel and Translation in the Late Twentieth Century*. It came to my attention in an article of the same name ("Deep Hanging Out") by Clifford Geertz as "localized, long-term, close-in, vernacular field research" in the October 22, 1988, issue of the *New York Review of Books*.

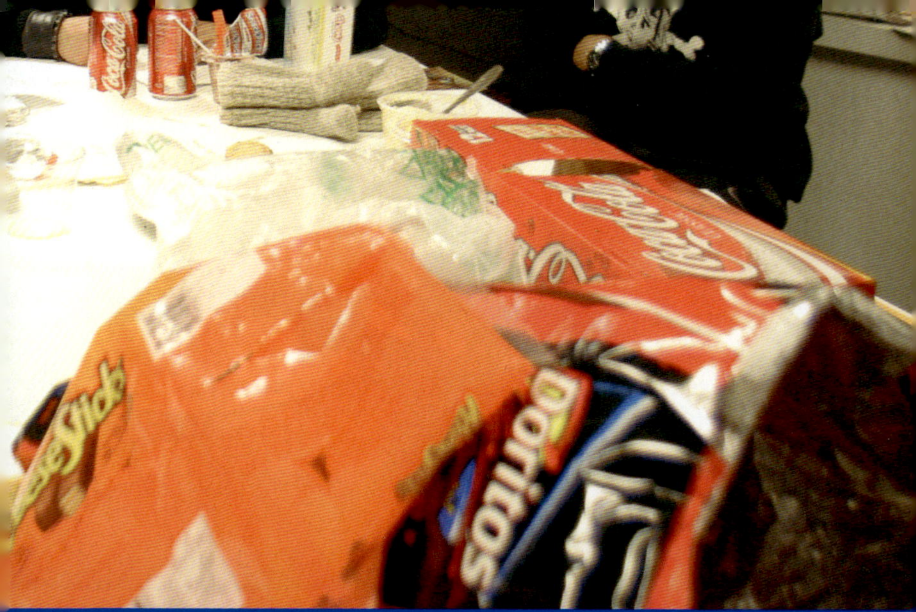
Coca-Cola
Doritos

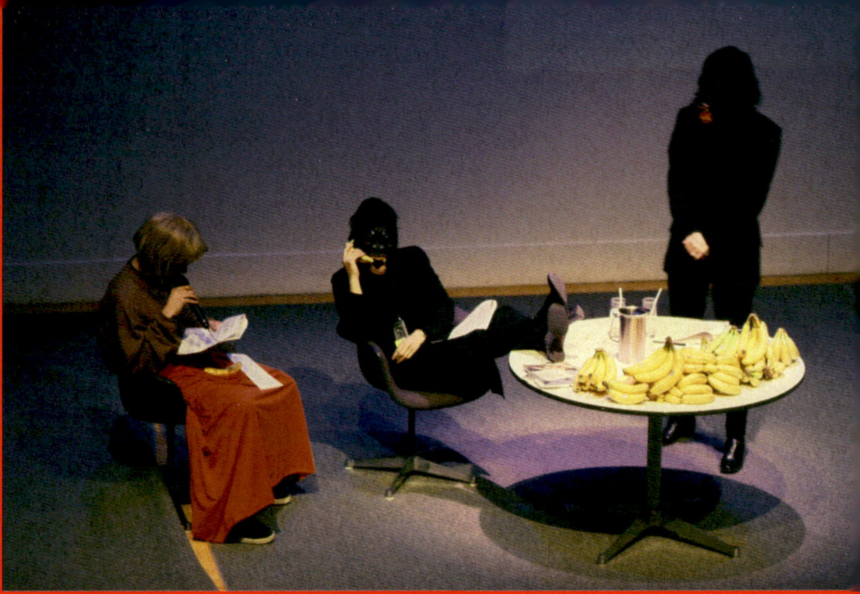

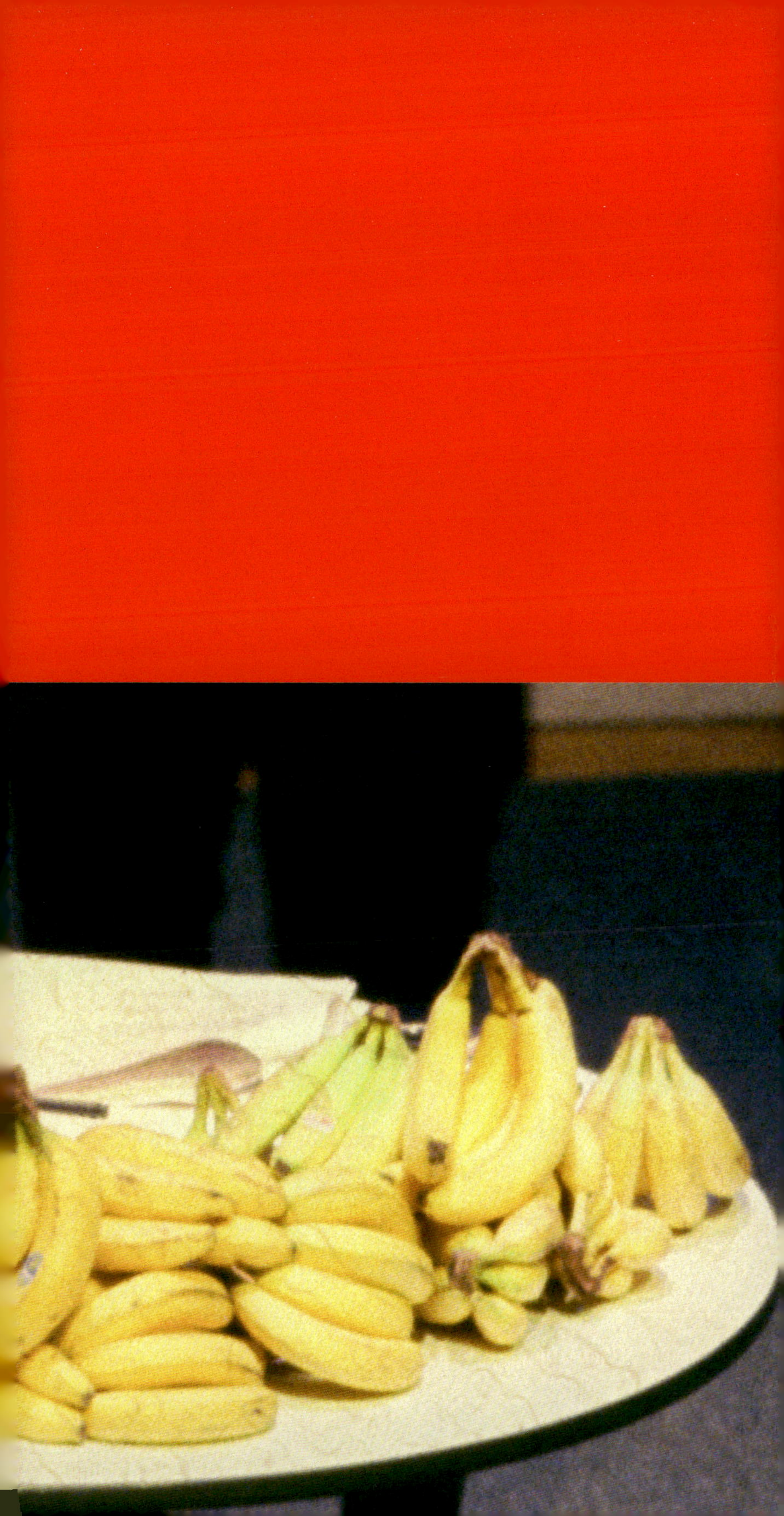

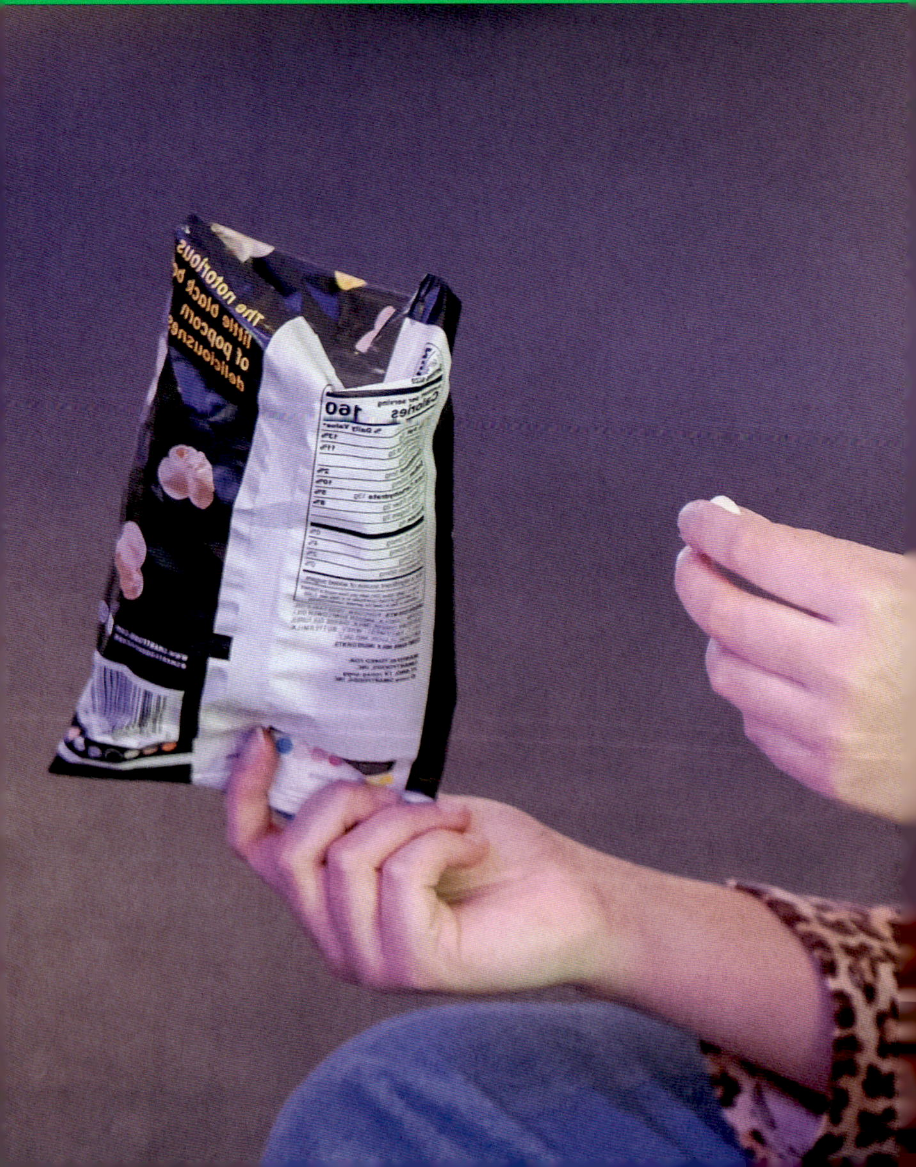

extra hangout time to establish that of being with. I spent two years with two cohorts to understand this critical piece. Perhaps weaving in moments of one-on-one conversations between each teen and me and increasing the frequency of my participation might deepen our relationship. Quite possibly, spending the same amount of in-real-life time without the anxieties and technologies forced by a global pandemic might accomplish it.

WACTAC is not the only site of intergenerational contact at the Walker. The galleries themselves constitute a site for potentially rich age-diverse encounters when acknowledged as such. Families—parents and kids, grandparents and kids—are a large segment of art audiences and offer a great opportunity to inquire, compare, contrast, and hold space for age-based points of view. Exhibition tours and gallery talks among age-diverse groups also provide an opportunity to pursue age diversity. Why not consider creating new age-diverse programming or turning teen-specific or retiree-specific programming into an opportunity for intergenerational encounters?

In settings where age-diverse cohorts might be encountering one another, each group's vocabularies (slang), identity concepts (race, gender, sexuality, functional diversity,[16] and neurodiversity), and/or behaviors (listening, communicating) may also affect the quality of age-diverse encounters. Preparing participants for the potential of these specific differences may also support clearer, more constructive, and more caring encounters.[17] But where might these encounters take place?

Art institutions—alongside public parks and public transportation—are one of the most naturally occurring age-diverse spaces. It is a sad truth that, even before the pandemic, the surgeon general sounded alarms about a "loneliness epidemic." Ironically, the highest reports of loneliness are among the youngest and oldest adults in our society—the two groups who might misunderstand one another the most may stand to have the most in common. If the pandemic forced art institutions to question their role in society, a critical role they can play in addressing mental health and ageism is through age-diverse programming. What might happen if institutions convened age-diverse groups weekly to snack, talk about art, and make TikToks about the artfulness of white walls and garbage cans? I imagine it would be nothing short of magic.

Ⓒ

16. "Functional diversity" is a term proposed by Javier Romañach and Manuel Lobato at the Independent Living Forum (Spain) in May 2005 to move away from the binaries of "abled" and "disabled." This term recognizes that all bodies have functionality but that those bodies, "with functional diversity, are different from most of the population, from the biophysical standpoint. Due to having different characteristics, and given the conditions of the context generated by society, we are forced to do the same tasks or functions in a different way, sometimes through third parties." And though the means may differ, the goal or action remains the same—to prepare a meal and eat it or to communicate, for example. And "the term 'functional diversity' corresponds to a reality in which a person functions in a different or diverse way from most of society." Romañach and Lobato, "Functional Diversity, a New Term in the Struggle for Dignity in the Diversity of the Human Being," University of Leeds Centre for Disability Studies, Independent Living Forum, May 2005, accessed July 27, 2022, https://disability-studies.leeds.ac.uk/wp-content/uploads/sites/40/library/zavier-Functional-Diversity-Romanach.pdf.
17. See 3.2.2. Intergenerational Tools for Constructive Conversation, page 461.

By Teens, for Tweens

Bio
Marie Hofer is the former youth and family programs manager at Crystal Bridges Museum of Art in Bentonville, Arkansas. She managed their Teen Council from 2019 to 2022, and created programs for and with high school students. Currently, Marie works in the museum's exhibitions department as an interpretation specialist.

Essay
As educators working in creative youth development, the phrase "by teens, for teens" is everywhere. It is the tagline on the Crystal Bridges Teen Council's social media account and an integral part of our teaching philosophy. The phrase is more than just catchy; it acknowledges that teens are cultural producers with distinct voices. Moreover, they are best positioned to advise the museum on topics of interest to their peers. Teens are experts in engaging their peer group; their insights are valuable when programming for various ages, including

the often-ignored middle school student audience. In the "by teens, for teens" model, we support the teen council as the primary producer of programs for middle and high school students.

Since middle school, teens in our council have matured dramatically, but that intensely transitional period of their life is still real and vivid for them. Additionally, many teens on our council have younger siblings in middle school. Because of this, teens are uniquely keyed into the interests of their younger counterparts. They remember the middle school experience and can advise us on programming for tweens.

At Crystal Bridges, we have expanded the "for teens, by teens" model and developed a "teens for tweens" concept where our Teen Council creates two large-scale Tween Nights a year. The council also advises us on topics for our Tween Studio classes. Not only does this continue to validate the expertise of the teens as cultural producers, but it fills a gap in museum programming. Tweens are often challenging to engage. They have aged out of more traditional family programming, having different interests, and needing more opportunities for social engagement. However, their maturity levels vary vastly, and they are not yet at the level to engage in some of the critical aspects of teen programming.

Working with the Teen Council to create fun and innovative programming for middle school students has been a successful part of our program for several years. While the Teen Council sees this type of engagement as very different from what they would present to their peers, they are excited to program for their younger counterparts. One of our former teen leaders, Helena, said:

> Planning Teen and Tween nights has been really rewarding, especially since I grew up going to Tween Nights. My favorite was the glow-in-the-dark Tween Night the council hosted when I was in seventh grade. I had the time of my life

dressing up and dancing. It was my first real dance experience, and I felt so heard and seen being able to dress up and do art activities as a new artist.

Like Helena, many council members went to these tween programs when they were younger and are excited to take on a new role as programmers, facilitators, and advisers.

Tween Night highlights the success of the "teens for tweens" model. Our Tween Nights are always themed, often something fun, accessible, and even a little quirky. This does not have to be based on an exhibition but can be a creative interpretation of our collection. Our Teen Council often chooses a theme with a costume element, which has been very popular with middle school participants. For example, our last Tween Night was marketed as "That '70s Party" and encouraged middle school students to dress up in their interpretation of the decade's style. These nights include a DJ, dancing, art-making, snacks, and engagements with artwork in our collection. On nights when our museum is closed to the public, we create a lounge for adults nearby yet separate from the tweens. The adult lounge allows shy tweens to have a support figure at the museum while still giving them room to build confidence and autonomy when engaging with their peers. This has been a way we accommodate the varying maturity levels of middle school students and allowed adults the opportunity to learn more about our tween programming. The council develops all the engagements for Tween Night and helps to facilitate the event.

This programming model has many benefits for both the tweens and our teen council:

Gives us a better understanding of tween interests and creates innovative programming. As mentioned before, teens have unique insight into the interests of tweens. Teens' creativity, humor, and willingness to play appeal to younger students who look up to our council.

Engages tweens at a transitional time in their lives, where there may not be as many engagement opportunities. We get positive feedback from middle school students and adult guardians who often express that programs available for their children have decreased significantly since aging out of elementary experiences.

Introduces tweens to the Teen Council and museum. As this is a large-scale social event, Tween Nights act as a welcoming, accessible entry point to museums and art. It also builds early recognition for our Teen Council. Many of the current members on our council came to a Tween Night when they were younger, which is how they initially learned about the council.

Helps the Teen Council grow their confidence. Tween Night is always the first large-scale event presented by the Teen Council. It is an excellent way to practice their event-planning skills before putting on a larger event for their peers. This event offers a lower-stakes opportunity to try new ideas and feel prepared to create Teen Night.

For Teens, by Teens: Public Event Planning

Bio

Araya Henry is the coordinator of teen programs at the Whitney Museum of American Art in New York. In this role, Araya coordinates all aspects of the museum's high-school-aged programs, including the national award-winning Youth Insights programs. Previously, Araya worked as the manager of youth and family programs at the Hudson River Museum in Yonkers, where she managed the national award-winning Junior Docent program, as well as coordinated family and outreach programs. Currently, she serves on the Greater Hudson Heritage Network board and the Junior Board of Part of the Solution.

Essay

Pipeline to Youth Insights Leaders
Our Youth Insights (YI) Leaders join us from our other Youth Insights programs, which include Artists, Arts Careers, and Introductions. The YI Artists program develops creative and conceptual

thinkers and offers teens the opportunity to work alongside artists-in-residence, who are artists on view, or whose work is related to a current exhibition at the Whitney.

In the program, students engage in gallery activities and discourse, and make art inspired by exchanging ideas. In the summer, the Whitney offers two intensive programs, Arts Careers and Introductions. Arts Careers allows teens the opportunity to meet and speak with arts professionals at the Whitney and in the NYC area. They learn about their peers, engage in discussions about art, and understand a variety of pathways within the art world.

Much like YI Artists, Arts Careers participants are meeting with Whitney staff to more intimately learn about their trajectory in the museum world. In addition, program presenters discuss current issues in the field and how the art world can become more inclusive and equitable.

Introductions is a free summer program for high school English language learner (ELL) students. The program welcomes teens to the Whitney to explore, discover, and discuss American art and create original works of art and writing. Teens represent the diversity of the world, and the museum galleries serve as a site for learning and building vocabulary together despite language barriers. Some of the program goals include:

Explore the concepts and queries artists respond to in their artwork
Develop English language skills through exploring aspects of identity
Build an English vocabulary glossary, or "word bank"; students are encouraged to use words in gallery inquiry discussions and define words together
Increase comfort and agency at the Whitney Museum and museum spaces in general

In YI Introductions, participants are encouraged to

bring their unique perspectives into the YI Leaders program. Participants bring a diverse set of ideas, intrinsic values, and a concrete understanding of museum programming for teens.

Over the summer, YI participants are welcome to apply and interview for the YI Leaders program. Several criteria are considered in selecting students, from attendance and contributions in past programs to application responses and recommendation letters.

Upon joining the YI Leaders program, students engage in an array of experiences, such as working with artists, discussing artworks and concepts with peers, visiting several sites, and making art inspired by contemporary issues. YI Leaders organize public programs and events for other teens from around NYC. In the event-planning process, they learn to develop and facilitate discussions and interactive art-making. YI Leaders primarily work to make the museum accessible to all young people. YI Leaders often collaborate with community partners and community-based organizations to broaden the reach of these programs.

Program staff have initial conversations with staff at community-based organizations to see if there may be opportunities for overlap or collaboration within our respective programming years. When planning a teen event, we first engage in a teen exchange to do icebreaker activities and discuss our respective organizations and the importance of programs for high school students at museums and community organizations. In a follow-up planning meeting, the group discusses the focus of the exhibition themes and concepts that can be highlighted from the show. We then establish goals for the event as a group, and based on the goals, the group is split into several smaller planning-committee groups.

Event planning is just one part of YI Leaders, in addition to meeting with artists and Whitney staff, spending time in the galleries, and planning drop-in workshops for their peers. Combined, these components are vehicles to achieve the program learning goals and outcomes, which include:

- Develop and practice critical thinking, project planning, time management, meeting management, agenda setting, group dynamics, team building, and collaboration skills. In the event-planning process, we work toward these goals by having the teens determine the planning committees, delegate tasks, share findings and progress in group meetings, create meeting agendas, and develop a timeline and checklist for events.
- Understand museum practices and develop decision-making skills. Students will understand how leadership skills are practiced in a collaborative and personal setting. In the event-planning process, we work toward these by having the YI Leaders assist in Open Studio workshops for families and teens, observing the program structures, and providing them with designated tasks they oversee for the duration of the workshop. Drawing on their experiences working with family and high school audiences of different age ranges and experiences, YI Leaders bring ideas and work experience into the collaborative planning process for teen events.
- Gain knowledge of anti-racist practices and disability justice through trainings. In the event-planning process, we work toward this goal by having museum staff lead trainings and discussions with YI Leaders.
- Gain knowledge of diverse cultures by working with museum visitors. In the event-planning process, we work toward this goal through YI Leaders' experiences working with visitors of various ages and experiences, including in program areas such as family programs and access programs and in events like Immigrant Justice Night and family events.
- Integrate lived experiences into program planning

and development. In the event-planning process, we work toward this by encouraging teens to share resources from their networks at school or outside of the Whitney and bring in their own interests.

- Learn how to practice team leadership through active group participation. In the event-planning process, we work toward this by having the leaders work together in smaller groups, creating space for all members to contribute ideas and report to the larger group.
- Develop a sense of confidence and belief in themselves and their ideas. In the event-planning process, we work toward this by validating all voices and providing the group autonomy to see their ideas come to fruition.
- Build a comprehensive set of practical skills and tools to rely upon through leadership practice. Throughout the year, YI Leaders are creating the meeting agendas, engaging in dialogue facilitation, and learning how to lead inquiry-based discussions, whether it be in the galleries or with an artist or group, and putting these lessons into practice.
- Learn how to effectively articulate their practical skills and tools on a résumé, in a college essay, through a portfolio, or during interviews. Throughout the school year, program staff host college-readiness workshops and trainings, in which YI Leaders can participate.

To begin the event-planning process, program staff reserve appropriate museum spaces and put together a PowerPoint deck of images that show the previous teen events for contextual examples, references, and inspiration. Since the YI Leaders program is a multiyear commitment, returning leaders can share feedback on prior events with new leaders. The group then has a conversation on teen events at the Whitney, hearing the perspectives of the leaders on what went well and what could be improved. In addition, attendee feedback is dissected to understand the highlights and shortcomings of the most recent events. An evaluation planning committee oversees the best ways to collect feedback at each event. Feedback can be collected via a Post-it Note wall, a Google Form, Mentimeter, or Poll Everywhere, to name a few. Although a few events take place annually, such as Halloween Teen Night, most events and programs are newly conceived. Some examples include Vida Americana Teen Night, 2022 Biennial Queer Teen Night, and Labyrinth Teen Event. In either case, the planning and activities always start from scratch. There are several questions discussed early in the planning process. These brainstorming questions include:

> Why are we planning this event?
> In what ways is this exhibition important to highlight?
> What do we want teens to walk away with?

Each public teen program incorporates a featured artist or exhibition presently on view. The YI Leaders come up with themes tied to the artist or exhibition; past themes have included Halloween Teen Night and Queer Teen Night. As part of researching the featured artist or exhibition, early in the planning process, curators join to discuss the exhibition's main concepts, answer questions, and discuss the curatorial process with the leaders. In subsequent meetings, the leaders are trained to lead object talks and inquiry-based tours of the exhibition. Program staff model the object talks and gallery inquiry-based tours and discuss the methods and reasoning behind these strategies. This work is also supported with a worksheet that helps guide teens in exploring the exhibition, researching the artist, compiling questions about the artist, and workshopping open-ended questions. The goal of the worksheet is to provide a springboard to developing the

YI Leaders' object talks or inquiry-based tours.

Committees are a significant part of the leadership development and event-planning process. Committees are formed throughout the planning process to move the group's goals forward. The program staff and the YI Leaders choose which committees must be formed. For example, Halloween Teen Night may have a costuming workshop, scavenger hunt, hands-on activities, and performances. Each aspect of the event will have a committee to plan the specific details and logistics of that activity. Committees are determined by the YI Leaders and other teen program collaborators based on the event goals. For example, for Biennial Queer Teen Night, one of the goals was to use text-based artwork from the exhibition to invite teens to create powerful posters and collages that can be used in the NYC Pride Parade. There was a planning committee specifically designated to bring this goal to life. As the planning process progresses, new committees can be formed to discuss additional developments. Each committee sets goals, has a checklist to move tasks along, and continuously reports back. These committees reflect the event's needs, and as one group's tasks are completed, additional committees can be formed to ensure that all aspects of the event are carefully planned and supported.

At the center of our work with the YI Leaders is the opportunity to work with contemporary artists. These artists work with YI Leaders to mentor, teach, and collaborate in the conceptual and logistical development of the teen events. This artist is considered a featured artist in the event and works with YI Leaders to develop a hands-on workshop inspired by the artist's practice. While formalizing a plan with the artist, we often explore quandaries in public programs. Here are some questions we consider:

How do we get teens into the galleries?
What are the educational takeaways of the

event?
How will teens learn about the artist and exhibition?
In what ways are we providing a safe space?
In what ways can we have effective outreach to bring in a diverse audience of teens?
How can this event be improved from the last?

In addition to collaborating with artists to create dynamic and engaging hands-on art workshops, YI Leaders often interview artists in artist talks known as Whitney Teens x Artists. In preparation for these talks, YI Leaders spend time researching artists, having inquiry-based conversations with program staff, and compiling a list of questions to ask the artist. Much like the event planning process, YI Leaders work in small groups to develop questions, a PowerPoint, and an outline to facilitate the discussion. These talks are sometimes open to the public, who can add their voice to the conversation by asking questions.

Queer Teen Night Checklist

For the Biennial Queer Teen Night, YI Leaders worked with Biennial artist Andrew Roberts, alongside community organizations The Door and Haus of Us to plan the various parts of the event. Teens met in smaller committee meetings, which were determined based on the established event goals. At the end of the planning process, each committee had to make a checklist in collaboration with program staff that listed the final tasks that needed to be completed the week of the event.

Artspace
☼ Make a test project as an example.
☼ Create a PowerPoint of images to show during the workshop.
☼ Make a day-of checklist for supplies and materials.
☼ Write out prompts for tabletop signs.

Theater
- Write out the prompt for the tabletop signs.
- Send, print, and cut out images for collage.
- Make an example of the project.
- Decide on what materials will be on the table and make a checklist for the day of the event.
- Make a design for photo wall.

Tour
- Finalize tour of LGBTQ+ Biennial artists.
- Practice tour with a peer.
- Finalize plan for distributing scavenger hunt before, during, and after the tour.

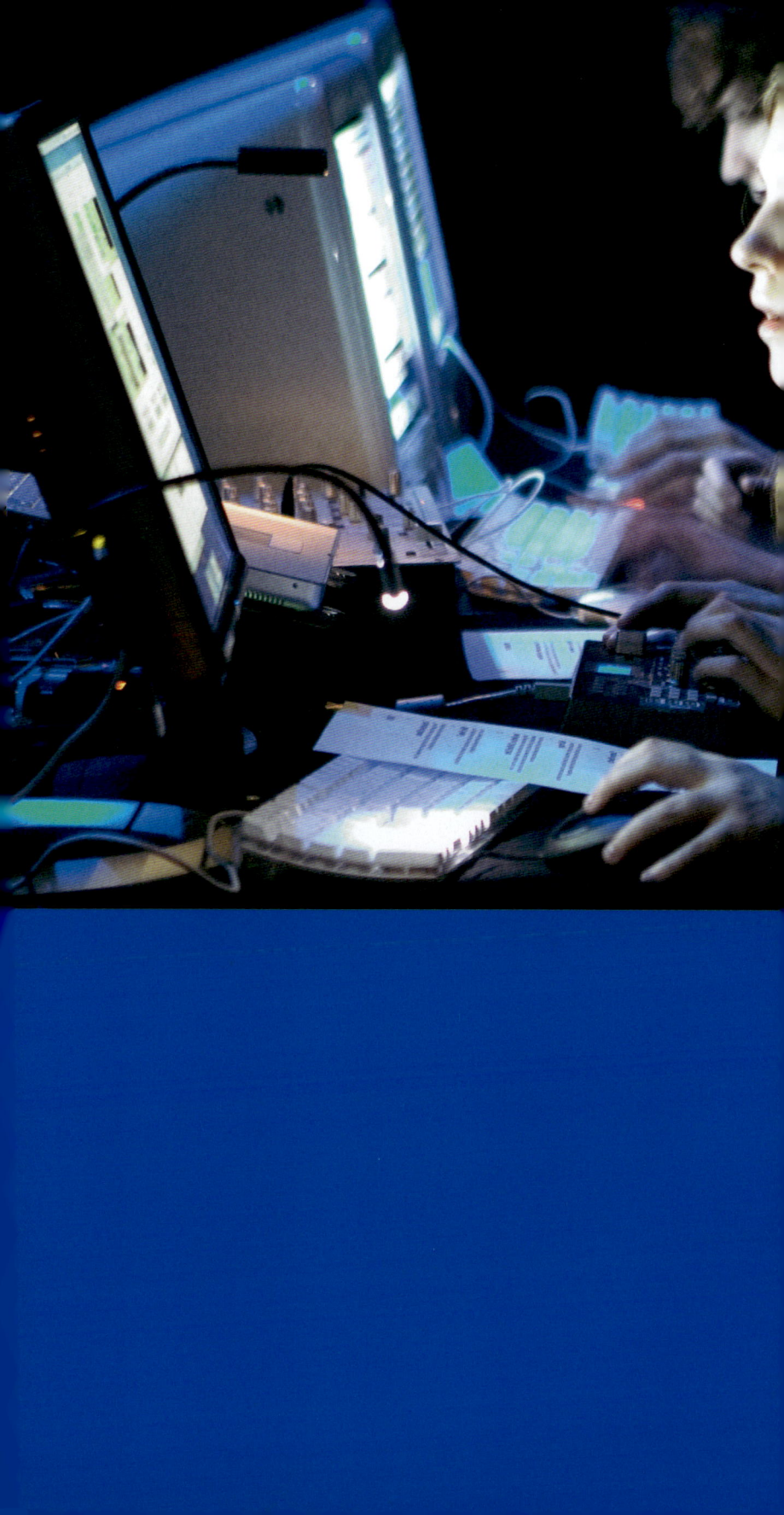

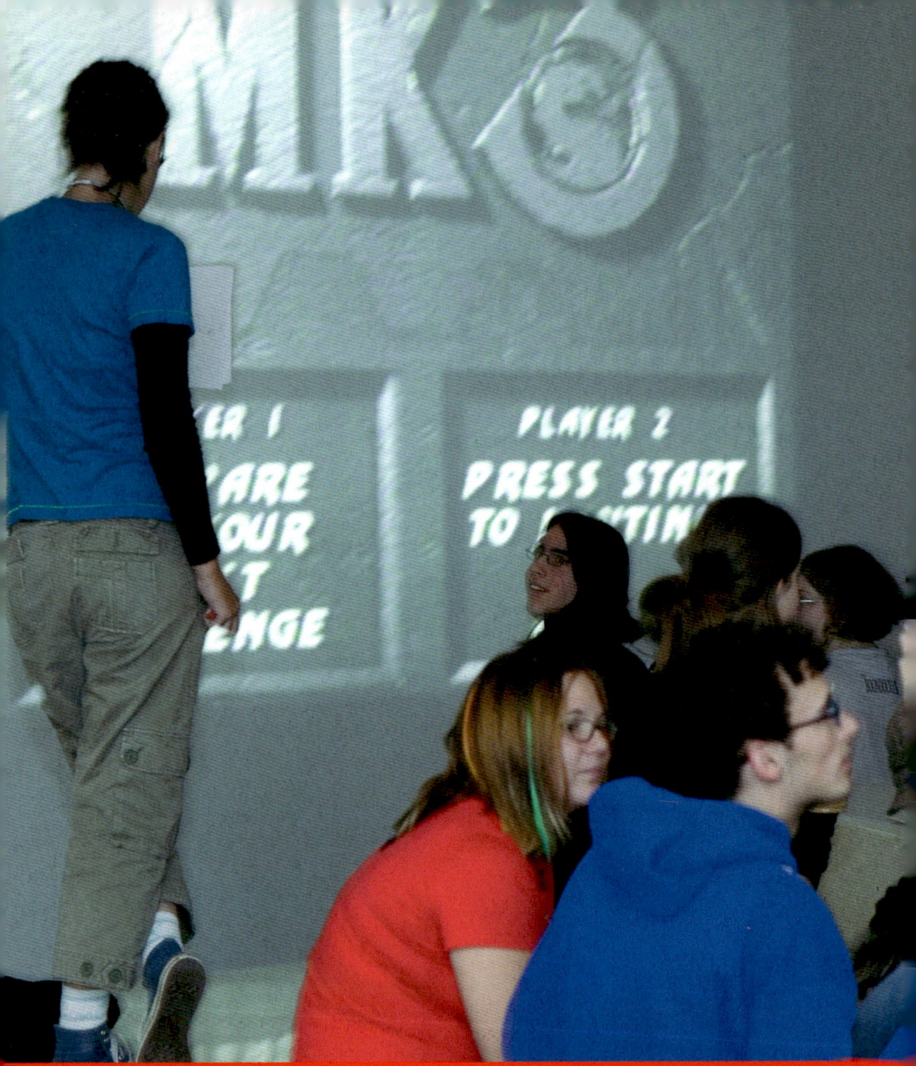
PLAYER 2
PRESS START

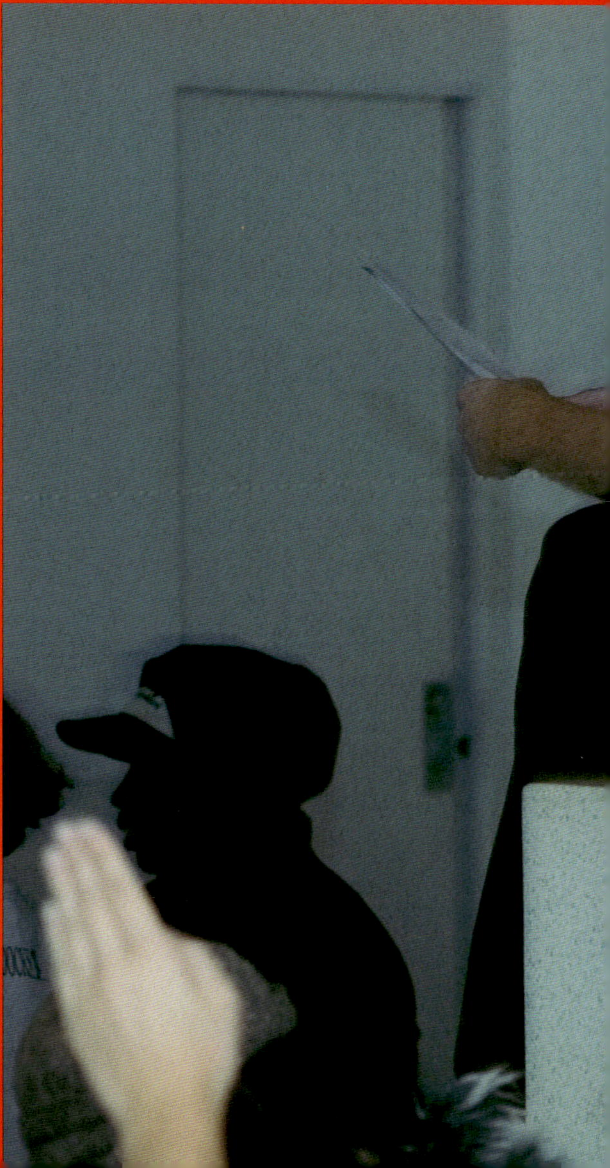

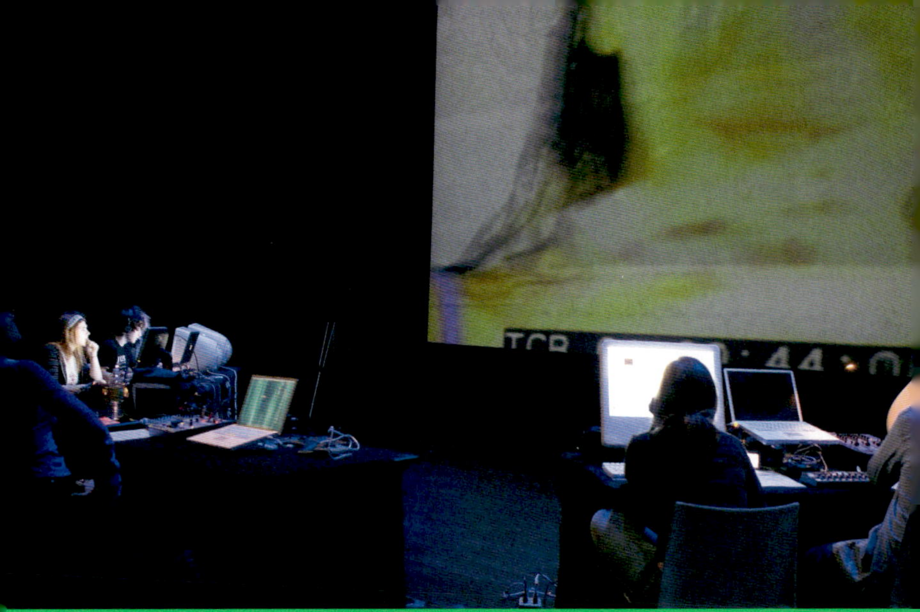

Planning for a Year of Programming

Bio

Simona Zappas (she/her) is the Youth Programs Manager at the Walker Art Center. In her work she designs and facilitates informal learning opportunities for youth. She collaborates with curatorial staff to bring a learning lens to museum public engagement with a social practice bent on programmatic strategy. Before this, she was the director of WFNU Frogtown, a low-power radio station in Saint Paul. Simona holds a BA with honors from Macalester College and a master of education from the University of Minnesota. Simona sits on the Saint Paul Neighborhood Network board and volunteers at Planned Parenthood as an abortion doula.

Essay

Planning for a year's worth of programming is no easy feat. Interests of groups change, exhibitions change, staff change, and so does the world. This may sound controversial, but as the Walker Teen Programs leader, I do not use the term *youth-led*.

I find it to be a fallacy. Facilitators hold significant programmatic gravity. We are the conduit of institutional information and policies; we select visitors, and manage schedules, documents, budgets, administration, and so on. Programs can still center youth and empower them by being *youth responsive*. This approach structures the year around learning goals and special museum-related experiences we try to offer each year (touring art storage, as a favorite example) in the Walker Art Center Teen Arts Council (WACTAC).

By planning around these containers, we can be flexible and have a tether to orient around the interests of the youth while keeping an eye on the scope of what is possible within our programmatic capacity. This helps maximize the potential to feel accomplished and satisfied with our collective work. In practice, for example, if we learn through conversations in the galleries that youth are interested in discussing the relationship between art and climate change, we might invite an artist to speak on the topic for a slot held for an artist visit a few months out. We will have scaffolded reasons for an artist visit but leave the exact artist open until we know the youth the artist will be speaking with. Alternatively, we might have an artist visit scheduled before meeting the teens due to the timeline of an upcoming exhibition. In this case, we will use our time with the teens to understand their interest or connection with the artist ahead of the conversation.

This document describes how we plan for a year and individual sessions by using our learning goals, the theory that unites everything. Moreover, how to not piss off all your colleagues in the process.

WACTAC is planned around learning goals developed with Dr. Yolanda J. Majors in Summer 2019. We focus on skill building over mastery of content. We are not concerned with youth leaving the program with an ability to name artists or art historical facts, but rather to leave feeling equipped to navigate institutions and confident in their abilities to approach artworks.

Learning Goal
Members can locate contrasts between lived, cultural, and institutional perspectives. Members are comfortable exploring these ideas while simultaneously holding that two varied perspectives can be true.

Measure
Recognition that disagreements are a learning opportunity, demonstrated by asking more questions instead of reacting with anger to different opinions.

Purpose
Throughout life, people will be presented with moments when texts, policies, or exchanges where their lived experience or identity will feel especially present—for better or for worse. By offering teens a safe space to explore these situations in a controlled context of viewing artworks that bring up various political and social issues, they can build their skills to navigate life's challenges.

⌑

Learning Goal
Build and maintain group connections.

Measure
Inside jokes, humor, eagerness to talk/share, collaboration.

Purpose
Group connections create positive feelings about the program and the institution. Teens will be more motivated to come and participate if they know they will have fun with their friends. Additionally, these build trust and comfort within the group, which allows for more exploratory sharing and better collaboration.

⌑

Learning Goal
Members can see how their ways of thinking can be rooted in a cultural or institutional perspective and can communicate the process of how they know that. Members will be able to apply this metacognitive framework to problem-solving.

Measure
Increased use of "I" statements, speaking from personal experience, and describing the "why" behind shared thoughts.

Purpose
Understanding how one's perspectives are formed better allows for space to see how other individuals' perspectives could differ from theirs. This is foundational for building empathetic conversations when disagreements spark. For example, if teens are arguing over the best chip flavor and there is a high contrast over Hot Cheetos, one teen might say, "I don't like Hot Cheetos because my family never really cooks spicy food, so my tolerance is low. That's why Cool Ranch Doritos are the best." I use this example because teens are gaining this type of practice constantly. Building in low-stakes opportunities for them to oxpress perspectives in these ways builds confidence to do so in higher-stakes situations.

◻

Learning Goal
Create a sense of ownership, connection, and comfort at the Walker and with arts institutions, and confidence in their ownership.

Measure
WACTAC visits, self-advocacy, mentioning artists, taking up space in the institution.

Purpose
Comfort in institutions at a young age means a life-

long connection with arts institutions. In WACTAC, we get excited when we see teens selecting to go into the galleries solo when they arrive early or relaxing in the lobby charging their phones. We hope this feeling stays with them so they know they can feel comfortable in museums no matter where they go.

⌑

Learning Goal
Members can infer meanings behind artistic choices and communicate their opinion on them and why they feel that way. Members can explain the impact of mediational tools on the meaning of a text.

Measure
Confidence in gallery discussions to name what they see using specific details.

Purpose
This is ultimately a textual literacy skill. Teens might begin to use this in language arts classes by being able to identify techniques like metaphors and how they contribute to the construction and meaning of a text. The same reading happens when they identify how a painter might use brushstrokes to communicate an emotion. This is teens' ability to interpret context clues to locate meaning in complex things like policy.

⌑

Achieving these learning goals positions the teens to obtain the learning outcomes below:

Learning Outcome
Members feel confident in their authority to analyze a text.

Measure
Approaching gallery works as texts, sharing opin-

ions in gallery conversations, little prompting or waiting on others to respond.

Purpose

There is a lot of pressure to "sound smart" in museums and life, and sharing thoughts on a text can be vulnerable. We tend to assume there is a "right" way. In WACTAC, we want to encourage teens to move beyond that pressure. We want to encourage them to embrace that they inherently possess authority and an ability to interpret, connect with, and despise artworks just by being themselves. In seeing their inherent abilities and hearing those of others, they become better equipped to see and react to the structures that set those belittling assumptions in the first place.

◊

Learning Outcome

Members will develop a more complex language and framework to understand, describe, and contextualize motivations for museum programs.

Measure

Applying information, like program names and staff roles, and citing curatorial decisions, learned from staff.

Purpose

Most teens join programs like WACTAC because they want to know how museums work. They might start with a question like "How do museums pick what art goes on the walls?" This might be coming from an interest in working in a cultural institution in the future. This goal satisfies curiosity and gives them insights into how institutions work, allowing them to self-mythologize, move ideas through, support audiences, and create an "us" and a "them" through processes and language. This helps them understand how to utilize resources in the future, either in college, at work, or in organizing.

⌘

These goals are achieved through taking iterative small steps, regular repositioning, and pivoting from staff. In WACTAC, we use weekly gallery discussions of artworks to test many of these skills, bring in different topics, and take note of the teens' interests. Before even considering what is on the plate for learning, we need to consider what teens are coming in with and what they are stepping into at the museum. We acknowledge that we have only two hours a week with the teens. We recognize that they are working on these developmental skills in school, working part-time jobs, caring for their families, and conversing with friends. We acknowledge that the space of the museum is charged and complicated, where power is up-front. The museum might feel stuffy, overly formal, stark, and full of unspoken (or yelled) rules to some teens, and to others it might be where they went with their families growing up. We acknowledge that teens often come in with comments on the money, cultural capital of attention, and an unwavering focus on what the teens have to gain, not the museum.

We organize the year with a big Excel sheet color coded by month. Each row is a weekly WACTAC meeting. The columns are labeled as follows:

Date
Session Summary
Activities
Materials Needed
Visitors

It is a *mess*. We change this *constantly* due to new ideas, opportunities from staff, and learning about the teens' interests, failures, surprises, and realism. We start the year with it filled out sparsely and then spend the rest of the year changing it. It is a way to organize and record our thoughts. Typically, we have an idea of a month, which changes as we get closer. One thing to keep in mind is that in arts institutions no one is working on the same calendar, so the planning calendar is an attempt to accommodate others while having your own to share and enforce. Over the summer, we put out a call to the whole organization to let them know we are taking ideas and want to hear about what they will be working on over the coming months to see where they might align with the teens.

The first month of the year is focused on the teens getting to know each other and their way around the building. Here are some key sections of this portion:

> Orientation: A day when the teens tour the building and get an overview of the program
> Family orientation: Family members have the chance to receive a program overview with staff
> Generating questions: The teens are tasked with listing all the questions and goals they have for the year
> "Ask me anything" with a curator: Teens *always* start with lots of questions for the curators
> Group norms process

This portion is focused on building their connections with each other. As a facilitator, I focus on making jokes and meeting their excitement for the year. Remember, you are the conduit for all their institutional information and model of how to behave; show them that it is okay to be silly. Jump on anything (barring teasing) that can be an inside joke to form bonding among them!

Once the teens know each other, we jump into planning our Teen Takeover event. Teen Takeover is a building-wide event where the Walker stays open late on a Friday night, admitting only teens. The WACTAC members select performers, art-making activities, decorations, and ways to activate the galleries. This is where we start to bring in other staff relevant to event planning, and they start to learn about institutional policies and think about their audience. This information can come into play later when they plan a second Teen Takeover in the spring, and as they begin their project, they have a sense of how long it can take to plan something and the many pieces that need to align. Planning the event brings the group together and gives them a major sense of accomplishment, as well as a vision of their impact and the scale of their new institutional prowess. Teen Takeover folds into the large program goals and Arts Platforming Action curriculum by giving the teens practice in balancing out ideas in collaborating toward a shared goal. They start to see how decisions, processes, and actions flow through the institution. It gives them a sense of the scale and multiple parties involved in pushing the event through. In planning Teen Takeover, we typically do the following:

> Meet with PR, marketing, and design staff
> Brainstorm vibe, food, music, swag, and activities
> Promote!

This varies based on institutional calendars, but following Teen Takeover, we have only a few weeks before we take our holiday break (aligned with the Minneapolis Public Schools' calendar). We use this time to jump into the collection. We spend lots of time in the galleries, touring storage, and meeting with artists. This is a chance to learn about the works and topics the teens are drawn to.

Following a two-week holiday break, we reconvene and typically begin with an evaluative conversation. We revisit their questions and goals from the beginning of the year and ask them to map out what they have learned and how we got there, create new goals, and share what they would like to see more or less of. Typically, this is when we get torn down a bit—we will hear what the teens hate and many more demands. This is also when teens may express frustrations with the program or the institution. It is healthy! It is good! It means they are learning and seeing how the institution can better serve them, and they see more ways to engage with the museum. This is where we get a strong sense of how they want to participate for the rest of the year or where they might have some big questions that we can start to use as guides for upcoming visitors, gallery discussions, and potentially their culminating project.

Following this period, we try to give them more institutional tools—we meet with staff on the highest levels of leadership, have a career day (like the ones in school, where a panel speaks), and bring in more artists to speak on their work. This is all meant to outfit the teens to prepare for their collaborative research project. This is an opportunity for the teens to generate a question they have relating to the museum where they would like to dedicate time and resources. Our biggest challenge is describing the scope to them. The goal is to see the resources available to them at the museum, use them for research, and create a satisfying product they can share. Our typical process for this is to support the teens in the following ways:

- Brainstorming questions and narrowing them down to one
- Figuring out the information they will need to answer it (we call this the five whys—what are the things you need to ask to answer this?)
- Mapping out the resources available to them (staff, artworks, facilities)
- Determining the output (a zine, TikTok videos, presentation to all staff)
- Determining measures of success

Once the project is wrapped, the teens jump into the final section of the year (hopefully) feeling satisfied and connected. They finish the year by planning a final Teen Takeover event—their big blowout. The second Teen Takeover is less focused on learning goals and seen more as another culmination of what they have learned and a chance to flex and celebrate it. Typically, we will have two weeks after Teen Takeover before the year ends—we will have a big party of their choosing (bowling, dinner, games), and we always do superlatives. This is a way to bring in a fun teenage trope and recognize the individual contributions of each member. I usually hand out a form with everyone's name and have each member write one for everyone, which I then combine and modify. We will get ones that range from "most likely to live in a villa surrounded by nature and then move to a brutalist mansion" to "most likely to be the main character on a sitcom and fist-bump Bill Clinton," "most likely to bully Morrissey," and "least likely to commit arson."

Day-to-day WACTAC meetings always follow the same structure. Even if we do different things in the meetings—brainstorms, artists visits, storage tours—we always maintain certain structures so that the teens

> always feel a sense of control and like they can know what to expect,
> can riff on the structure to make it their own,
> feel a sense of ritual and that they are entering a distinct space, and
> have time to mentally transition from school.

Our meetings run from 4:30 pm to 6:30 pm. People are always late. There is always traffic. Greet everyone by saying hello and giving their names as they enter—let them know you welcome them into the space and ask how their day was. We always kick off the meetings by asking the teens if they have any announcements or something boring to share. This is a great way to bring the group together and let them know we care about their lives outside of

1.1.6.

meetings. Every session begins with a "go around" question—we ask silly questions to warm up the teens to listening, sharing, and recalling. This is where inside jokes are made, hot takes are given, and connections are made.

After the go-around question, facilitators make announcements and give an overview of the day. This gives time for anyone who is late to not miss out on important information. Every WACTAC meeting looks different, but we aim to vary activities and spaces to keep minds active. This means nothing goes on for more than an hour or so. The beginning of the meeting takes about fifteen minutes. We typically have speakers or main content like Teen Takeover planning from 5 pm to 6 pm and might break for a game or a check-in. We always allot thirty minutes to go into the galleries and discuss an artwork—this is where the work that builds the learning outcomes happens!

Keep pivots in mind. If things are not working, change the space—check in on their energy levels.

When putting together your agendas and lesson plans for individual meetings, consider the following:

- Are there preexisting skills you are expecting the teens to possess?
- What have you learned from the wants and interests of the teens? How can you incorporate them?
- What are your learning goals, objectives, and intended outcomes?
- How is this lesson scaffolding to the next? What skills have you been preparing leading up to it? How are you scaffolding the components of the lesson?
- What behaviors are you modeling? How are you doing it?
- How will you know the day was a success? What are your measures?
- Are you using an in-language, vocabulary, or concepts that might need an explanation?

Can you connect the teens with additional resources on a given topic? For example, can you have books on an artist's work available for discussing an artwork? Can you share links to the artist's website or an interview of theirs?
What materials will you need?
What can you change in the future?
What is your backup plan?
Where do you have room for input?

If you follow all of this, you will have the perfect year!

Consensus + Conflict:
A Reflective Facilitation Guide

Bio

Grace Needlman (they/she) is a cultural worker and maker preoccupied with questions of collective imagination and agency. As the Manager of Studio Programs at Marwen, Grace supports artists and youth in building inspiring learning communities through art. Grace's puppet designs have appeared in theatrical productions across Chicago. As a company member at Rough House and Chicago Puppet Lab Co-Director, Grace works to create equitable pathways for puppeteers in Chicago. Previously, Grace managed family and youth programs at the Museum of Contemporary Art Chicago, where they worked to put museum resources in the hands of Chicago youth and fostered connections between artists and intergenerational publics. They publish and present on youth agency, collaboration, and queering museums. Grace graduated with a BA in fine art from Yale University and an MA in contemporary art theory from Goldsmiths University of London.

A group of teens gather for their weekly meeting. They sit in a big circle and discuss the agenda for the day and all the decisions that need to be made as they work toward a public event. From the outside, this might look like any other meeting that happens in any other organization throughout the day, but the process that this group takes to reach consensus is often very different from how other discussions play out. Many groups use some variety of consensus facilitation, working to make decisions collectively and as nonhierarchically as possible. How collective discussion is facilitated in teen programs defines the character of the group, the learning that takes place there, and what happens in moments of conflict.

"Facilitation" means to *make easier.* Collective processing is some of the most challenging and magical work we do. It can be frustrating to listen to a large group of people and make decisions together; the facilitator's job is to make that work easier. There are many excellent, in-depth facilitation guides available.[1]

If you are new to facilitation, please start by doing some in-depth research. Consider the history of how nonhierarchical facilitation has been developed, and seek training outside of your museum. Look for spaces that have traditions of working in nonhierarchical ways—for example, mutual aid networks, Quaker meetings, anarchist activist groups, circle keepers, transformative justice groups, and anyone working in the tradition of popular education.[2]

This piece of writing is not a comprehensive facilitation guide but a companion reflection on why facilitation is critical and what makes it unique within a museum teen program context. It explores how

1. My favorite facilitation guide is from Seeds for Change, a UK-based group whose book on consensus facilitation is available in paperback, as a website, and as a free PDF at seedsforchange.org.uk.

the basic skills, roles, and tasks of facilitating group decision-making can lay the groundwork for exploring socially engaged art and navigating institutional critique and conflict.

The Power of Facilitation

Developmentally, adolescence is a time of finding yourself, specifically in relation to the social systems and histories that surround you.[3] Social scientists laud the value of third spaces,[4] those outside the "first space" of home and the "second space" of work or school. Even more than others, teens need spaces that are not home or school where they can build independent friendships and connect with adults who do not carry the authoritative baggage of parents or teachers. They need spaces whose rules they can shape based on their strengthening values and understanding of justice and history. Creating a space with teens is a visionary, liberatory project. The spaces we create together get to be the best version of society we can imagine, often in opposition to the spaces in which teens spend the majority of their time.

Most spaces we spend time in, both as teens and adults, are organized around an explicit hierarchy that structures how discussions are held and decisions are made. Parents have more power to make decisions than their children. Curators have more power to make decisions at a museum than gallery

2. Mariame Kaba and Shira Hassan, *Fumbling towards Repair: A Workbook for Community Accountability Facilitator*s (Project NIA / Just Practice, 2019); Mariame Kaba, J. Cyriac Mathew, and Nathan Haines, *Something Is Wrong: Exploring the Roots of Youth Violence* (Project NIA, 2010), https://project-nia.org/uploads/images/Something_Is_Wrong-Curriculum.pdf; Lisa M. Landreman, ed., *The Art of Effective Facilitation: Reflections from Social Justice Educators* (Sterling, VA: Stylus Publishing, 2013).
3. In framing eight stages of psychosocial development in *Childhood and Society* (1993), Erik Erikson describes adolescence's core conflict as between "identity and role confusion."
4. Third space theory is attributed to Homi K. Bhabha.

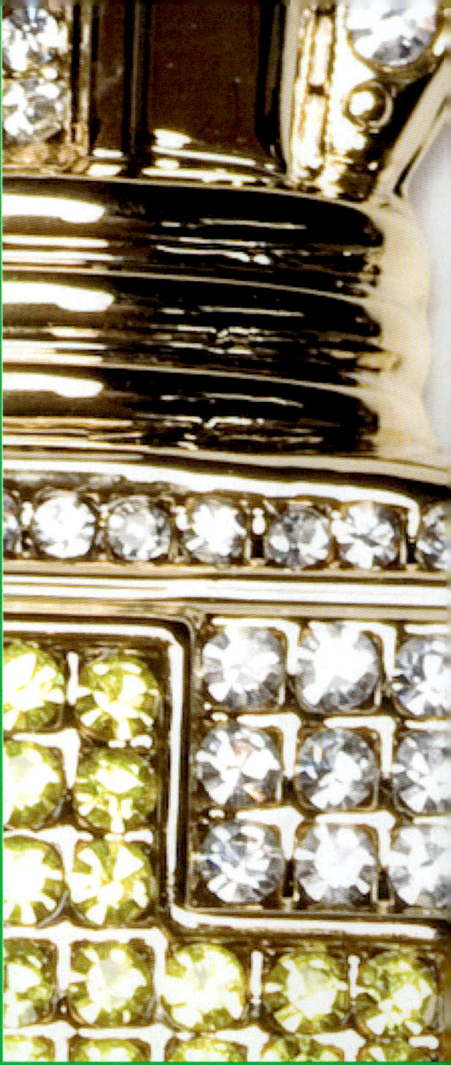

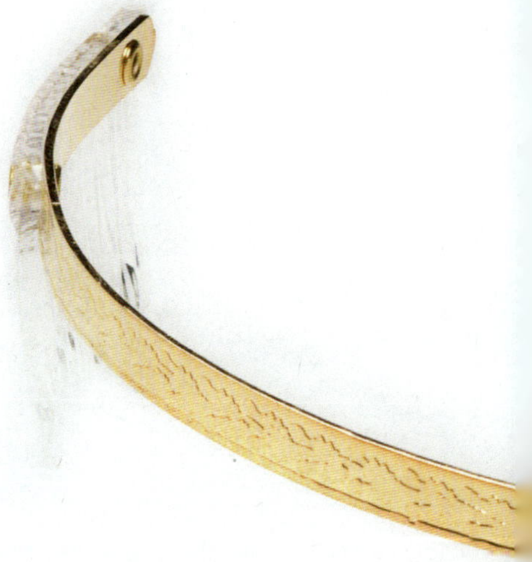

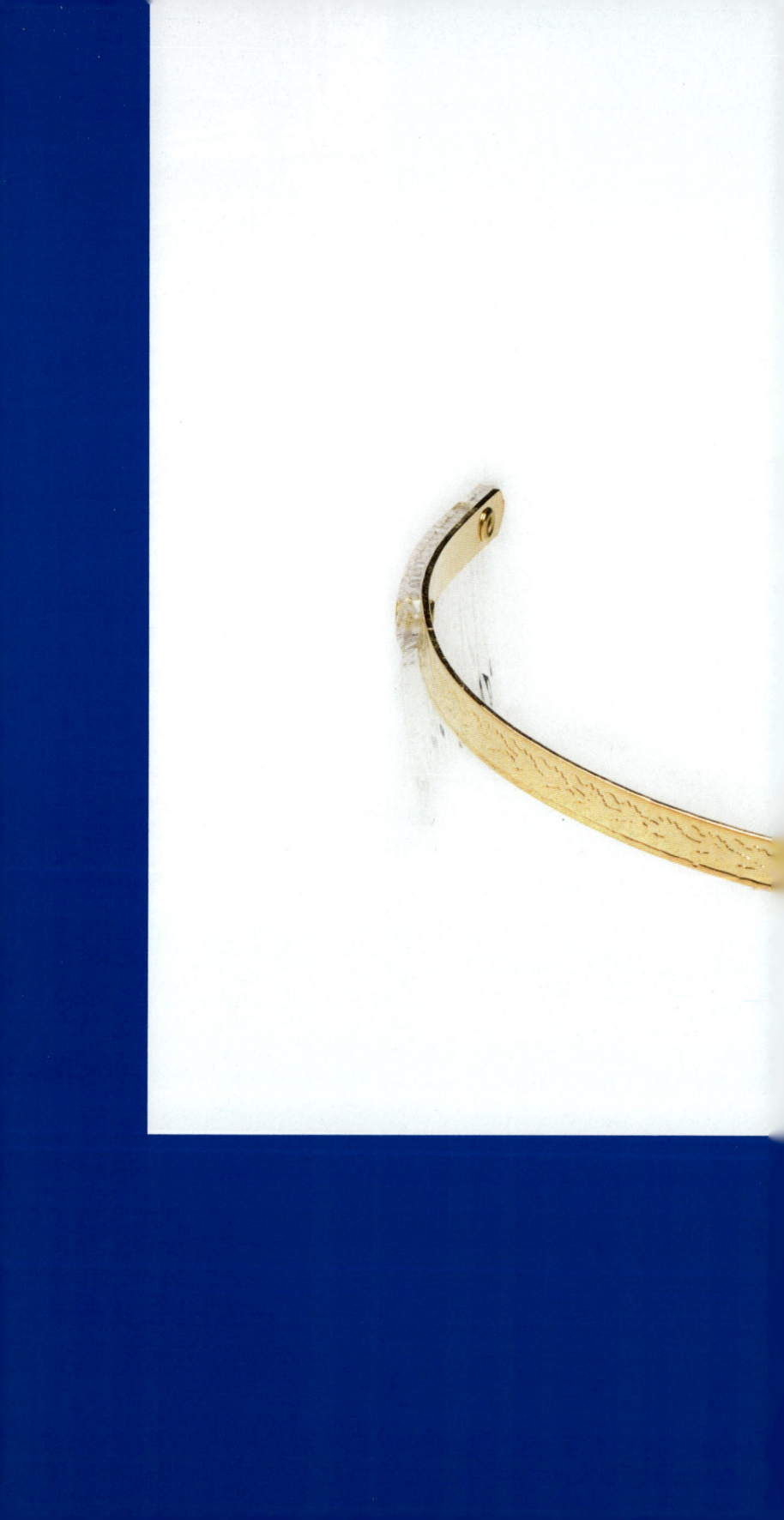

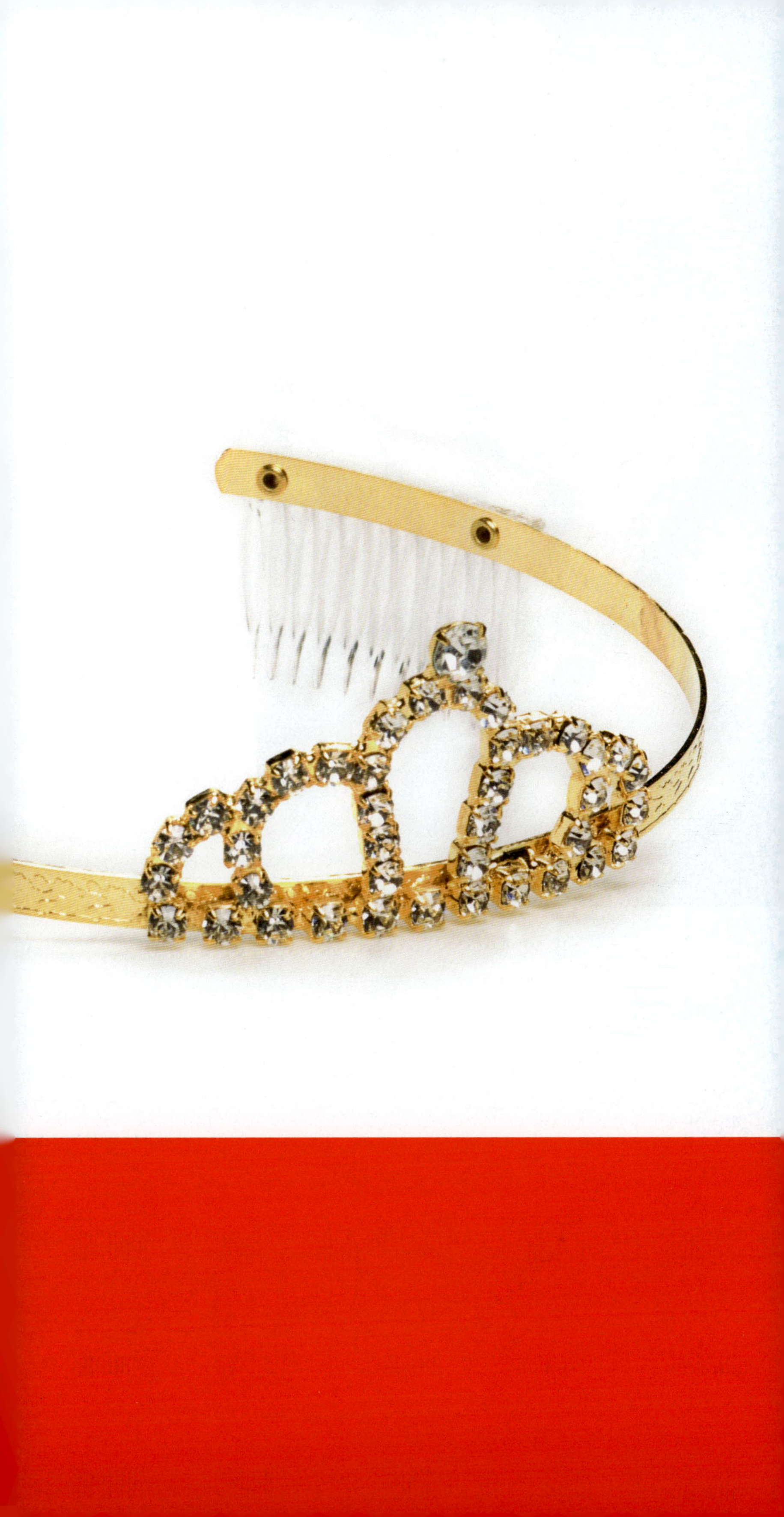

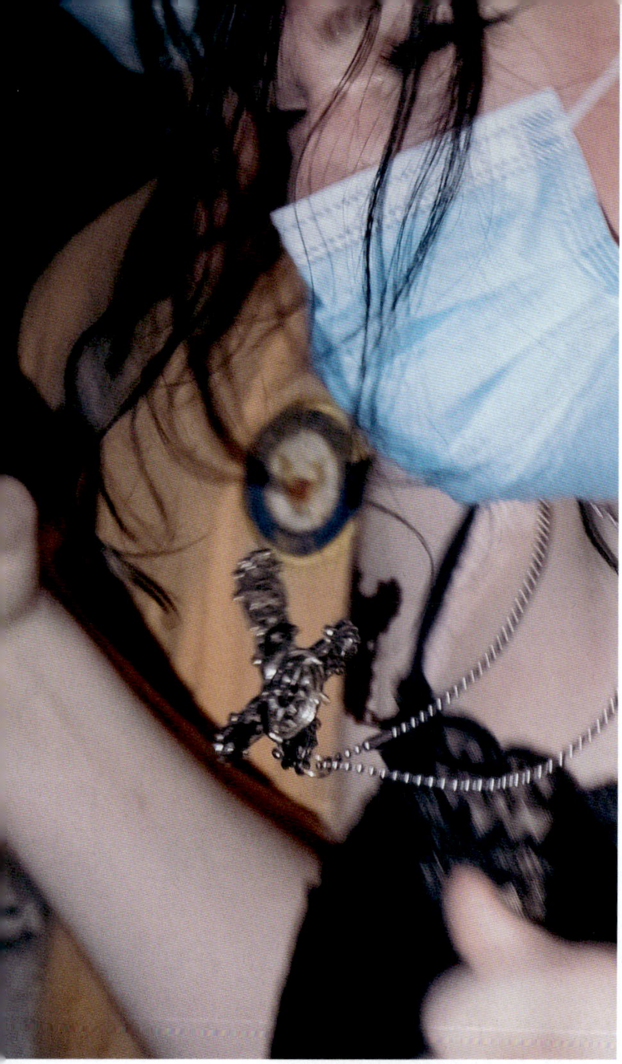

guards. These hierarchies are often appropriate and necessary and, at the same time, oppressive and frustrating. One of the most important things we can do as teen programmers is to offer alternatives, spaces intentionally organized in as nonhierarchical a way as possible. In order to have open and meaningful conversations about art, which, if we are being forthright, will almost always come back to conversations about dimensions of social power, the way power is held in our groups is important. Distributing power in a way that questions the norm also supports the core goals of building community and helping individuals discover their agency and creative or critical voices.

In practice, you are unlikely to gain robust experience participating in nonhierarchical facilitation techniques from historically hierarchically organized institutions. As staff members working with teens, we spend our days in meetings with colleagues and evenings or weekends in meetings with teens. The differences between the norms and practices employed in each of these spaces are essential for establishing authentic youth leadership and attending to potential conflicts between teens and their institutional host.

For facilitation to have the most significant impact, anyone in a group must be able to step into the role of facilitator. Initially, you might find facilitation practice useful for your own teaching or group stewardship, but the greatest impact comes from introducing these practices to teen participants. Many young people are naturally skilled collaborators and have a will to collaborate that many adults could learn from. A few simple tools can amplify this inherent agency. From the very start of the year, you can scaffold opportunities for young people to learn how to facilitate their own spaces.

Sometimes, at this point, a question arises: Why are young people learning facilitation in a museum; aren't they supposed to be learning about art? Facilitation can be part of a conversation about contemporary art. It grows from the same histories and strategies of popular education and liberatory pedagogy that underpin the last several decades of social practice and, by extension, museum public programming. How Pablo Helguera outlines the levels of participation explored in socially engaged art, and his "tentative taxonomy" is useful. He describes "collaborative participation" in which "the visitor shares responsibility for developing the structure and content of the work in collaboration and direct dialog with the artist."[5] Young people who learn the skills of facilitation can extend those skills to invite others into the creation of collaboratively participatory processes. The skills have ripple effects within the programming teens create for museum audiences, the way museum staff observe and learn from youth-led processes, and how teens create collaborative or consensus-based spaces beyond the museum.

The Goals of Facilitation

Facilitation helps groups stay focused and positive and reach a decision everyone can live with. More importantly, it does this to center the decision-making power within the group, not on an individual leader.

Facilitation sets the groundwork for authentic collaboration by creating a space that explicitly points to how power operates in group decision-making. Because of that, it is important to talk explicitly about power and oppression when your group begins developing facilitation skills. Teen group leaders should be prepared to lead conversations about different aspects of oppression and power. This can take many different forms, depending on your knowledge and personal experience. One simple activity that you can use as an inroad into conversations about power and oppression with your young

5. Pablo Helguera, *Education for Socially Engaged Art: A Materials and Techniques Handbook* (New York: Jorge Pinto Books, 2011).

people comes from an anti-adultism workshop led by youth from the Chicago Freedom School.[6] This can be done in discussion, in small groups, through journaling, or as a mingling activity.[7] Share with a partner: *a time an adult made you feel powerless; A time an adult made you feel powerful*. What does it feel like to be powerless or powerful?

Facilitation keeps the conversation accountable to the group's shared agreements. Creating group agreements at the start of any group experience is fundamental to facilitation and, at this point, standard practice.[8] For example, someone facilitating might say, "Please remember that we all agreed to respect each person and their lived experience, so make sure you are speaking from your experience and not making assumptions about someone else or speaking for them."

As a nonhierarchical practice, facilitation relies on a set of roles that are divorced from specific individuals. Anyone can step into any facilitation role at any time. Teaching youth to hold these roles can help youth hold authentic power and create a shared

6. This is another good place to seek training and professional development. Groups like Chicago Freedom School lead trainings for adult allies working with young people. Learn more at their website: https://chicagofreedomschool.org/workshops/rev-up-institute-spring/.

7. A mingle activity is when participants are invited to walk around the room, moving through and around one another, periodically stopping for short one- to two-minute conversations, and then switching partners. Mingling is a great icebreaker because it gets people up and talking to others. Navigating through space with and around one another builds physical awareness of social space and the relatedness of the group.

8. Here are a couple of articles on creating brave space agreements: Christopher Rogers, "A Celebration of #LetUsBreathe's Brave Space Agreements," *Identity, Education, and Power* (blog), March 31, 2017, https://medium.com/identity-education-and-power/a-celebration-of-letusbreathes-brave-space-agreements-seeding-abolition-as-pedagogy-into-the-9f77f0b9f0ce; Felicia Holman and Ellie Mejía, "Safe Spaces, Brave Spaces and Why We Gon' Be Alright," City Bureau, December 19, 2019, https://www.citybureau.org/notebook/2019/12/19/safe-spaces-brave-spaces-and-why-we-gon-be-alright.

language for talking about hierarchy and power.[9]

As teen programmers, many of us are ethically drawn to creating a nonhierarchical space for and with teens, somewhere totally different from the kinds of hyper-hierarchies often operating in homes and schools. Operating any group without any hierarchy is arguably impossible. People come with different amounts of experience at different times and levels of commitment. For teen groups, hierarchies are even more structural, with one or two adult stewards who are employed and paid to ensure the safety and learning of the youth participants.

All facilitation roles support the goals of facilitation, while the facilitator holds the bulk of the activity, and sometimes the facilitator is the one doing all these roles. The roles vary in complexity and visibility and rely on a core set of skills. Here are some standard roles that many groups use. There is nothing sacred about these roles, so feel free to adjust or add to them based on your specific group's needs.

The facilitator takes responsibility for the process and quality of the conversation. They are responsible for setting up the conversation with an agenda and all the space and materials necessary for success. Like an emcee or chairperson, they set the stage, introduce, summarize, and move the group forward. Sometimes a cofacilitator joins in to share this role.

The timekeeper ensures enough time has been set aside in the agenda for each task and keeps the meeting on time.

The notetaker records what happens in the meeting both for review afterward and to help the facilitator summarize and ask clarifying questions during the meeting.

The vibes checker attends to the energy in the room. How are people feeling? Do they need a stretch

---

9. For more information, see 1.2.4. Respect Is...Activity by Simona Zappas on page 185.

break, a deep breath, or a snack? Was something said that hit a nerve and requires a pause?

The doorkeeper attends to anyone entering or leaving an in-progress conversation. They quietly recap what is happening so that the person entering can participate, and acknowledge anyone leaving so they feel valued.

Of course, the primary responsibility for reaching consensus lies with the participants. The whole group must put their trust in the facilitation process and defer to the facilitators to guide it.

Qualities of a Facilitator

Respect: Remember everyone in this room has something equally amazing to share.

Active listening: Listen to whoever is speaking with your whole body! Be aware of your eye contact and body language.

Awareness: Even as you are listening actively, be aware of the whole room. Take in the body language, mood, tone, comments, and direction of everyone in the group.[10]

Confidence: Trust what you sense is going on with the group and act decisively when needed.

Assertiveness: Be comfortable jumping in to respectfully get the conversation back on track or mediate someone who might be being disruptive.

Understanding: Ensure you understand the group's goals and what has been said. It is okay to ask clarifying and follow-up questions.

Neutrality: If you use your power as a facilitator to sway the conversation in your favor, then you erode the group's level playing field and trust in the role of the facilitator. Neutrality does not mean you do not have an opinion or are unbi-

---

10. There is a concept in theater called "soft focus," which is a practice of being aware of everything around you evenly, without focusing on one thing in particular. We can think about facilitation as a form of soft focus, an acute awareness of the emotions, feelings, and needs of those around us without desire or need of our own.

ased, just that you commit to not contributing your opinions while you are the facilitator.

Nothing is more precious than the trust of your teens. Without their trust, your space cannot support the bravery required for collaboration and critique. No matter how committed you are to breaking down hierarchies, you have power that the youth in your program do not have. Unlike mutual aid or activist networks, your work with teens is held and framed within a program structure in which you have been hired as a full- or part-time employee, and teens are participants. It is important to think through your own relationship to holding this power and be transparent about that with young people. You cannot maintain their trust if you are not honest about decisions that are your responsibility to make. Learn to say "no" in a trustworthy way.

Trust young people, so you can be open about the power that you hold, why, and how you are thinking through the decisions that are yours to make. The group's trust in the facilitator is premised on the understanding that they will not abuse their position by directing the group's decision-making. For an adult program steward, this is the quality of facilitation that creates the foundation for shared power and trust. This is an opportunity for you to truly hand the power over to young people, but it must be authentic.

Preparing to facilitate in a way that authentically centers teen voices means preparing ahead to know exactly when your opinion matters or does not. For example, at the Museum of Contemporary Art Chicago, one of the most powerful decisions we handed over to young people was the choice of whom to hire as the next adult staff member to support their program. This grew from the annual practice of teens reviewing applications and making selections for the following year's cohort. We extended group review and discussion strategies, and members used their facilitation skills to lead a group interview with finalist candidates. Making space for young people to collectively make the final decision required up-front work. Staff had to review first-round candidates through the contextual lenses available to us as adult staff. Youth trusted us to make the first round of selections and send them a short list because they trusted that when we sent them that list, they were free to choose whomever they decided on as a group. It is not authentic to facilitate a conversation where you, as a staff person, really hope the group will choose one candidate and then guide the conversation in that direction. If you have strong feelings about a specific candidate, you must enter the conversation as a participant to make your voice heard. Before you step into the role of facilitator, gut check that the following statement is true: "Whatever decision the group makes is okay by me."

Facilitation in Action
Prepare the Room

Markers, large paper, your group norms posted, and an ideas box can be great additions to a space. Consider whether it would be helpful to have a "talking stick" or other tools available in the room. Sometimes offering drawing materials, pipe cleaners, or other small fidgets is nice. Consider when and if you would like to have snacks and water.

What is the physical shape of the conversation? Sitting or standing in a circle allows all participants to see everyone else and play an equal part in the conversation. Consider if you want to give the group choice if they are sitting, standing, lying on the floor, and so on. Adult leaders will often help set the stage for conversations, but the facilitator needs to notice if people are straying or sitting outside the circle.

If this is your first time together, consider communicating some basic needs and norms. Tell folks where the restrooms are. Are they able to just go when they need to? Or would you like them to notify you? What is the expectation for cell phones? Hand raising?

Set the Agenda
Consider who decides what your group will discuss or work on. Who sets the agenda? Is it always the adult facilitator? When can teens set their own agendas? In any session, it is crucial to make sure that everyone knows what topics are on the table, what the group is trying to decide through this conversation, and how much time there is. Making the agenda visible—printed, written on a whiteboard, or sent out in advance—is a way of sharing power. It externalizes the group's road map, so it is not just in your head. If youth are facilitating a conversation, work with them ahead of time to create a proposed agenda to bring to the group for additions and adjustments. You can also build an agenda together as a group at the start of your session. Figuring out what needs to be decided and how long each step will take are invaluable skills for any project.

Here is an example agenda from the day our group chose collaborators for a public event.

(10 min) introduce applicants
(40 min) discuss applicants and discard obvious "no projects"
(5 min) break
(40 min) discuss remaining applicants and vote
(10 min) assign liaisons for chosen projects
(10 min) recap and set next meeting goals

Summarize
In one or two sentences, restate points made and how they add to the central question or focus of the conversation. You can rely on the notetaker to remind everyone what has been discussed and what decisions have been made. It can be helpful to introduce facilitation skills by inviting young people to summarize and recap during conversations you are facilitating.

Help Everyone to Participate
Respectfully remind people to be aware of how

much time they speak in the conversation. Invite quiet folks to participate and help talkative folks take a breath and make room for others. Be assertive about limiting overtalking and drawing out quiet people.

Taking hands: If many people have their hands in the air, list everyone who wants to speak and let them know in which order they should speak. ("I saw Ale's hand, then Efrain's, then Anushka's.") Try to take hands in the order they were raised, but also pay attention to people who have not spoken as much and ensure they get space.

Pay Attention to the Energy of the Group

Pay attention to how people are feeling. You will be able to tell by body language, eye contact, expression, and how often people speak up. Sometimes you can feel it in the air when people are frustrated or sleepy. Try taking a break or introducing a different conversation structure when people seem to be losing focus. See if there are decisions or items on the agenda that can be tabled for later if the meeting is really stalling.

Parking Space

Even as you try to keep the conversation on topic, many great ideas will come up. Have a space—a large poster or a shoebox with slips of paper—on hand to collect all the ideas that might come up during the discussion that does not directly relate to the goal or focus of the conversation. Remind participants to use this idea box or parking space, especially if the discussion gets sidetracked.

Take Action Points

Action points are tasks given to group members to complete after the meeting. For example, a member might volunteer to create a Facebook event for an upcoming public event. Make sure the group decides what, how, who, when, and where for every action point.

Challenge Put-Downs, Discriminatory Remarks, and Disruptive Actions

As the facilitator, it is your job to call out language or actions that do not support our agreements to respect each other. Remember that if someone is disrupting the process, the problem is their behavior, not them as a person.

This can be the most challenging task for a facilitator. It is easier if the group regularly reminds one another of their shared agreements. Our group started a practice of reading our shared values together at the start of every session. Interrupting disruptive behavior could look like repeating a value to the whole group, "Please remember that we all agreed to listen, so let us all check in with ourselves and make sure we are keeping an open mind to others' opinions." It could look like calling a pause and giving everyone a moment to clear their heads. If something truly offensive was said, it is often helpful to call it out immediately, take a break, check in with individuals, and then address it as a group.

Temperature Checks

There are a number of ways to check in on a group to see how close they are getting to consensus, especially if there are quiet voices in the room who have not been heard on a particular topic. Temperature checks can be verbal, nonverbal, written, or anonymous. We often use hand signals to gauge how individuals feel (twinkling our fingers up high for support, in the middle to indicate remaining questions, or down low to show continued disagreement). Many groups use a variation of their own hand signals. You can also stop and take a quick anonymous poll or Post-it poll, or even a hand-raise.

Change It Up!

Sometimes a large-group discussion is not the best way to get things done. Often, it is essential that the whole group hears the introduction and sets the agenda for a meeting together. Then, consider using other forms of decision-making.[11]

Small groups: How groups break up can depend on the conversation and context. Inviting people to get in groups with others they might not know so well can be helpful. Explain clearly the goal of the groups. Write that goal or driving question where all groups can see it. Offer regular time checks, so groups know how much time they have remaining.

Go-around: Make sure the question to be addressed is clear and how long each person will have to speak. It is also good to begin a session with a go-around. If people are asked to speak in the first five minutes of a discussion, they are more likely to participate.

Physical break: Sometimes, if people are frustrated or sleepy, getting the group on their feet to stretch or run around is good. If you sense the topic is losing people's attention, do not be afraid to let it go, even if it does not feel resolved. If it is essential, you can return to it later in the conversation or try tackling it in a different form.

Humor: Notice if tensions are running high or people are zoning out. Making a joke releases bad energy and gets people refocused quickly.

Change of space: If you're able to, changing rooms can help a lot. Teens have to get up and walk to the new space, and the change in scenery is more powerful than you would expect.

Facilitating Conflict

Facilitation can help us navigate conflict both within our groups and as groups come up against museum

---

11. See 3.1.3. Setting Boundaries and Making Pivots in this publication on page 382 for more on making pivots.

policies or other experiences they find challenging. Using facilitation to address internal conflict is well-documented in restorative and transformative justice resources. Facilitating peace circles or accountability processes is a higher-level skill that requires further training. It is worth building your skills in this area to support transformative processes around interpersonal harms arising from misunderstandings, insensitivity, or disrespect. Always be aware of your boundaries, and do not hesitate to call in support from professionals and parents or guardians around serious issues like mental health or bullying. Be honest about your own limits and about the limits of what you and your group can facilitate.

It is perhaps more likely that, over a year, conflict will arise between teens and *the museum* than between individual members of the group. Facilitation can be a valuable tool in navigating conflict between teens and the other decision-makers in an institution.

As stewards of teen programs in museums, we often navigate what can feel like a tenuous line between our colleagues and our teens. It takes practice and nuance to understand where our responsibilities lie, where to honor youth decision-making that might challenge institutional norms, and where to step back. Maybe the teens are considering whether to publicly address a politically sensitive topic in their art. Maybe they want to put posters critical of the president of the country up in a gallery. If you feel nervous or uncomfortable with a potential group decision, assess what is at stake for you. What is actually at stake? Are you afraid of losing your job? Is that an actual possibility or just a fear? Consider what is at stake for the museum. Make sure you are asking, "What is the concrete danger? What is the risk of public debate? Of scandal?"

Sometimes youth challenge museum norms or policies directly. If you have done your job and created a space where young people feel ownership and have learned to take agency within the museum, they will take a stand when they disagree with something.

Here is an incomplete list of potential sources of conflict between teens and staff:

> Sometimes, museum staff make decisions that do not align with the values teens have developed in their groups.
>
> Teen programs are facilitated nonhierarchically. Most museums operate in a traditional, corporate structure. Border crossing between these structures can happen multiple times within one program session and can rub against each other.
>
> Teens and museum staff operate with different norms of communication. Staff might prepare a formal email or presentation as a sign of respect, while teens might receive the tone as distant or impersonal.
>
> Teens and staff might have different ideas of how, where, and with whom to showcase their work.
>
> Teens and staff operate on different schedules.
>
> Social media might be a standard, low-stakes form of everyday communication with teens. Social media might be a carefully crafted and regulated part of a communications strategy to museum staff.
>
> Teens and staff may interpret museums' mission and values differently. The gap between what a museum is working toward being and where it currently is can frustrate teens. Sometimes this aspirational work is hidden in processes, upcoming programs, or other internal changes that are less visible or less meaningful to the teens.
>
> Teens are present in a museum for only a brief few years, at the most. Institutional change can take much longer.

Remember, critique is an expression of love. When teens speak out, it shows how much they care for and esteem the group and the museum. How do you help administrators hear the critiques of teens with gratitude? How do you establish respectful pushback when faced with the absolute righteousness of teens? Facilitation can help bring youth and administrators together because it makes explicit the way power functions in discussion and decision-making.

In facilitated conversation, you can introduce rules and boundaries in a way that does not undermine the personal agency of individuals or the shared nature of the space. It can help to redirect the group by offering hypotheticals, asking questions, or rephrasing proposals on the table. As with group agreements, you can have conversations about how teens would like to be informed of what else is going on in the museum that they might not see on a daily basis and return to that in later conversations.

Sometimes, young people do not have their facts straight. Sometimes, there are things they cannot see. This is true also of your administrators and yourself. It goes in all directions. You can have obstructed or limited vision as well. Key facilitation strategies like maintaining the neutrality of facilitation and checking your biases can help establish ways to challenge young people supportively. It can give your group a shared language around how and when you assert something.

Contribute factual and contextual boundaries that you have access to that the group may not have with the clear statement that these are external facts and not opinions. For example, if the group is planning an event and wants to do something out of budget or that may not be physically accessible for many visitors, it is your responsibility to bring their awareness to those facts. Help teens understand that museum staff are not crushing their dreams or underfunding their work; help teens understand that by sharing what you know.

If you approach hard conversations with candor and respect, teens will understand if you have to set hard boundaries or cannot offer specific answers to their questions.

- Be a present, vulnerable human being. Speak from your own experiences, and honestly share your motivations and priorities.
- Give real information. Even if you cannot offer a definitive yes/no answer to any of their questions, they will appreciate your explaining what processes and information you're taking into consideration as you explore their question.
- Invite their thoughts and recommendations, listen, and attempt to understand their perspectives.

These reminders go for any adult who might speak with young people.

Working through any conflict with your museum is easier if teens have already been introduced to staff who are part of making organizational decisions, so *the museum* is humanized. Inviting staff to participate in youth-facilitated conversations is a way to build trust and rapport. Remember, teens and administrators have different modes of communication. Try not to have the first time you meet your directors be in a moment of crisis. Get to know them early on.

Consider your role as a mediator and translator between these communication forms. For example, you might need to remind a director that the energy and feeling of the conversation is often as important as the content discussed. Be generous with your colleagues. Introduce them to the practices of the group. Let them know that the group sits in circles, which helps physically establish the idea that everyone in the conversation, regardless of age or position, has something valuable to contribute. Tell them that the group prioritizes introductions and opportunities to speak from personal perspectives and experiences. Remember that most adults spend most of our time in spaces where modes of interaction are not centered on agency or community. Sharing facilitation practices beyond your teen group can offer your colleagues alternatives and change how your museum functions.

Ultimately, it comes back to trust. Facilitation can help you build trust with your group, predicated on open conversations about power and backed up by consistent respect for the mutually agreed-upon process. With this foundation, your teens will be better prepared to make collaborative decisions, create participatory experiences, and navigate challenging situations and conflicts.

☺

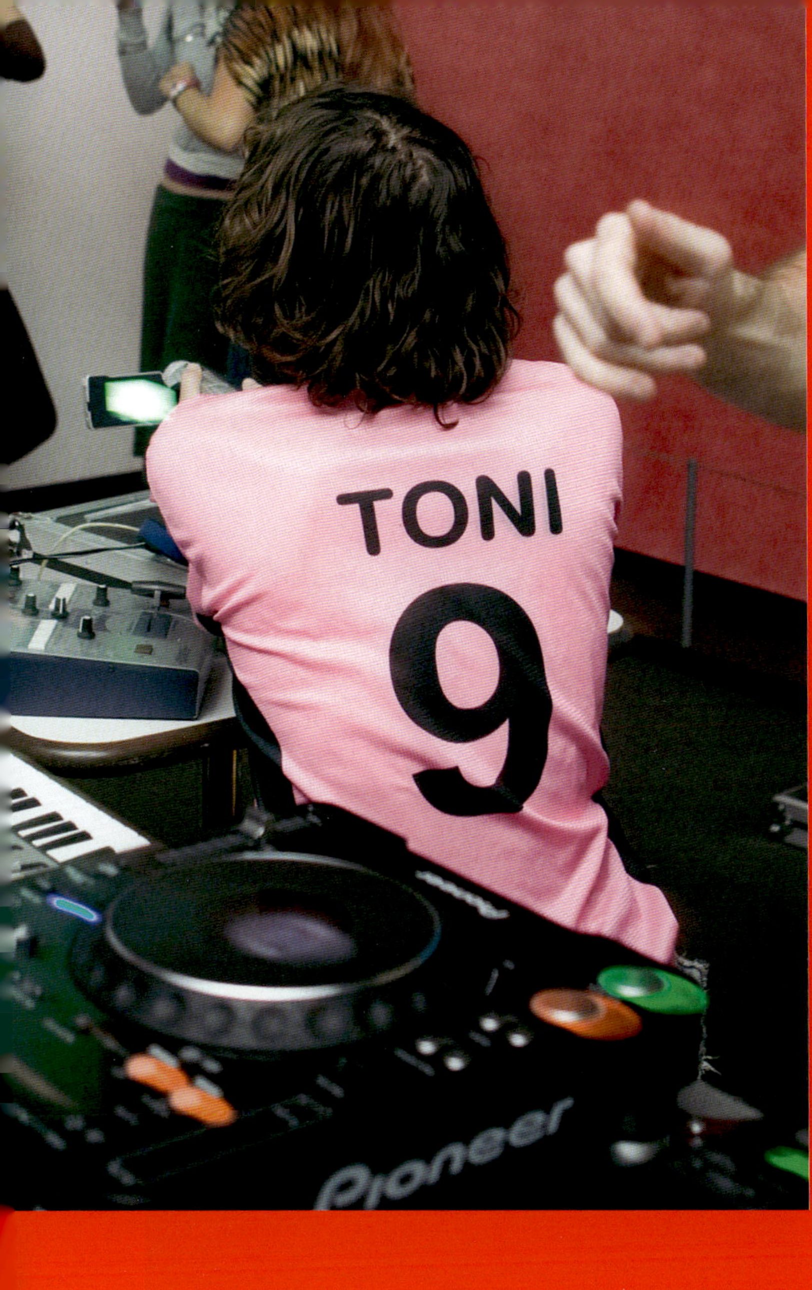
TONI
9
Pioneer

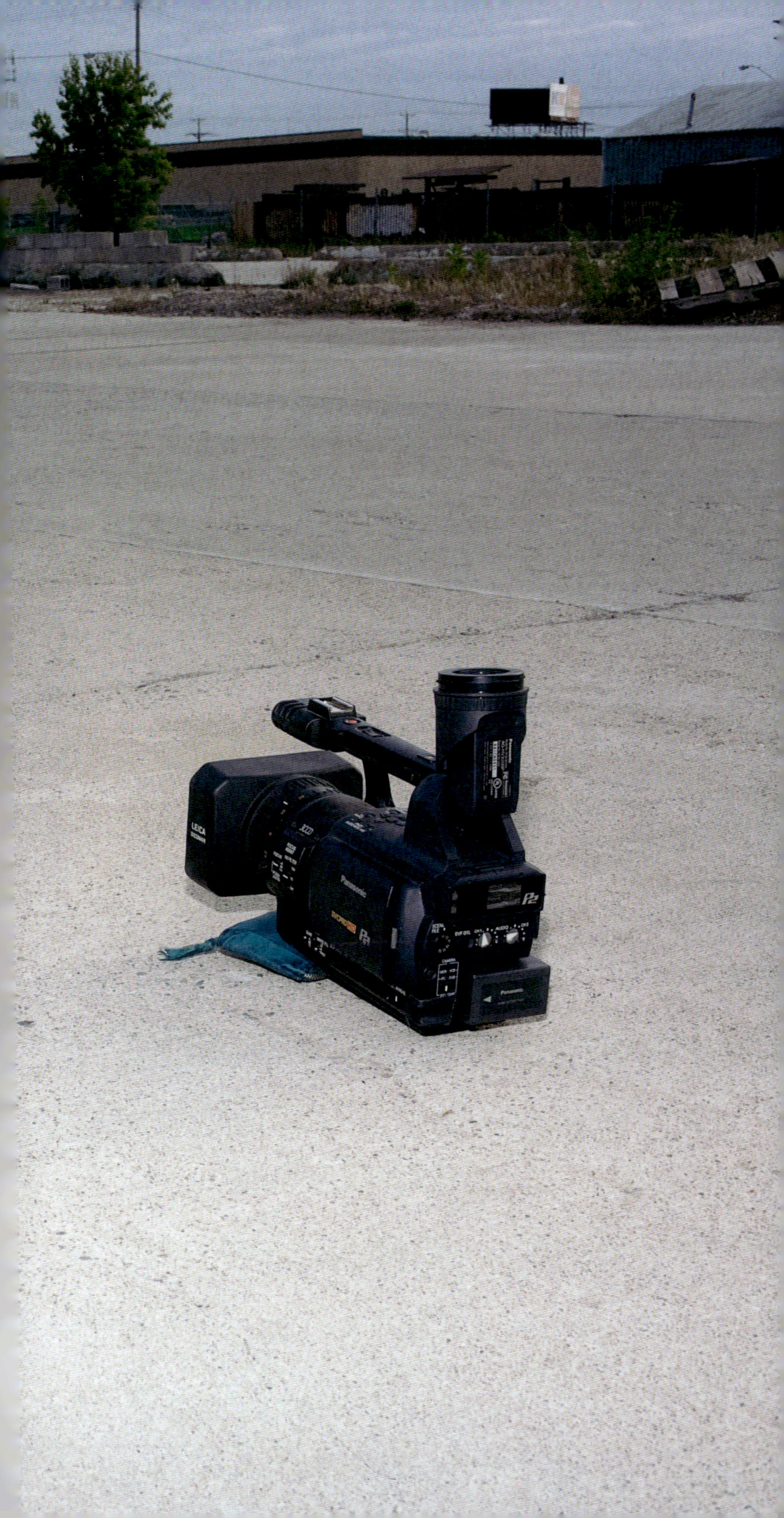
LEICA
Panasonic
P2

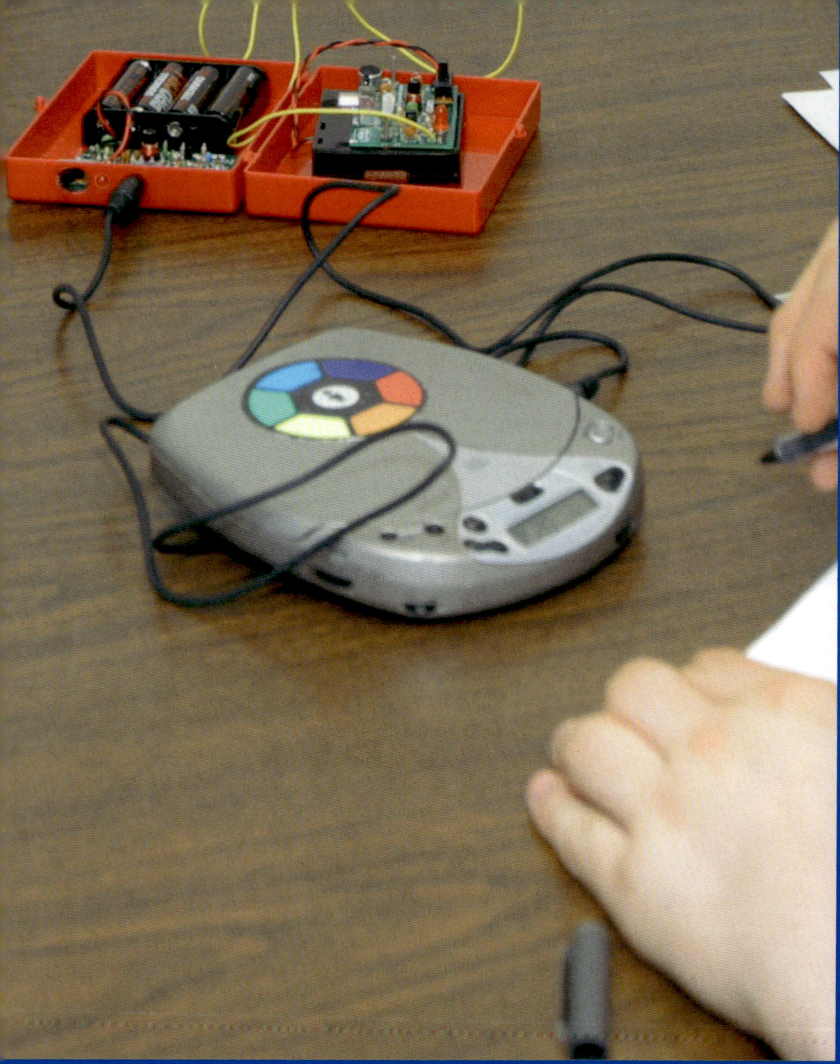

1.2. RESOURCES

1.2.1. WALKER ART CENTER TEEN ARTS COUNCIL (WACTAC) 2022-2023 ONBOARDING MATERIALS

Simona Zappas, Walker Art Center

Bio. Simona Zappas (she/her) is the Youth Programs Manager at the Walker Art Center. In her work she designs and facilitates informal learning opportunities for youth. She collaborates with curatorial staff to bring a learning lens to museum public engagement with a social practice bent on programmatic strategy. Before this, she was the director of WFNU Frogtown, a low-power radio station in Saint Paul. Simona holds a BA with honors from Macalester College and a master of education from the University of Minnesota. Simona sits on the Saint Paul Neighborhood Network board and volunteers at Planned Parenthood as an abortion doula.

Introduction

The following resources are materials used to onboard WACTAC members in new cohorts. These examples were taken from 2022–2023.

1.2.1.1. WALKER ART CENTER TEEN ARTS COUNCIL (WACTAC) FAMILY FAQS

This sheet is provided to family members and guardians of Walker Art Center Teen Arts Council (WACTAC) members at the onset of the program year to provide context for the program.

Welcome to WACTAC! If you have any questions, please feel free to reach out to Simona, Youth Programs Manager.

Email.
teenprograms@walkerart.org

What is WACTAC? WACTAC is the Walker Art Center Teen Arts Council. The program began over 25 years ago and has inspired other museums nationally and internationally. WACTAC is a behind-the-scenes learning program aiming to introduce a contemporary art museum's social, cultural, and internal functions to teens while providing opportunities to connect with art and artists. WACTAC takes a skill-based approach and aims to be led by the participants' passions. The council is made up of a diverse group of high school students from all around the Twin Cities who come to the Walker weekly to discuss art, plan events, meet artists, and create original projects.

When/where does WACTAC meet, and what precautions are in place for COVID-19 safety? WACTAC meets at the Walker Art Center on Thursdays from 4:30 pm to 6:30 pm. The Walker is located at 725 Vineland Place. We offer participants free parking vouchers and bus tokens. We plan to meet in person for the foreseeable future. We will pivot to virtual meetings if it is deemed best for group safety. WACTAC members are expected to wear a mask during meetings.

Are there perks? Each month, the Walker will recognize the participation of the members with a $100 prepaid US Bank debit card (see Participation Recognition FAQs doc for more info). WACTAC members also receive a four-year Walker membership and free tickets to performances and screenings at the Walker.

Do they have to come every week? What happens if they're sick/on vacation? Yes! Weekly attendance at WACTAC is expected! Being sick or missing a week is OK, but members are expected to give the facilitators at least 24-hour notice. This is a fast-paced program, and each meeting builds off the last. If a member has three absences in a month, their spot in the program will be in jeopardy. If a member has more than three unexcused absences, their place in WACTAC will be in jeopardy.

Who runs WACTAC? WACTAC is facilitated by Simona Zappas, Youth Programs Manager. Simona has managed Walker youth programming for over four years, has recently led national training on youth engagement in museums, and holds a master's degree in education.

How does this look on a résumé or college application? WACTAC is a very competitive program that can be listed as an extracurricular activity. Many other museums and organizations have youth councils, so colleges and employers recognize what participants gain from these programs. You can expect your members to gain skills in teamwork, event planning, research, and confidence in collaborating with people different from them. WACTAC staff are always happy to write recommendation letters.

Will you provide devices if needed? Yes. As a safety protocol, we may host meetings virtually. If a member needs a device to access the internet, they will be lent an iPad from the Walker Art Center free of charge. There is no need to show proof of requiring the device. Members should contact Simona if this is needed.

What are the meetings like? The content of WACTAC meetings varies, but we spend time planning events for other teens, meeting with other Walker staff members to learn about their careers, doing art-making activities with local or international artists, or viewing art. Most of the year will be dedicated to a group research project. The WACTAC members will explore a topic of their choosing, contributing to the enhancement of the Walker as a whole.

Is there homework? Not usually. At times the members may be asked to do short, optional activities at home, like designs for posters, but we try to keep the content in the meetings. Success in the program comes from weekly attendance, participation, and keeping up with weekly emails from Simona.

Will they make friends? Yes! WACTAC is very focused on the teens building relationships with each other and forming a group bond. We hope that, above all else, WACTAC is a fun experience that they look forward to coming to each week!

What is my role now? Sit back and relax! Remember, WACTAC is the members and their responsibility. Family involvement from this point on is not expected or required. We encourage you and your family to visit the Walker when you can! We are always happy to get free tickets for you!

1.2.1.2. WALKER ART CENTER TEEN ARTS COUNCIL (WACTAC) WELCOME LETTER

This letter is sent to Walker Art Center Teen Arts Council members upon acceptance into the program to provide an official feel.

[Date]

Dear [WACTAC Member],

Congratulations and welcome to the Walker Art Center Teen Arts Council! For the next nine months, you will be part of a diverse team of peers that will meet every Thursday at the Walker from 4.30 to 6.30 pm. Over the course of the year, WACTAC will collaborate and build new ideas about arts engagement, plan events, connect with artists, and learn about the behind-the-scenes goings-on at an internationally celebrated museum.

Walker Mission. The Walker Art Center empowers people to experience the transformative possibilities of the art and ideas of our time and to imagine the world in new ways.

Teen Programs Mission. Teen Programs create and support the interactions with and connections to contemporary art and artists of our time. Walker Teen Programs seek to provide vehicles for young people, ages 13–19, to safely ask complex questions, voice their own ideas and opinions, and explore their own creative potential.

Before WACTAC begins, we have two orientations.

Family Orientation. [Date] at the Walker Art Center. This optional event is for WACTAC parents and guardians only. It's a chance for them to learn more about the program. If your family member needs translation services, please contact Simona.

WACTAC Orientation. [Date] at the Walker Art Center. This event is mandatory for all WACTACs. If you require any accommodations, please contact Simona.

The first WACTAC meeting. [Date] at the Walker Art Center.

This packet includes mandatory forms that need to be signed and turned in by the first meeting. There are also some helpful sheets with information about the Walker and WACTAC. If you have further questions about anything at all, do not hesitate to reach out to Simona. Congratulations and welcome to the team!

Sincerely,

Simona Zappas
Youth Programs Manager
Walker Art Center

1.2.1.3. WALKER ART CENTER TEEN ARTS COUNCIL (WACTAC) PERMISSION FORM

This form is distributed digitally to Walker Art Center Teen Arts Council (WACTAC) members and their caregivers at the onset of the program year as a safety measure to obtain consent for their participation in the program.

This form collects essential contact information, and permissions for participating in WACTAC. This form must be completed by the WACTAC member and their parent or guardian before the first meeting on [date].

Please contact Simona at teenprograms@walkerart.org with any questions.

Participant name:
Participant mailing address:
Participant email address:
Participant phone number:
Participant birthday:
Participant school:

Parent/Guardian name:
Parent/Guardian phone number:
Parent/Guardian email:

Emergency contact name:
Emergency contact relation to WACTAC member:
Emergency contact phone number:

I give my child permission to participate in the Walker Art Center Teen Arts Council (WACTAC).

● Yes
● No (Contact Simona)

I understand that participating in WACTAC is my child's responsibility. They are responsible to attend weekly meetings and keep up with their correspondences. Failure to do this could result in being asked to leave the program.

● Yes
● No (Contact Simona)

I understand that in participating in WACTAC my child will engage in conversations and view artworks that I give the Walker Art Center permission to photograph and film my child for documentation and evaluation purposes.

● Yes
● No

I give the Walker Art Center permission to share pictures or videos of my child on social media or in marketing materials.

- Yes
- No

Does the participant have Wi-Fi at home?

- Yes
- No
- Sometimes

What devices does the participant have access to?

- Phone (shared)
- Phone (not shared)
- Computer (shared)
- Computer (not shared)
- Tablet/iPad (shared)
- Tablet/iPad (not shared)

1.2.1.4. WALKER ART CENTER TEEN ARTS COUNCIL (WACTAC) RESPONSIBILITIES AND REQUIREMENTS

This form is sent digitally to Walker Art Center Teen Arts Council (WACTAC) members at the onset of the program year as a means to communicate base expectations for candor in the program.

Being a member of the Walker Art Center Teen Arts Council (WACTAC) is a great opportunity for personal growth and learning that should be taken seriously. This document outlines the basic behavior expectations of council members when participating in WACTAC programming.

WACTAC Meetings. WACTAC occurs *every Thursday evening of the school year from 4:30 to 6:30 pm, unless notified otherwise.*

Commitment to Inclusion. Our goal for WACTAC is to make the Walker a welcoming and safe space for teens of all backgrounds and identities. We welcome differing viewpoints in WACTAC, but our actions should never come at the expense or exclusion of an individual or a group of people because of their identity or belief. There is always space for learning and expression in WACTAC, but making statements meant in harm or offense toward a person or group's identity will not be tolerated.

While you are participating in WACTAC, you are expected to follow the Walker's Inclusion Statement:

1. As a contemporary art center, we believe we have a greater imperative to reflect the world in the work we do and to represent a multiplicity of voices about the times in which we live.
2. We depend on a diverse set of viewpoints to enact our mission and reflect the audiences we serve now and in the future. We believe this array of views, internally and externally, makes for a better experience.
3. We will only be able to fulfill our mission and achieve our strategic plan by embracing the opportunities: to make all people feel welcomed throughout the organization; to create bridges; and to help provide a greater understanding.

Attendance. WACTAC members are expected to attend each week. Occasional absences are OK, as long as the member provides program staff with advanced notice. If a member misses more than three meetings in a month, their spot in the program will be up for discussion. If a participant has more than three absences without notice, their spot in the program will be up for discussion. WACTAC follows the Minneapolis Public Schools calendar for holiday breaks.

All WACTAC members must call, text, or email prior to the meeting if they are going to be absent. Please call, text, or email Simona at least 24 hours in advance if you have a pre-existing conflict with a WACTAC event. In the event that you are sick or something unexpected comes up, please call/text before the meeting to let Simona know.

If you have five unexcused absences, your place in WACTAC will be up for discussion.

Social Media. WACTAC members are expected to post on our Instagram and TikTok (@walkerteens). This is our best way to tell people about our events. It's also a great way to share your interests, what's happening behind the scenes, and more.

Remember that when you are posting on social media, or any online content, you are representing WACTAC and the Walker. The rule of thumb is to only post content you would be OK with a teacher seeing and that does not use offensive or explicit language. If any member breaks this, the post will be removed.

Events.

WACTAC Events. WACTAC members are expected to attend all WACTAC events such as Teen Takeover. Some events may be on other evenings or weekends.

General Walker Events. As a WACTAC member you have access to free and discounted tickets to Walker events. We encourage you to take advantage of this opportunity! If you want tickets to something, let Simona know and she will do her best to get them for you for free (no guarantees unfortunately)

Drugs/Alcohol/Controlled Substances Policy. It is a policy of the Walker Art Center and WACTAC to ensure that members do not come to meetings under the influence of alcohol or drugs; consume alcohol while at the Walker; or possess or consume drugs while at the Walker or on-site. *Failure to comply with any part of this policy can be cause for dismissal and/or termination.*

Safety and Misconduct. Feeling safe at the Walker is incredibly important. To ensure that our meetings are a safe space, *any harassment, misconduct, or violence is cause for immediate dismissal and/or termination.*

The Walker defines harassment as intimidating, hostile, or offensive behavior toward someone based on their gender, race, color, national origin, ancestry, religion, disability, age, or sexual orientation. These behaviors include insults, comments, touching, emails, and other electronic communications.

If you ever feel that you've been harassed while you're at the Walker, please talk to Simona.

Your signature below reflects your understanding of what has been laid out in this document.

Printed name & signature:
Date:

1.2.2. SNACK CURATORS

Jorge Espinosa, Museum of Contemporary Art, Los Angeles

> **Bio.** Jorge is an artist, musician, educator, and designer based in Los Angeles. He is one of the two people responsible for the teen program at the Museum of Contemporary Art, Los Angeles (MOCA), and coordinates MOCA family programs, consisting of in-person and online art-making events and projects for people of all ages and experience levels. In addition to his educational occupation, he is active in his visual and sound art practice.

Introduction

Each week, in the Museum of Contemporary Art, Los Angeles (MOCA) teen program, a teen intern is selected to curate food and drink for the meeting. Through this activity, teens develop organizational and creative skills related to managing resources, communicating, and working in a group. Having food and drink available for our students at weekly meetings goes beyond the basic need of giving them energy after a long and exhausting day at school; it also achieves these distinct programmatic goals:

- Eating together provides a special opportunity for the group to relax, break the ice, and learn more about each other, including their interests, where they come from, their cultural backgrounds, and other stories about who they are.
- The Snack Curator Project seeks to open an informal space for exchange among our teen interns and facilitate community building toward the program's objectives.[1] Having a snack on hand during meetings helps the group's concentration,[2] and balances the group's energy. We have found

---

1. Some of the MOCA teen program objectives are to develop communication skills necessary to express themselves and function well within a diverse group; to learn multiple strategies for including and encouraging everyone's ideas, opinions, and participation; to effect positive social change by fostering model citizen contributors; or to develop skills for lifelong learning.

that snacks help us improve our ability to focus, making us more alert and open to learning and participating. Eating, apart from its primary functions,[3] like nourishing and providing energy, is something that gives pleasure and comfort. It is a pleasurable activity that could be enhanced in a relaxed atmosphere surrounded by friends. According to the *Atlantic*,[4] the average American eats one in five meals daily in the car, and many families eat together only once every five days. Due to the generalized conditions of our daily life, it is becoming a rarity for many families to eat together. In most cases, we are replacing the people around us with screens, making it increasingly difficult to relate to one another and converse with people at our tables, including those we love.

Eating in the company of our classmates and colleagues can be a special experience. At MOCA, we think it offers another opportunity to reinforce key elements of our program objectives, like developing our communication skills, increasing our ability to function well within a diverse group, viewing our contributions as important, and thinking of work as an enjoyable experience. Snacking also allows us space to talk about other topics that are not necessarily present in the weekly agenda yet are extremely helpful in building camaraderie.

Unstructured moments benefit shy kids who might feel uncomfortable talking in large groups, or about topics they are not fluent in. Space can help them gain confidence and discover new affinities with their peers. The simple moment of sharing snacks, which happens just minutes before our meetings officially start, offers a unique chance to nurture our small learning community, and becomes a great pretext for many new and unexpected ideas to flourish.[5]

---

2   Harvard School of Public Health, "The Science of Snacking," accessed December 15, 2022, https://www.hsph.harvard.edu/nutritionsource/snacking/.

3   "The Function of Food," in Food and Nutrition: A Handbook for Namibian Volunteers (Windhoek, Namibia: Ministry of Higher Education, Training, and Employment Creation, Namibia, and the Food and Agriculture Association of the United States, 2004), https://www.fao.org/3/a0104e/a0104e06.htm.

4   Cody C. Delistraty, "The Importance of Eating Together," *Atlantic*, July 18, 2014, https://www.theatlantic.com/health/archive/2014/07/the-importance-of-eating-together/374256/.

All teens in the program are expected to be snack curators at least once in the school year. At the program's start date, each teen signs up for a week, during which they are the snack curator. The appointed intern receives an envelope with twenty dollars in cash one week before the meeting date. The teen must bring their snacks of choice the following week while bringing the shopping receipts and change, if any. Snack curators must consider all the logistical aspects of their duty. For instance, if they drive a car, they will have more flexibility and choices, including what and where to purchase snacks. Alternatively, if they use public transportation or depend on a friend or family member for access, they must carefully plan and coordinate with everyone involved in the process. If transportation is a problem, the teens should reconsider the "menu," so to speak, and buy something easy to store and bring to the museum. As part of the planning process, snack curators check with the whole group to see if there are any dietary restrictions or allergies. We want to ensure everyone feels safe and included; we do not want to leave anyone out of the experience due to dietary restrictions.

Snack curation is an exceptional problem-solving exercise and serves as training for more complex projects, such as Teen Night. Teen Night is the program's culminating event, where students plan and host a celebratory event at the museum for over nine hundred local Los Angeles high school students.[6] Not only do our students need to consider the food served at the event, but they also have to coordinate and plan art activities, DJ sets, decorations, student art exhibitions, and each facet of the event. For most of our interns, this is their first time working on projects like these, and it would not be surprising that some of them may be confused about what or where to buy everything needed for snack curation. At the beginning of the school year, the two program managers explain the aspects of the role, and we model

---

5 "Free play will help your child develop a flexible mind. This is crucial, as it will prepare them for moments later in their life when they have to face unexpected challenges. This is especially important in their teenage years." Andy Earle, "The Importance of Unstructured Play in Your Child's Life," *Emile* (blog), accessed December 15, 2022, https://www.emile-education.com/unstructured-play/.

6 Teen Night attendance: In 2018 and 2019, attendance at Teen Night was over 900 teens per night. In 2020 and 2021, the program shifted to a virtual event with 5,000 visits to the mocateens.org website in a month. In 2022, at our first in-person event in two years, we decided to reduce our capacity due to COVID-19 restrictions to 450 attendees.

by acting as a snack curator at our first meeting.

Generally speaking, our teens tend to buy packaged food and products that are ready to eat as it is convenient and saves preparation and cleanup time. But we are not opposed to the possibility of serving something more elaborate, as long as the result is tasty and feasible, considering the limitations in space, ventilation, and time. If our interns accept the challenge and decide to put their time and energy into preparing something unique and intricate, we fully support them. We have seen a variety of homemade dishes at our meetings, and some teens opt for family recipes or something that represents part of their culture and identity, making this activity another excellent opportunity to understand more about our community.

Nevertheless, in most cases, the menu is much more straightforward and consists of vegetables such as carrots or celery, cookies, potato chips, pita bread with dip, sweets, and fruit such as tangerines, bananas, or grapes, and in some cases drinks such as lemonade. We always have filtered water available and tea or other infusions. We avoid sodas and food with artificial flavorings, but the latter is not always possible. Part of this assignment is to find and bring the best available options. It is not just a matter of looking for something nutritious or healthy but also something that makes our students feel good and bonded, even if it is not the most recommended food for an ideal diet. Remember that this is just a snack, and we do not intend to replace any of the important meals of the day. Our sessions are in the late afternoon, during which most of the teens have had lunch already and are likely to have dinner after our meeting.

When the day of the assigned session arrives, the snack curator must arrive a few minutes early to prepare the table where the snacks will be laid out and wash utensils and food items properly. Our Thursday meetings usually take place in the museum's boardroom, so we need to be extremely careful and respectful of the space. It is important that nothing is spilled, that all liquids, drinks, or sauces are in a safe container, and that we have all the essential cleaning implements ready in case of an accident. There is a small kitchen across the boardroom; dish preparation or cleaning must be done there, but it is forbidden to cook any food on-site. Everything must arrive ready to eat from home or the supermarket.

Once our meeting is over, everyone helps clean up. All recyclable material and organic leftovers should go to the corresponding containers. It is important to leave the space as we found it. The snack curator is in charge of cleaning and returning all the trays, bowls, or kitchen implements taken from the kitchen.

Snack curation might seem very simple, but this combination of structured and unstructured time and activities contributes enormously to the program. By the end of each year, our students have gained the confidence to communicate clearly, work together, and build community. The growth is palpable, and they relate to each other through the bonds that they have shared.

In conclusion, by the end of each program year, the objectives we intended to reinforce with the snack curators exercise are met, such as developing communication skills, creating an atmosphere where multiple ideas and opinions are welcomed, creating an opportunity to break the ice, and sharing the space in an unstructured and informal setting. Small activities and projects like these allow our students to exercise different problem-solving skills, in an original and inventive way, problems that are not always simple. The teen program seeks to develop relevant skills through complex and eye-catching projects, such as Teen Night, as well as in ordinary, everyday moments, which can sometimes go unnoticed. Building a strong team that can work well with a diverse group of students from Los Angeles who have not been exposed to the same life experiences is only possible if we break the ice, bond with each other, and make opportunities for students to be themselves. And what better way to do it than by eating snacks together!

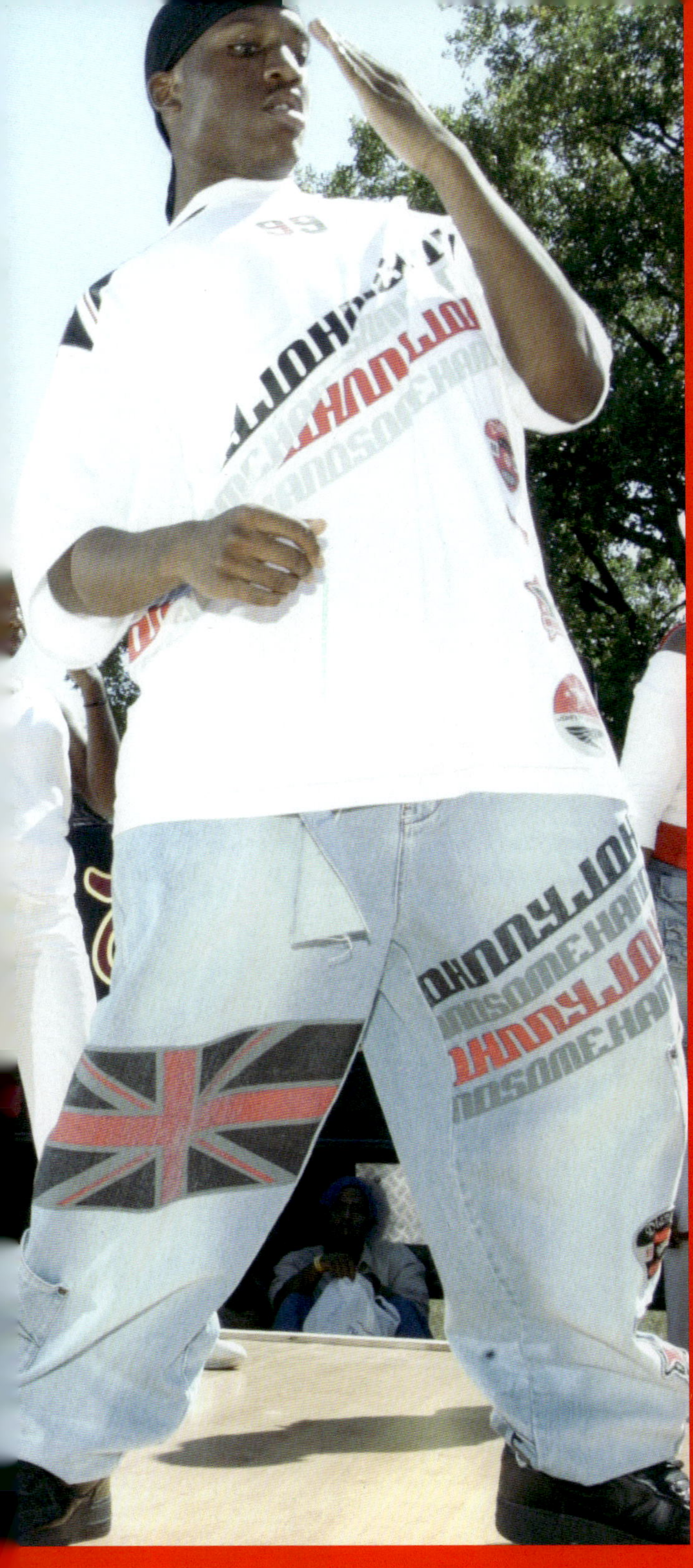

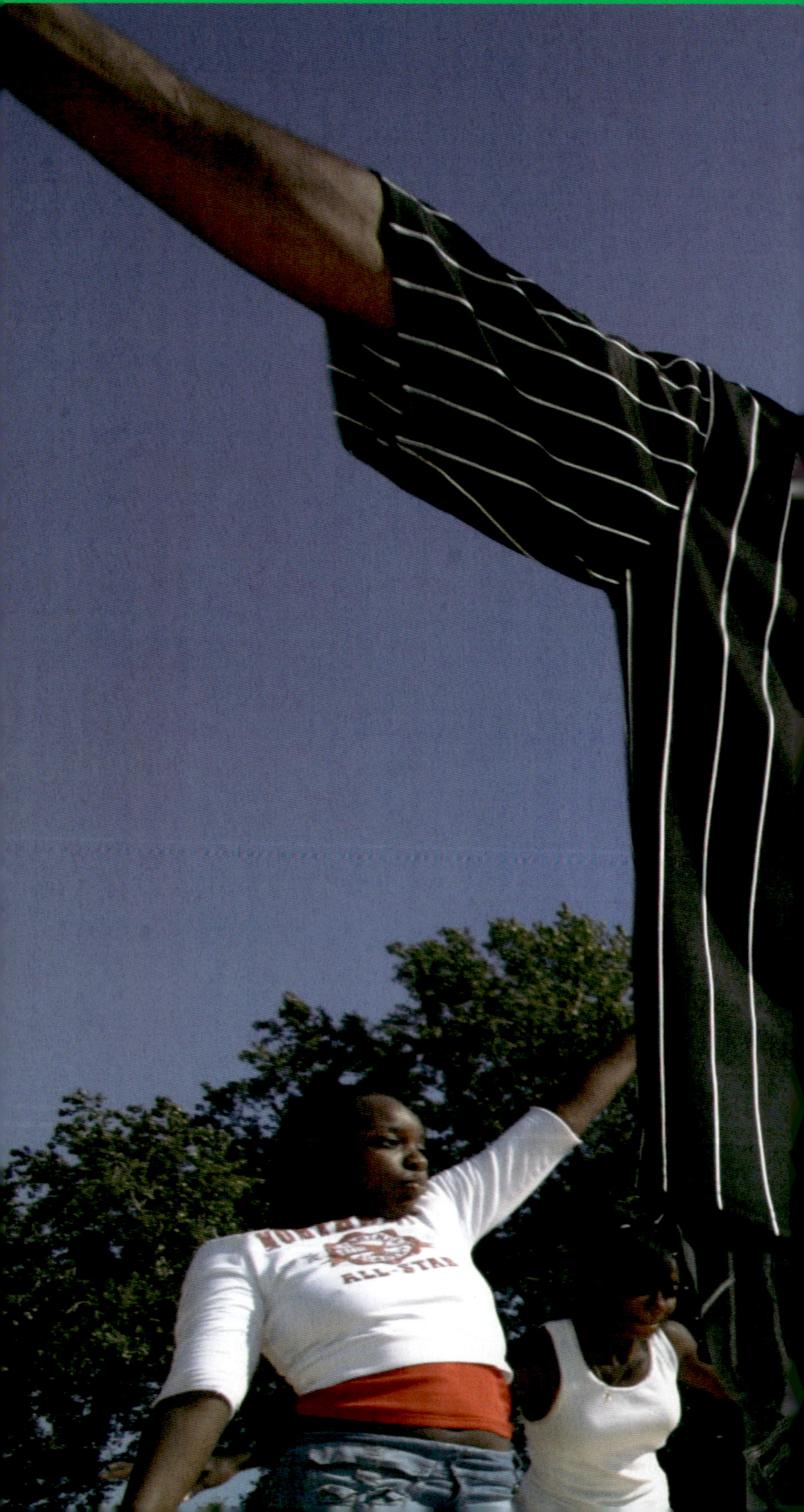
ALL-STAR

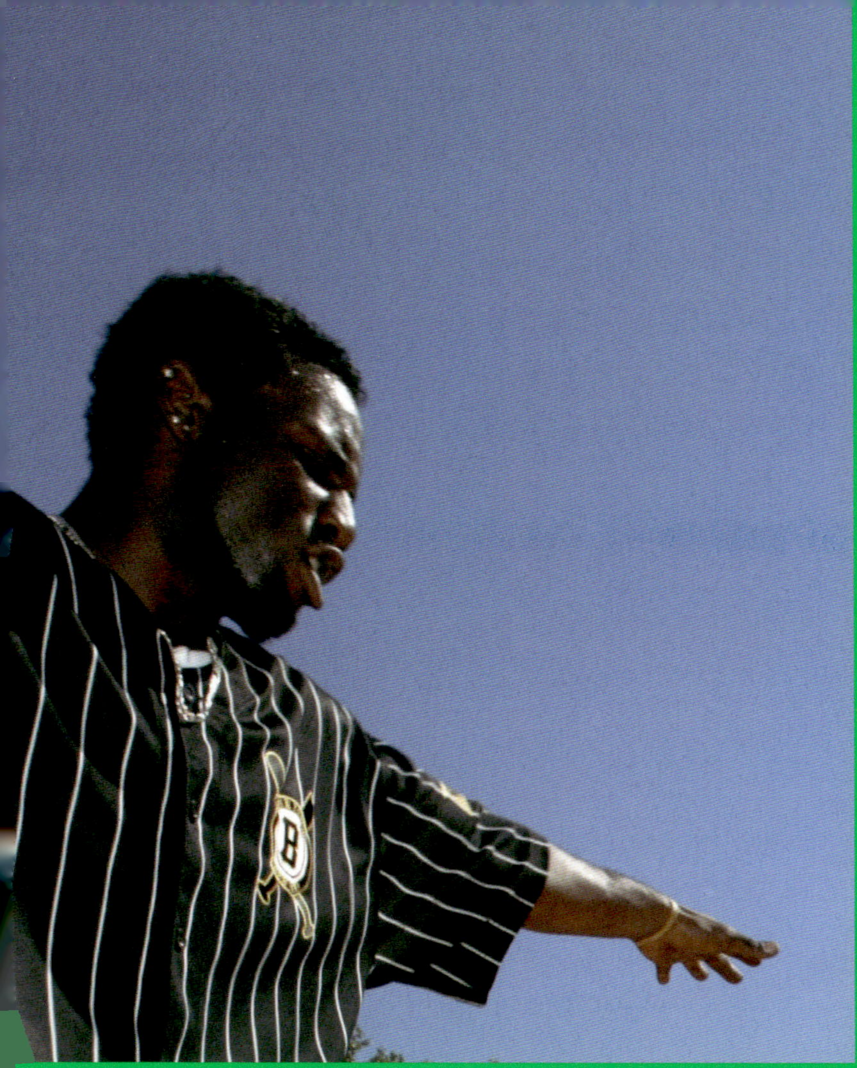

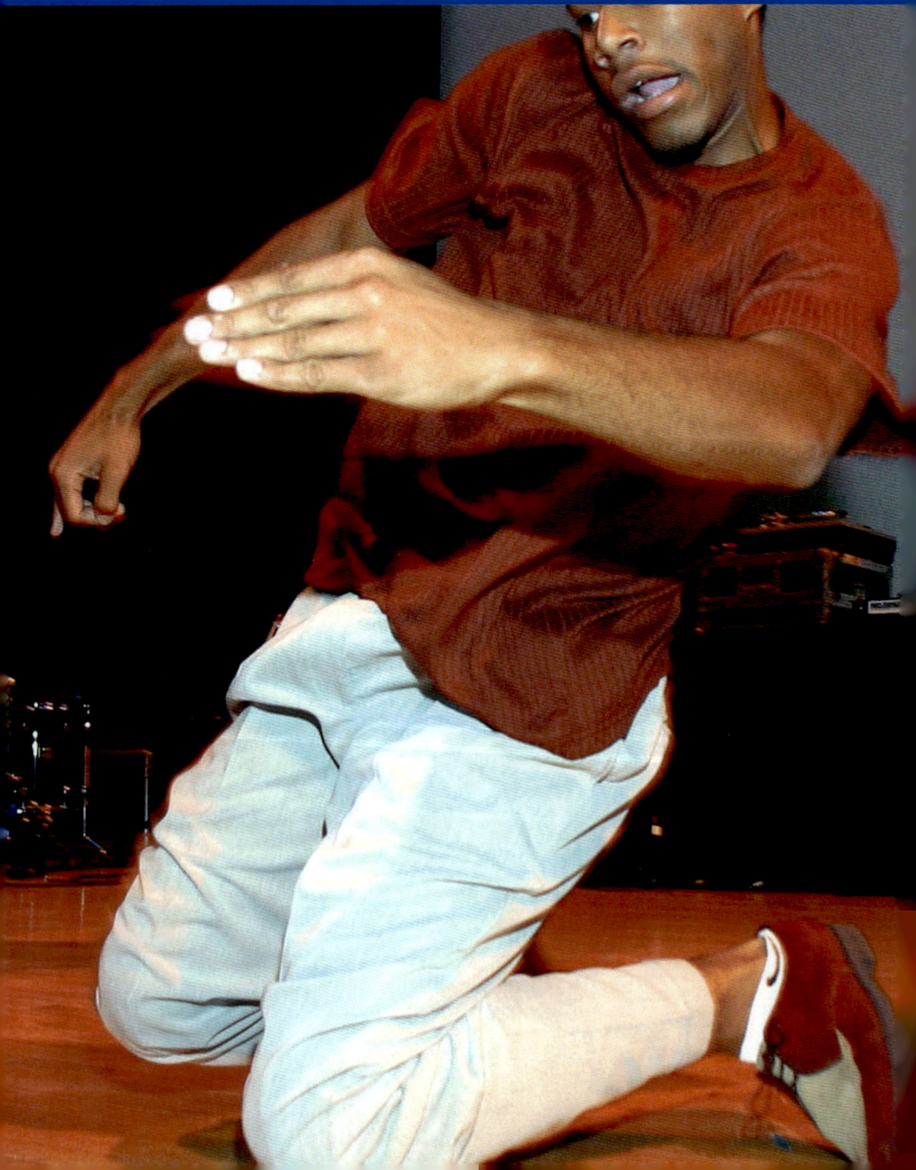

1.2.3. BREAKING THE GRID

Jorge Espinosa, Museum of Contemporary Art, Los Angeles

> **Bio.** Jorge is an artist, musician, educator, and designer based in Los Angeles. He is one of the two people responsible for the teen program at the Museum of Contemporary Art, Los Angeles (MOCA), and coordinates MOCA family programs, consisting of in-person and online art-making events and projects for people of all ages and experience levels. In addition to his educational occupation, he is active in his visual and sound art practice.

Introduction

Guide for a Zoom activity with simple instructions but not-so-easy solutions.

Learning Goals. Using surprising outcomes to facilitate problem-solving and physical interaction in a remote digital environment.

Remote working and learning are here to stay with or without a pandemic. Even though it is (at the moment?) not the same as in-person meetings or courses, group video calls offer many pedagogical benefits.

It is great to have the opportunity to talk to people who might be far away or unavailable to come to our area physically. For people who have family and friends hundreds of miles away, as I do, video calls make the separation more manageable and help us feel more connected.

Before March 2020, I don't think I knew that Zoom existed. I was aware of FaceTime (which I used weekly with my family) and Google Hangouts. With the latter, I remember a few years ago proposing to some colleagues to meet remotely, so I could avoid a long ride and the hustle of finding parking. They agreed, but I could read in their faces that they thought I was an eccentric person. Nowadays, it's really hard to find someone who's not using this tool.

The sad thing is that we spend too many hours in front of screens, working, hanging out with friends, talking to loved ones, or watching entertainment online. After too many months of this new reality, we are exhausted, using the same interface over and over, making us feel that we are in a very long meeting because everything looks the same: a series of horizontal rectangles with more or less the same content inside. Staring at the rigid grid of Zoom for many hours can be hard. It is boring, and everything looks identical, aside from a few background changes.

At the Museum of Contemporary Art, Los Angeles (MOCA) teen program, we noticed the fatigue our students were experiencing after eight hours of Zoom classes for school. So we tried to implement a few changes in our meetings. Some changes were simple, like changing from "active speaker" to "gallery view" or allowing the teens to be off camera at specific times.

At the beginning of our meeting icebreakers, we tried to do something that involved more body or voice, or something forcing us to be more physically active. As an aside, I recommend this for in-person meetings as well. Most museum teen programs take place after school, so youth come from eight hours where they are following specific behavior and social rules. Doing something that allows for some physical difference and release can help transition into the program time and space.

The "Breaking the Grid" activity is a problem-solving activity for groups of four to sixteen participants. It works better in groups made of even numbers. The goal is to connect adjacent rectangles using paper or cardboard cutouts to create new geometrical figures that do not follow the interface's stiffness. Before the activity, you have to prepare a few things in advance, and the "coordinator" of the activity should get familiarized with Zoom's interface and vocabulary to describe its various components to the participants.

Materials. The materials you will need are designed to be very accessible.

- Use a letter-size piece of paper (I recommend using plain white paper to have some unity with the rest

of the pieces created by other participants); other paper will do in a pinch
- A writing utensil
- Two pieces of tape
- Scissors

Activity

First, participants will need to create an arch. The strip could be around 1.5 inches to 2 inches wide.

Then participants can cut a strip with the remaining paper. Use the leftover paper from the previous shape. It could be 8.5 inches by 1.5 to 2 inches wide.

Once they have two pieces of paper, add the masking tape in order to create a handle for the pieces. This will make it easier to hold the figures on the screen.

Once everyone is on the call and with their cutouts ready, you will need an icebreaker coordinator. This person will give the first instructions and answer all the questions about the activity. This person will ask everyone to switch into gallery mode and to rearrange their windows in the same order so we all have the same people in the same place. Click and drag the windows to place them in the right position (this is not possible on all devices or versions of the software; please try to update to the latest version of Zoom). If this is not possible for one participant, make sure to offer instruction and support for them. The group must follow the instructions to order everyone consistently on their personal screens. Be considerate that some folks might be on phones or tablets and have different interfaces.

And now you are all set and ready to play!

The goal is to connect any of your cutout shapes with the people around your screen. Collectively you will create ovals or other more complex geometric figures.

> This is not always easy; enjoy the process, and think that imperfection is inevitable but beautiful!

1.2.4. RESPECT IS... ACTIVITY

Simona Zappas, Walker Art Center

Bio. Simona Zappas (she/her) is the Youth Programs Manager at the Walker Art Center. In her work she designs and facilitates informal learning opportunities for youth. She collaborates with curatorial staff to bring a learning lens to museum public engagement with a social practice bent on programmatic strategy. Before this, she was the director of WFNU Frogtown, a low-power radio station in Saint Paul. Simona holds a BA with honors from Macalester College and a master of education from the University of Minnesota. Simona sits on the Saint Paul Neighborhood Network board and volunteers at Planned Parenthood as an abortion doula.

Introduction

A common practice in social-justice-oriented youth learning is empowering young people by trusting them to determine some behavior expectations for the group. This helps them stay accountable to each other because

- it can create ownership they feel over "the rules";
- it can allow for more horizontal leadership because not all of the expectations will be delivered or administered by the adults in the room; and
- it can encourage being part of an in-group and intentionality around the space.

These practices are common across youth work and go by many names—group agreement, accountability agreement, ropes, and the WACTAC way. Whatever you call it, it is common to keep it written and posted in the meeting space, revisit it as a living document, and ask the youth how they want it collectively enforced.

In the Walker Art Center Teen Arts Council (WACTAC), we typically write ours two to four weeks into the program so that the teens know each other a bit and have some footing around the norms at the museum. Rather than writing the group agreement raw, we use a scaffolded process that encourages the youth to think about how everyone has different ways they want to be treated and how common words, like "respect," mean different things in different contexts to different people. For example, someone who went to a school where teachers are called by their last names might be uncomfortable calling adults by first names, versus someone who went to a school where they call teachers by their first names might find calling someone "Mr. Smith" a power imbalance.

This process has teens break down respect in different contexts, think about who is setting the bar for it, and think about what makes them feel respected and how to hold space for others having a different idea. I like to say we are "making the stone feel stony" in taking the time to think about what a word we commonly use really means.

> *Please note.* This guide is adapted from an interactive Google Doc used by the 2020–2021 WACTAC. This can easily be adapted for in-person use with large sheets of paper.

Begin by introducing the activity—simply describe the goal and why you are writing everything out.

Background

Hi, everyone! We will use this as our working document to determine our group agreement (or whatever we want to call it). We can use this as our guiding expectations of how we would like to show up and have others show up in the space of WACTAC. This might mean certain behaviors, like asking each other not to be on our phones or not using certain words, or it can be positive things, like we all agree to tell one joke each meeting. This will be a living document that we will all be able to refer to during meetings as a reminder of how we expect ourselves and each other to show up in meetings and how to hold each other accountable and call each other back[1] when boundaries are crossed. We can edit it whenever we want—this is a collective agreement that we all have shared ownership over, but whatever is added or taken off must be decided in conversation with the group. The group agreement can be long, it can be short, it can contradict itself, it can be whatever y'all feel supported by. I hope that we come up with something through consensus and feel positive about what is included. We will keep our notes here to make the process visible.

> ### *Activity 1*
>
> Take some time to reflect on when you were part of an intentional community. What made it intentional? Write down a description of an intentional community you were part of. If you do not feel like you have been in one, how would you define an intentional community? We will ask volunteers to share what they wrote or what they wrote about.
>
> **Ask the group to reflect on this personally on paper or in journals you provide.**

What is an intentional community?

---

1   Ultimately, it is up to the facilitator to enforce and manage safety and boundaries in the program. Asking the youth what they think are effective ways to encourage growth and discussion over punishment is a great idea, but facilitators should never put the expectation of responding when a boundary is crossed on youth. We can support them in respectful disagreement, but beyond that, it is simply not their responsibility. See page 382 for 3.1.3. Setting Boundaries and Making Pivots for advice on pivoting and making boundaries.

Activity 2

As a group, we will add some words to describe what it felt or looked like to be part of an intentional community.

If the group shared out what they wrote, you could populate these lists (posted for all to see) with terms you pull from what folks shared, or people can popcorn out ideas.

Intentional communities feel like...

Intentional communities look like...

Activity 3

When we use certain words, we unintentionally assume others have the same definition. We will use this activity to unpack the word "respect." This will help show how the word has different social and cultural meanings that change based on individual experience, cultural values, and the context in which the word is used. You may have conflicting definitions in your groups, and that is okay! The goal here is not to gain consensus; it is to highlight that words can have differently experienced definitions that can all be true. We will share what we wrote and noticed while working in our groups.

Break into small groups and ask the teens to start listing their thoughts. Each group can do one space. I like to premake groups to encourage friendships across the cohort rather than folks falling back onto cliques. I try to vary the groups as much as possible and think through how I can ensure a balance of personality types in each group. This can be challenging at the beginning of the year, so another option is to randomize them slightly by asking the teens to count off by three.

1.2.4.

Group 1—Respect in school means...

Group 2—Respect at home means...

Group 3—Respect with my friends means...

Activity 4

Let us write our group agreement (or whatever we want to call it). This will be a living document that we will all be able to refer to during meetings as a reminder of how we expect each other to show up in meetings and to hold each other accountable when boundaries are crossed. We can edit it whenever we want—this is a collective agreement that we all have shared ownership over, but whatever is added or taken off must be decided in conversation with the group.

1.2.4.

WACTAC [Year] Group Agreement

1.2.5. WALKER ART CENTER TEEN ARTS COUNCIL (WACTAC) "GO-AROUND QUESTIONS"

Simona Zappas, Walker Art Center

> **Bio.** Simona Zappas (she/her) is the Youth Programs Manager at the Walker Art Center. In her work she designs and facilitates informal learning opportunities for youth. She collaborates with curatorial staff to bring a learning lens to museum public engagement and a social practice bent on programmatic strategy. Before this, she was the director of WFNU Frogtown, a low-power radio station in Saint Paul. Simona holds a BA with honors from Macalester College and a master of education from the University of Minnesota. Simona sits on the Saint Paul Neighborhood Network board and volunteers at Planned Parenthood as an abortion doula.

Introduction

We kick off every Walker Art Center Teen Arts Council (WACTAC) meeting with at least one "go-around question." These are silly questions that the WACTAC members come up with, and we ask everyone in the group to go around in a circle and answer. The questions have a few goals:

- It is a repeated ritual that they can expect each week to mark the start of a meeting
- They practice sharing about themselves, speaking to the group, and listening
- Teens might share an opinion and find connection in it
- It builds laughter and humor in the group that can lead to long-term bonding

> These questions have become a calling card of WACTAC—nearly every staff member at the Walker now knows that if they're meeting with the teens, they better be ready to share something about themselves, like their favorite sauce.

Activity

Here's a record of some of the questions generated by the 2020–2021 WACTAC cohort. They can be used at any time.

- What's your favorite board or card game?
- What is a creative project you've been working on?
- What is your favorite beverage?
- What is your favorite costume?
- Describe your outfit in one word.
- If they had to make a reality show about your life, what would the show be? What would be the scripted series?
- What is the funniest thing that ever happened to you?
- Do you have any UFO stories that happened to you or someone you know?
- Do you have any ghost stories that happened to you or someone you know?
- What's been bringing you joy?
- What movie do you recommend?
- What's the weirdest thing in your house?
- What type of rock are you?
- What's one on-brand thing that happened to you this week?
- What's your favorite type of cheese?
- What pro-tip do you have?
- What chemical are you?
- What are three things you love?
- What kind of potato are you?
- What's your favorite sandwich?
- Why are you tired?
- What would your superhero name be?
- If you could smell only one thing for the rest of your life, what would it be?
- Say you're independently wealthy and don't have to work—what would you do with your time?
- The '60s, '70s, '80s, '90s, or '00s: Which decade do you love the most and why?
- What fictional world or place would you like to visit?
- You can have an unlimited supply of one thing for the rest of your life—what is it?
- If you could choose any person from history to be

your imaginary friend, who would it be and why?
- What is the grossest smell?
- What's your biggest hype/entrance song?
- What fashion trend should come back?
- If you had a talk show, who would be your first guest?
- What would be the title of your autobiography?
- What is your cell phone or computer background right now?
- What is something dumb you hate?
- What is your pitch for *Shark Tank*?
- What's one of your biggest pet peeves?
- What is the best candy? What is the worst candy?
- What animal would you want to have and what would you name it?
- If you were a lemonade, what flavor would you be?
- What are you thankful for?
- If you had to commit a crime, what crime would you commit?
- If you could make one thing legal, what would it be?
- What's the best costume you have done?
- What song are you feeling like today?
- What's your favorite game?
- What's the worst movie you've ever seen?
- If your laugh were a color, what would it be?
- Who is your favorite cousin?
- What after-school activities are you in?
- What's your least favorite kind of soup?
- What's the worst nightmare you've ever had?
- What is one city you want to visit?
- If you could travel with only one mode of transportation, what would it be?
- What's your favorite flower?
- What's one word to describe your brain?
- If you could eat only breakfast, lunch, or dinner foods for the rest of your life, what would you choose?
- If you were a Pokémon, what type would you be?
- What's the weirdest book you have ever read?
- What kind of snack food are you?
- What's your favorite limb?
- Who is your favorite actor?
- If you could have only one type of sauce for the rest of your life, what would it be?
- What was your favorite childhood cartoon?
- If you could wear only one color for the rest of your

life, what color would you choose?
- Do you prefer digital or analog clocks?
- What is your favorite subject in high school?
- What is a vegetable that represents you?
- What are your hopes and dreams?
- If your life were a book, what would the title be?
- What does your personality smell like?
- What should our go-around question be?
- What is the longest New Year's resolution you have kept? What is the shortest?
- What's something that's making you happy right now?
- What are your weekend plans?
- What is your favorite color of Play-Doh?
- What is your favorite fish?
- What is something weird you did as a kid?
- What is one thought that makes you happy?
- What is a weird piece of trivia you know?
- What kind of stuffed thing are you?
- Do you prefer to sleep in a cold room or warm?
- What is the best accessory and why?
- What is your favorite crystal?
- What is your favorite type of weather?
- What is your least favorite dinosaur?
- If you were a puppet, what kind of puppet would you be?
- What is something good that happened to you this week?
- If you could be born with another body part from another animal, what would it be?
- What planet matches your personality?
- What outrageous lawsuit would you like to bring forward?
- What time of the day do you like best?
- What crime would you do?
- What TV show would your life be?
- What is your favorite pastime?
- What was your favorite show as a kid?
- If you were a taco, what kind would you be?
- What is a boring fact or something boring about you?
- What Harry Potter house are you?
- What piece/type of art do you want to live in?
- What was a weird thing you were obsessed with as a kid?

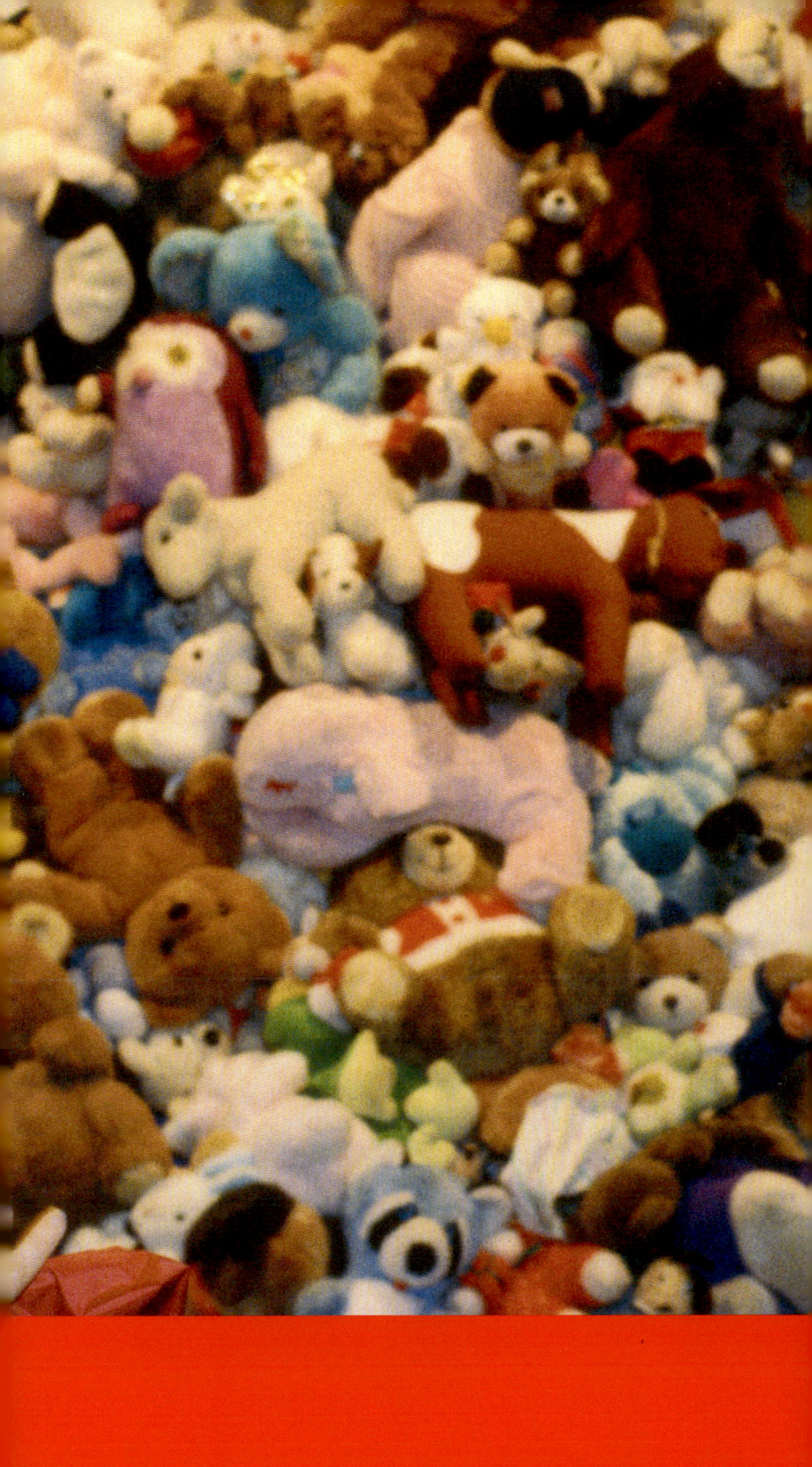

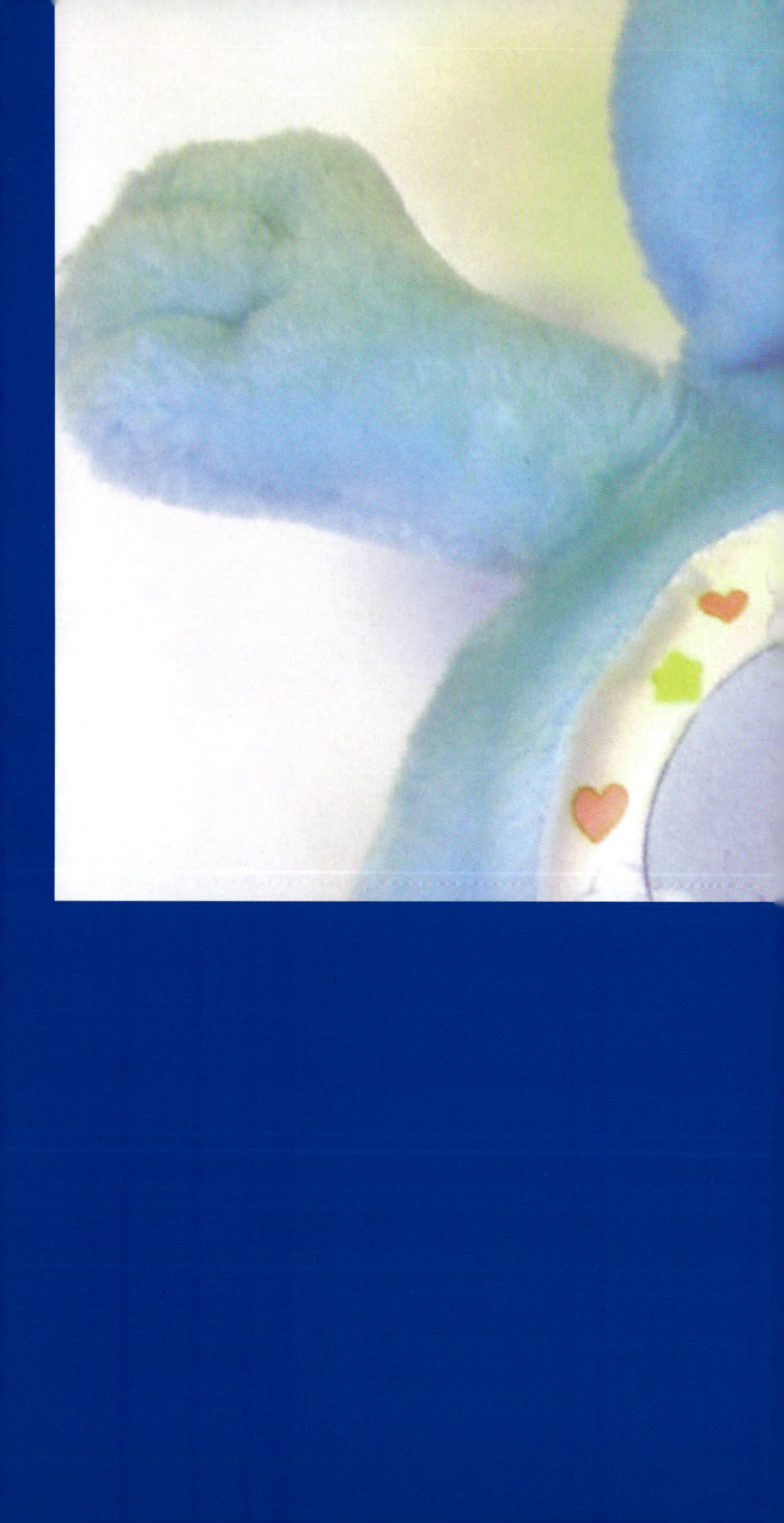

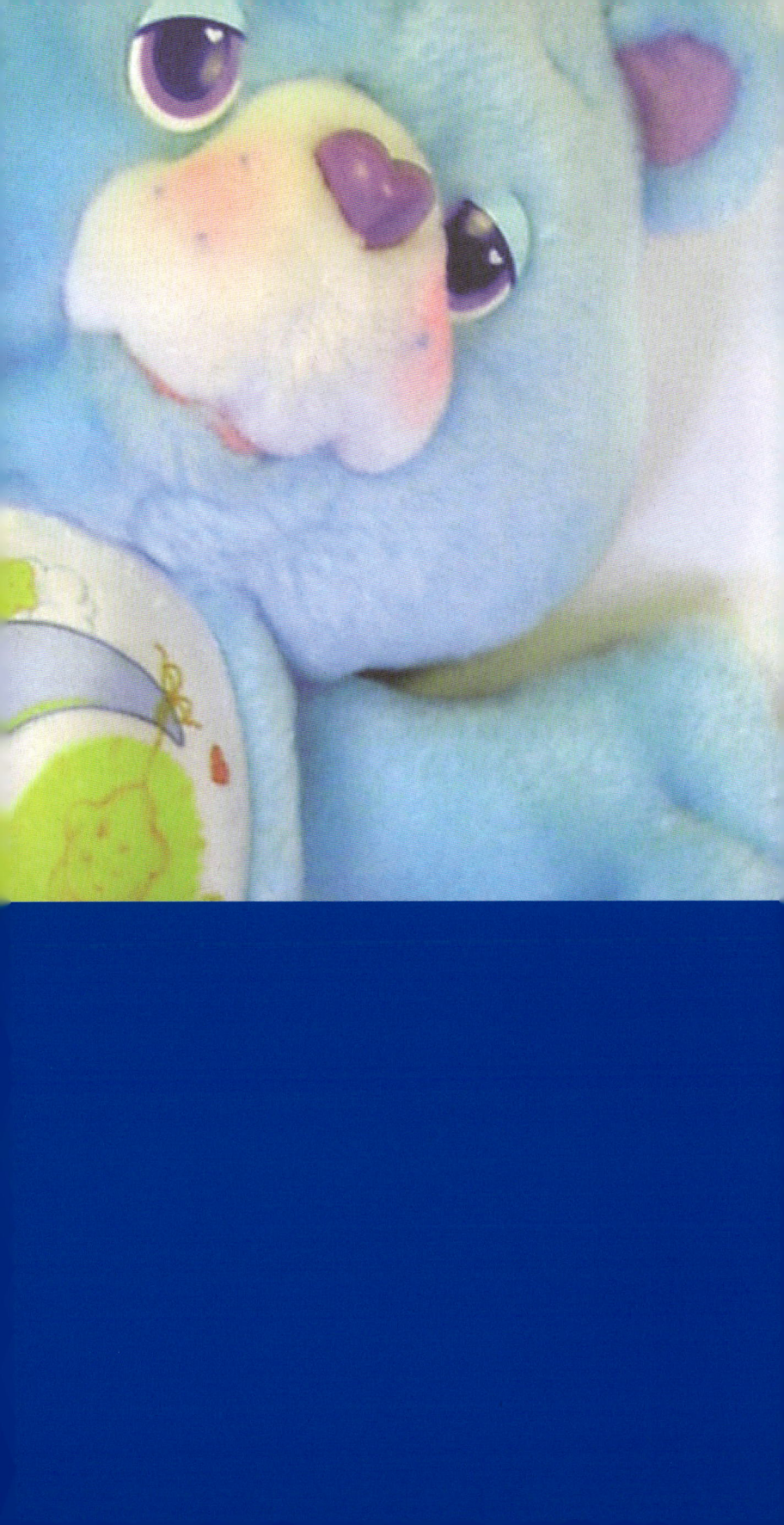

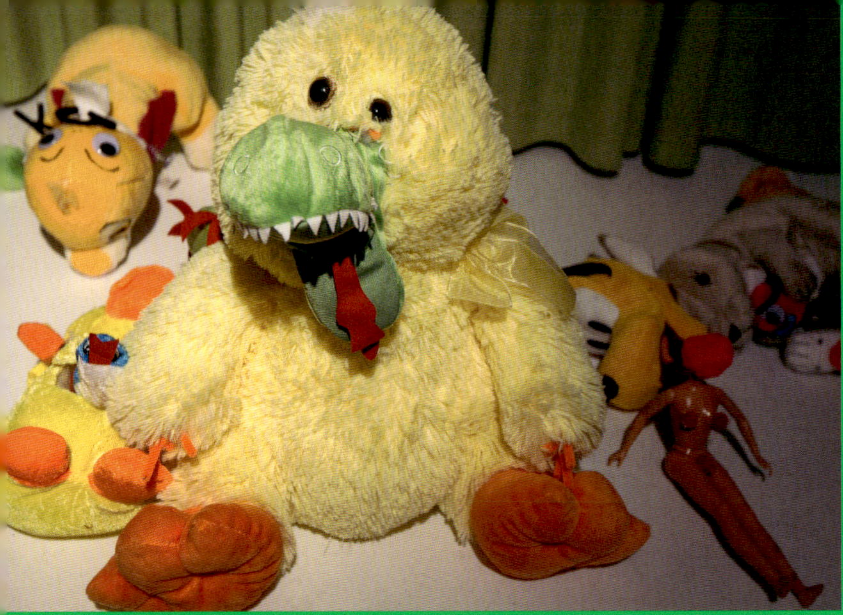

- What is an irrational fear you have?
- What hairstyle would you try?
- What is your favorite cereal?
- If you were a form of a pickle, what form would you be?
- What is a joke you know?
- What commercial jingle gets stuck in your head?
- If you were a My Little Pony character, what would your mark be?
- What is a nickname you have?
- Come up with a question to ask the next person.
- What is your favorite gas station food?

1.2.6. BUILDING CONNECTION THROUGH CREATIVE ICEBREAKERS

Nohemi Rodriguez, Institution of Contemporary Art, Boston

> **Bio.** Nohemi Rodriguez is a Chicana artist and educator born and raised in Houston, TX. She graduated from the University of Texas, where she completed a thesis on collaborative art-making with adolescents of the Amani community. In collaboration with young people, she developed a "toolbox" for facilitators to consider when collaborating with teens. She now works at the Institute of Contemporary Art/Boston, where she collaborates with teens to imagine how they hold space in the museum for other teens. She loves Tajín on mango and watermelon.

Introduction

Using creative icebreakers facilitated by young people can deepen connections among the group and distribute holding of space among all members. When young people design icebreakers for each other, they create them based on their interests and experiences.

Why should young people lead icebreakers?

- Invites young people to design and hold space for the group
- Deepens collaboration among group members
- Encourages teens to create meaningful connections with and for each other based on their own interests and experiences
- Engages folks in critical thinking by inviting them to problem solve as they guide others through icebreakers or participate in icebreakers

Background

In Spring 2022 two educators reached out asking for advice on building group collaboration and connection. They shared that the young people they worked with had challenges collaborating, connecting, and facilitating space. I experienced the same challenge in my work in Fall 2021.

Young people on the Teen Arts Council (TAC) at the Institute of Contemporary Art/Boston (ICA/Boston) began to be in physical space together after two years of social isolation. TAC is a group of twelve paid teens from the Boston area that serve other teens by creating space to engage other teens with contemporary art at the ICA/Boston. They organize events throughout the year to connect with teens, including seasonal Teen Night, where teens take over the museum. I connected with three members, Nathan, Scania, and Jazz, and we created a workshop that would prepare young people to lead icebreakers in their groups. This workshop models three different icebreakers and then invites young people to create and facilitate their own. We pre-created some icebreakers; others we revised and made our own.

Agenda. We will go around the space and share:

- names
- pronouns
- something creative you did today

Overview of Time Together

- We are going to spend time together doing icebreakers. We will move our bodies, create poems, and make art.
- We will then debrief by talking about our experience. This conversation will help inform how you build your icebreakers in pairs. Yes! You all will be designing your own icebreakers today!
- We will end by doing everyone's icebreaker!

Activity 1

Title. Transformation: Rock, Paper, Scissors
Written by. Jasline[1]
Duration. 15–25 minutes (may vary depending on the size of the group)
Materials. Stickers

Instructions

1. Begin by asking the group: Do folks know how to play rock, paper, scissors? (Rock beats scissors, scissors beats paper, paper beats rock.)
2. Do a few practice rounds of traditional rock, paper, scissors until everyone feels confident.
3. Explain that this icebreaker involves a twist. Everyone in the group will find an opponent to play rock, paper, scissors with. With each opponent, they will play traditional rock, paper, scissors. The opponent who loses each round will go down one "transformation level." Dinosaurs who lose turn into chickens. Chickens turn into eggs. The winner of each round goes up a transformation level.
4. Model with the group the three transformation levels that folks will use to communicate their bracket in the tournament.

- Participants all start out as dinosaurs. Do this by placing your arms out and walking like a dinosaur.
- The next level down is a chicken. Chickens walk around flapping their arms, pretending they have chicken wings.
- The final level down is an egg. To be an egg, you need to make your body into an egg shape, however that feels most comfortable for your body.

5. Explain that eggs who lose are eliminated and get a sticker from the facilitator when they are out. The game continues until there is one Egg (first place), Chicken, and Dinosaur winner (third place).
6. Do a practice round with the group so folks can practice transforming up and down a level.
7. Start an official game!

---

1 Jasline modified the icebreaker after experiencing a version of it during one of our TAC meetings.

Activity 2

Title. Poetry Activity
Written by. Scania G. Imagined by JFD[2]
Materials. Paper, pencil, speaker, phone or computer

Instructions

1. Begin by passing out paper and a pencil to each person.
2. Share the following prompt: Write a four-line poem that rhymes. You have 2.5 minutes.
3. Set a timer and keep the time.
4. Share when folks have 1 minute left to wrap up.
5. Bring the group back together and share the plot twist that all will rap your poem to a preselected beat.
6. Each participant shares.

Activity 3

Title. Mindful Color Play through Silhouettes
Written by. Nohemi R. & Mithsuca B.[3]
Duration. 30–60 minutes
Materials. Paper, watercolor paints or markers, pen

Instructions

I invite folks to…

1. Adjust your body so that you feel more comfortable.
2. Take a deep breath.
3. Draw three silhouettes on your paper that represent

---

2 The icebreaker was imagined by TAC member JFD for one of our TAC meetings. JFD has experience in music production and sound design, and they enjoy reading. They invited TAC to create tiny songs, be vulnerable, and share them with the group. Scania then documented this icebreaker.

3 The activity was developed in the summer of 2020 in the context of social distancing during the COVID-19 pandemic, the murder of George Floyd, and community protesting police brutality against Black bodies.

the body. These can be any size/form/shape.
4. Fill the first silhouette with a visual representing how you feel in this moment.
5. When you are ready, put down your materials and close your eyes.
6. *Instruct the group to practice alternate nostril breathing.* This creates a relaxed, harmonious feeling as it balances the left and right hemispheres of the brain. It is often suggested to be practiced before bed or when feeling tense. To do it:

- Sit in a comfortable position. Breathe relaxed, deep, and full as you practice.
- *Inhale* through the left nostril. (Close your right nostril with your right thumb.)
- *Exhale* through your right nostril. (Close your left nostril with your right index or ring finger.)
- *Inhale* through your right nostril. (Close your left nostril with your right index or ring finger.)
- *Exhale* through your left nostril. (Close your right nostril with your thumb.)
- *Repeat.*

7. *Share with the participants.* While you continue to breathe deeply and focus on your breath, select drawing materials and fill the second silhouette with a visual that represents what you are experiencing, highlighting sensations, emotions, and so on, throughout continuing to center your breath. When you finish, close your eyes, sit back, and return to alternate nostril breathing.
8. The last silhouette represents the body after meditation. *Ask folks:* How do you feel? How does your body feel?
9. *Thank the group for doing the exercise and invite them to write and respond to the prompt:* I feel most present/mindful when... Write for fifteen minutes. Then share. Tell the group that they do not need to share everything and can choose the parts they feel comfortable sharing with the group.
10. *Share out.* Would folks like to share in a large or small group and then share as a squad?

Conclusion

Reflecting on practice and creating new icebreakers.

Spend some time encouraging the group to reflect on the experience of doing the creative icebreakers.

Ask questions. What was the experience of participating in these icebreakers like for you?

- What did you enjoy most when doing the icebreakers?
  What makes a good icebreaker?
  What should be included when designing an icebreaker?
- What did you enjoy least when doing the icebreakers?
  What should be left out when designing an icebreaker?

Creative constraints for your icebreaker: Please share with the group that they will now build their own icebreakers!

- Get into pairs or groups and create an icebreaker.
- Allow thirty minutes to design an icebreaker and be ready to lead.
  Your icebreaker should last five to ten minutes.
  This icebreaker should encourage people to connect.

Each group then presents its icebreaker to the entire group.

Debrief as a group

- What did you learn from leading icebreakers?
- What are things to be aware of when leading icebreakers?
- Share one word that describes how you feel in this moment.

1.2.7. TWO ACTIVITIES FOR TAKING UP SPACE

Grace Needlman, formerly at Museum of Contemporary Art, Chicago

> **Bio.** Grace Needlman (they/she) is a cultural worker and maker preoccupied with questions of collective imagination and agency. As the manager of studio programs at Marwen, Grace supports artists and youth in building inspiring learning communities through art. Grace's puppet designs have appeared in theatrical productions across Chicago. As a company member at Rough House and Chicago Puppet Lab Co-Director, Grace works to create equitable pathways for puppeteers in Chicago. Previously, Grace managed family and youth programs at the Museum of Contemporary Art Chicago, where they worked to put museum resources in the hands of Chicago youth and fostered connections between artists and intergenerational publics. They publish and present on youth agency, collaboration, and queering museums. Grace graduated with a BA in fine art from Yale University and an MA in contemporary art theory from Goldsmiths University of London.

Introduction

For teens to feel comfortable hosting experiences for the public in the museum, they must feel comfortable themselves. Often, our programs are good at carving out special spots or clubhouses for our teens in safe corners of an education wing or back office. It can be harder to make the galleries themselves feel like home. In order to change the vibe of a museum, pilot new interpretative practices, make the space more welcoming for other young people, or curate exhibitions or events, teens must feel at home and in power in the public spaces of the museum.

Here are two activities to help your group claim space in the galleries while exploring the artwork and building community. They draw on performance and critical theory to consider the feelings and politics of being an embodied human encountering a work of art in a physical place. They can be fun and vulnerable and require intentional consideration and care for the group. Remember that the museum's space is coded, arising from histories fraught with tensions around class, respectability, cultural imposition, policing, and appropriation. How we show up as human bodies within a museum dramatically influences how we encounter the artworks on view.

Even in its most playful form, drawing attention to your physical body in a museum can come with risks. Traditional modes of safekeeping in museums, for the good of the artworks and visitors alike, often use the strategies and language of policing. Guards in uniforms can be intimidating and triggering, especially to young people and people of color. Drawing attention to oneself in a public space can get youth, especially youth of color, incarcerated or killed.

In order to safely hold space for young people to begin taking up space in the museum, it is very important to do the following:

1. Prepare the group. Do these activities only with a group that has already spent time behaving "normally" in the museum. It is also essential to know your group and already have agreements about comfort, consent, and access needs in place. Before facilitating, consider how to adapt these activities for folks with different physical or sensory abilities.
2. Prepare the guards. Make sure you have spent time in the galleries getting to know guards and demonstrating your trustworthiness and respect for them and their work. Please ensure you go around to each guard individually before the activity so they know what to expect and can explain the activity to concerned or curious visitors. Ideally, anytime you are doing anything in the galleries, attend the guards' morning meeting to give them and their managers a heads-up.

Activity 1

Tableau vivant, or living picture, is a French game from the 1800s and a classic of gallery learning. It is a fun, low-pressure way for teens to begin performing in the gallery while looking closely at works of art. This game can help engage folks who enjoy learning and processing ideas or experiences through movement. It can also help groups build a shared language around public experience and performance. It is a good tool for early in the year when teens are still getting comfortable looking at and talking about art and being together in the galleries, and can be an early step toward building the confidence to facilitate experiences for museum publics.

The goal is to show the story of an artwork using your body. Doing this with figurative artwork is pretty intuitive. It is the same as the TikTok fad of remaking famous artworks in your home. Creating a tableau vivant of an abstract work, where the story or forms might be less obvious, with only your body in space, can offer increased challenge and interest. In this case, the "story" might be more about composition, energy, or flow. The challenge also increases with 3D and 4D works. How do you create a tableau vivant of a sculpture that changes shape as you walk around it, a video, or a sound piece? As the artworks you respond to become more complex, encourage participants to describe composition, rhythm, weight, volume, energy, or flow. You can find patterns or major gestures in the most abstract works. Then explore ways of stretching, compressing, twisting, balancing, or holding energy in your body to represent what you observe.

Be mindful of differing levels of comfort that folks might have with performance being in their own bodies. Depending on how young folks sign up for your museum program, they may or may not have any idea that they will be asked to "perform." It could be challenging for folks working on building their confidence. How much you encourage individuals to push their comfort zones might depend on how important it is to your program that all teens engage visitors, speak publicly, or facilitate group experiences. Versions of this activity that do not involve performance still support conversations about artwork, community building, and unconventionally inhabiting the gallery. For example, doing large-scale gesture drawings in the galleries could work for folks who are excited about drawing. You could also bring simple blocks or found objects into the galleries to make ephemeral sculptures in response to artworks. There is no single correct way to do this; just have fun!

Title. Tableau Vivant
Written by. Grace Needlman
Learning goals. Creatively respond to an artwork. Have fun building community. Be introduced to public performance.
Duration. 1.5 hours
Materials. An exhibition to explore with open space to move around, timer, paper, pencils (optional).

Instructions

Introduction (5 minutes). In this game, we will make living pictures, or tableaux vivants, in response to artworks in the gallery. This is a game that folks have been playing for hundreds of years. It is like charades, but instead of acting out a picture, we will make silent, frozen scenes that tell a visual story.

Warm-up. Collective tableaux. Choose an artwork the group is drawn to, or have one prechosen that works well with the activity. You can decide whether to tackle a figurative or abstract work, depending on what kind of challenge your group is up for.

Talk about the artwork (10 minutes).

Prompts for conversation.

- Gather around the artwork. Look closely.
- What is going on in this work?
- How does it make you feel?
- What are the bodies? What are the key relationships?
- Describe the composition. Describe the energy, emotion, or movement.

Two tableaux and share-back (10 minutes). Split the group in half. The groups have five minutes, working separately and simultaneously to create a tableau representing the artwork everyone was just looking at. After five minutes, the groups perform their tableaux.

Discuss. What did each group choose to focus on in the artwork? How did they use their bodies—for example, levels, composition, and audience perspective?

Small Group Tableaux.

Group making time (15 minutes). Divide into groups of three to four. Each group has fifteen minutes to choose an artwork in the gallery and create their own tableau. Make sure to remind everyone of gallery safety before setting out.

Performance (15 minutes).

Variation A. Each group takes the "stage" and holds their tableau for one min. The other groups try to guess the artwork the group chose.

Variation B. Each group holds their pose for five minutes, while the other groups draw them. The drawings can then be collected into a shared zine.

Debrief (10 minutes). Circle up with the whole group.

- How did making the tableaux change how you understood the artwork?
- How did viewing other groups' tableaux change how you understood the artwork?
- How did doing the activity change how you felt in the museum's physical space?

Activity 2

Museums are spaces full of rules, some explicit and some unspoken. Some rules exist only in the minds of the visitors. Most museums do not actually require visitors to whisper. Many museums welcome visitors sitting on the floor, sketching, or looking at artworks from unconventional angles, as long as these activities do not endanger other visitors or the artwork. One of the most special features of teen-led museum events is the energy, noise, music, fun, and sense of exploration that permeate the galleries. Youth-led days feel unlike any other day. Teens lead meditation, card games, immersive storytelling, dance circles, and political soapboxes, all of which are well within the museum's rules but transgress brilliantly the rigidity and quiet that often characterize the "norm" in the galleries.

Getting there, figuring out how to make the museum a more welcoming place for young people, means unpacking ways in which it might not currently be so welcoming. Often, museum rules explicitly alienate young people by reproducing practices of policing that alienate or threaten young people in many public spaces. It can be helpful to start these conversations in spaces young people know well, especially in the classroom.

The writings of bell hooks offer many relatively accessible inroads into conversations about how power and oppression show up in the physical and social shapes of the spaces we inhabit daily. She writes:

> As a black woman, I have always been acutely aware of the presence of my body in those settings that, in fact, invite us to invest so deeply in a mind/body split so that, in a sense, you're almost always at odds with the existing structure, whether you are a black woman student or professor. But if you want to remain, you've got, in a sense, to remember yourself—because to remember yourself is to see yourself always as a body in a system that has not become accustomed to your presence or to your physicality.[1]

This activity offers an inroad into testing the boundaries of museum norms through a close reading of bell hooks and a Fluxus-inspired gallery game. This activity asks for a lot of vulnerability and should be done only with a group that has already done significant trust building and built up a rapport with the guards and other staff who are often charged with "policing" galleries. Trying to do this activity too soon or with a new group can be very destructive. Even so, there is always the risk that

---

[1] bell hooks, "Building a Teaching Community: A Dialogue," in *Teaching to Transgress: Education as the Practice of Freedom* (New York: Routledge, 1994), 129–65.

visitors will respond in ageist, racist, or just generally negative ways, and youth and facilitators need to be ready to support one another in responding to that.

Still, if facilitated with care, this activity can become a transformative experience of taking power and enacting change in the museum. If well stewarded, the feeling of real risk associated with doing something transgressive in public can be energizing and galvanizing.

Title. Unspoken Rules
Written by. Grace Needlman
Learning goals. Think and talk about what makes museums welcoming or uncomfortable, have fun building community, be introduced to public performance.
Duration. 1.5 hours
Materials. Timer, small pieces of paper, pencils, a hat (for choosing prompts), a bell, printed copies of bell hooks selection, an exhibition to explore with open space to move around, a suitable space for an in-depth discussion.

Important note. This activity is about the relationship between spaces and our actions. The space in which you facilitate this activity is important. Think about whether to do the discussion in the gallery or another space. A group conversation in a gallery can be a performance that challenges or changes the space. On the other hand, consider it, for your group, It might be better to talk about spaces that make us uncomfortable in a secure, private space.

Instructions

Discuss (30 minutes). How do the unspoken rules of a space affect how we act and feel in that space?

Read inspiration text (15 minutes). Choose a reading, video, or artwork highlighting how physical and especially institutional space shapes social performance. For example, read an excerpt from the chapter in bell hooks, *Teaching to Transgress*, about disrupting the norms of a classroom together.

Consider printing out pages for each person and having volunteers read a few lines at a time in a circle. Make sure to pause along the way to clarify any language that might be unusual or inaccessible.

Discuss (15 minutes). Prompts.

- How does this reading relate to your experiences at school?
- Does the type of spatial control exist in other places in your life?
- How does it show up in the museum?

This can be done as a whole group or in small groups with a share-back in the larger circle.

Generate prompts (15 minutes).

Remind everyone of the actual rules of the museum and take time to talk about why they exist. Think about things you want to be able to do in a museum that would break the norms of the space—the norms, not the rules.

What are the unspoken norms of the museum? (Write a list together on a large piece of paper.)

- How do they make you feel?
- How do you want to be able to act in a museum?

Think about what you want to be able to do—what you would do in a museum to feel more at home, more yourself—not just what you feel like you cannot do but would not want to anyways.

Some examples. Ask a stranger about their interest in an artwork, high-five a guard, slowly and carefully do yoga stretches in front of a calming painting, cry.

Write your action on a small piece of paper and put it in the hat.

Perform (30 minutes). At this point, make sure your group is in the gallery. It should be a gallery with plenty of space to move around. Ensure you have checked in with the guards and know the space's visitors.

Divide the group into two.

Invite Group 1, those who are comfortable, to pick a prompt out of the hat randomly.

Give Group 1 two minutes to move around the gallery trying out different ways of performing their prompts. Encourage them to find one way of performing their prompt that they can sustain/repeat for a few minutes.

When two minutes are up, ring the bell.

Tell Group 1 to begin to perform all at once and keep performing until the bell rings again.

Tell Group 2 to walk around the gallery and witness Group 1's performances.

Give it five minutes. Gather the group. Applaud for Group 1.

Group 2 now chooses prompts from the hat, has two minutes to explore, and then five minutes to perform while Group 1 witnesses.

Debrief. In a circle, discuss:

- How did performing feel?
- How did witnessing feel?
- How did your actions influence the tone and space of the gallery?

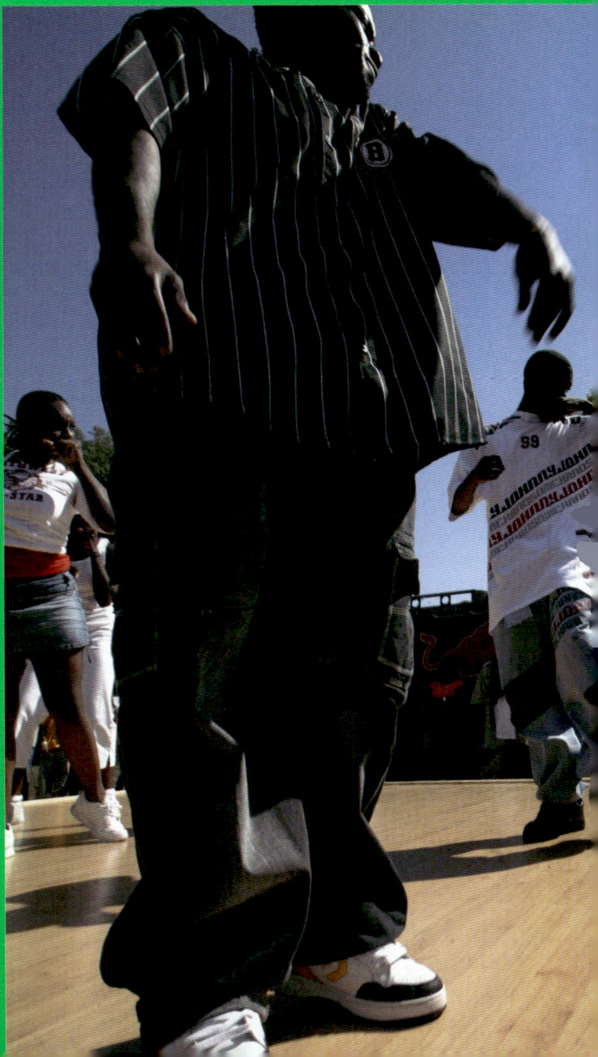
99

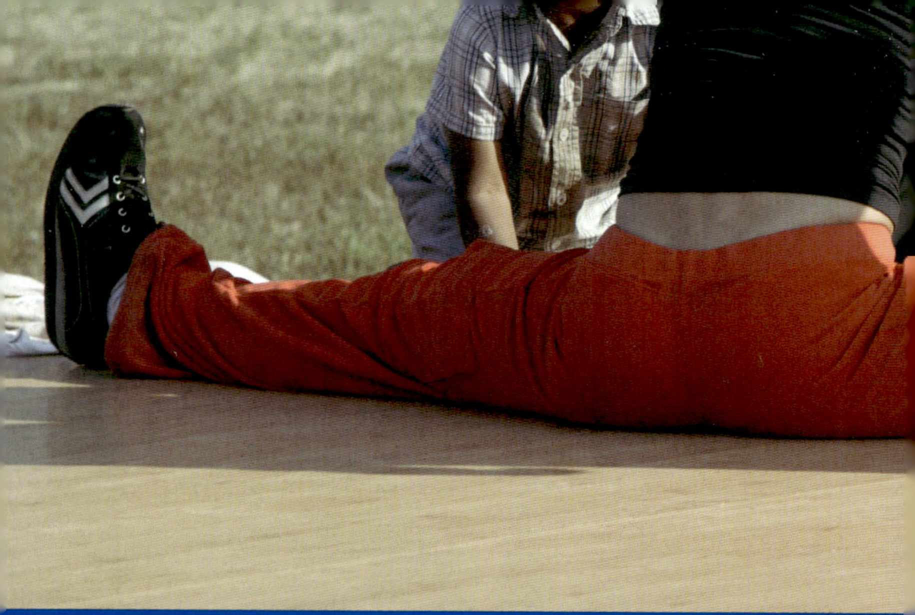

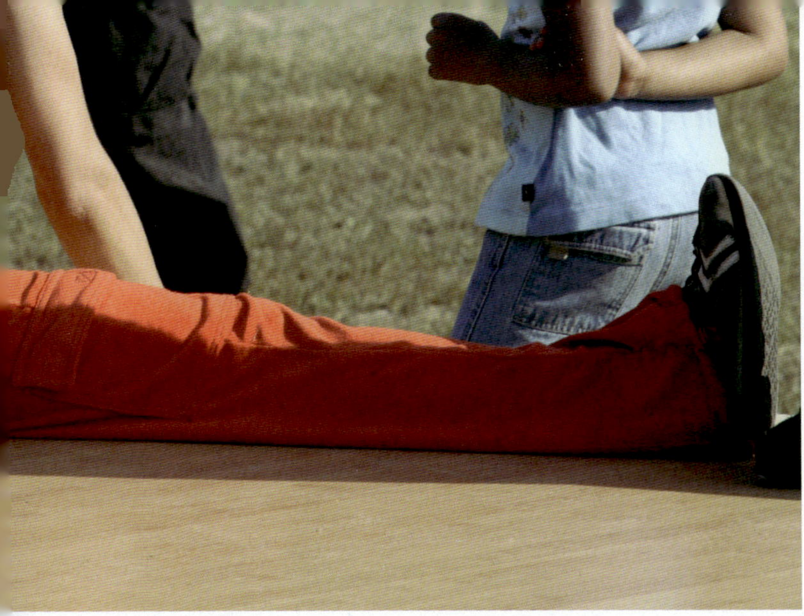

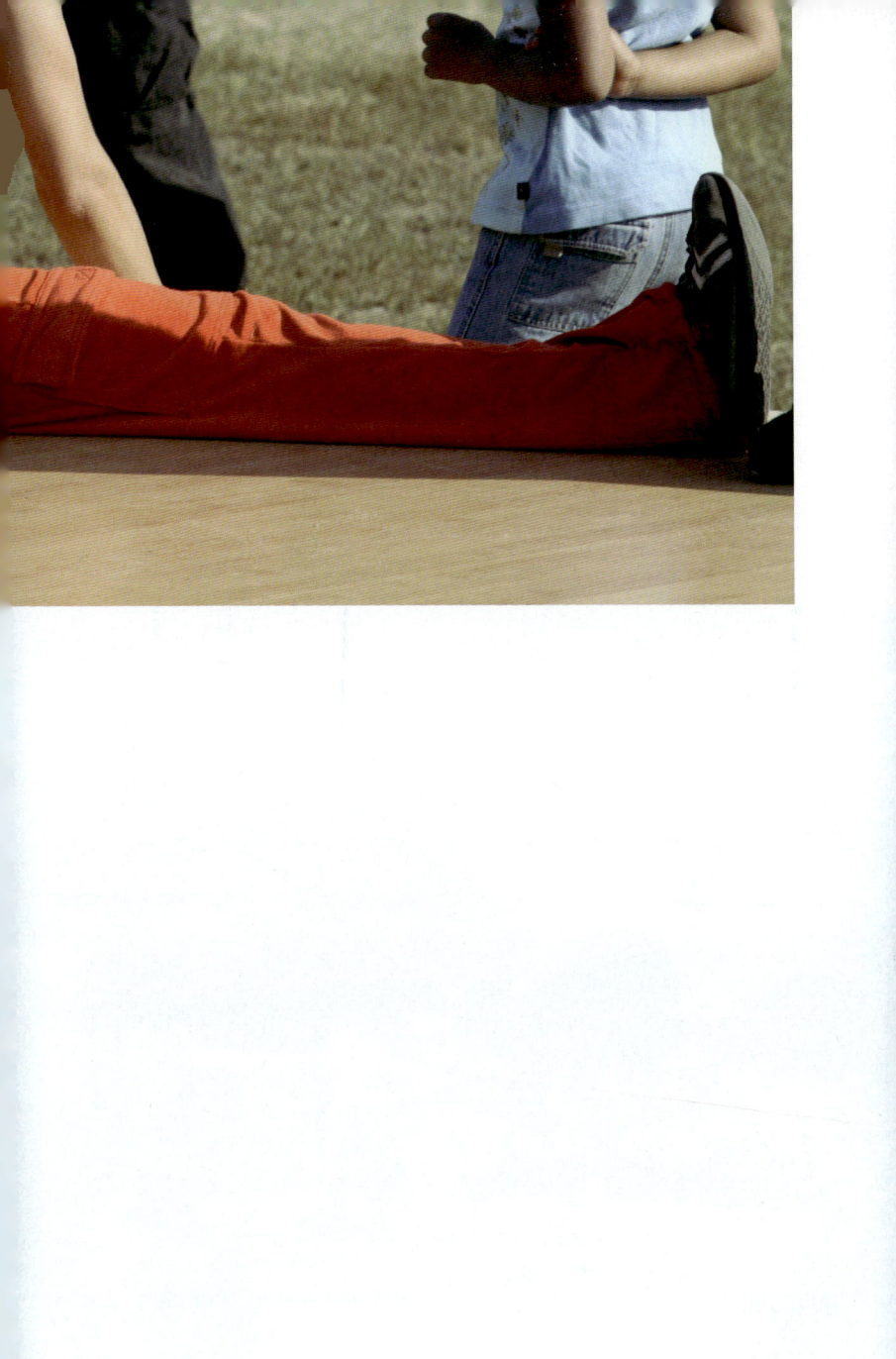

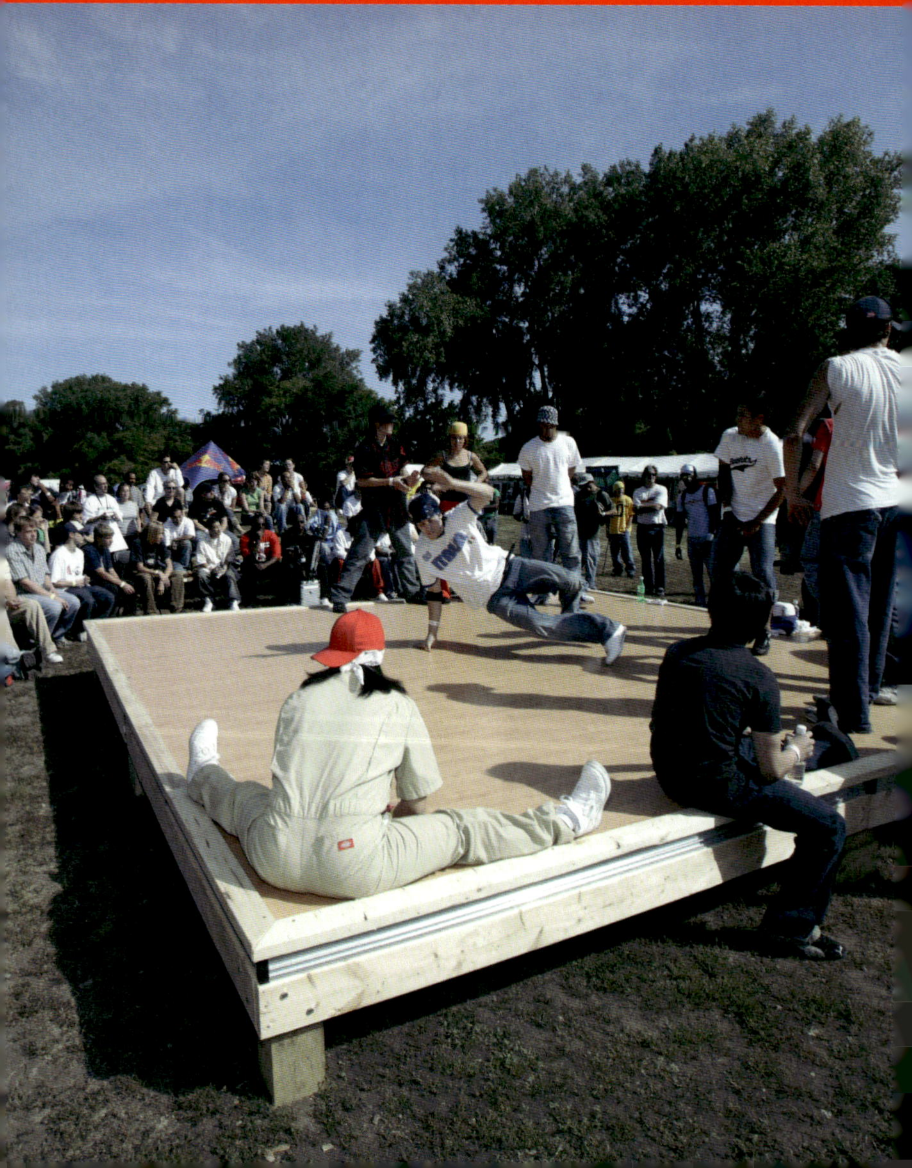

2

Prac-
tice

Introduction

In this section, you will find pieces on what and how teens learn in museum teen programs from educators' perspectives. Topics range from building literacies out of school, facilitation tips, ways to connect teens with museum collections, and a range of lesson plans developed by artists.

  With works by
Dr. Yolanda J. Majors, Michelle Antonisse, Melissa Katzin, Grace Needlman, Lauren Bína, Sean J. Patrick Carney, Savannah Knoop, Andreas Laszlo Konrath, Mollie McKinley, Stephen Kwok, and Simona Zappas

Essays, Reflections & Advice

Dr. Yolanda J. Majors 2.1.1.

Museums as Youth Opportunity Spaces

Bio

Yolanda J. Majors, PhD, is the founder and CEO of the Hurston Institute for Learning and Development. Dr. Majors's scholarship has focused on child, youth, and community learning. She is the author of the book *Shoptalk: Lessons in Teaching from an African American Hair Salon* and over two dozen articles and book chapters on social contexts for learning development. After Dr. Majors became a tenured professor (at the University of Illinois at Chicago), her focus shifted to designing and supporting out-of-school spaces of learning for youth and adults. Her award-winning work has led to numerous corporate and organizational partnerships and, in 2019, the establishment of the Hurston Institute for Learning and Development (HILD). Through HILD, Dr. Majors provides instructional design support, research, evaluation, design-based research, and workshops worldwide for classroom and community educators. Dr. Majors writes a weekly advice column and facilitates online seminars and discussion forums for educators, administrators, and graduate students at hurstongroup.com.

Essay

In 2018 I partnered with the Walker Art Center to (1) address the lack of specificity in how art museums and youth educators understand and talk about the relationship between their teaching methods (the conscious scaffolding of experiences and conversations) and the empowerment and learning of youth, and (2) provide a professional-development model for the advancement and dissemination of data-driven practices. Much of my work, in and outside of the Walker, has focused on bridging the divide between in-school (IST) and out-of-school (OST) learning for youth by drawing attention to opportunity spaces of doing and learning. Opportunity spaces are youth-serving OSTs that provide practitioners, youth, and families with science, technology, engineering, arts, and math (STEAM) related engagement opportunities that are geographically available, socially equitable, accessible, and at the right learning level.[1] Opportunity spaces offer people a chance to move across borders and boundaries, to engage around something shared and valued, decode it in some way, and make new meanings around it.

My scholarly work is built on researching what it means to know and teach in and outside of classrooms, which has shown (1) the inadequacies of focusing on schools as the sole lever of change in our pursuit of equitable, healthy learning environments for youth; (2) the availability and affor-

1. Nichole Pinkard, C. K. Martin, and S. Erete, "Equitable Approaches: Opportunities for Computational Thinking with Emphasis on Creative Production and Connections to Community," *Interactive Learning Environments* 28, no. 3 (2020): 347–61; Yolanda J. Majors, *Shoptalk: Lessons in Teaching from an African American Hair Salon* (New York: Teachers College Press, 2015); Nichole Pinkard, "Freedom of Movement: Defining, Researching, and Designing the Components of a Healthy Learning Ecosystem," *Human Development* 62, no. 1–2 (2019): 40–65.

dances of communal learning resources and tools that derive from youths' social and cultural backgrounds and communities; and (3) how youth learning across places and spaces ties directly to their involvement in social networks and events critical to their development and identity shaping.[2]

Since the 1980s, educational scholars have argued for the need to address the continuity or discontinuity between in-school and out-of-school time (OST) in children and teens' lives. Since then, a robust body of research has documented the issues that can emerge when we focus on learning as something that happens only in schools, providing effective descriptions of practice demonstrating how classroom participation and language-related structuring limits youth engagement. Unfortunately, far less work has been done to document and harness proactive ways in which OST youth opportunity spaces promote learning and development in ways that are not limiting or siloed but instead move freely across space and time. Even more so, less work has been done to understand what it means to teach and to learn in an opportunity space that is a public-serving venue for the arts—like the Walker Art Center.

What is more important than documenting and understanding the kinds of learning that occur in opportunity spaces is *applying* what is learned to use. In my work with the Walker, we wanted to create a framework that guides art-informed spaces' design and literate practices to engage teens in problem-solving. We spent two years reimagining the program that moved beyond "wouldn't it be cool if teens did something in the museum" into something that provides both teens and art educators with the opportunity to take up the encounters they share, the identities they resist and create, and the literate skills they display, along with the lessons learned from their collective and complex

2. Majors, *Shoptalk*; Pinkard, "Freedom of Movement," 40–65.

social readings of art and the world. Educators, artists, teens, and patrons actively constitute a kind of counter-public in the museum's public space. Day-to-day images, obstacles, and dilemmas encountered in the museum and the world are shaken and stirred. Collectively, teens can reread, reshape, rename, and redefine not only the art piece but their experiences and place in the world—transforming the museum into a creative arena through a process that is not just fun but also includes problem-solving and problem posing. The result is an interpretative artifact that is multi-voiced and multiscripted, that guides, informs, and propels those who simultaneously create and witness it into action.

The culmination of my work with the Walker Art Center was Arts Platforming Action (APA)—praxis for navigating and creating an arts-focused opportunity space for teens, the means and tools designed to support that learning,[3] and an aim to address the nature of youth learning and arts-based facilitation. Before the work of APA can be done, young people must consider what it takes for them to get to and participate in the museum. When beginning my work with the Walker, there was little to no exploration to understand and address the challenges to participation in learning they face beyond the anecdotal (much growth is still needed here!). Youth with different histories of participation will vary in their repertoires for engagement. Historians of science and art, as well as social scientists who examine youth participation in everyday practices, have shown that voluntary learning calls on a broad spectrum of methods and contexts through which learners acquire and advance their skills, knowledge, and sense of direction toward goal achievement across the lifespan.[4]

Fundamental to all points along the opportunity space, the learning spectrum is the human capacity for curiosity—the desire to engage, know, and

3. Majors, *Shoptalk*.

do beyond life's challenges, what is immediately evident, or within current practice. This desire for learning through participation motivates youth to engage available resources drawn from their repertoires in the process of exploring what one can learn by seeing, thinking, and doing. However, most curricula tend not to focus on what may be different entry points based on (1) the physical, domain-specific, and conceptual *boundaries* that can impede or enhance learners' freedom of movement and (2) the cultural, social, and economic borders that establish the value of the assets of one teen learner. We cannot determine if such a form of movement and participation differs based on ethnic/racial and language differences among youth, because such questions are generally not raised.[5] When youth participate in OST opportunity spaces like museum teen programs, they are moving across several differing borders:

1. The social and cultural borders that exist within and across institutions
2. The economic and ideological borders that penetrate and inform in-school and out-of-school learning opportunities
3. The pedagogical borders of arts-based practices that influence teaching, learning, and transformative action

APA takes up the phenomenon of cultural and social border crossing not as a problem but rather as an opportunity. First, it acknowledges that for teens, who daily act to move across the socially, culturally, and politically constructed and imposed divides (borders) that help to distinguish cultural groups and

4. Shirley Heath, *Words at Work and Play: Three Decades in Family and Community Life* (Cambridge: Cambridge University Press, 2012); Majors, *Shoptalk*; Barbara Rogoff et al., "Firsthand Learning through Intent Participation," *Annual Review of Psychology* 54, no. 1 (2003): 175–203.
5. Pinkard, "Freedom of Movement," 40–65.

language communities from one another, there is the requirement of a certain set of skills by which to navigate. While all people move across social boundaries, APA distinguishes cultural, linguistic, and social borders from social boundaries:

> Borders are features of cultural differences that are not politically neutral. Boundaries are transformed into borders when one world's knowledge, skills, and behaviors are more highly valued and rewarded than those within another.... When boundaries exist (even when the sociocultural components of teens' worlds are different), movement between worlds can occur with relative ease—that is, social, psychological, and academic costs are minimal. Alternatively, when students encounter borders, movement and adaptation are difficult because knowledge and skills or particular ways of behaving in one world are more highly valued and esteemed than in another. Although it is possible for teens to navigate borders with apparent success, these transitions can incur personal and psychological costs invisible to their teachers and others.[6]

For many teens, their fate often lies at the mercy of inequitable socioeconomic and cultural landscapes surrounding them and their families; our recognition of such borders is insufficient. While others have focused on the border-crossing experiences of youth who must negotiate family life, peer interactions, and school, teens often engage in a special kind of cultural-border crossing that happens across the lifespan as people negotiate a range of cross-cultural, cross-economic encounters beyond their control. Thus, any exploration into the kinds of safe-space engagements made possible by their involvements in arts-based, museum-led activities must also take up the situatedness of their unique experiences, as well as the norms, tools, roles, and

6. Patricia Phelan, Ann Locke Davidson, and Hanh Cao Yu, *Adolescents' Worlds: Negotiating Family, Peers, and School* (New York: Teachers College Press, 1998).

structures they draw on as a part of their cultural tool kits. APA concerns itself with how youth learn across places and spaces, with an acknowledgment that such learning ties directly to their involvement in social networks and events critical to their development. Our vision is that APA provides youth and educators with the means and the tools by which to not only recognize such borders but to navigate and transform their experiences of moving between and across them.

The lack of connectivity between OST programs and school settings presents a glaring opportunity to create a learning ecosystem that supports students as whole learners. The challenge that presents to teachers and facilitators alike is the issue of transferability of learning. Learning tasks and the skill uptake that facilitates that is not exclusive to classrooms or art museums; they are not performed and do not exist in a vacuum. However, the challenge lies in understanding; understanding that the skills required to interpret an art piece are similar to skills required to interpret informational texts in science, however different the application may look.

The kinds of skills that teens and art educators display in service to engagement are not neutral, cognitive skills but a kind of appropriated tool kit that includes systems of values, language, discourse, and modes of reasoning or meaning-making and constructing individual and shared identities in the public, social world. Leveraging the art space and its works with the goals, challenges, and dilemmas teens face requires a holistic head, heart, and hands approach to instruction.

The *head* refers to aspects of youth education that spring to mind as educators and facilitators think about the program's content: domain-specific theories; theories of adolescent learning and development; research literature on identity and cognition; historical, social, and cultural narratives. The *head* work draws upon and integrates theories of teaching and learning and scholarly evidence to highlight the work and traditions at the bedrock of our endeavors.

The *heart* refers to the passion and energy at the core of the work among teens and art educators alike. The *heart* requires attention, emotion, spirit, reflection, intuition, and ethical purposes. The heart also summons the toughest and most intriguing questions about why something like youth teen programming is needed, how to achieve and display personal authenticity, how to discern right from wrong, and how to confront personal and social fear, anger, and injustice.

The *hands* point to the actual in-the-world work. Some of that work goes on in the face-to-face and virtual settings of museum teen programming, public and private workshops, and community engagements. Handwork also continues in the just-in-time experiences of group projects and active learning. Handwork focuses on the collaborative design of learning experiences and offers specific exercises, agendas, assignments, visual aids, and web-based activities that have proven effective in helping people engage, and institutions build capacity.

The kinds of teaching and learning that occur in OST spaces are essential. However, we do not intend to lose sight of the work and challenges schoolteachers face, who often refer teens to museum programs. In addition to lacking time, support, and resources, most urban classroom teachers struggle to "close the gaps" to support their students outside their four walls precisely because of this shortfall. Teachers want to support their students as whole human beings who learn, succeed, and excel in environments outside of school. However, when so much is demanded of their skills inside the classroom related to school outcomes, it is not difficult to imagine that one person cannot also support student learning in other capacities when so much is demanded of both their work and time in support of their classroom pursuits.

Opportunity spaces for learning exist all around

us but may look different based on context, culture, location, background, and resources used to guide learning and understanding. But the question remains: What does it mean and look like for the young people who cross these borders of learning spaces and contexts?

The disjuncture between these borders is well-documented and persistent. The meaning-making resulting from OST programs like the Walker's Teen Arts Council is pivotal and tangential to the learning that is being asked of students across domain-specific activities in school. However, how does the disjuncture between OST and IST settings affect learners' ability to transfer skills, concepts, and tools across spaces? This is my continued work and what I would like to see in action across the field.

☺

Michelle Antonisse

Talk Time with Teens

Bio

Michelle Antonisse is a Los Angeles-based artist and educator. She is currently manager of teen and school programs at the Museum of Contemporary Art (MOCA). Michelle has worked with organizations such as Honduras Children, Burgundy Center for Wildlife Studies, Big Basin Redwoods State Parks, the Norton Simon Museum, Los Angeles Public Libraries, Angel's Gate Cultural Center, the National Children's Museum, and China's Hangzhou University of Commerce to explore concepts of art and environment with people of diverse backgrounds and ages. Michelle also runs experimental environmental education workshops called "Into the Field." These practices explore the vast intersections between art, science, and critical thinking by centering reflective practice and conversational, student-centered learning. When not teaching, Michelle can be found looking closely at moss, boogie boarding, or cuddling with her dog, Wolfgang.

Essay

A teen programmer's greatest resource for teaching and building community is teens' voices themselves, how they intersect, overlap, conflict, and run in parallel. They might sing in harmony that they are there to learn, that they care about art, that they even want to grow and know each other, but the nuances of each voice, its timbre of experience, the way it oscillates and moves in connection to others, will only add to the overall vibe, character, and sound of your program.

Teens in most of these programs are self-selecting and are usually excited to learn and engage. Even so, the teens in your program will likely have varying interests, experiences, expertise, and personalities. Many of these programs have an implicit aim to create conversations across demographics and to help teens value a multiplicity of perspectives. This practice encourages better friends, citizens, workers, artists, and lifelong arts advocates.

Many of our teens' applications talk passionately about transformative art experiences; even if these are short and infrequent—there is a seed of interest. Our program seeks to grow that seed into a rooted, lifelong connection to art that continues to challenge ideas through social exchanges with artists, artworks, and other audience members.

Artworks are conversation pieces we rely on as tools for catalyzing these exchanges; they provide shared phenomena to help articulate how we all might experience the same object, or moment, differently. One person's interpretation is intrinsically limited by their individual lens. When you enjoy art in pairs or a group, that shifts, and you can peer into a more holographic, multi-lensed experience of art and, ultimately, the world. One way to get this perspectival shift is to read didactics, attend a tour, or do research. Many people in museum spaces seek a curator, historian, or the maker's point of view. In teen programs, it is important to lean into the social

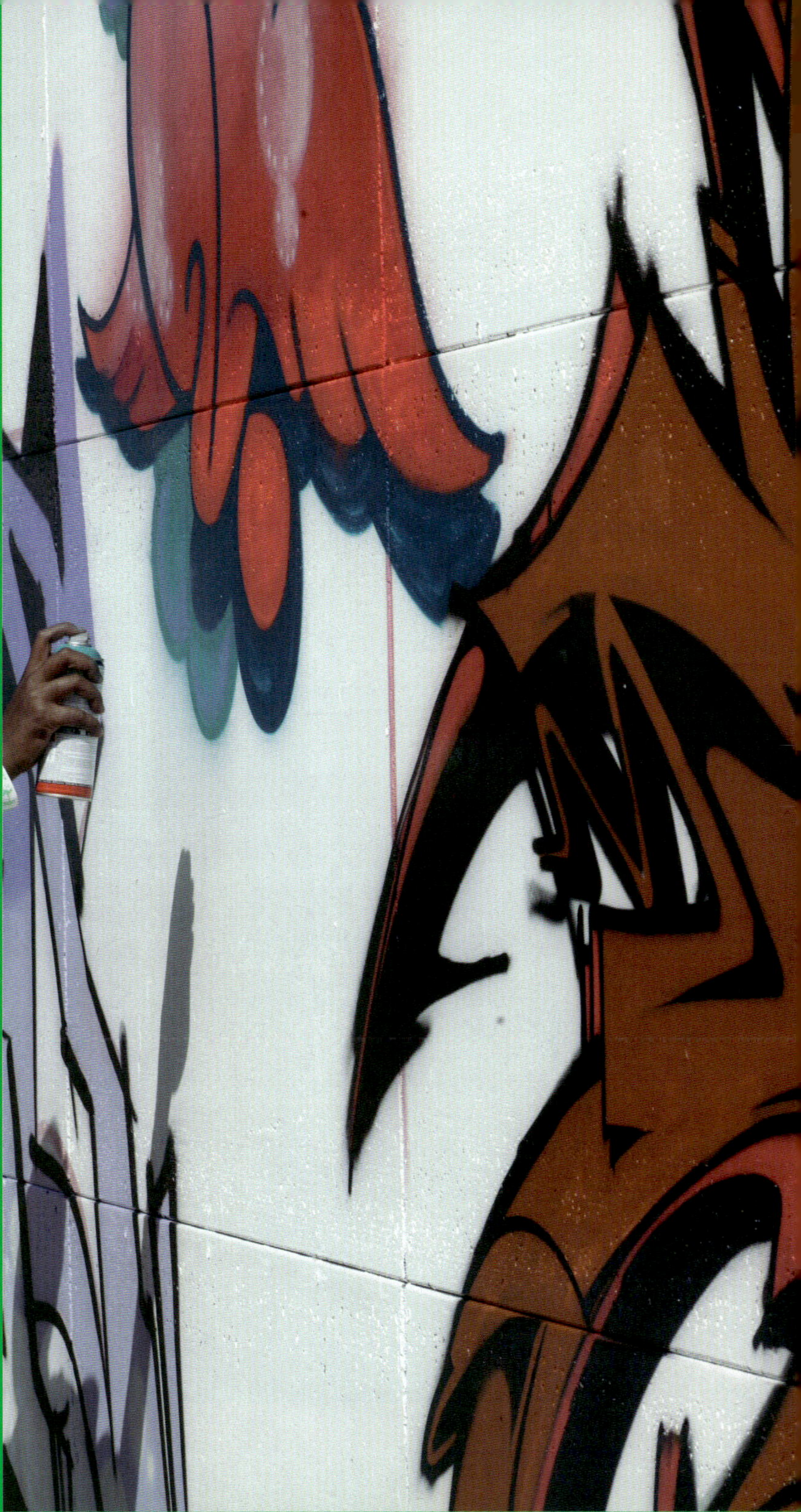

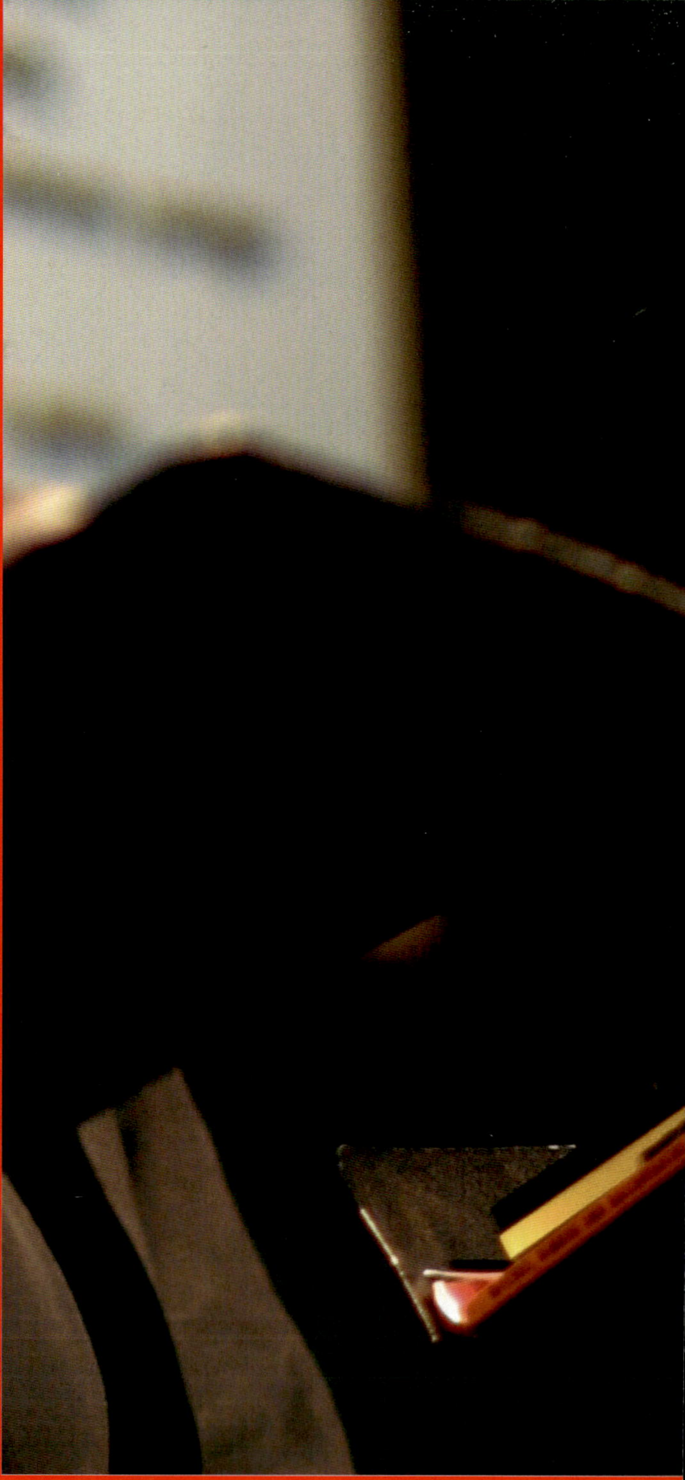

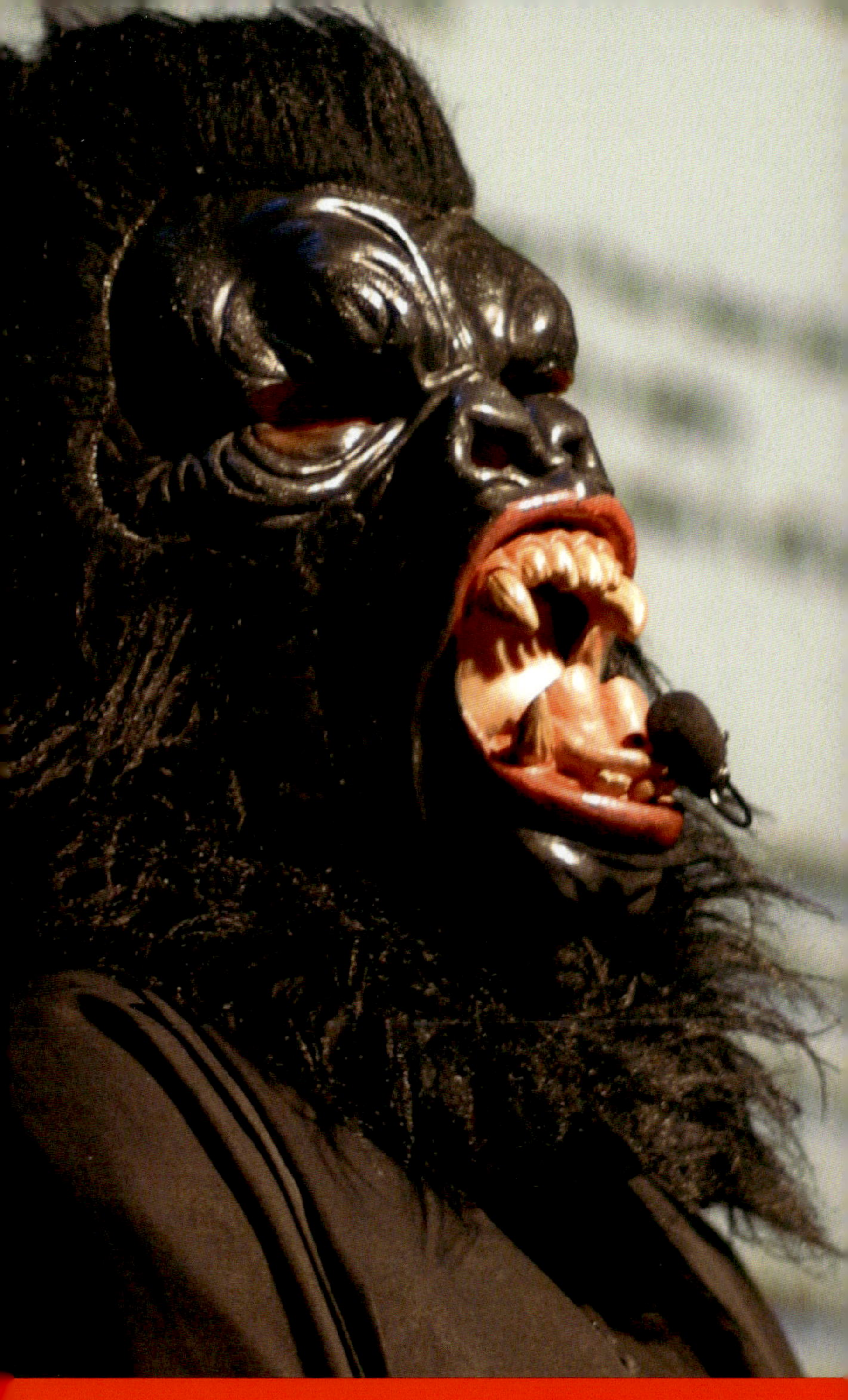

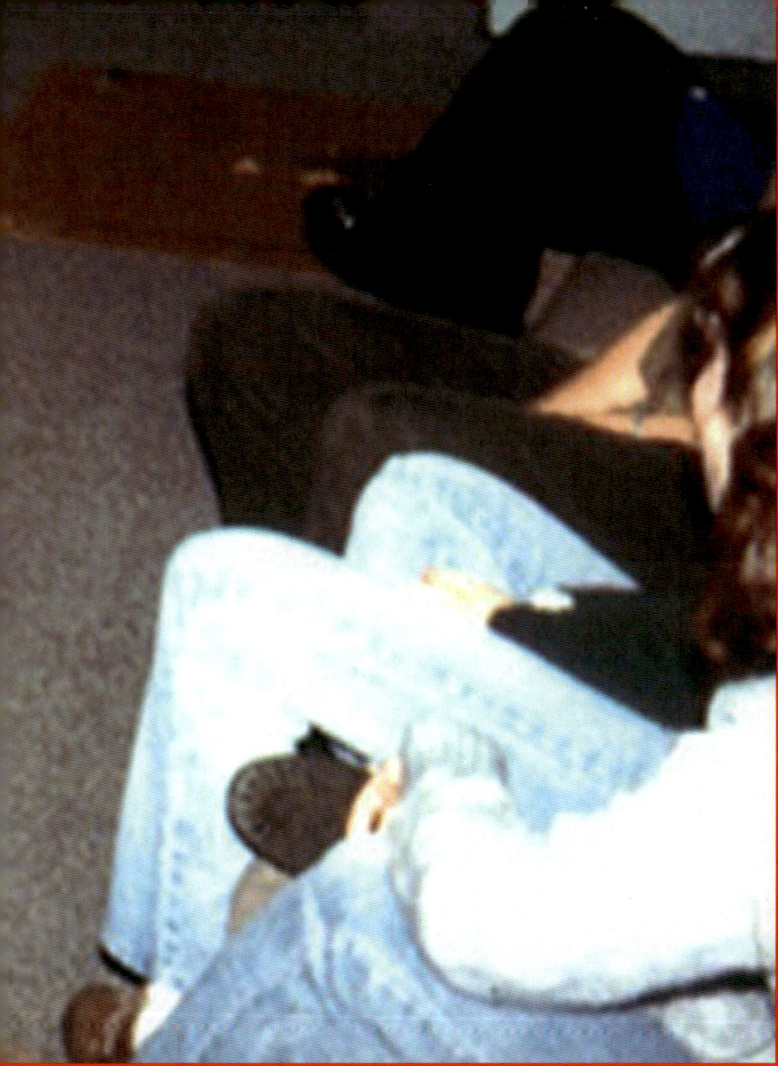

meaning-making experience of artwork instead of privileging voices with historical authority and power.

Of course, excitement and interest should not be discouraged—teens often ask voracious and exciting questions and bring in external research—this is great! But an authority figure adding information into these conversations (especially when not asked for) can create the impression that some interpretations are more valid than others. This can imply that the information provided is some key to the "correct" meaning-making.

At the Museum of Contemporary Art (MOCA) in Los Angeles, California, we primarily use Visual Thinking Strategies (VTS),[1] a student-centered, dialogical pedagogy developed by Abigail Housen and Philip Yenawine. All of the educators in our department have had extensive training and reflective practice in this conversational teaching strategy, and we center our teaching practice on its values. VTS asks that if you lead the conversation, you excuse yourself from the social process of meaning-making. The facilitator (like the curator, historian, or maker mentioned earlier) has a perceived authority in the space; their point of view may negate the thoughts or opinions of others, shutting down what could be an open, accepting, and expansive space for imagination, community, and criticality. Also, centering teens' voices makes their ability to interpret artworks visible to them, centers their identities, and reveals them as "experts." It is also a critical practice to move perpetually deeper into centering teen voices without adding what you might believe is pertinent or essential information. Perhaps the most significant benefit of this strategy is that it creates a container for conversation without dictating the shape of the conversation itself.

Two of the greatest tools at the disposal of a VTS practitioner, and the center of this practice,

1. Philip Yenawine, *Visual Thinking Strategies: Using Art to Deepen Learning across School Disciplines* (Cambridge, MA: Harvard University Press, 2013).

are paraphrasing and using what VTS practitioners often refer to as "the second question," or "Q2." Paraphrasing what you hear is a way to restate ideas, sometimes using vocabulary related to art. For example, the facilitator or VTS practitioner might say, "I hear you talking about the composition." Sometimes metacognitively framing what the viewer is doing ("It sounds like you are wondering about the artist's intention") can be helpful. If there are places where you could clarify ideas further, you can ask, "What did you see that makes you say [something they said]?" This pushes viewers to provide evidence for their opinions and interpretations and to invite others to see their thinking patterns. To build on that trust and vulnerability within the group, try linking students' comments together when you see connections; this will model respectful disagreement and practice community building by weaving people's ideas together. As former MOCA educator Iris Yirei Hu puts it, "In a VTS discussion, divergence is what makes a conversation fruitful."[2] Through highlighting agreement and confluence, as well as moments of cognitive diversity and disagreement, the VTS facilitator models the intrinsic value of difference. This social process of VTS not only shows respect for myriad positionalities but implies that they are, in fact, necessary in order to more completely grasp the layered and complicated "meaning" of an artwork.

While we use VTS, there are many inquiry-based pedagogies, such as Bloom's taxonomy, an educational framework that catalogs language around asking questions, or the Socratic method, a technique in which the facilitator asks questions until assumptions are revealed. These methodologies all center student voices and help a facilitator to "get out of the way" and allow students to puzzle through texts together. If you are not familiar with these techniques, take some time to look them up, try them out

2. Yenawine, *Visual Thinking Strategies*.

(in the case of VTS, you can attend a training), and, as important as the previous two steps, make time to reflect on how it went. Try having a conversation with another educator or write in a journal. Consider what worked, what did not work, what felt off, when people seemed the most engaged, and when people seemed distracted or bored. This reflective space will help you improve regardless of your personal teaching practice. It will help you continue to listen closely, center teen voices, and create containers for emergent communities of practice.

☺

Melissa Katzin

From Bellini to Basquiat: Equitable Education Practices in Encyclopedic Museums

Bio

Melissa Katzin is the Manger of Family Programs and Group Experience at the High Museum of Art in Atlanta, Georgia. She develops and implements family and teen programming, including free family days, early learner programs, and Teen Team. Previously at the High, she served as the youth and community programs coordinator, managing summer camp, community workshops, and other programs for children. Before joining the High in 2017, Melissa was an art instructor at the Johns Creek Arts Center. Melissa holds a bachelor of arts degree from the University of Georgia and received her master of arts in art history from George Washington University.

Essay

The Teen Team program at the High Museum of Art in Atlanta, Georgia, was established in 2011. Staff continuously adapt to the changing needs of teens and expectations on and from the museum. The underlying goal of building the Teen Team's familiarity and knowledge of the museum's collection and special exhibitions remains a constant North Star to guide the ever-evolving work. With works of art on view as a foundation, Teen Team participants can better speak about the museum as a whole. This is achieved by supporting the teens in leading object-based tours and developing and implementing art-making projects based on artwork in the collection, and encouraging them to discover their passions within the museum's galleries. Creating a balanced curriculum takes significant effort with seven collecting areas (African, American, decorative arts and design, European, folk and self-taught, modern and contemporary, photography). However, when successful, it creates a more balanced and connected experience for both the teens and the museum.

Anecdotally, many of the young people who have been part of the Teen Team program for the past few years have self-reported to have received much of their art education from social media. Big names like KAWS and Yayoi Kusama, Ai Weiwei, and Daniel Arsham are initial draws for teens entering the museum's galleries. These are often artists whose work is easily accessible and visible. Some Teen Team members come to the program with a laser-focused passion for other collecting areas, like folk art, or a specific medium, like photography. One of the many objectives of an encyclopedic museum is for visitors to recognize the throughlines, connections, and contrasts between time periods, cultures, geographic areas, and mediums. We, as educators, have the opportunity to cater to the current interests of teens by using them as jumping-off points and leverage to achieve our goal of guiding teens to find an appreciation for multiple collecting areas.

For example, for the 2021–2022 Teen Team, during their eight-week summer intensive, the project was to create self-guided tours for young people to use when they visit the museum. The final products were a museum-wide scavenger hunt titled "The Mystery of the Museum's Missing Cat" and an audio guide with an accompanying map titled "Art 101." Both tours gave nearly equal space to each collecting area at the High. The creators put significant amounts of thought into making it as equal as possible given their constraints.

Compared to previous years, the Teen Team members in the summer of 2021 were primarily concerned with creating this equity, with minimal prompting from the adult educators in the program. These teens were regularly encountering ideas of identity, inclusion, community, and diversity in their everyday life—they brought these ideas with them into the program, confronting these topics of belonging and access in the museum space. They encountered these concepts as they began their year in the program and continued to build on and express these ideas as the educators encouraged this exploration.

Affected by protests, politics, and the COVID-19 pandemic, the 2021–2022 Teen Team was exploring their place and power in the world. They aimed to give all young people a sense of belonging in traditionally white, middle-class, and male-dominated institutions. To find their place within the museum and help teen visitors find their place, the Teen Team explored how their own backgrounds, interests, and passions could be found within the gallery walls.

Breaking Ground, Making Ground
The first week of the summer intensive, like the beginning of any program with teens, is filled with icebreakers and team-building activities. Most of these are pretty standard, changing a little each year based on staff and new ideas. But every year, without exception, the teens are tasked with researching a specific collecting area. Through observation and exploring the museum's website and presenting their findings to the rest of the Teen Team, we want the teens to begin getting to know each other and the galleries simultaneously. We hope this cre-

ates comfort with the space and each other, and an understanding of the museum context.

The teens were split into seven groups of two or three each and chose one of the seven collecting areas from a hat. Their directive was to present their collecting area at the end of the week, and they were required to include the kind of art in that collecting area and where it could be found in the museum. Then, the teens were let loose to discover—at this point in the program, they knew very little about how to get around the museum; or if the teens were regular visitors, they were not considering the demarcations between the different collecting areas. The teens could use our museum map and website and ask staff members questions. The majority went off into the galleries to discover their own way.

With the 2021–2022 Teen Team, presentations of each collecting area ranged from PowerPoints to posters, with each set of teens choosing their direction. The teens focused on European art chose five artworks representing the collecting area. The teens with African art created a poster with images of the galleries. Other groups focused on providing directions to their collection, especially decorative arts, distributed throughout the museum. Each year that we do this exercise with the teens, it is the beginning of the teens building close relationships with each other and one collecting area—they have created a feeling of ownership by being responsible for introducing the other group members to their galleries. Through this project, each Teen Team member gets to know their collecting area on a deeper level but also learns about what other teens find interesting about the collections they present.

Curators and Collections
Every summer, the Teen Team meets with individual curators for an hour-long session, during which they do a deep dive into each collecting area. The Teen Team staff usually schedules these sessions in the months before the program's start, and they

take place throughout the summer, depending on the curators' schedules. We keep the directive for these sessions simple: show the Teen Team your collecting area. No additional information is provided to the curators except for a brief overview of the Teen Team program. If a curator asks for additional clarification, our staff directs them to explore their galleries to allow the teens to learn more about them and their collecting area. While sometimes frustrating for curators, this ambiguity leads to more open conversation and allows our teens to better understand the curators, their careers, and their collecting areas. By having curators lead the tours of their respective areas, it encourages the teens to recognize different hierarchies and systems of authority within the museum. While our instructional staff could facilitate these collecting area overviews, the teens must connect with the staff who oversee the respective galleries; as such, the teens begin to understand the roles different staff play and hopefully become interested in various areas within the museum.

The structure of the gallery sessions has significantly varied—some curators have elected to provide more formal tours, while others focus on the practices of the collecting area as a whole, key works, or a new rotation in the galleries. In the summer of the 2021-2022 Teen Team, the newly hired curator of African art used the time to discuss her plans for exhibitions and future collecting practices. During the session with the curator of African art, our teens were able to ask questions about provenance and possible repatriation of objects—questions they had already begun asking our education staff. In providing these exclusive opportunities with the curators, the teens go behind the scenes and gain a more comprehensive understanding of each curator and their collecting area.

Each year, a different collecting area becomes popular among the Teen Team, and there appear to be clear ties between the popularity of a collecting area and the curators themselves. By giving the curators free rein over their sessions with the Teen Team, the time with each curator is singular and unique, allowing the teens to make personal connections and discover the commonalities with these additional staff. Additionally, multiple Teen Team members in the past have gone on to study art history or work toward a curatorial practice in part because of the personal relationships they have cultivated with specific curators. By allowing curators to imbue their in-gallery sessions with their own passions and ideas, the teens can better connect with the artwork within the museum.

Discovering the Unknown
Teen Team members are tasked with creating and giving tours of our permanent collection to other teens as part of their design and implementation of programs. Some years, these tours have been the concentration of the summer intensive, but whatever the focus, they are always a part of the summer curriculum. Creating self-guided tours was their main project in the 2021–2022 Teen Team summer, supplemented by planning their monthly teen workshops and Teen Night.

How we teach the teens about giving tours, and some of the tours themselves, are designed to help our Teen Team members find additional connections to their favorite artworks or artists or explore their passion in a newly discovered gallery. We start creating a tour by helping guide the teens to look closely at art. We provide them with the basics of Visual Thinking Strategies (VTS)[1] and Artful Thinking[2] routines and then go into the galleries to learn about these strategies in front of artworks and practice with each other. Visual Thinking Strategies, created by psychologist Abigail Housen and museum educator Philip Yenawine, focuses on three main questions to promote visual literacy: what's going

1. Philip Yenawine, *Visual Thinking Strategies: Using Art to Deepen Learning across School Disciplines* (Cambridge, MA: Harvard University Press, 2013).

on in this picture, what do you see that makes you say that, and what more can we find? Artful Thinking, developed by Harvard University's Project Zero, contains multiple thinking routines, such as "I used to think…Now I think…" and "I see, I think, I wonder." Both Artful Thinking and Visual Thinking Strategies use the subject matter at hand—in this case, art—to provide the catalyst for inquiry and foundation for deeper exploration.[3]

When our 2021–2022 Teen Team went off to practice close looking, or intensive visual observation, with their peers, they split off into small groups and spread throughout the museum. Some immediately went to their favorite galleries to search for new meaning, but many intentionally traveled to parts of the museum they were less familiar with, exploring nineteenth-century American art and British ceramics, Ellsworth Kelly paintings, and African Kente cloths. By showing the teens that we could discover context and interest through the artwork itself, without prior research or study, the teens felt empowered to talk with their peers about art on which they had little or no background information—and this, in turn, provided them with the agency, autonomy, and tools to provide those same experiences for our visitors.

Through this exercise of having the Teen Team explore galleries with minimal or no prior knowledge of artists, movements, or specific artworks, they begin to build confidence in talking about art through close-looking strategies alone. While their final tours were steeped in art-historical research, they were rooted in visual inquiry—they almost always started with a moment of looking closely at the artwork or asking what the visitors noticed first. Additionally, when the teens gave in-person tours at Teen Night or their monthly workshop, they were able to facili-

2. Shari Tishman and Patricia Palmer, *Final Report: Artful Thinking* (Cambridge, MA: Harvard Project Zero, 2006).
3. For more information, please visit the Project Zero website at http://www.pz.harvard.edu/projects/artful-thinking.

tate these gallery experiences almost entirely using Visual Thinking Strategies or Artful Thinking routines, stepping into the role of facilitator with sometimes little time or context with which to prepare. By beginning the tour-building process with close looking rather than research, the Teen Team felt confident that they could discuss essentially any artwork in the museum, that they were able to root every experience in the visual evidence, and that they were knowledgeable about what they were giving their tour on through the visual evidence alone.

Letting the Art Talk Back

Our teens are regularly asking questions that our education staff might not know or be able to provide the answers to—everything from questions about why the museum paid for an artwork they could make themselves to how the institution supports artists who identify as Black, Indigenous, and people of color. As educators of teens in a cultural institution, our staff often feels that in order to address the need to answer questions concerning museum practices around access, inclusion, diversity, and current events, we must not give biased responses or allow personal leanings to influence the teens' thoughts on these subjects. We encourage the teens to consider different viewpoints to every question they ask and every answer they receive; our staff infuses their discussions and inquiry with twenty-first-century skills, encourages their critical thinking, communication, and leadership abilities. Our staff gives ample room for the Teen Team to have open discussion and dialogue, giving each teen space to vocalize their ideas and likely come across others with different viewpoints.

And every year, our teens want to discuss some difficult personal, political, or emotional topics during the program as they get to know each other and our staff. One of our roles as educators is to stimulate inquiry and adjust those conversations to be within the museum's framework. We want our teens to feel comfortable having these conversations in the museum and to see that it is a generative space to have them because of the prompts and affordances of using artwork to ground the conversations. For example, viewing artworks by artists representing diverse identities can encourage teens to consider multiple perspectives and experiences and build empathy or validation through representation. Connecting teens' experiences and questions to artworks or artists can make the idea or topic more accessible to other teens who might have different perspectives without minimizing or discounting the range of experiences in the room. This method of perspective taking removes the onus from the teens and puts it back on the art.

This method of relating conversations, especially challenging ones, back to the art assists the Teen Team members when they are creating their guided and self-guided tours. By demonstrating how current events, social justice topics, and big feelings can relate to our visual culture, the teens can use those strategies to have similar conversations in their gallery experiences.

Taking Perspective

While our staff recognizes that many of our Teen Team members are familiar with the museum before they begin the program, the methods used to create interest across collecting areas help the teens know the galleries intimately and personally. The foresight of collecting area equity (and the recognition of its shortcomings) was ingrained in the Teen Team members from their very first week in the program. It became part of the vocabulary, how we see the museum's collection as a whole, and in its parts; it is the lens through which we show others what the High has to offer. From creating the summer curriculum to scheduling meetings with the curators, our staff intentionally guide the teens to see each collecting area as equally essential and to help them facilitate experiences for teen visitors with fairness and equality.

Of course, we want teen visitors to find their own interests in the galleries, but part of the Teen Team's mission (and thus part of our mission as educators) is to help others become familiar with the unfamiliar. Our goal is that what they learn in the Teen Team program can become part of their experiences outside of the museum and that their inquiry of art will lead to an inquiry into the world around them. It might be that 2021 teens were more aware of divisions, striving for equity, and trying to create balance in their uncertain young adult world. Undoubtedly, these concepts are inherent within this generation, but we cannot discount our role as educators of these young people in helping them explore these concepts.

By introducing the Teen Team members to each collecting area—taking ownership through researching and presenting to others, making it personal by meeting the curator behind the collection, exposing the unknown, and questioning everything along the way—they can find their own personal connection in each gallery of the museum. And then they can do that for others.

Our staff's methods for the 2021–2022 Teen Team program were not drastically different from any previous year—the basics were essentially the same, with curator-led tours, close-looking activities with varied artworks, collecting area deep dives, and reframing conversations to be through the lens of art. However, the outcome was markedly different, with the fifteen participants showing real intentionality in their choices.

Creating self-guided tours for teen visitors took many iterations throughout the summer. Initially, each Teen Team member designed their own tour, personalized to their interests. Nevertheless, those tours morphed as the summer continued: the individual teens turned into two groups, and their ideas combined to encompass most collecting areas.

The scavenger hunt group, "The Mystery of the Missing Cat," wanted to create a tour for some of our younger teens and preteen visitors, combining art history, close-looking activities, and a bit of whimsy. The scavenger hunt took visitors to seven artworks within the museum: an American portrait of the museum's namesake, a European painting, an American landscape, two African objects, a mixed-media artwork by a folk artist, and a contemporary painting. Their decision not to include artwork from the photography collecting area was based on logistics. The photography collection is rotated in and out of the galleries more often than other objects on view, and the teens wanted the scavenger hunt to be relevant for a more extended period than those rotations would allow.

The "Art 101" self-guide was in response to our Teen Team members not knowing where anything was when they had to present on collecting areas the first week of the summer intensive; they wanted to create a guide for someone unfamiliar with the museum, but still wanted to impress their friends with their art and museum knowledge. Their audio guide and accompanying map gave an overview of five of the seven collecting areas within the museum, moving geographically through the galleries—European, American, African, folk and self-taught, and modern and contemporary art. Their reason for not including the photography collecting area was the same as the scavenger hunt group's. For the decorative arts collecting area, the "Art 101" audio guide discussed decorative art objects as they explored the other collecting areas, as those artworks are incorporated into those galleries.

These methods of establishing and investigating collecting area equity were especially apparent as the 2021–2022 Teen Team planned for their spring Teen Night. When developing the event, an "around the world" theme was the front-runner, hoping to bring teen visitors to all corners of the museum. It was scrapped for a neon theme, incorporating the colors of a KAWS exhibition with other brightly colored art in the permanent collection. To our educators, this was a clear measure of success, as the Teen Team was deliberate about using popular art as an entryway into the museum for teens—they used the KAWS special exhibition to attract visitors to overlooked parts of the museum as a framework for conversations about art as commodity and pop culture, and all through their own inquiry and consideration.

The educators leading the program guided the teens in discovering their own connections within the museum, supporting them through inquiry and discourse. The methods used by the educators ranged from encouraging open dialogue, facilitating projects that imbued a sense of ownership for the teens, and creating spaces for the teens to investigate and explore ideas with diverse groups of museum employees. Through these methods, the 2021–2022 Teen Team was able to probe the galleries for a way to relate to the institution, much like they were probing society to find their own place, voice, and potential to enact change.

These are our four key strategies to guide teens in building connections and deepening understanding across all collecting areas:

1. Creating interest and enthusiasm around distinct collecting areas through research and gallery exploration.
2. Connecting with the people behind the art by meeting with the curators of each collecting area.
3. Building confidence and understanding when talking about art through close-looking inquiry and practice.
4. Using art as a foundation for dialogue to find deeper understanding or as a catalyst for topics and ideas relevant to the teens.

Alex Chung Vargo & Devin Malone

With
Sean J. Patrick Carney, Savannah Knoop, Andreas Laszlo Konrath, Stephen Kwok, and Mollie McKinley

Performer, Producer, Conduit: Artist Educators in Conversation

Bio
Sean J. Patrick Carney (born in 1982 in Michigan) is a writer in Berkeley, California. He is a frequent contributor to *Artforum* and *Art in America*, and his writing has also appeared in *Vice*, *High Country News*, Glasstire, Artnet News, and *Foundations*.

Bio
Alex Chung Vargo is an arts administrator and museum educator based in the Hudson Valley, NY. She is the senior manager of learning and engagement at Dia Art Foundation, designing, producing, and evaluating programs that center all participants' interests and lived experiences in pursuit of transformative learning opportunities and in collaboration with artists. She holds a BA in art history from Oberlin College and an EdM in the arts in education from the Harvard Graduate School of Education.

Bio
Savannah Knoop is a New York-based artist, writer,

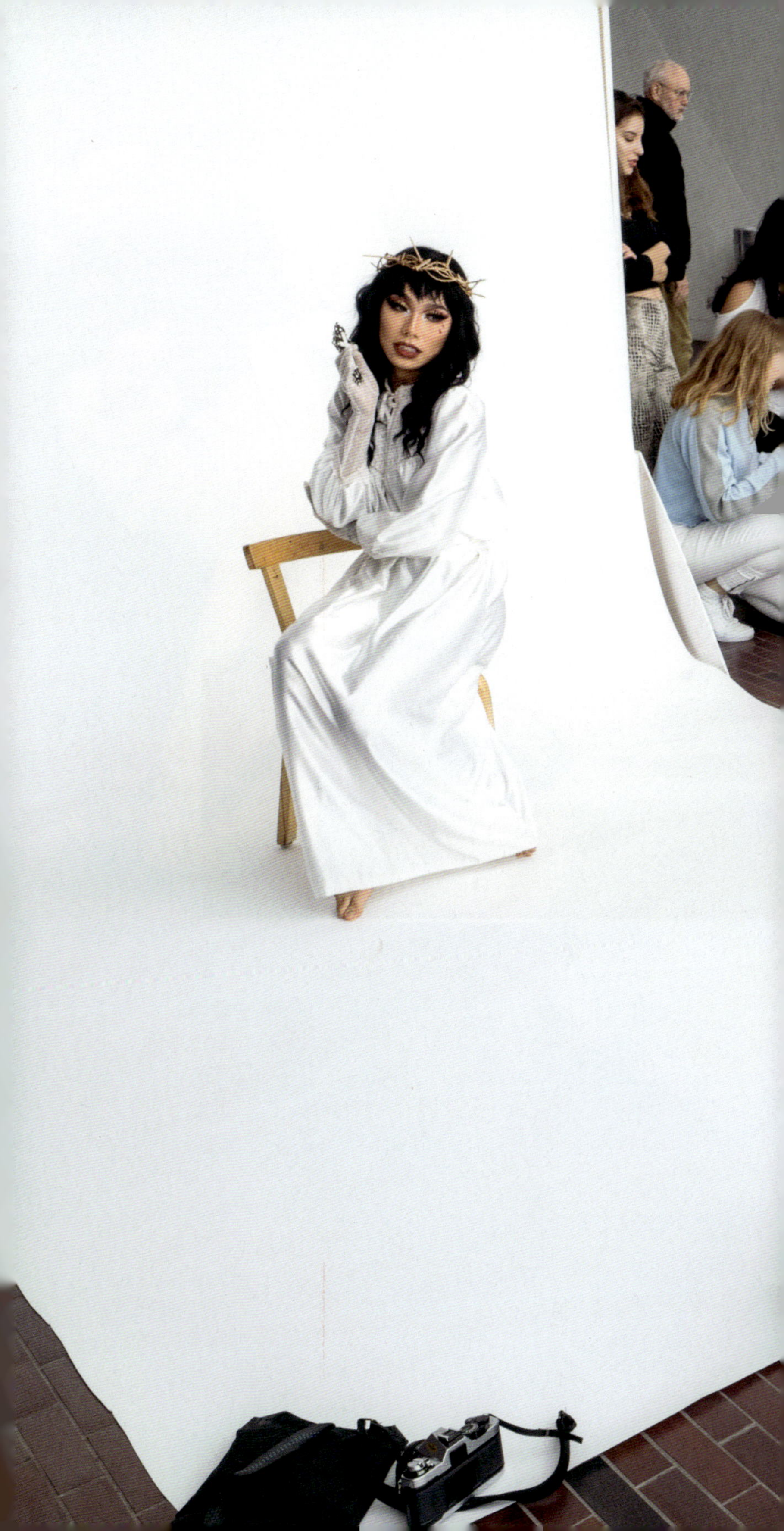

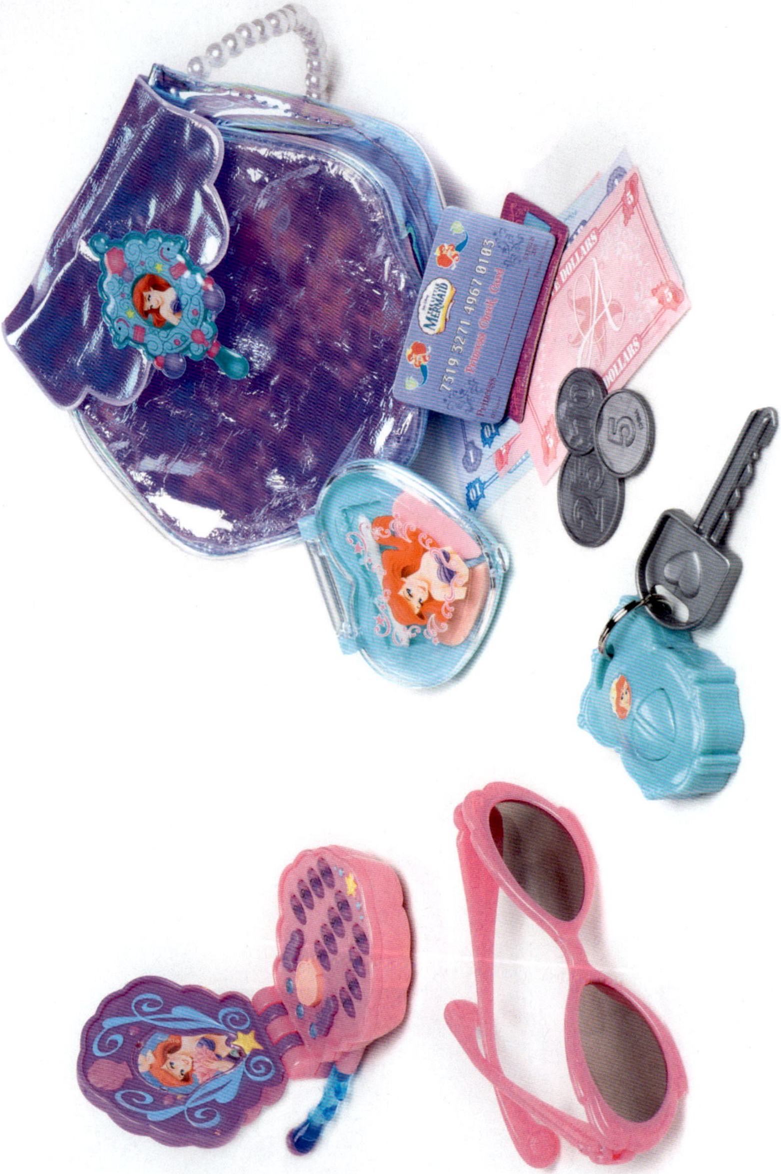

and educator; they have exhibited their work and performed at venues such as the Whitney, MoMA, the ICA Philly, and the Leslie-Lohman Museum. In 2007, they published their memoir, *Girl Boy Girl: How I Became JT LeRoy* (Seven Stories Press), and adapted it into a screenplay, coproducing the resulting feature-length film, *JT LeRoy*, with director Justin Kelly (Universal Pictures, 2019), starring Kristen Stewart and Laura Dern. Their short film, *The Tumbler*, premiered at BFI Flare in 2022, released on Aspect Ratio Films. They are working with multimedia artist Brontez Purnell and director Ro Haber to adapt Purnell's second novel, *Since I Laid My Burden Down*, into a feature-length film.

Bio

Andreas Laszlo Konrath is a photographer and artist educator who utilizes the zine format as a vehicle for many projects, citing community building, exchange, and collaboration as key inspirations and motivators. Andreas's zines have been archived in collections at the ICP Triennial, the Getty Research Institute, the Metropolitan Museum of Art Library, the MoMA Library, and the Yale University Library. Andreas regularly contributes as a visiting artist to FIT, ICP, Parsons School of Design at The New School, Pratt Institute, Red Hook Labs, and SVA. He has organized zine workshops for Fondation Louis Vuitton, Gavin Brown's enterprise, Penumbra Foundation, Red Hook Community Justice Center, and Tasweer Photo Festival Qatar. Keeping a connection to the community, Andreas recently codeveloped a progressive web app—SHRIMP ZINE—that allows users to create zines for free on their smartphones, bringing a new creative and collaborative access point to digital natives.

Bio

Stephen Kwok makes experimental events incorporating sculpture, live performance, digital media, and text into participatory systems. He has exhibited his work at Seoul Museum of Art; Surplus Space, Wuhan; Haus der Kulturen der Welt, Berlin; Center for Performance Research, Brooklyn; Julius Caesar Gallery, Chicago; Contemporary Arts Center, New Orleans; and Lawndale Art Center, Houston, and has participated in programs at Delfina Foundation in London, the Canadian Centre for Architecture in Montreal, and NEW INC in New York. He lives in Brooklyn, teaches design at Brooklyn College, and serves as the Curator of Public Engagement at Dia Art Foundation.

Bio

Devin Malone (they/them) is a cultural producer based in San Francisco, California. Malone has produced education and public programs at the Fine Arts Museums of San Francisco, Dia Art Foundation, the Museum of Modern Art, and the Studio Museum in Harlem, among others. Drawing on queer, anti-capitalist, and Black radical study, Malone develops multimodal engagement programs that emphasize fostering sustained, collaborative relationships with historically underserved museum audiences. They hold an MA in museum and exhibition studies from the University of Illinois, Chicago, and a BA in anthropology from the University of Illinois at Urbana-Champaign. They are the Director of Public Programs and Community Engagement at the Fine Arts Museums of San Francisco.

Bio

Mollie McKinley is an interdisciplinary artist whose work translates invisible healing processes through the visceral phenomena of nature. She unites the earth's ecological health with the health of human bodies through symbols of contemporary medicine, such as infusions. She combines materials such as salt, glass, neon, photographs on textiles, and text in collaboration with these elemental intelligences. Her work has been shown at Fridman Gallery, NADA, Pioneer Works, Independent Curators International, the Museum of Arts and Design, Momenta Art, Field Projects, Anthology Film Archives, and others. She was awarded a fellowship in glass at Wheaton Arts and a two-year fellowship in sculpture and glass at Alfred University. McKinley holds a BA in photography from Bard College and an MFA in sculpture / dimensional studies from Alfred University. Her works are held in private collections, as well as the permanent collection of the Samuel Dorsky Museum.

Introduction

Dia Teens, a multisite program serving high school-aged youth in the Hudson Valley and the five boroughs of New York City, finds its purpose and methodology in the foundational ethos of the Dia Art Foundation. Since the 1970s, Dia has pledged commitment to realizing ambitious artworks through full participation and collaboration with artists in all stages of the creative process.

In this spirit, Dia Teens centers participants as the authors and protagonists of their own creative and intellectual trajectories both within and beyond Dia. Young people co-construct a peer community around their shared and ever-evolving ideas, questions, and priorities.

While teen participants are encouraged to remain with the program over several consecutive years, artist educators work with each site's cohort for a maximum of one year. These artist educators support the group in articulating ideas, developing creative projects, and identifying the critical questions through the design and delivery of an emergent curriculum, which functions as a supportive and evolving framework within which teens exercise their individual and collective voices.

Informed by the artist educators' own creative practices, the organizational context of Dia, and the young people themselves, this open-ended structure invites both the educator and youth participants to learn and experiment in community with one another. The collaborative relationship between the teens and artist educators embodies the program's core values of care, vulnerability, reciprocity, and intimacy.

> On November 16, 2021, five former Dia Teens artist educators gathered in New York City with Devin Malone and Alex Chung Vargo, two Dia program administrators, to reflect on how they approached their roles and navigated some of the opportunities, questions, and tensions that arose from this work. The following conversation has been edited for clarity and length.

Conversation

Alex Chung Vargo
For someone who might not know, what or who is the Dia Teens artist educator? What is the relationship with the teens like, and how did you think about power, positionality, and agency within this dynamic?

Savannah Knoop
I think of artist educators as a kind of conduit—we act as a component of the group that provides boundaries to push against through listening and collective problem-solving. The artist educator facilitates flexibility and change according to the group's desires.

Mollie McKinley
The role of power for a Dia Teens artist educator was interesting because it's the closest I've come as an educator to dismantling vertical hierarchies. It felt a lot more horizontal—the program's structure supported more of a horizontal power structure. I think part of that is because the teens aren't getting grades from us; there isn't some kind of ultimate rubric that they have to meet. And so, within that openness, you can create new power structures where there isn't this sense of the artist educator being in charge. We're older and can share what we know with the teens, but we ask that the teens engage in a reciprocal exchange of ideas and expertise. That is one of the most

exciting parts of the Dia Teens program.

Andreas Laszlo Konrath

To jump off that idea about hierarchy, I'm thinking about how I positioned myself when I walked into that Dia Teens space. When I come in, I don't assume I have more information than anyone else. Even though I am facilitating and creating a curriculum, I must remain open to learning. We come into the space as learners, not as just educators.

Stephen Kwok

One of the essential things about Dia Teens is that the group stays the same, and the artist educators cycle through every year. By having the teen cohort stay the same, I think you are naturally put in a position as an artist educator to be humbled by the fact that there's so much that's already gone on by the time you come into the group. The mantle is being passed on to you, so you really need to learn about the existing relationships and dynamics.

I don't know if this language is still used, but I think we were called "artist allies" for a time. I think the idea of not being an "educator," per se, or being an ally, someone who is working alongside the teens, is a really important part of how I attempted to build and maintain relationships throughout the year working with the teen program. Although I was facilitating, I would always do my best to participate. It creates a more lateral situation between the teens and us.

Sean J. Patrick Carney

I'm trying to think of a good analogy. And it's funny because the vocabulary I want to use is so institutional. I'm trying to draw this other kind of analogy based on what everyone said, and I'm thinking about a recording engineer, producer, or someone working with a group of musicians that already have a sound and vision. Our job is to tease out some of the more exciting elements or nuances of their performances or capture things they're not super aware they're doing intuitively. Coming in as an educator to a group with a rapport felt like that to me, where I ask myself, "How do I help your sound achieve its height, width, and depth sonically? I can't teach you to play your instruments, but I can help shape this or that."

    I'm also thinking about who I was before I came to Dia Teens versus who I was when I came out afterward. I had a lot of experience with alternative education programs. Teens are socialized and trained to be obsessed with particular types of rubrics of success, and I had always thought, "Oh, I'm going to help them break that." And then I realized very quickly, coming into Dia Teens, that I was carrying those rigid expectations, too, and I needed to drop a lot of my own presumptions. As you all said earlier, "dismantle" is a good word. I thought I had it all figured out, and then I walked into Dia Teens and realized, "Oh no, this is really building the plane while I'm flying it." It was exciting and has forever changed how I put a syllabus together or work with students.

ALK
    Sean, going back to this idea that as a quote-unquote adult it is presumed that we have it figured out and have the answers, but we're coming in and saying, "I don't have it figured out." The important thing is being willing to say, "I don't know," and being honest. It's a way of connecting with the teens and being vulnerable ourselves, which worked for me to admit, "I actually have no idea what the hell I'm doing right now."

SaKn
    I like that analogy, too, because there is a level of investment for us as facilitators, or "producers"— we are always hemming and hawing about all the details—that's our role, to think about the structure and how that relates to their live feedback within the group, as well as the order of operations. We're holding/recording the sort of open chaos, the open form that everyone is collaborating and working within. Maybe we're taller, and

we're older, but we're not not learners when we come in or leave the room.

MM

I love the mention of vulnerability. That's important and was foundational to me. Having an authentic relationship with the teens and feeling like we could go into a space that was less about the things we already knew. Like you, Andreas, one of the first things I told them was "I don't necessarily know more than you do, and we're going to be on a journey of unknowing together."

Maybe we can't totally dismantle all the structures because we are still working under the guise of a museum. We're still in an organized society. We are still playing by some of these inherent rules. We are trying to find the sweet spot structurally between some of those dismantling processes and some of the radical openness and vulnerability. There are some structures, even within this experimental environment, that keep it functional and keep us accountable; as Sav is saying—there are stakes. It is not a no-stakes environment, and I think that's important. There is this sense of creating a certain kind of energy. And I also love the analogy of the producer. What is this continuum that I jumped into? What does that energy feel like that we've been working with? What is it right now? What do I have to bring that can open up new learning and creating spaces with these particular human beings?

StKw

I was just going to mix a metaphor, which I apologize for! You know when you're hosting a dinner party, and you do the preparation so that when the guests come, you can actually hang out. That doesn't always happen (it rarely happens for me), but that's always an aspiration. It's a desire to set up optimal conditions for learning so everyone can just dive in.

The other thing that I've wanted to think about is that the vulnerability in my position was also really welcome because I didn't have to perform in my own position. I'll speak for myself in saying this, but I find an inherent discomfort with the idea that I should enter a classroom as an educator and be accountable to have all the answers or to know more than anyone else and to be able to tell you what to do. So as a participant in the Dia Teens space, it was nice not to have to perform that because it feels like a performance whenever I am asked to do that.

ALK
Yeah, it's probably also quite refreshing for the teens to experience a relationship with an adult that doesn't have that kind of authority of knowledge. In this alternative space, they can perhaps build a relationship with an adult differently, and I think about how I can be something different for them, not better or worse, but something that's an alternative.

Going back to the idea of vulnerability, openness, sensitivity, reciprocity, and being a conduit is this constant back-and-forth. In those traditional spaces, as Stephen said about performing, the teens are also performing. They're performing learning. And perhaps Dia Teens is a place where they don't have to perform learning; they perform being. Or not even performing, they can just be.

SJPC
I feel like we did that, too, as educators. Stephen and I'd just talk about how we were freaking out! That was so different from my experience at other educational institutions, where you feel like there's a performance, even with your colleagues. Also, when Mollie came in after me, we talked about my experience and what it was like to work with teens. It felt okay to be vulnerable with my colleagues too.

MM
The co-performances of teacher and student are thrown out the window. I am not expecting the teens to visually show me that they get what I am

talking about, that they like what I'm talking about, or that I'm pleasing them.

SaKn

I'm nodding my head off right now.

MM

It's okay! They can check out. Things happen outside of the program. I had to trust them and let go of many of those visual cues. In other, more formalized institutional teaching settings, it can feel very performative, like you're on a stage, and it can be exhausting. I think it takes away from the actual learning process.

SaKn

The teens are going to look bored.

Devin Malone

It's about relinquishing the need for instant gratification. There were moments of frustration where you, Sav, were like, "I don't know if they're like really feeling what's happening right now. I'm feeling a little stressed out." And we talked about the fact that the things that you're teaching them or learning with them are things that might hit years later. That can be frustrating, in a way, because you're the person who's there right now. But it stays with them.

SaKn

It is true. We immediately let go of these weird structural things in Dia Teens. Conventions like the idea of one person standing behind a desk and others sitting and facing them become psychedelically strange. As you let that go, those performances slip away, or, perhaps more honestly, rearrange themselves.

Because I did feel like I would be performing *other things* with them or for them, to almost sort of get the ball rolling. This other performativity gets going, where you're saying, "Could it be like this?!" In other words, you might be performing, but there's no set script. You find that you are putting on a lot of different hats. It's exciting, too, because you feel it's such a different world of choreography than the traditional top-down institutional kind we are accustomed to.

ACV To pick up on some of these thoughts about undoing the structures of more traditional educational environments and relationships, let's talk about the approach to curriculum in Dia Teens. At various times we've referred to the curriculum as a road map, a blueprint, a playground. I'd love to hear from you all about how your understanding of an emergent curriculum evolved from when you started as an artist educator to when you finished or up until now. And was there any part of the curriculum development process that surprised you?

ALK The part that I always found the hardest in my role was building the curricular arc. I had to learn to appreciate and embrace those unexpected, unknown moments. It helped me move forward, especially in my second year of Dia Teens; I embraced that a lot more.[1] The first time around, I was pretty strict and structured, and I didn't know how to let go of things. My learning around the curriculum was definitely about letting go.

MM I really appreciated how collaborative the curriculum editing process was with the learning and engagement team. I was able to create an experimental curriculum bordering on a manifesto. It was a kind of text about experimental pedagogy and methodology, and it became something functional through a very care-driven and rigorous editing process. It was our guidebook and detailed how everything was going to unfold. There were parts that I was really uncertain and insecure about.

1. Savannah and Andreas worked with Dia Teens for two years during the COVID-19 pandemic. While artist educators typically work with the program for a single year, these two artist educators continued with the program for a longer duration to minimize the program's disruption as it moved to virtual sessions from March 2020 to June 2021.

With specific sessions, I was so worried, thinking I had to have this tight document. But I also had all these ideas that I didn't know where to cite all of them. They just fell into the curriculum, into this long, beautiful, written piece that we all put so much care into.

SJPC

When I started as an artist educator, I thought I knew what an emergent curriculum was. It was something that I thought I was doing beforehand, and I realized in retrospect that what I was making was responsive syllabi. I would think about the context—this place, these people, something like that—but making something that was in progress the entire time was eye-opening. It made me aware of the presumptions I had as an educator about structure and expectations and how institutions encourage particular types of responsive curriculum while requiring a PDF of your syllabus two weeks before meeting the students. I understand why that happens organizationally, but I think that doing something in real time with a group of people made me aware of the conditioning of art education. So much of my teaching up to that point, totally subconsciously, was fear based and based on expectation and performance. Mollie, you used the word "insecurity"; it seemed like a failure when the Dia Teens curriculum had to change—I must have done something wrong. And then, after the fourth or the fifth time I redid my curriculum for Dia Teens, I realized that that was just what was happening. We were responding to what the teens were doing. We were seeing them. We were participating with them.

And it's definitely hyperbolic and dramatic to say that I had a fear-based pedagogy, but I was flipped out that the teens might see that I was a sham. So getting rid of that, I thought, "Oh, wow, this is cool."

MM

And actually, the only failure would be inflexibility

and not constant revision.

StKw

Many of the questions I have now as an educator, which emerged or crystallized when I was working at Dia, are around how much structure to provide and how much openness to leave. I generally err on the side of less structure and more openness, and maybe that is something that emerged out of working with Dia Teens.

The premise of my curriculum was to have the city be a collaborator with us. I remember it was called Site x Subject, and the subjects would author or reclaim a site or have agency over how a site operates and is experienced to actually make an impact. Because of that initial structural decision to be so site based and out in public, we constantly improvised because we couldn't control many places where we met. We did this one playwriting session in a food court early on that set the tone for the year, and we realized that sometimes things would go wrong because we couldn't control if the security guard wanted us to leave. We had to build in the idea that things might not work, which infused our entire year.

In terms of what surprised me, I've found that as I go into other teaching spaces, if I am firm in my belief that the openness of the structure is intentional, then you can get students, participants, and other people on board with you and with that type of framework. It is this open-ended *intentionally*. It is this open to error *intentionally*. Some people will still think it's messy.

SaKn

It feels like structured improvisation, where you have all of these parameters built into the open-endedness. It's always a mix of very loose and very tight at the same time. For me, it felt very emotional. There'd be weird moments of almost unconscious panic. I would set up all this stuff for a session, and then we'd just throw it in the bin.

One example happened this past summer

when we explored the politics of pleasure. It came from this idea of doing workshops where you would have these sensations.[2] You might each take a Szechuan peppercorn and listen to a thing and rub some sandpaper and silk while you're eating dark chocolate. I had built out this whole thing, and the whole curriculum was based on this initial idea. And we tried the workshop; they were like, "I hate dark chocolate!" They were like, "Blech, eww, what are you doing to me? Why are you torturing me this way?" And then we found a different way to do it. They created their own version of it.

The structured improvisation was really real! I'd tell the teens about a working theme, and they would say, "I hate that. Let's do this!" And this is sort of what you hope for. It's nice to acknowledge the emotional aspects and to be scared of something and do it anyways. It opens up a lot of doors in an emergent curriculum. There are many unknowns. There's a lot of awkwardness. We're opening up the room to the chaos of the city or the chaos of each other. That's part of the magic of having everyone together and present in all those twists, turns, and changes.

ALK
You're in this paradox of preparation and flexibility, and the risk-taking is the doing. That's where the exciting stuff happens when you embrace spontaneous moments that completely take you away from your original idea and derail everything you wanted to touch upon. I learned to embrace that and allow for a certain amount of risk-taking, play, flexibility, and spontaneity, which all depend on trust.

SaKn
Right. At first, you can feel like you created a plan that didn't work, but nothing is ever lost. In my summer curriculum, I realized that we somehow

---

2. See page 312 for Savannah's complete 2.2.3. Sensorium Workshop.

covered all the bases. All the things we wanted to cover got pulled back in by the group in their own time and rhythm. It's like the difference between practice and praxis—practicing something and then actually doing it in the real world. There are always a lot of weird twists and turns, which happen every time. How you imagined it, and then how it plays out.

MM

The risk-taking that you're talking about, Andreas, is so important, and it relates to the risk of an individual studio practice also. These emergent curricula are related to our identities as artists and our individual research and practices—it is so intimate.

I'm coming back to the idea of vulnerability. What is essential to put in the curriculum? What is the vital experiment that we're going to do together? There's something so precious about this time spent with these teens, and you want to make the experience open enough. What is the most critical use of this collaboration? What feels really vital? What needs to happen right now in the world? What needs to happen right now in my practice? What parts of my practice can be translated into a conversation like this? It does start to feel like collaborative research, in a way. You're letting them into your practice and vice versa.

The free-fall feeling has the same energy as wondering if anyone will come to your party! Are the teens going to get it? Are they going to like it? You have to keep shedding the expectation that they'll perform learning for you. That's a fascinating editing process, trying to figure out what is important about my practice that translates into pedagogy. What is essential for these human beings to interact with right now? What do I have to offer that is compelling and may pull us out of mundane reality in an exciting way?

SJPC

I'm thrilled you said that. I felt like "editing" was

like simmering under the conversation. I keep thinking about learning to collectively and collaboratively edit and relinquish the control of your individual editorial vision as you work with the teens. You can't be precious about what is left on the cutting-room floor.

MM

And like Sav said, even what's left on the cutting-room floor has an uncanny way of finding its way back into the curriculum in magical, mysterious, and confusing ways. It felt like there was some kind of container or some phenomenological field that I still don't understand—it hovers above all of our articulate analyses of what was happening. It's like the magic of theater or, again, structured improv. Something magical really does happen in that container, and not everyone can make sense of it. It doesn't happen every day or every week, necessarily. But those moments hit really powerfully and propelled us to keep experimenting because something weird and incredible happened last time.

StKw

One of the most challenging parts of the curriculum development process was articulating a set of driving central questions. To build off what Mollie said, I was drawing from my practice the entire time as I formed and conceived the curriculum. It became about trying to articulate what questions I was asking in practice rather than the answers I had come up with as artworks to address those questions. And then you have to figure out how to communicate those questions in a way where people actually share that question with you and are personally invested as well.

I landed on "How can we encounter everyday environments from a position of personal power? What creative strategies can we develop to empower ourselves?" And whenever I would make a choice in a particular session that felt like it was approaching an answer to these critical questions, it usually didn't go over the best. For one session, we went to Times Square, and it was just chaos; it wasn't working, and maybe that's because I was trying to provide an answer to that question rather than a different way to pose it or a different opportunity to engage with it. Writing that question was the most challenging part of the entire process, but one that I'm really thankful for now.

ALK

Regarding drawing from your practice, I did find that, over time, we developed some momentum, and the sessions began to feel like they were building themselves versus me pushing them along. I started introducing things that were not connected to my own practice but ideas I wanted to explore and experiment with myself and with the teens. The program allowed me to broaden my thinking because it almost felt like I had limited resources in terms of what I knew and what I could do. So, I started being able to take some risks, too, in introducing new themes, following these little seeds of ideas. It's allowed me to try out other things I was maybe too afraid to try by myself. I've become more open about what I want to explore as a creative person.

SaKn

Do your own prompts. For the next ten years. [laughs]

StKw

Yes! There are moments where you would create a prompt of some sort and think to yourself, "How would I do that?" You create a situation where you don't know how you would meet that as a participant. That's exciting. Also, scary.

SJPC

As I went through the process of writing this curriculum and collaborating with the teens on it and getting their feedback and changing it, I did start to feel a kind of permission to bring in these other topics or ideas that maybe were intimidating to me

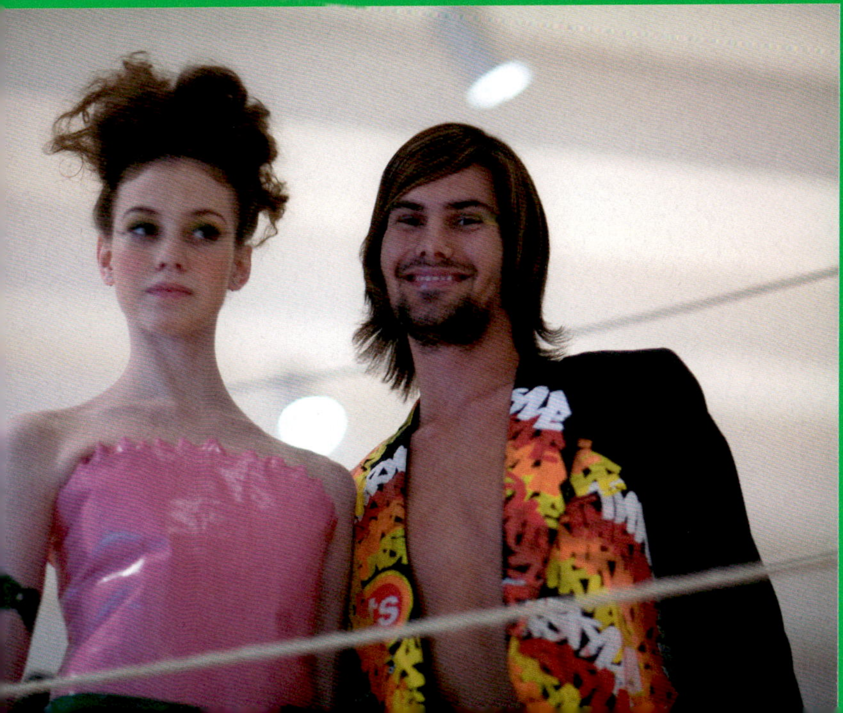

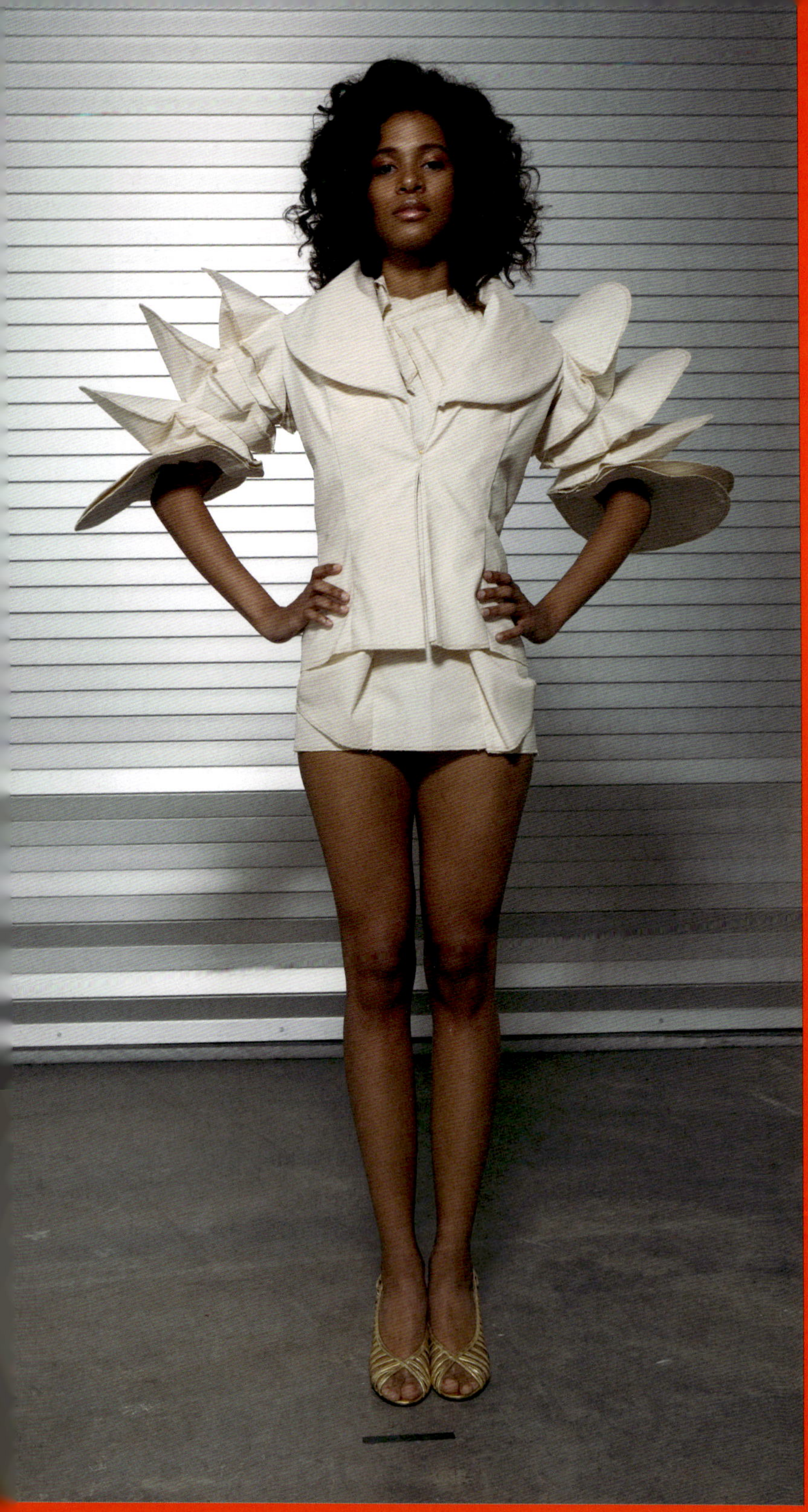

or I felt were not in my wheelhouse. Coming out of Dia Teens is a 180-degree change in what I make as a cultural producer. I realize that Dia Teens is my hinge point, which was not the point of teaching, of course, but just shows that the teens had a profound impact on me and my practice. The parts of my practice that the teens responded to helped me realize what was interesting to me and why. I had shifted my whole paradigm about what I wanted to investigate or what I thought was interesting to others, and they were receptive and critical and really changed what I do.

MM
Yeah, it changed what I do too. Working with the teens profoundly changed who I am and how I move through the world. It just felt like we're all in this together, learning how to be better humans. It was so real and lacking bullshit and really tender while also being quite profound at the same time. I'm not even sure I can articulate how it has changed my practice now that I'm trying to put it into words. I just know that there's a fundamental distinction in how I even perceive myself, before and after having worked with the teens. There was a sea change because it required me to embody my practice in a totally different way than I had before. That's what I was trying to say earlier: there's something about talking about this in this kind of intellectual, thinky way, but there's such a somatic resonance with this program. It really exists in a physical space and in the body in an incredibly specific way.

SaKn
Yes! I think that is connected to what I was saying about performance, that you're not doing the usual performances, but you do start to perform *something* that I think is connected to highlighting where the group draws connections and themes. I would catch myself "performing" these gestures almost as some sort of ontological baton to pass off to someone else in the group. We're trying to

be crowdsourcing those, or the teens should be generating them. At first, it felt like I had pulled some sleight of hand or something, but I wasn't trying to trick them, and they eventually latched on to it. Eventually, the teens and I settled on the understanding that prompts were something to push against. It helped us.

StKw

I also think about absence as a strategy. Sometimes my absence would be a good thing. There would be moments in my curriculum where I would really try my best to outline what I had prepared—what was available in the room, how time would flow, things like this—and then I'd try to take a step back or be completely absent. As much as we want to reroute and dismantle some of these hierarchical structures, we can still be seen as a quote-unquote authority figure, however diffuse or dissolved, to our students. So, just not being in the room or so hands-on and present can offer the teens a new kind of freedom.

Then I'd return almost as an assistant toward the end of the session or workshop to offer some of my expertise, like around installation, for example. I figured out that the balance between structure and openness is the hardest part of the program.

SaKn

I remember one moment with Melanie. I think we were talking to a group of new teens, and Melanie said, "No, no, you just take the prompt, and you do whatever you want with it. Don't worry; there are no wrong answers." Like, "Don't worry, it will be great no matter what."

I love when the teens just do whatever they want with the prompt. That's always the goal—the score.

ALK

That exploration is the whole point. There is no pressure to come up with a correct solution. It should only feel authentic to you as a human.

There is no grade; there is no criticism. I just encouraged the teens to get away from right and wrong because every session is just an opportunity to experiment, take a risk, and try.

ACV

That reminds me of one of our reflection conversations, Andreas, where you described feeling some kind of success when, during studio time, teens would seek you out to ask your opinion about something they were working on. I think that's connected to what Stephen was saying about becoming an assistant to the teens, becoming a resource for them to deploy. These are all ways to recognize those moments when teens feel empowered or enfranchised when they claim space for themselves.

   To wrap up, is there anything you would like to pose to this group?

SaKn

We can do with this what we like, but what are some specific gestures that felt like they opened up this space that we always try to cultivate together—your hits? Are there any things that felt like they worked every time?

StKw

I didn't do this at Dia, but I have tried it in subsequent programs: students really love it when I pair them based on their astrological compatibility. They love it! It helps to establish how you, as the artist educator, are participating and locating yourself in the group and a larger cultural context, especially if you do that early on. Pointing to the outside—pointing to relationships, my friendships, how I participate in the world—can be an equalizing force and make more things feel permissible in the space.

SJPC

I think the most successful icebreaker I led was asking, "What's a meme that needs to die?" The teens immediately shifted from social participants to cultural critics. They put stuff on blast! I was amazed. They went around, and all of them instantly knew, "This one!" And I was like, "Oh my God, I've been posting cringe."

Conversations around art and art learning are connected to all these other cultural pockets with signs and signifiers. And the teens have particular lived experiences that produce a certain kind of identity position, and I want them to feel enfranchised to articulate their point of view. I have been thinking for years about why the meme question made them respond so immediately. It has something to do with how we can support them in feeling like they have specific cultural authority and that their point of view is interesting.

They're generating all of the funny things. They're determining what culture is.

MM

I had no language around memes until I interacted with these teens, and it was a way of getting into their world and saying, "Yes, this is just as valid, if not more so, than all my weird ideas that I've done all this research on." They come in with a completely fresh take on so many cultural things, and it was critical to give that a lot of airtime and allow it to drive our inside jokes and aesthetics.

SaKn

When we were talking about how much we value the teens' honesty and perspectives, and about the distinction between right and wrong, good and bad, and the choreography of all that, I also was thinking about the question of ethics and care within the group. I felt like the teens were also always playing within that realm of their own ethics, not the ones inherited, and part of this felt like it was exercised through trolling one another. Care for one another and care for yourself were so profoundly woven into these gestures. It was interesting because while they would say things like "You're a moron because you like Kanye West!" to one another, at the foundation, there was sort of an ethic around being with each other—as if to say, nobody's perfect, and we're still here.

DM
That comes from a place of intimacy, right? You get to that place of ribbing your sibling or your close friends because you have that familiarity, that intimacy. You have that groundwork of trust from the beginning. You can recognize that if I say you're an idiot because you like Kanye, you realize that I still love you and that I don't actually mean that. There's shorthand that's produced by intimacy.

SJPC
I just remembered when we'd do Art Chopped, and some of the teens would be the competition judges, and they would just annihilate each other's work.[3] It was so funny. The judges would get up and walk around and just be like, "This is meaningless!" But there was so much care and trust there; it was about comedy and humor. They were roasting each other in a safe and structured way because nobody actually had time to make anything good. It was all nonsense. It was so cool to see them do that.

MM
All these points that we've been talking about in this part of the conversation have to do with this intersection between care and critical thinking, and respecting the role of critical thinking and honoring how you foster that in a group of young people. The process of developing a point of view in Dia Teens is different because we've created this little ecosystem built on care, safety, respect, and even the way they interact with one another physically.

For example, when one of the teens did not feel okay, they would be on the floor in a pile on the pillows hugging each other. They would make this puppy pile and knew how to coexist with the

3. See page 308 for Sean J. Patrick Carney's 2.2.2. Art Chopped lesson plan.

puppy pile and with critical thinking. Critical thinking is one of the most essential parts of maintaining their agency and authority as young people.

SJPC

Part of what is neat about the teen program, in particular, is the framing that you don't have to consider yourself an artist to participate in it. The metrics for success in Dia Teens are about inquiry, criticality, and a slow burn of understanding that's going to click for one of them three years from now. Maybe. And that's totally cool.

It's such a funny dynamic. They're on this kind of precipice of something big that's going to happen, but we get them in this spot where they are not at home or school, so you do get to experience this tenderness and this playfulness at the same time. It's such a weird, special spot to goof around in and figure out your position, point of view, and criticality, and feel like, for the first time, that you can say anything. And maybe it isn't the first time for everybody, but it is for some.

SaKn

To return to the puppy pile, laying on the floor really did so much work. I feel like a place where they could lie on the floor and be themselves and then be given a MetroCard at the end of the day—

MM

Like you can get a snack and lay down. You are given full permission to be a human being rather than being at school, where there's a certain way that your body has to be. And not just your facial expressions as you're listening and responding, but you have to sit in a chair, you're not supposed to touch each other, and there's a specific time to eat. So just allowing for some of that humanness to come in, with the puppy pile and group lunches, did so much of the work, just sitting on the floor on giant pillows together and allowing your body to be super exhausted or whatever it needed to be in that moment.

StKw
    It makes me think of how important it is to adjust the elements of the space and the material context. We had students who would come an hour and a half early because of their schedule, so that flexibility and time and space really lends itself to creating an environment where the teens can say, "Yeah, this is a resource that I have at my disposal. I know this space; this space is mine." You build that up over time but also through gaining intimacy with flexibility and touch, through the sensory experience as well.

SaKn
    Yeah. And then they're like, "I'm gay, by the way."

SJPC
    Yes! Working with young people, group care is essential. Once, before a Dia Teens public event, the group discussed what pronouns to use in front of each other's parents. And everyone was like, "Got it, cool." It was incredible, and they did that on their own. They really do cultivate these spaces.
        I'm getting all warm and fuzzy.

ACV
    It's going to end in tears.

SaKn
    As it always does.

©

2.2. RESOURCES

2.2.1. GALLERY CONVERSATION LESSON PLANS

Lauren Bína, formerly Walker Art Center

> **Bio.** Lauren Bína recently worked as a lead educator in the Public Engagement, Learning, and Impact Department at the Walker Art Center in Minneapolis, MN. She received a BS in art education and a BFA in darkroom photography from the University of Wisconsin–River Falls. Bína holds Minnesota and Colorado state K–12 art teaching licenses. She is currently based in Denver, CO, where she plans to continue her career in museum education.

Introduction

Each week, the Walker Art Center Teen Arts Council (WACTAC) members spend around thirty minutes discussing a work of contemporary art. When possible, we aim to have these conversations in the galleries to build teens' comfort in those spaces and to connect them with our collection and works on view. Despite all the other goals and moving pieces in a museum teen program, art remains at the center and drives participation. Art talks are facilitated by the Walker educators, who are trained to provide inclusive, inquiry-based conversations for a broad range of learning styles and participant needs. The educator guides the group through a series of observations, discussions, research, and reflection to analyze contemporary artworks and develop well-reasoned interpretations. A selection of the Walker educator training topics and resources for those topics can be found below:

- Visual Thinking Strategies (VTS)
- Universal Design for Learning (UDL)
- Teaching Artistic Behavior (TAB)
- Visual, Auditory, Kinesthetic, Tactile (VAKT)
- Child Development

Benefits of Art Talk

The selected artworks are typically pulled from the museum's permanent collection or special exhibitions on view at the museum. This allows participants to gain familiarity and make personal connections with the institution's collection and collecting practices. Facilitators select artworks based on several factors—sometimes they will be driven by the media or content interests of the teens; sometimes they will be connected to a particular thematic discussion topic or visiting artist or staff member, or a selection of "greatest hits" of artworks that typically elicit robust discussion and opinions. No matter the reason driving the selection, there is always consideration over whether a piece needs content warning, additional scaffolding, or a sensory warning for elements like light and sound. As the program year goes on and facilitators get to know the youth, we have more reference points for their interests, which help us select pieces.[1]

In addition to becoming familiar with the collection, art talks prepare the group for the research project by developing critical-thinking skills, like identifying problems or biases, gathering information, communicating their ideas, and evaluating an artwork based on the data they have collected and observed. Art talks teach participants how to ask thoughtful questions and how to start answering those questions. This curiosity often flows into asking questions about other aspects of the museum and how institutions, like the Walker Art Center, function.

How to Select an Artwork

Artworks are selected to introduce participants to a variety of mediums, techniques, ideas, messages, moods, identities, and perspectives within contemporary art. Participants should be able to see a reflection of themselves in the artwork and the artists selected throughout the program. At the beginning of the WACTAC year, the facilitator selects a few artworks to focus on and then later opens up the artwork selection to the participants.

The selected artworks are scaffolded so that participants can gain comfortability in the galleries and with each other at the beginning of the program before tackling artwork that may involve more sensitive topics. Starting the year with goofy, fun

---

[1] For more information, see 1.1.6. Planning for a Year of Programming by Simona Zappas on page 121 in this publication.

artworks and low-stakes activities can help build comfort. For example, an abstract sculpture like Rachel Harrison's *Jackson* can help students build the skills needed to discuss more complex artworks like Kerry James Marshall's *Gulf Stream*, which focuses on race and representation within the art world.

As stated earlier, throughout the program the art talk facilitator will understand the participants' interests and note any specific artworks, artists, and concepts the group is drawn to. Artworks are then selected based on the interests and requests from the youth.

Art Talk Structure

Art talks are typically structured using five components: observations, discussion questions, context, activity, and evaluation. The order of these components can be mixed and matched to suit the artwork and group discussion needs. This framework was developed based on observations of hundreds of school tours given at the Walker Art Center as an interactive way for youth to develop their own ideas and build on the ideas of others to form their own opinion about an artwork. Each component is broken down below, with a couple of examples of how these components can be used when talking about art.

Observations. Making observations about artworks can help participants develop skills to understand what they are looking at, what they think about it, and why they think that. Observations lay the groundwork for further understanding and discussion. This component is most frequently used at the beginning of art talks before the participants are introduced to important information about the artist and artwork. This encourages participants to develop their own thoughts and opinions that are not influenced by the interpretations of others. The questions during this component encourage close looking and can be used with any artwork. Some examples of questions used during the observation component are listed below.

- What do you notice?
- What is your initial reaction to this artwork?

  - Do you like this artwork right away? Why or why not?
  - Is this something you would stop and look at in a museum, or would you walk past this artwork? Why?

- What does this artwork remind you of?
- How would you describe the mood of this artwork? Why?
- What questions do you have about this artwork?

Discussion questions. Discussion questions can be used between the considering context sections to break up the context and check for understanding, or they can be used after all the information has been given. These questions encourage deeper thinking about an artwork and are designed with the specific artwork and its context in mind. General discussion questions and tips for facilitating group discussions are listed below.

General discussion questions. The following discussion prompts can generally be used for discussing any artwork.

- What might this artwork tell us about the time and place in which it was created?
- What story is being told in this artwork? Who is telling that story?
- If someone found this artwork in one hundred years, what would it tell them about the time we live in now?
- How would this work be different if _____?
- We just learned that _____. How does that affect the way you think about this artwork?
- In that quote, the artist says _____. What do you think that means? Do you agree with that statement? Why or why not?

Facilitation tips. Repeat the responses that participants share. Paraphrasing participant responses can offer more processing time for the whole group and help validate those who share. Different ways to facilitate conversation for different scenarios can be found below.

- If participants have long responses, pull out a few key ideas and paraphrase their responses. For example: "You are pointing out a couple of different things about this artwork. First, you mentioned the monotone color scheme, and then you shared that the artist might have felt isolated because he grew up on a small island surrounded by water."
- If participants share something new that you haven't thought of before, share that. "So, you're saying that the swirling lines in this artwork remind you of a tornado? I haven't thought of that before but can totally see that now!"

- If participants share short responses, encourage them to expand on their ideas. For example: "You mentioned that this painting reminds you of a warm summer day. What do you see in the painting that makes you say that?"
- Try opening up participant responses for the entire group by asking related questions. For example: "You shared that the sculpture of a car looks like it has been in a car crash. Does anyone else agree with that statement? What do you think happened to this car?"
- If participants ask questions, try opening their questions up to the rest of the group. For example: "It sounds like you are asking why the artist chose to make this painting so large. What do you all think? How would this artwork be different if it was small enough to fit in your hands?"

Ways of responding. Try mixing up the discussion by having participants respond to the artwork in different ways. A few examples are listed below.

- *One-word response.* Have each participant share one word that comes to mind when they think about the artwork or ask the participants to respond to a discussion question with only one word. After hearing everyone's responses, ask volunteers to share why they selected the word they did.
- *Anonymous written response.* Have participants respond to a discussion question by writing down their thoughts anonymously on a note card. Then collect the note cards and read them out to the group. Discuss the similarities and differences in the responses.
- *Timeline.* After sharing a discussion question or statement about an artwork, offer two responses. Then create an imaginary line on the ground and assign a response to each end of the line. Ask the students to stand along the line based on their responses. For example: "If you agree with that statement, stand on the right. If you disagree, stand on the left. If you are not sure, stand somewhere in the middle." Then ask volunteers to share why they chose the spot they did.

Context. In this component, the facilitator shares some context about the artist and the artwork. It can be helpful to share a photograph of the artist or share a quote directly from the artist. In cases where there is a lot of context, break up the information with a few discussion questions.

The context typically includes an artwork's who, what, where, when, why, and how. For each section, consider the message or ideas presented in the artwork and what information is relevant to understanding the artwork. Not all of the sections will be relevant in understanding every artwork. Each of these sections are broken down with examples below.

Who. Share information about the artist who created the artwork.

- For example, Angela Two Stars is a Dakota artist from Minnesota. This is important context to share because Two Stars creates site-specific sculptures incorporating words and phrases from the Dakota language into her artwork.

What. Share what kind of medium the artist used to create the artwork. This may be obvious for certain artworks, but for others it can provide context relevant to understanding the artwork.

- For example, Ellen Gallagher's *DeLuxe* features collages using vintage magazine advertisements aimed at changing the physical appearance of Black audiences. This is important context because the artwork focuses on identity and the complex role hair plays in Black culture.

Where. Share any relevant information about where the artist is from or where the artwork was created.

- For example, the photographs of Lorraine O'Grady's *Art Is...* were taken during a performance the artist did at Harlem's African American Day Parade. This is important context because the artist and her friends held gold frames around audience members as if they were an artwork.

When. Share any relevant information about when an artwork was created.

- For example, the film *Semiotics of the Kitchen* by Martha Rosler was created in 1975. This is important context because the film is part of the feminist art movement and focuses on the artist's frustration with gender roles at the time it was created.

How. Share any relevant information about the process the artist used to create their artwork.

- For example, in Tseng Kwong Chi's *East Meets West* series, the artist dressed up in a Mao suit and took self-portraits at important landmarks around the world. This is important context because the artist describes how people saw him wearing the suit and assumed he was an important political figure. Tseng was treated differently and gained access to places and events he might not have otherwise.

Why. This section brings together all of the above context sections and provides information about why the artist created their artwork and why they made the artistic choices they did.

Activity. Activities create opportunities for participants to connect to the artwork in different ways and can support different learning styles. They can be used at any point during an art talk and can vary in length and materials. A list of activities that can be used for each of the art talk components can be found below.

Observation Activities

- *Thirty-second search.* Have participants stand with their backs facing the artwork. Then have them turn around for five seconds and look at the artwork. After the five seconds are up, have them turn around, and ask them what they noticed. Repeat this process for fifteen seconds and then again for thirty seconds.
- *Jump inside.* Invite participants to imagine that they could jump inside this artwork—what else might you see? What would you hear? Smell? Taste? How would you feel?
- *Word poems.* Hand out a long strip of paper to each student and ask them to write down one word they would use to describe the artwork. Then have participants get into groups of three or four and have them pass their paper to the person to their left. Now ask them to read the word they just received and write a sentence or phrase about the artwork using that word. Then have the group read their sentences to each other and arrange them into a poem. Have each group share their poem with the large group.
- *Back-to-back.* Have two participants sit back-to-back, one facing the artwork and the other facing away from the artwork. The participant facing the artwork describes what they see to the participant facing away from the artwork. Then the participant facing away from the artwork draws what the artwork could look like based on their partner's descriptions.

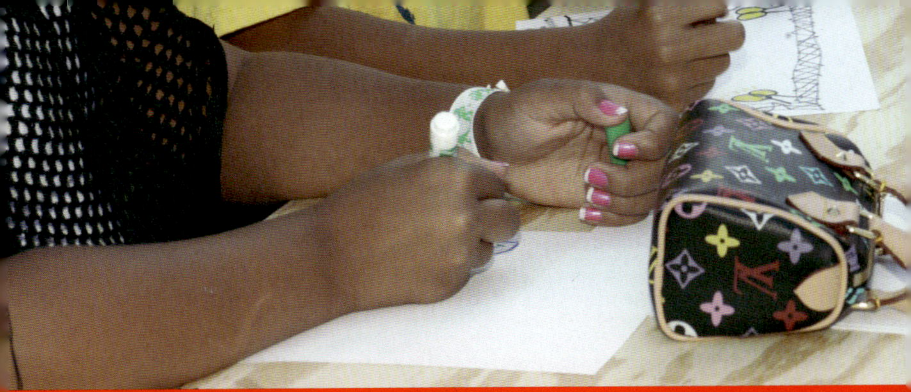

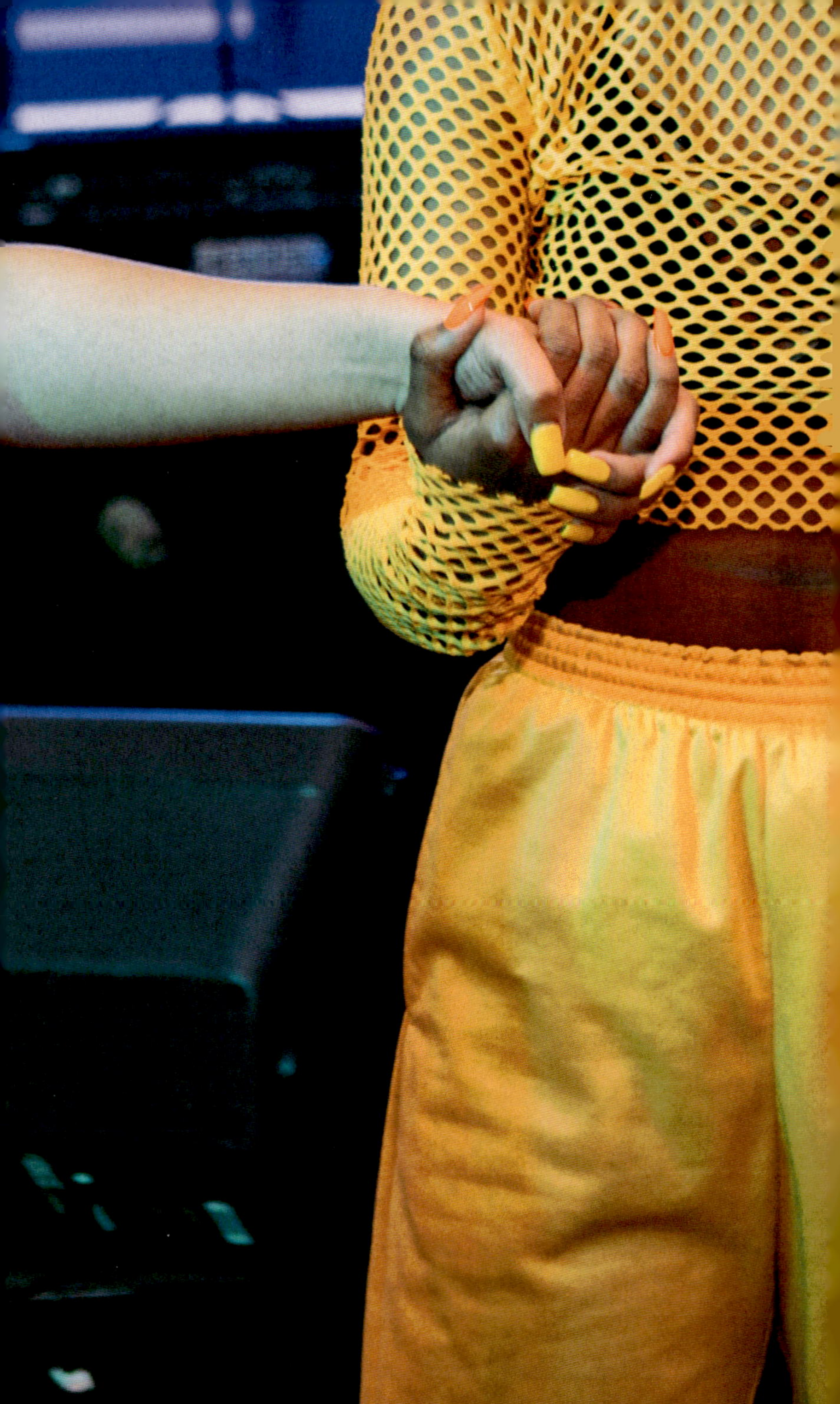

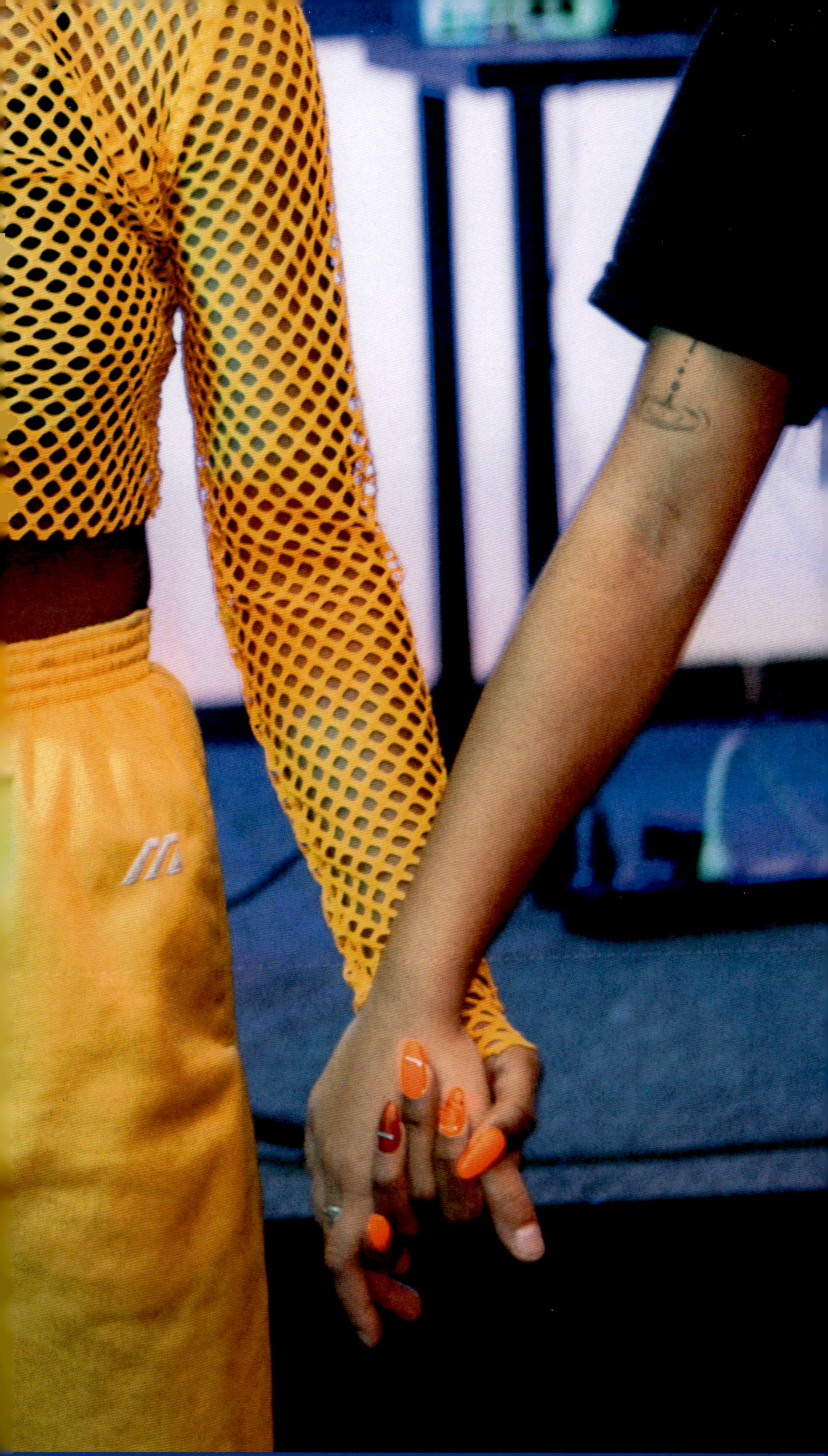

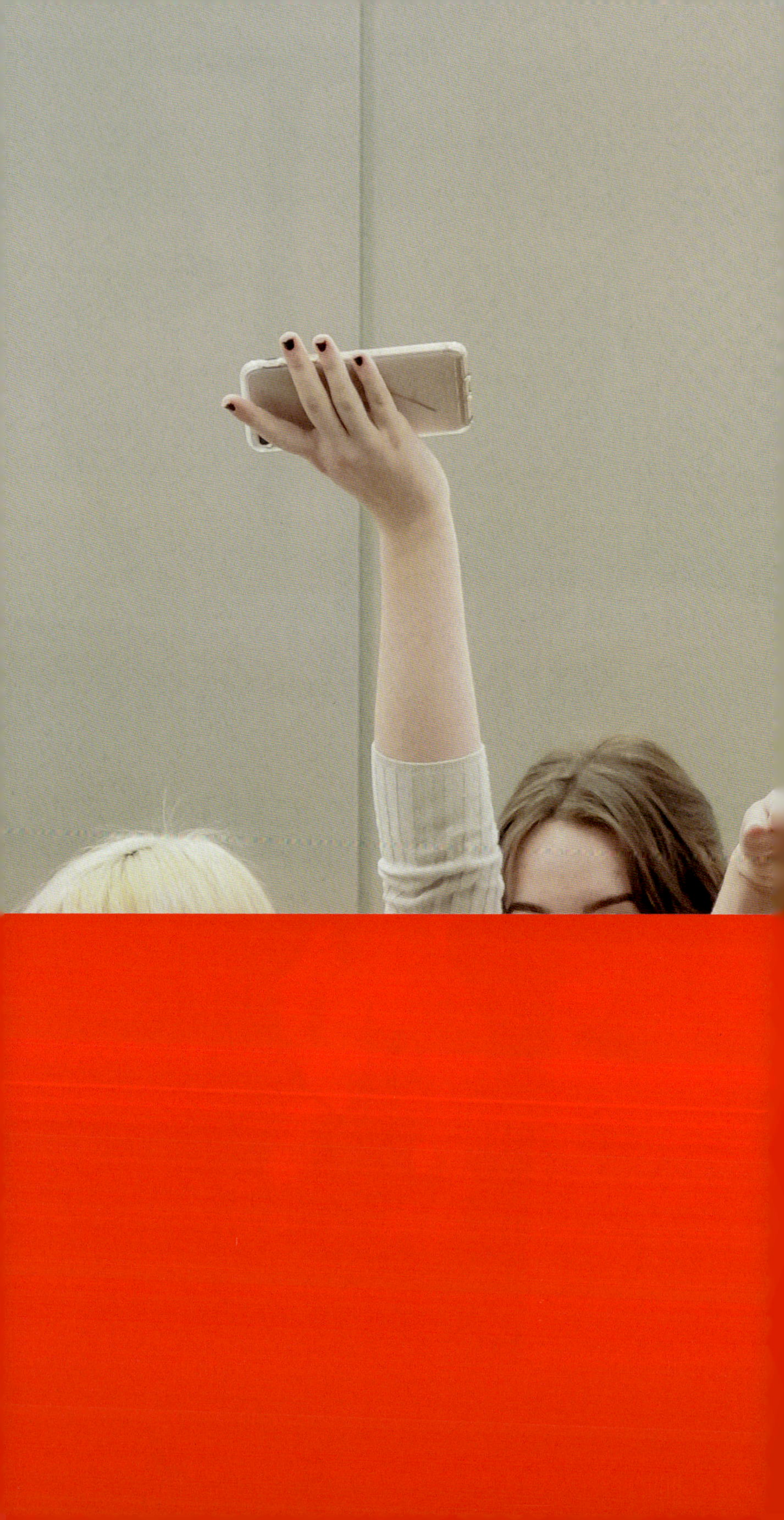

Considering Context Activities

- *Research.* Invite participants to come up with a question they have about the artwork. Then ask them to conduct some short research to try to answer their question. Participants can research the artwork by reading the didactic, looking at the artist's or museum's website, or reading preprinted articles about the artwork.
- *Artist quote or video.* Hearing directly from the artist can provide some helpful contextual information. Share a quote by the artist or a video of the artist working in their studio or talking about their work. Then discuss what stood out in the video or quote.
- *Investigate.* After sharing a sentence or two about the context of the artwork, ask students to take on the role of art investigators and search for a few clues in the artwork that support the context information just given. If they are struggling to find any evidence in the artwork, have participants sketch out what they would add to the artwork to make that message or idea stronger.
- *Drawing activity.* If the artist uses a specific process for creating their artwork, like painting from memory or only using horizontal lines, try creating a drawing exploring the same process the artist uses. Then reflect on how it felt to try out that process.

Discussion Question Activities

- *Think-pair-share.* Ask participants to think about their responses to a discussion question on their own for a minute. Then have them pair up with a partner and share their response. Finally, have the participants share their responses with the entire group.
- *Journaling.* Ask students to respond to a discussion question by writing or sketching their responses on a piece of paper. Then have volunteers share their responses with the group.
- *Agreement cards.* Hand out a set of cards to each participant, one green and one red. While the discussion is happening, ask students to hold up the green card if they hear something they agree with or the red card if they hear something they disagree with. Ask students to expand on their thoughts as needed.
- *Number calling.* Have participants break up into groups of

three and assign each participant a number one through three. Then give the students a discussion question and a couple of minutes to discuss the question in their group. Call out one number and have the participants assigned to that number share a summary of what the group discussed.
- *Concentric circles.* Have participants form two concentric circles. One circle should be facing inward and one facing outward so that each participant faces another. Ask a discussion question and have the pairs of participants discuss their answers with each other. Then ask the outside circle to rotate, so everyone has a new partner. Repeat the same discussion question or ask a new one.

Evaluation Activities

- *Score cards.* Give participants a set of ten note cards with the numbers one through ten written on the cards. One number should be written on each card. Then ask students to give the artwork a rating by holding up a number card—one being the lowest and ten being the highest. Discuss why participants rated the artwork the way they did.
- *Emoji sentence.* Ask participants to evaluate an artwork using only emojis. Encourage them to use at least five different emojis to share their thoughts about the artwork.
- *Venn diagram.* Hand out a Venn diagram worksheet to each student, or ask them to draw a Venn diagram on a piece of paper. Ask them to write or draw things they like about the artwork in one circle. In the other circle, ask them to write or draw things they don't like about the artwork. If they think of something they like and dislike for different reasons, have them put it in the center. Then ask participants to share some main ideas from their Venn diagram.
- *3-2-1.* Have students pair up with a partner or work in small groups. Ask them to share three things they like or dislike about the artwork and why, two things they learned about the artist or artwork, and one question they still have about the artwork.

Evaluation. Evaluation is where participants form an opinion about the artwork informed by their observations, discussions, and understanding of the artwork's context. The evaluation component should be used at the end of the art talk so that participants have as much information as possible. The facilitator should clarify that it is okay if participants do not like the artwork; they should just work on explaining why they like or do not like something. Some examples of questions used during the evaluation component are listed below.

- Do you like this artwork? Why or why not?
- Has your opinion changed at all since you first saw this artwork? Why?
- What artwork did you connect with the most today? Why?
- What is a question you still have about any of the artwork we looked at today?

Art Talk Example 1

Artwork. Kerry James Marshall, *Gulf Stream*, 2003.

Observations. This artwork is a painting by an artist named Kerry James Marshall. Let us start by making some observations or listing what we see when we look at the artwork.

- What do you notice?
- What does this artwork remind you of?
- What questions do you have about this artwork?

Context. Here is a photograph of the artist who created this painting. His name is Kerry James Marshall, and he is interested in how Black people have been represented in art history. According to a 2019 study by Williams College, 85 percent of the works in the collections of all major US museums are by white artists.[2] For most museums, less than 3 percent of their collection is by Black artists. This means museums have not been collecting as many artworks by Black artists as white artists, which is a big problem and something Kerry James Marshall

---

2 Chad M. Topaz et al., "Diversity of Artists in Major US Museums," *PLOS ONE* 14, no. 3 (March 20, 2019), https://doi.org/10.1371/journal.pone.0212852; Hakim Bishara, "Artists in 18 Major US Museums Are 85% White and 87% Male, Study Says," *Hyperallergic*, June 3, 2019, https://hyperallergic.com/501999/artists-in-18-major-us-museums-are-85-white-and-87-male-study-says/.

addresses very directly in his artwork. The painting we are looking at together now is one example of this!

Activity. Kerry James Marshall's painting from 2003 is based on a very old painting by a white painter named Winslow Homer from 1899. Let us break up into small groups of three to four and compare and contrast Winslow Homer's painting with Kerry James Marshall's version. I will hand each group a printed version of Winslow Homer's painting and give you all a few minutes to discuss it in your groups.

Discussion questions. Let us come together as a large group and share what you discussed.

- What similarities did you find?
- What differences did you find?
- How would you describe the mood of each painting? Why?
- What stories are being told in each painting? Who is telling those stories?

Context. I will be sharing a couple of quotes that Kerry James Marshall has said in interviews. Hearing directly from an artist can give us a lot of helpful information when we are trying to understand their artwork.

"When you go to an art museum, the thing you are least likely to encounter is a picture of a black person."[3]

"My introduction to art history was like everybody else's. You see an art history book that has works by Rembrandt and Leonardo da Vinci and Michelangelo. Yes, these things are great. But I don't see a reflection of myself in any of these things I'm looking at."[4]

---

[3] Barbara Isenberg, "For Kerry James Marshall, the Mission Is Clear: Bring Portraits of Black Life into Very White Art Museums," *Los Angeles Times*, March 7, 2017, https://www.latimes.com/entertainment/arts/la-et-cm-kerry-james-marshall-20170307-htmlstory.html.

[4] CBS News, "Kerry James Marshall: Depicting the World as He Sees It," *Sunday Morning*, June 4, 2017, https://www.cbsnews.com/news/kerry-james-marshall-depicting-the-world-as-he-sees-it/.

Discussion questions. Let us spend some time unpacking these quotes and the context of this artwork.

- How does this new information change the way you think about this artwork?
- What is your experience learning art history?
- Do you think the way we teach art history will change in the future? Why or why not? What changes would you like to see?
- Why do you think Kerry James Marshall decided to transform Winslow Homer's painting in this way?

Evaluation. Now that we have spent some time observing, discussing, and learning more about this artwork's context, we are prepared to evaluate the artwork.

- What is your overall opinion about this artwork?
- Do you like it? Why or why not?

Art Talk Example 2

Artwork. Martha Rosler, *Semiotics of the Kitchen*, 1975.

Observations. The artwork we will be discussing today is a video. We will spend some time watching the film together and then make some observations about what we are noticing.

- What is your initial reaction to this film? Do you like it right away? Why?
- What is happening in this film?
- How would you describe the mood of this film? Why?

Context. Let us learn a little more about this artwork and the artist who created it. This work was performed for the camera in 1975 and shows the artist Martha Rosler standing in a strangely bare kitchen surrounded by kitchen appliances and utensils. She moves through the alphabet and assigns each letter to a common hand tool in the domestic kitchen space, which has often been designated as a space for women. Rosler pokes fun at these gendered spaces and demonstrates each tool in an intense, sharp manner, reflecting her frustration with oppressive women's roles.

Discussion questions. Let us think about that information a little more deeply and start defining some of these words that are coming up.

- How do you define gender?
- What comes to mind when you think about gender roles?
- This film [video] was created in 1975, almost fifty years ago! Do you think gender roles were different when this film was created? How so?
- How might they change in the future?

Context. The title of this artwork is *Semiotics of the Kitchen*. Semiotics means the study of signs and symbols and how they are interpreted. In this performance, Martha Rosler exaggerates the movements one might typically make when using these tools. Exaggeration converts each movement into an almost robotic image of the performer and the tool. Rosler was responding to the cooking shows that were becoming common on TV in the 1960s and 1970s, aimed mostly at women, teaching them how to become good housewives based on their kitchen skills.

Discussion questions. Let us discuss that information a bit more.

- We learned that Rosler parodies, or pokes fun at, cooking shows from the 1960s and '70s. Why do you think she does that?
- How do you think Martha Rosler felt about gender roles? What do you see in the artwork that makes you say that?

Activity. Rosler uses movement and body language in this film to express her frustration. Based on that idea, we will play a quick game similar to charades. We will start by writing down an emotion on a slip of paper. For example, you could write down *excited*, *skeptical*, or *terrified*.

I will collect all the paper slips and put them into a bag. Now think about an activity you are used to doing daily. It could be walking your dog, brushing your teeth, or reading a book. Once you have your activity, draw an emotion card from the bag without showing anyone. Then act out your activity but using the emotion on your card. For example, you might have to act out brushing your teeth but be very skeptical about it. The rest of the group will try to guess what activity and emotion you have.

Discussion questions. Let us reflect on that experience.

- How did it feel to act out something you do every day, but in a different way?
- How else do artists express emotions in their artwork?

Evaluation. Now that we have spent some time discussing this artwork, let us evaluate it.

- What is your overall opinion about this artwork? Why?
- Has your reaction changed at all since we first watched it? How so?

2.2.2. ART CHOPPED

Sean J. Patrick Carney, Dia Teens

> **Bio.** Sean J. Patrick Carney (born in 1982 in Michigan) is a writer in Berkeley, California. He is a frequent contributor to *Artforum* and *Art in America*, and his writing has also appeared in *Vice*, *High Country News*, Glasstire, Artnet News, and *Foundations*.

Introduction

> Read to all participants: Four artists. Three exhibition models. Only one chance to win.
>
> The challenge: create a fantastic body of work from the mystery art supplies hidden in these boxes before time runs out. Our distinguished panel of judges will critique the contestants' work, and one by one, they must face the dreaded chopping block. Who will win the title of Art Chopped Champion, and who will be chopped?

Art Chopped is a simple concept: take the format of the Food Network cooking competition show *Chopped*, in which contestants are given identical boxes of ingredients over three rounds—appetizer, entrée, and dessert—and they compete to make the best dishes. Today, we substitute art supplies for groceries.

Background

Sean J. Patrick Carney first staged Art Chopped at New Release Gallery in New York City in the summer of 2015. Later that fall, he reimagined Art Chopped as a class at the Bruce High Quality Foundation University, culminating in a ridiculous public finale at Art Basel Miami Beach. Since then, Art Chopped has taken place in all kinds of places, and it is clear that teens, in particular, innately understand the performative, persona-based satire that makes the game critically funny.

Activity

Title. Art Chopped
Written by. Sean J. Patrick Carney
Learning objectives. Have fun and build community. Be silly, irreverent, and un-precious with art-making.

Materials and setup

Art supply "pantry" that artists can use at all times; your pantry may include paper, tape, scissors, markers, wire, paint, brushes, string, scrap wood, and so on. These can be leftover materials from a previous project, items from a coworker's desk, or products selected from the local dollar store.

Nine mystery boxes in total, prepacked with supplies unique to each round; the mystery boxes within each round must be identical to each other, organized in this fashion:

- *Round 1.* Four boxes, each with four oddball art supplies; boxes must be identical
- *Round 2.* Three boxes, each with four oddball art supplies; boxes must be identical
- *Round 3.* Two boxes, each with four oddball art supplies; boxes must be identical

Five tables or surfaces: four tables for artists; one table for judges / presentation of work.

Roles

- *One host.* A teen, artist educator, or staff person.
- *One to three judges.* Teen program participants, visiting artists, curators, instructors, alumni of the program, etc.
- *Four artist competitors.* Individuals or teams.
- *Audience.* The rest of the group.

Run of show, led by the host

Introduction to the competition. The three rounds on *Chopped* are appetizers, main course, and dessert. In Art Chopped, the rounds are as follows.

1. *Group Show.* You are contributing a single artwork to a show with many other artists.
2. *Solo Exhibition.* You are showing several works of art in a show that features only you.
3. *Career Retrospective.* You are being celebrated with an extensive show featuring work from throughout your career, including your newest work and perhaps your most ambitious work.

Introduction to the competitors. Introduce each artist—or team of artists—to the audience.

Note: Ask teen competitors to jot down a few exaggerated or fictionalized bullet points about themselves beforehand for their introductions.

The rules of the game. At the start of each round, prompt each artist to simultaneously unpack their mystery art supplies from the boxes.

Each round is only five minutes long! As the competitors work, periodically ask them why they compete in Art Chopped.

Note: Hamming it up is, of course, encouraged. The time limitation encourages the teens to lose themselves in the game; there is no time to overthink art-making in Art Chopped, and what results is, frequently, incredible work.

Ending a round. At the end of each round, invite the artists to present their work to a panel of judges. The judges may ask the competitors pointed, challenging questions.

Note: Encourage artists to improvise their five-minute artwork's explanations—the more convoluted, the better! Everyone intuitively starts to perform various reality-TV and art-world archetypes.

After viewing everyone's artwork, excuse the artists from the room. The judges then discuss the artworks in the context of a given round's exhibition model loudly enough for the audience (and maybe the artists) to hear. Judges may consider aesthetics, technical proficiency, and conceptual rigor.

The judges then confer quietly, deciding whom to chop, and secretly share their decision with the host.

Invite the artists back into the room and announce who is chopped. The judges provide the artist with a brief explanation, and then the game moves into the next round. The entire game lasts three rounds.

Ending the game. At the end of the Career Retrospective round, one of the two remaining artists is crowned Art Chopped Champion, a distinction which, the host should point out, is wholly meaningless.

2.2.3. SENSORIUM WORKSHOP

Savannah Knoop, Dia Teens

Bio. Savannah Knoop is a NY-based artist, writer, and educator; they have exhibited their work and performed at venues such as the Whitney, MoMA, the ICA Philly, and the Leslie-Lohman Museum. In 2007, they published their memoir, *Girl Boy Girl: How I Became JT LeRoy* (Seven Stories Press), and adapted it into a screenplay, coproducing the resulting feature-length film, *JT LeRoy*, with director Justin Kelly (Universal Pictures, 2019), starring Kristen Stewart and Laura Dern.

"What would I be doing with my time and energy if I made decisions based on a feeling of…yes?"[1]

Activity

Title. Sensorium Workshop
Written by. Savannah Knoop
Learning goals. Creating boundaries creates a focus, it makes specific parameters clear around what you are feeling, and how; what you like and do not like, want and do not want. If it is a yes, explore the yes further. If it is a no, that leaves room for a yes elsewhere.
Materials. Journals, dark chocolate, lemons, Szechuan peppercorns, 50-kHz-frequency sound composition, laptop or phone (and additional speaker, if desired), sandpaper, smooth fabric squares.
Location. Program space, ideally with access to a kitchen.

---

1 adrienne maree brown, *Pleasure Activism: The Politics of Feeling Good* (Chico; Edinburgh: AK Press, 2019), 23.

Instructions

- Test the audio, and prepare and arrange the materials before the workshop. Make adjustments to the edible materials based on any allergies or food sensitivities in the groups.
- To start, consider that this is a collective sensorial act.
- Describe the activity to the group and offer the opportunity to opt out of anything that pushes past sensory safety.
- Throughout the workshop, all group members should use note-taking to try to document and deconstruct the experience. In your notes, make columns for the different movements of the workshop. Especially take note of the pros and cons of what you discover while participating or not participating.

Lead participants through these sensory experiences.

A plate of cut lemon wedges.

1. Squeeze your nose with your fingertips; with your other hand suck on a lemon. Take notes. Describe the flavor profile, where you feel the sensation, and any thoughts or desires to act after it.
2. Release your nose. Describe the difference in sensation; any thoughts or desires that come to mind after the action.

A plate of dark chocolate and Szechuan peppercorns.

3. Let a piece of dark chocolate melt on your tongue along with a Szechuan peppercorn. Roll it around so that the flavors mingle and melt together. Take notes of the flavor profile and where you feel it in your body.

50-kHz sound wave turned on.

4. While playing the 50-kHz sound wave piece, describe what you feel. How do the sensations change? Where do you feel this vibration in your body?

Cut sandpaper squares.

5. While rolling the chocolate around your mouth, rub your fingers across a piece of sandpaper. Take notes on the sensation.

Smooth silk swatches.

6. Roll your fingers along a smooth piece of fabric. How does the taste change? Discuss what you experienced.
7. Brainstorm a sensorial tour you would like to have the group try out.

Considerations and questions for discussion.

- What did you gain while participating or not participating? Please share which parts were which and why.
- What did you notice about the relationship between senses being accentuated and tamped down?
- What boundaries were established around what senses?
- What specific words, diagrams, and illustrations came up for you?
- What connections can you draw between adjectives of textures, taste, and smell? Do you find that you associate smoothness with sweetness, bitterness with roughness, and so on?
- Where in your body do you feel these experiments beyond the sense that is being activated (or deactivated)?
- Do any emotions come up while moving through these exercises?
- Side question: During the first days of the pandemic, were there certain sensations that became more accentuated? Colors, sounds, textures, and so on?

2.2.4. STUDIO SYSTEMS

Andreas Laszlo Konrath, Dia Teens

> **Bio.** Andreas Laszlo Konrath is a photographer and artist educator who utilizes the zine format as a vehicle for many projects, citing community building, exchange, and collaboration as key motivators. Andreas' zines are archived in collections at the ICP, the Getty Research Institute, the Metropolitan Museum of Art Library, the MoMA Library, and the Yale University Library. Andreas has organized zine workshops for Fondation Louis Vuitton, Gavin Brown's enterprise, Red Hook Community Justice Center, and Tasweer Photo Festival Qatar. Andreas cofounded SHRIMP ZINE, a free web tool that allows users to create zines on their smartphones, bringing a new creative and collaborative access point to digital natives.

Introduction

The following exercises were introduced as participatory practices—some daily, some weekly, all ongoing—that acted as throughlines for a summer intensive at Dia Beacon, during which teens met four days a week for five weeks. Collectively, the exercises invited us to consider how our creative work can not only reflect ourselves, our identities, our desires, and our viewpoints but also how it could be considered an invitation—a doorway—for collaboration, connection, and curiosity.[1]

Activity 1

Signs of Love Group Collage

Inspired by Ree Morton's 1976 complex visual orchestration *Signs of Love*,[2] for the duration of the summer, we shall co-create an ever-expanding wall collage as an open-ended proposition, expressing our feelings or thoughts on any given day for one another and the group. Part theatrical presentation, part individual/group stream of consciousness, this wall collage will encapsulate our time together by signaling love for ourselves and one another.

We can also reference Lorraine O'Grady's *Cutting Out the New York Times*[3] series of twenty-six cutouts or found newspaper poems made by O'Grady on successive Sundays, from June 5 to November 20, 1977, as another way for us to experiment with adhering language to the walls of our studio.

Activity 2

Library Exchange

Throughout the year, we will provide a library exchange where the teens can bring their favorite books they want to share and encourage others to read. We will check in regularly and see if anyone has anything they want to add and ask what they find so special about each book. Additionally, we will ask if anyone has spent time with anyone else's book and how they found the experience, compare notes, and open a discussion about why we like books.

---

1 Excerpted from *On Wandering: Reflecting in the Third Space*.
2 Ree Morton, *Signs of Love*, 1976, installation, acrylic, oil, colored pencil, watercolor, and pastel on nitrocellulose-impregnated canvas, wood, and canvas with felt, Whitney Museum of American Art, New York.
3 Lorraine O'Grady, *Cutting Out the New York Times*, 1977, installation, toner ink on adhesive paper.

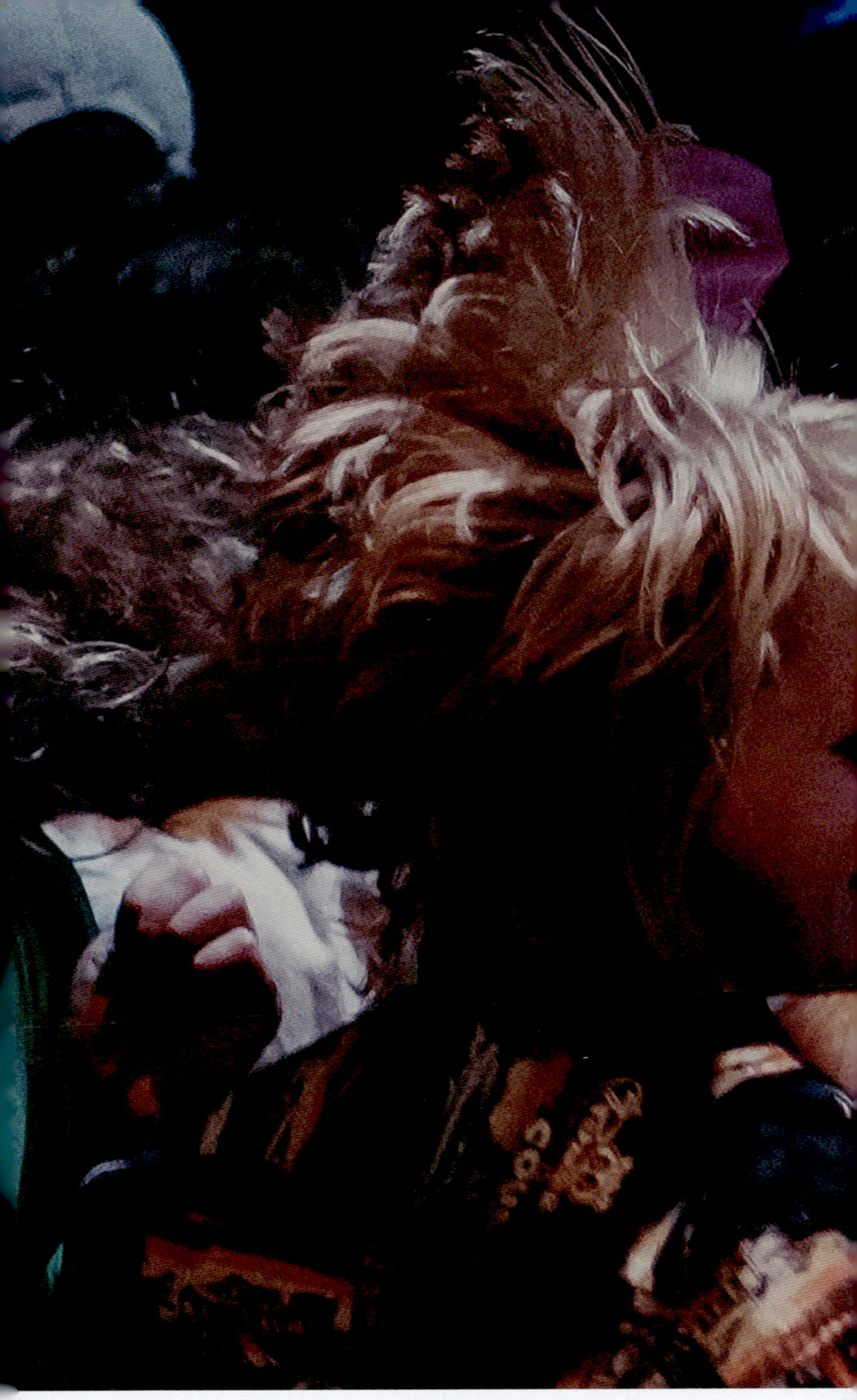

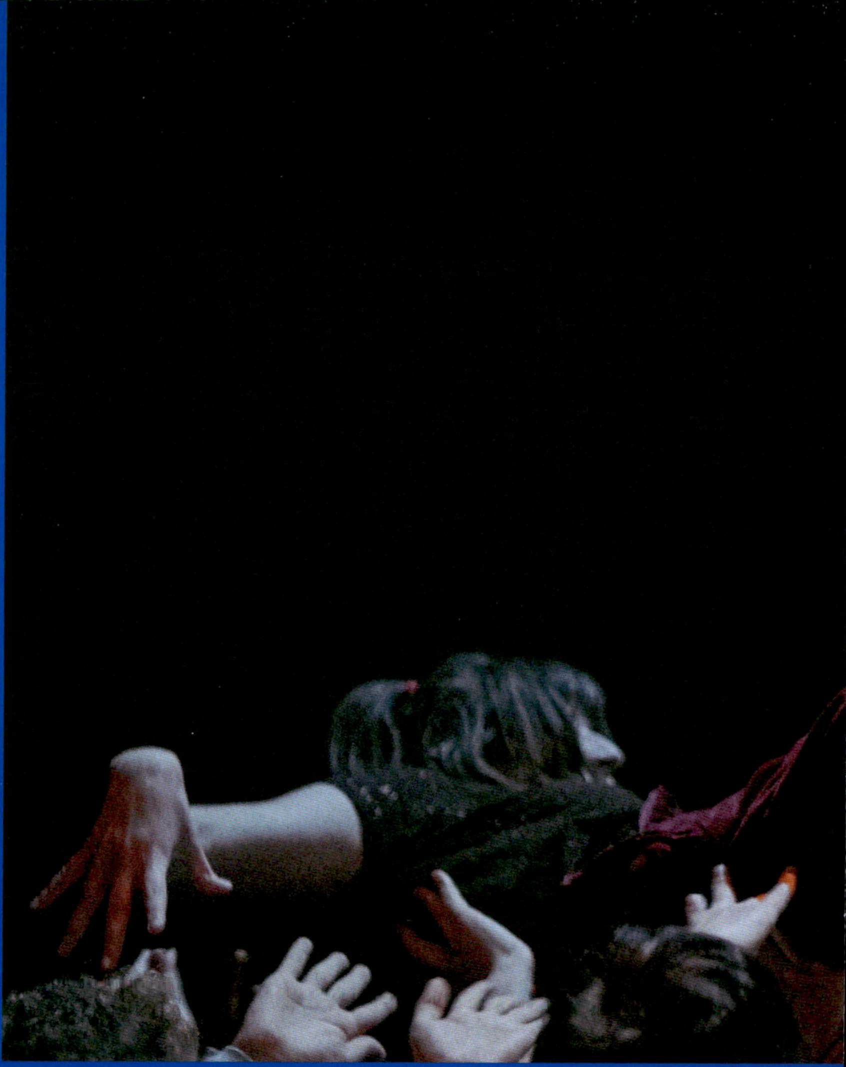

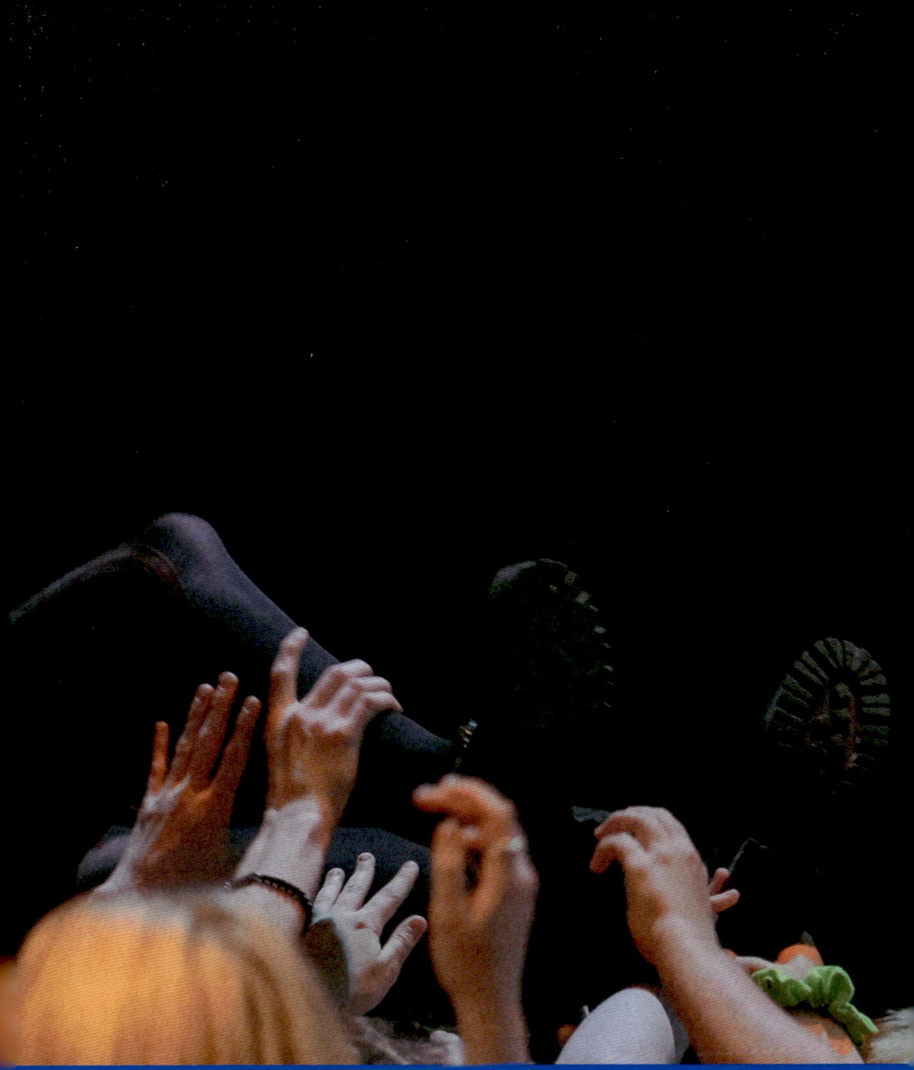

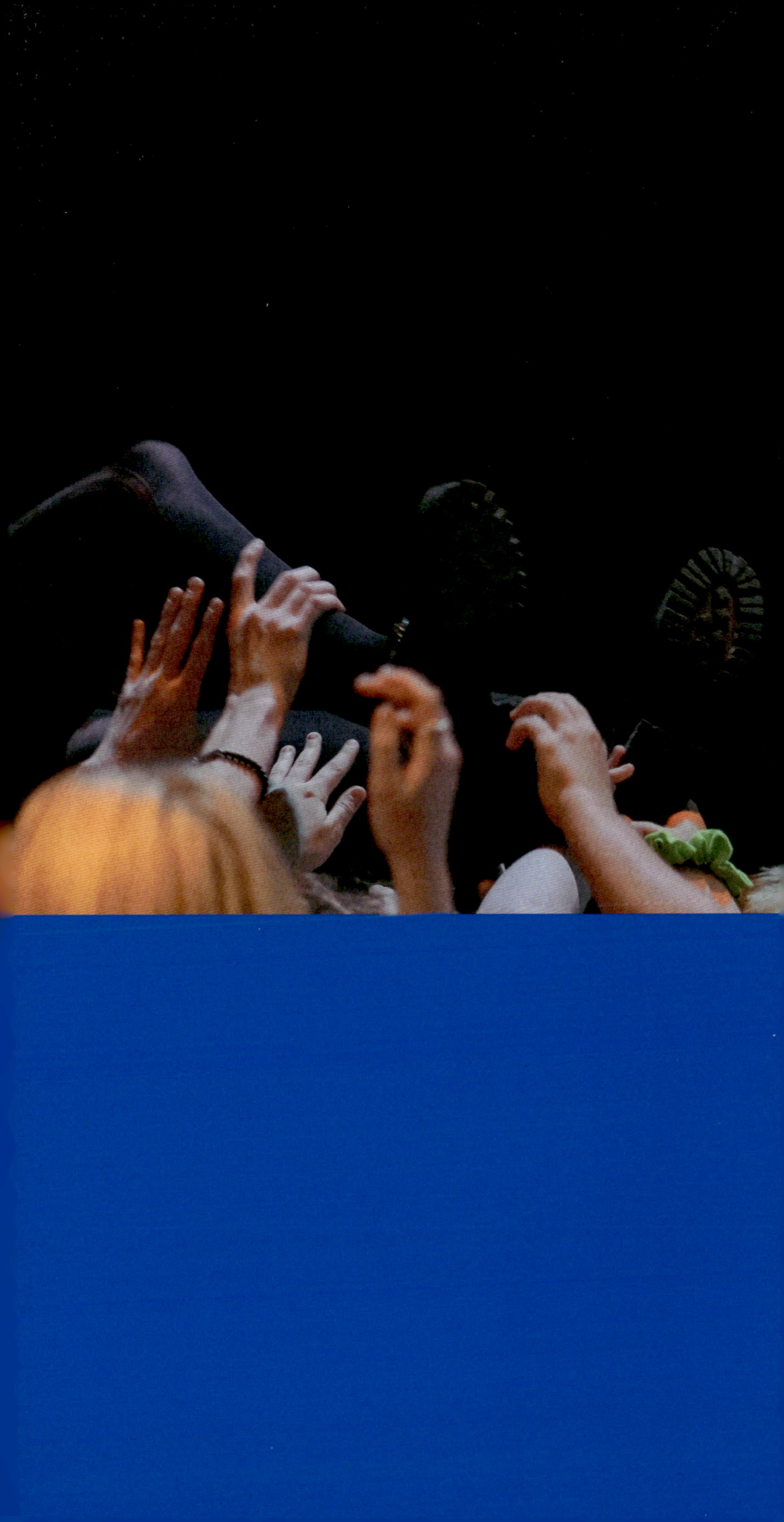

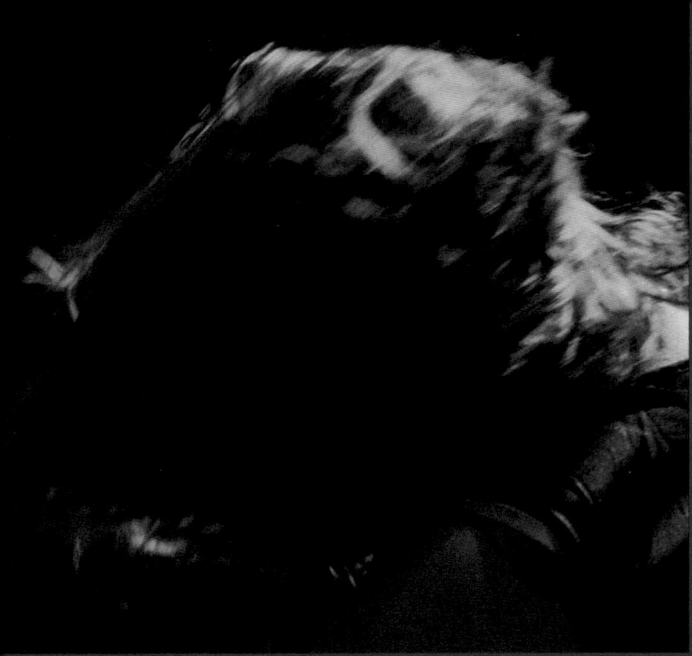

Activity 3

Supper Club/Lunch Rota

Each session, a different small group of teens will take ownership of the day's lunch rota (a rotation of duties), creating a ritual around food and our eating time.[4] Two teens collect the lunches, and two prepare the space and set the lunch vibe—for example, choose the music, set the lighting, make placards with everyone's name, decide where each will be seated, and leave each person a little message or a drawing for that day on their plate. When the food arrives, the host group will set out the lunches and invite the rest of the group to dine together.

Activity 4

Affirmation Cards

Each week the teens will be assigned a partner, and at the end of the week they will give a note to that person describing something that they did that inspired them, that excited them, or that they related to in some way. We will keep track of our affirmation partners by listing names at the beginning of each week on the board and referring back to previous weeks to ensure everyone gets a different partner each time.

---

4 Judy Chicago, *The Dinner Party*, 1974–1979, installation, ceramic, porcelain, textile, Brooklyn Museum.

Activity 5

Pins of Desire

Each week we will set a task of creating button pins for ourselves and each other that encapsulate something that we agree on as a group.[5] This could be a series of words that we think set the tone or vibe for how we feel on those days, or it could be a saying, a political statement, or a poem even. The pins could just be colors, drawings, found images, or something else entirely, as long as the group consensus is that it represents us fully at that moment.

---

5   Daniel Martinez, *Museum Tags: Second Movement (Overture) or Overture con Claque—Overture with Hired Audience Members*, 1993, six offset lithographs on metal museum admission tags.

2.2.5. BODIES AND NATURE, MARBLE AND FRUIT STUDIO PROMPT

Mollie McKinley, Dia Teens

Bio. Mollie McKinley is an interdisciplinary artist whose work translates healing processes through alchemy and phenomenology in nature. She works with salt, glass, neon, photographs on textiles, performance, and text. Her work has been shown at Fridman Gallery, NADA, Pioneer Works, Independent Curators International, the Museum of Arts and Design, Momenta Art, Field Projects, Anthology Film Archives, and others. McKinley holds a BA in photography from Bard College and an MFA in sculpture/dimensional studies from Alfred University.

Activity

Title. Bodies and Nature, Marble and Fruit Studio Prompt
Written by. Mollie McKinley

Learning Goals/Objectives.

- Get out of our heads and into the flow of making with nontraditional materials
- Investigate contemporary artists whose works relate to nature, landscape, performance, and the body
- Engage with the work of other artists and identify new creative forms to incorporate into our own practices and/or develop creative critiques
- Experiment with new and natural materials, ideally locally sourced
- Create works of art that can be photographs of objects, small solo performances, small installations, videos, or other forms
- Build confidence with innovating in the studio as individual artists

Materials. Clay—plasticine, or something softer, rocks or marble, wood, fruits and flowers, string, glue, wire, photographic image

> Educator note / pedagogical challenge: Can we lose the anxious preciousness of uninterrupted studio or making time? Usually, in Dia Teens, we avoid this by having a quick challenge that lasts an hour, so there isn't the time or pressure to make something perfect. Today, we will find a way to get deep into a material by having a full day of studio time with organic materials. We will play with the boundaries of boredom, an important generative space. As young artists, how can we feel permission to make something big or ambitious?

Critical Questions.

> Educator note: These are the driving questions behind this lesson plan. They inform the artist educator's choice making around planning and facilitation, and they may or may not be posed directly to teens during the session.

- What is the relationship between our bodies and nature?
- What is the relationship between nature and gender?
- What is the relationship between nature and dis/ability?
- Why has nature been gendered as feminine? Do we agree? If not, how can we redefine it?
- Is nature nonbinary?
- What is the "augmented body"?
- What implications does it have for the idea of "natural"?
- How have contemporary artists used the land and the organic as subversive material in relation to the body?

Artist Inspirations.

Laura Aguilar
Nairy Baghramian
Roni Horn
Nona Inescu
Lorna Simpson

Instructions.

Warm-up (5–10 minutes)

Writing prompt. When did *my body* show me something unexpected about how I perceive the world? Think about a moment when your ideas or reality shifted in a direct relationship to your body. Maybe you were sick or injured, or you pushed your body to a limit in an athletic pursuit. Maybe it did not happen; feel free to write fictionally and go into sci-fi realms!

Educator note: Asking teens to think about their body—both its potentiality and limitations—might be difficult and triggering for some. For this reason, we introduced this studio prompt later in the year after we had invested time into getting to know each other as individuals and as a group. Teens were encouraged to prioritize their own well-being and artistic interests and to adapt the prompt in any way they wanted. Throughout the session, the artist educator should do one-on-one check-ins with teens to ask how they are doing and pose questions to deepen and potentially complicate the process.

Prompt 1. Artist Fan Club Response Piece (30 minutes)

A selection of printouts of contemporary artists' work, curated in relation to the day's questions and concepts, are shuffled and posted on the board. There are over thirty images in the selection. Each will have the artist's name and the artwork written on the back.

Each teen takes an image or two that interests them and makes a response piece to it. The response piece may use similar forms, colors, and ideas or provoke a kind of movement and/or series of words.

The activity introduces teens to artists in a new way, where they can gravitate toward something intuitively, respond to it, and explore what drew them to the work. It is intended to be more engaging and student driven than a slideshow or lecture.

Prompt 2. Augmentation and Extension (1.5 hours)

Using the organic and man-made materials provided, create something that is an extension of your body. If you use clay, you must also use two other materials in what you make.

Ask yourself the following questions: How can I use objects from nature to assist my mobility? My perception? The way I navigate space? Can some of these materials become tools, garments, or devices? Can a sculpture be performative and not just a motionless object? Is it an object for the present day? Or maybe it is for the future or an alternate reality?

To avoid preciousness, we will discuss in the introduction of this prompt that all of the sculptures will be destroyed at the end of the session. We will photograph each object, but the work must be ephemeral.

2.2.6. AN INCOMPLETE DICTIONARY OF ART IN ACTION

Stephen Kwok, Dia Teens

> **Bio.** Stephen Kwok makes experimental events incorporating sculpture, live performance, digital media, and text into participatory systems. He has exhibited his work at Seoul Museum of Art; Surplus Space, Wuhan; Haus der Kulturen der Welt, Berlin; Center for Performance Research, Brooklyn; Julius Caesar Gallery, Chicago; Contemporary Arts Center, New Orleans; and Lawndale Art Center, Houston, and has participated in programs at Delfina Foundation in London, the Canadian Centre for Architecture in Montreal, and NEW INC in New York. He lives in Brooklyn, teaches design at Brooklyn College, and serves as the Curator of Public Engagement at Dia Art Foundation.

An Incomplete Dictionary of Art in Action is a deck of cards comprising verbs commonly used to respond to "what is this work doing?" The deck is a tool or resource for discussing or facilitating discussions about works of art.

> The deck is incomplete, and each deck has blank cards. On the backside of each card is the definition of the verb.

Activity

Title. An Incomplete Dictionary of Art in Action
Written by. Stephen Kwok
Learning objectives. Practice discussing works of art and the way works of art can function or engage with ideas, space, and people.
Materials. Make your own card deck. Instructions below.

Using the Deck

When viewing an artwork, pull a card from the deck to express what the artwork is doing. How does the artwork utilize this verb? See examples below.

The Deck

1. *Transform.* Metamorphize, change completely.
2. *Reveal.* Make previously unknown information known to others.
3. *Illustrate.* Explain or make clear using visuals.
4. *Translate.* Convert into another language or form.
5. *Express.* Convey an emotion.
6. *Play.* Engage in an activity for enjoyment.
7. *Intervene.* Interrupt, come between to alter the course of events.
8. *Activate.* Initiate, set something in motion.
9. *Punish.* Inflict a penalty upon.
10. *Celebrate.* Acknowledge with a social gathering.
11. *Entertain.* Provide (someone/audience) with amusement or enjoyment.
12. *Memorialize.* Preserve the memory of; honor publicly, commemorate.
13. *Create.* Construct, produce, build.
14. *Hypnotize.* Capture the whole attention of (someone); fascinate.
15. *Investigate.* Carry out a systematic or formal inquiry to discover and examine the facts of.
16. *Advocate.* Publicly support or recommend a particular cause or policy.
17. *Display.* Give a conspicuous demonstration of.
18. *Sit.* Does nothing.
19. *Implicate.* Points at, implies a relationship with.

For Example

"The work plays with color."
"The work activates the neighborhood."
"The work translates the architecture into a sound."
"The work expresses the artist's inner conflicts."
"The work transforms the space."
"The work celebrates queerness."
"The work memorializes civil rights leaders."

PLAY	Engage in an activity for enjoyment.
BORE	Make (someone) feel weary or uninterested by dullness.
REVEAL	Make previously unknown information known (to others).
CELEBRATE	Honor or praise; pay tribute to.

2.2.7. EVALUATION AND VIRTUAL FACILITATION TIPS GRAB BAG

Simona Zappas, Walker Art Center

> **Bio.** Simona Zappas (she/her) is the Youth Programs Manager at the Walker Art Center. In her work she designs and facilitates informal learning opportunities for youth. She collaborates with curatorial staff to bring a learning lens to museum public engagement and a social practice bent on programmatic strategy. Before this, she was the director of WFNU Frogtown, a low-power radio station in Saint Paul. Simona holds a BA with honors from Macalester College and a master of education from the University of Minnesota. Simona sits on the Saint Paul Neighborhood Network board and volunteers at Planned Parenthood as an abortion doula.

Introduction

Evaluation. Evaluation can feel stressful at times. When writing grant reports or developing data for presentations on our programs, it often comes into play in museum teen programs. Because of this, evaluation might feel removed from our work or something you do at the end of a program. I am here to promote and celebrate evaluation as one of the best tools to grow as facilitators and to offer free ways to do it.

Some considerations to reimagine your relationship with evaluation.

1. Define success and its measures while remembering that success is a moving target. To zoom out, evaluation is measuring something's success against a certain set of predetermined criteria. So, to evaluate something, we need to understand what we mean when we say something is successful. Start from the get-go by defining what success means for a certain project by considering the context and stakeholders. Different stakeholders will have different measurements and different contexts. Ensure you recognize all stakeholders (the youth, funders, facilitators, coworkers, families, etc.).

For example, the Walker Art Center Teen Arts Council (WACTAC) members, who attend the program, will have a very different vision of what makes a successful event versus the officer from the granting foundation that funded it—both measurements are valuable. There can be many definitions and measurements of success, but it is essential to recognize that they will vary between stakeholders. As we learn from programs, what we measure and how we do it will continue to change. Evaluation is a means to know how to apply change and better use our resources; dynamism in our definition can be a sign of success. Evaluation never decreases success; it only shows how things are growing.

2. Evaluation is most meaningful when you build it in as a regular practice. Saving all evaluations for the end of a fiscal year or a report deadline does not give you much time to act on what you can learn from the evaluation. Suppose you need to track specific data for reports. I suggest that you schedule regular times for yourself to keep up with it. If this is not as much of a concern for you, build in meaningful reflection time. This might mean scheduling meetings with colleagues to hear how projects go, sitting down and writing to reflect on past meetings with teens, or building it into your meetings with the teens with simple activities.

3. Here are some of my favorite ways to do this:

- Keep a document that's a short log of each WACTAC meeting. As I pack up my things at the end of a session, I like to write a short paragraph of what we did, things that went well, or things that didn't. Consider it like a diary or field notes.[1] It is a nice work/life boundary tool as well because it can feel like you are unpacking your day before heading home.
- Ask the teens at the end of meetings to give a thumbs-up or thumbs-down on what they thought of the meeting or do a one-word checkout. For more nuanced information, ask for their rose (something that went well), bud (something they are excited about), and thorn (something that did not go well) during the meeting. That offhand data is excellent for planning the next session. In WACTAC,

---

1 For more information on fieldnotes and how to write them, see Robert M. Emerson, Rachel I. Fretz, and Linda L. Shaw, *Writing Ethnographic Fieldnotes*, 2nd ed. (Chicago: University of Chicago Press, 2011).

we do a big midyear evaluative conversation where we put up a piece of butcher paper and ask the teens to write/draw what we have learned so far, how we got there, and remaining questions. Try this out and use this information to inform the second half of the year.
- Give your teens regular surveys. Use the same survey each time and make it clear who will review the data and its use. In WACTAC, the data is used for facilitator feedback and grant reports. Be clear with teens on what grants are but clarify that their feedback will not jeopardize funding. When writing your questions, remember the definition of the success you and the other stakeholders want to learn about, the measurements, and who the stakeholders are—are they the teens? You? Your supervisor? The funders? Consider how you are sharing it too. Will it be more beneficial to have numbers or quotes for your stakeholders? Will this be information you would like to share with the teens? Should it be anonymous? In WACTAC, each survey question ties back to a specific learning goal or outcome or asks for direct feedback on specific projects.
- It's important to remember that evaluation is the best tool for improving your performance as a facilitator— it is measurable feedback! You can ask a colleague to observe a meeting if you want to get really intense about self-evaluation. Give the teens a heads-up and let them know you are the one being observed, not them. Alternatively, you can (with permission from the teens and clear communication of its use) video record the session and review it to see moments where you think learning happened.
- If you plan an event with your teens, I recommend building in evaluation from the get-go. Start your initial planning discussing with the teens to determine how they're defining a successful event and how they'll know it. In WACTAC, the teens have developed some of their own tools for evaluation. One year, they set a goal of wanting to learn more about the teens who came to our Teen Takeover event and designed an activity where attendees could use a piece of yarn to wrap around their answers to questions about their identity, like the zip code they live in, grade, and favorite subject in school. The activity could show us overall trends (a lot of people at Teen Takeover love art class) or individual snapshots

(a ninth grader from 55407 who likes science class). At the same Teen Takeover, the teens wanted to encourage folks to talk to new people, so they designed an activity where teens could fill out a form describing themselves. Folks were given a form to fill out upon entry, handed a filled-out form, and tasked to find the person who wrote it. Completed matches could be turned in for a special swag item. The returned forms gave us a sense of how many folks talked to each other. Evaluation does not need to be dry! Teens are great at designing participatory approaches to collect data, and it is essential to support them in finding the information they care about because it is another way for them to take ownership of the event.

My final note on evaluation is that it is only as meaningful as it is applied. Take what you learn to heart and consider where and how you can apply it. Some things can be immediate; some require strategic, structural, and long-term planning. If you get negative feedback, know that you can only go up from there. As I said, evaluation is only as meaningful as it is applied.

Virtual. Virtual programming is now an expected and accepted part of museum teen programs. Typically it is used as a pivot for health and safety due to the COVID-19 pandemic. Alternatively, it can be a deliberate choice for access due to transportation and distance barriers when done to leverage the benefits and setbacks of platforms like Zoom or Google Meet. Virtual programming can be as effective as in-person programming. Here are a few tips and suggestions to help cultivate that impact:

1. *Consider the space teens are meeting in.* It is safe to assume that most teens will be joining virtual programming from home, a space with a different meaning to each person. Being at home can blatantly lay out folks' material and economic conditions, which can be vulnerable for everyone. Many teen councils are designed to bring together a diverse group of teens, including socioeconomic diversity. In your group, you may have teens joining the virtual program in a space with visible markers of wealth or lack thereof. Consider that everyone will have different levels of comfort regarding their space. I recommend avoiding show-and-tell type games, encouraging cameras only for conversation/engagement, but still leaving them optional. Beyond what is on the screen of someone's home, teens may share devices, have spotty

internet, care for siblings, or have a lot of activity going on at home. Communicate an acceptance of that from the start of each meeting by saying, "Let us remember to be patient that being at home might mean Wi-Fi going out, pets and siblings joining us, or interruptions. That is all okay with me; please give us a heads-up in the chat if you can, if you need to step out for a minute."

2. *Be mindful of pronouns.* Thinking back to the last point, we do not always know many details about home situations for teens, and one thing that may be different about home versus in-person programming is the name and pronouns teens feel comfortable with and prefer using. When virtual in WACTAC, we (the facilitators) always encourage the teens to put their preferred name and pronouns in their Zoom (the platform we use) name. We always direct the teens to do this at the beginning of the meeting and always give instructions for desktops, tablets, and phones (another tip—always differentiate for the range of devices teens might be using). Some teens might use a different name or pronoun at home than in WACTAC. When pivoting to virtual, I often drop in an open invitation to teens to signal that we will build intentionality around their wants and needs to accommodate this difference in use. Simply sharing at the beginning of a meeting (either verbally or in the chat), or if you have a group chat or weekly email, something like "If you would like me to refer to you differently in virtual meetings, please let me know" or "Please put the name you would like us to use in your Zoom name" can open the door for youth. Being intentional with how you share this invitation is essential because opening it can create anxiety about being outed for some teens. If teens use different pronouns, just refer to them by their name; if teens use a different name, ask them what they are comfortable being called. Ask the teen how they would like this shared with the other group members.

3. *Use breakout rooms.* One thing that can be lost moving from in-person meetings to virtual is unfacilitated time for teens to interact with each other. Many video conference platforms have great breakout-room options where the teens can spend time together in smaller groups. If you open breakout rooms, always give them clear instructions on the task at hand. Bounce between them. Even though the goal is adult-free time, it can still be good to check in to ensure there is not any conflict. Sometimes a way to prevent this is to provide a low-stakes activity with simple instructions. Virtual can

feel awkward for some, and a complex activity can be frustrating without the facilitator answering questions. Give sufficient group time because some internet connections may make it harder to join them.
4. *Incorporate a tech survey.* If you may be doing some virtual meetings during your program, consider adding a tech survey to your onboarding paperwork.[2] This lets you know what technology, Wi-Fi access, and devices teens have access to before they need it. Gathering this information at the onset of your program year allows you to plan.
5. *Provide hot spots and devices.* If you can, designate program funds or arrange with your team to provide devices or purchase hot spots or Wi-Fi extenders for teens. Many teens do not have devices or reliable internet at home. If they need this to participate, it should not be a barrier to entry. In WACTAC, we lend teens iPads for the year with permission locks from our IT department so they cannot download apps. The teens are welcome to use them for WACTAC work and simply need to return them at the end of the year. We ask them to sign the usage and return agreement. If needed, we will purchase Wi-Fi hot spots or boosters for teens that they can keep. No proof of need is required.
6. *Use the chat!* I will be real with you. After returning from a year of virtual programming to back in person for WACTAC, I have missed the chat every day. The chat is an incredible tool that I used for a variety of things:

- Private messages to check in with teens if something felt off. It is a great, quick de-escalation tool. I also used it to make pivots and plans, and to check in with my cofacilitator on the fly.
- Anytime we gave directions, asked questions, or shared useful information, we could put it in the chat.
- Links! For a WACTAC meeting, we often mention artists, events, programs, and more. With the chat, we could seamlessly add them into the conversation!
- Jokes! Side conversations! Questions! The WACTAC chat was always lit. Encourage this kind of usage by modeling it.

---

[2] See 1.1.2. Walker Art Center Teen Arts Council (WACTAC) 2022–2023 Onboarding Materials on page 162.

7. *Variation.* Some tips might feel like reminders after working through the pandemic, but I cannot stress enough the importance of varying content and keeping up the pace when virtual. In WACTAC, we shortened the meetings when we first pivoted to virtual to accommodate for some of the monotony of meeting online (remember, teens may be coming from an entire virtual school day) and found that, without being in person, we gained back a lot of time that was usually taken up by transitions and side conversations. Keep the content flowing by adding lots of little components to the meetings. Find ways to make things interactive (polls, Jamboards, games, etc.). Remember that it can be more challenging for folks to pay attention online, so if you have content that is building weekly, find ways to make it memorable through interaction or build in time to recap.

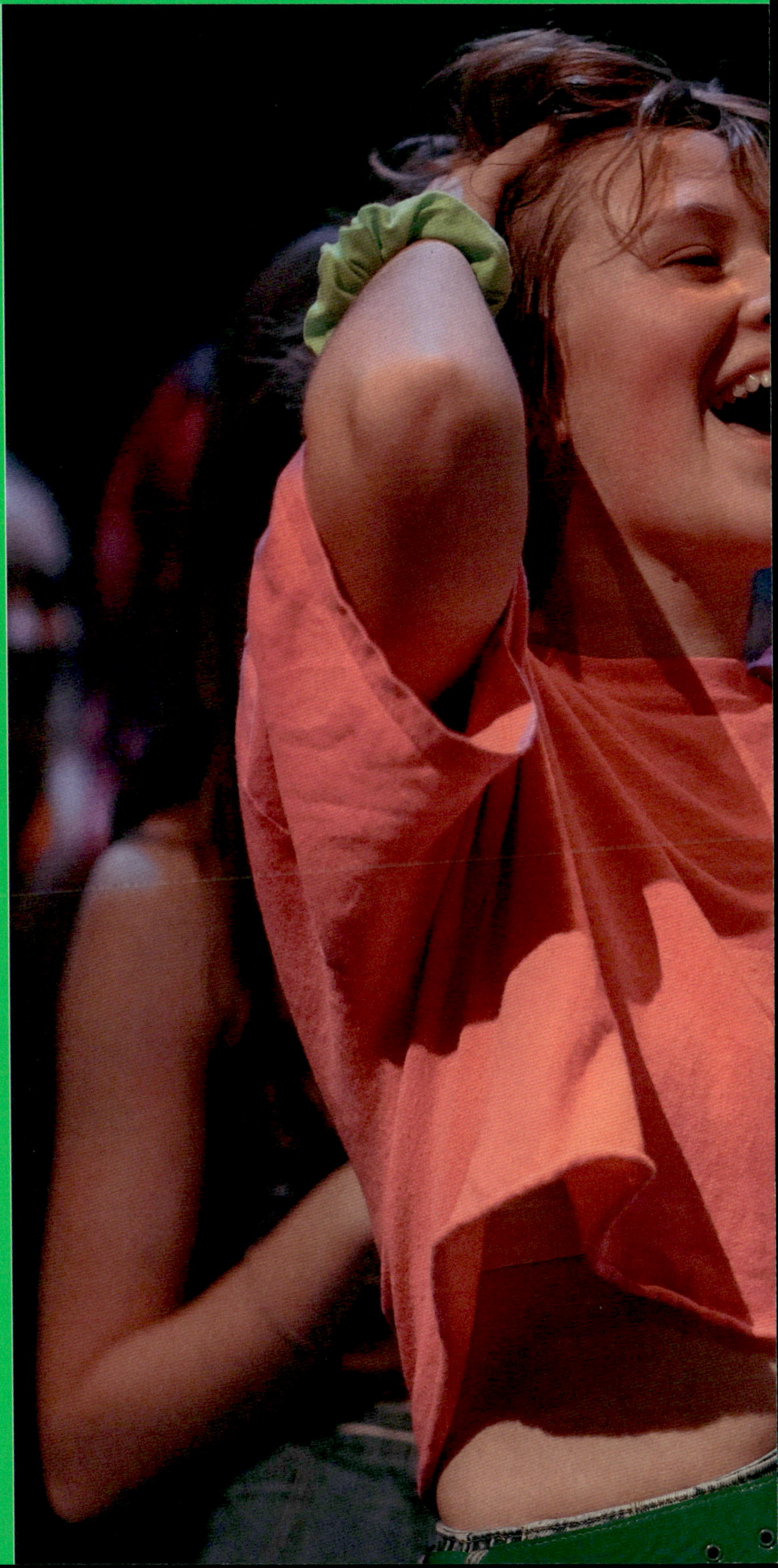

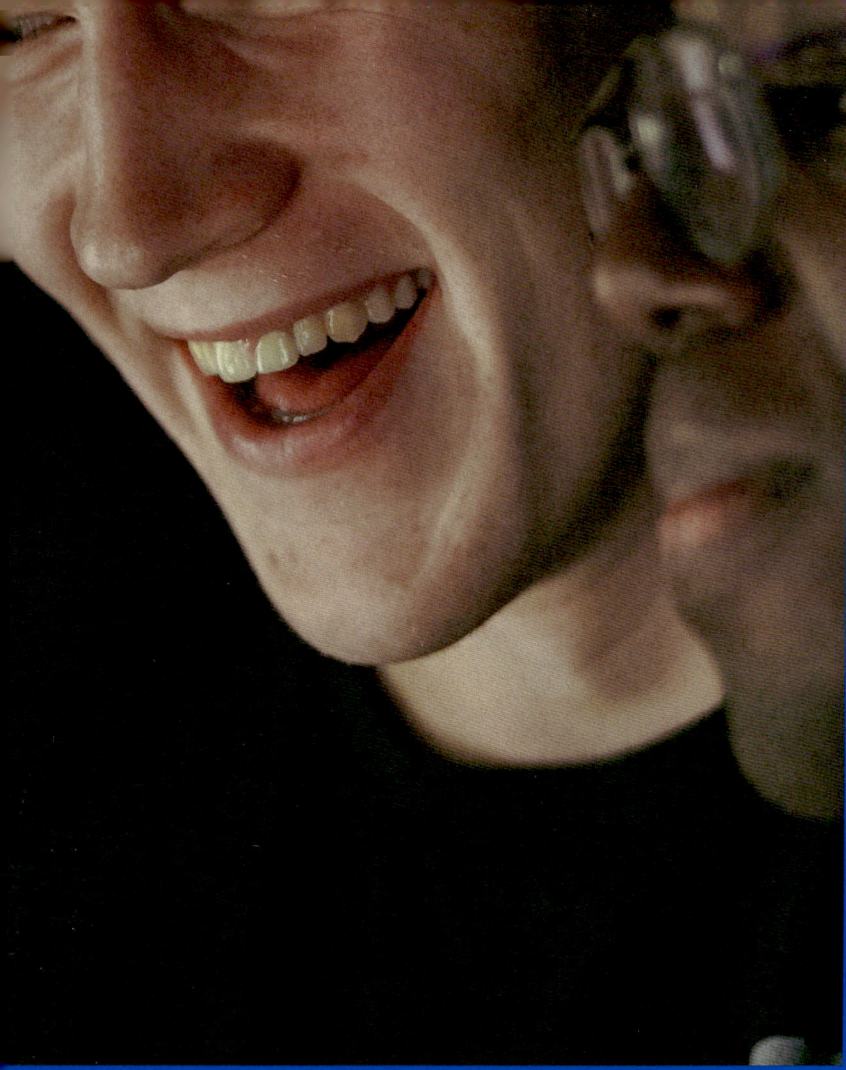

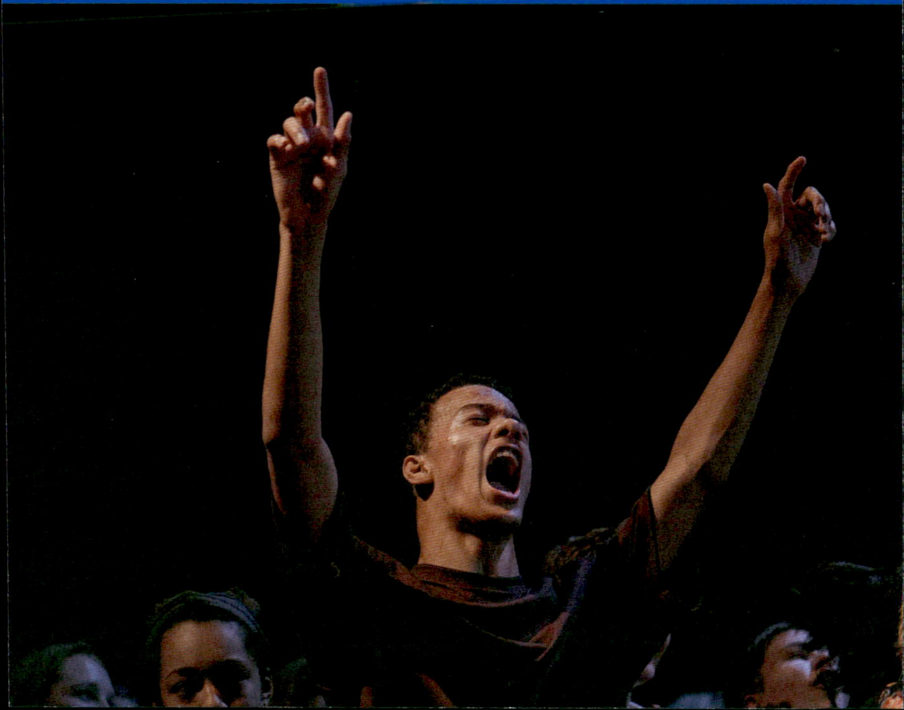

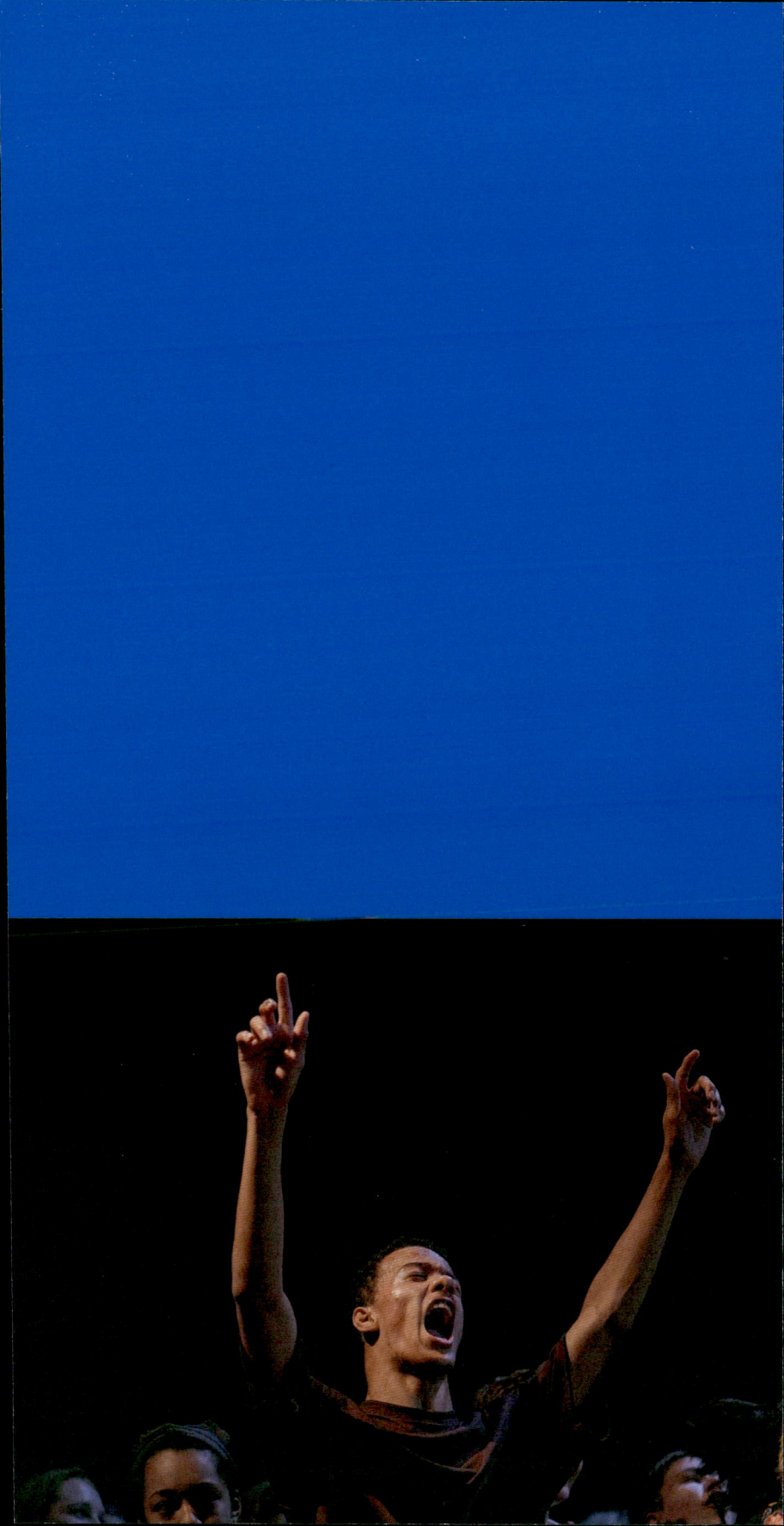

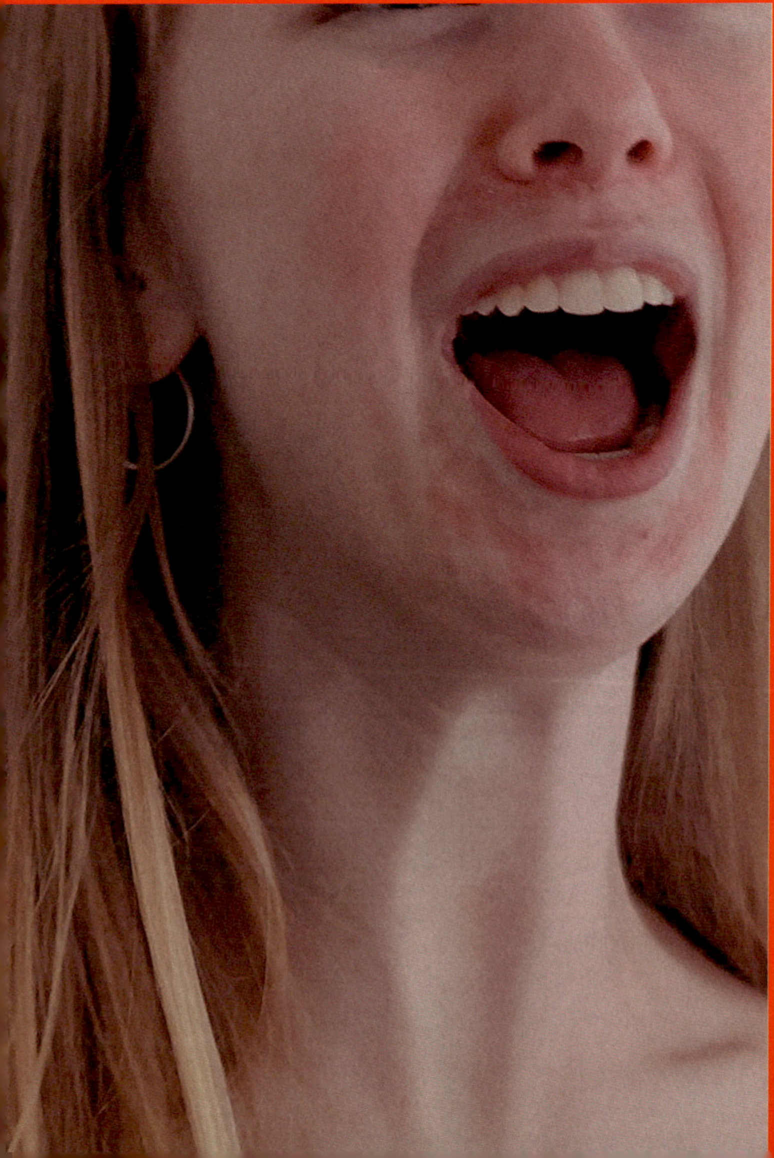

3

Big Feelings

Introduction

In this section, you will find pieces on the messy, contrasting, beautiful, and complex emotions when navigating relationships with your identity, youth, coworkers, politics, and lives in and outside the museum.

    With works by
Dr. Kendall Crabbe, Simona Zappas, Dr. Yolanda J. Majors, Jo Higgins, Nisa Mackie, Sir Lyra Hill, Jeremy Kreusch, Amanda Hunt, and Nancy Nowacek

Essays, Reflections & Advice

Dr. Kendall Crabbe & Simona Zappas

Positionality and Pedagogy

Bio

Dr. Kendall Crabbe, PhD (she/her), is the director of the bachelor of fine arts with an emphasis in art education program and a faculty supervisor for preservice art education students at the School of the Art Institute of Chicago. She is also the assistant editor of *Art Education: The Journal of the National Art Education Association*. Kendall earned her PhD in art and visual culture education at the University of Arizona. She employs participatory pedagogies in graduate, undergraduate, K–12, museum, and community-based contexts. Kendall's scholarship focuses on Youth Participatory Action Research (YPAR) in the arts. Current projects include longitudinal research to center youth experiences, stories, and perspectives in co-created programs.

Bio

Simona Zappas (she/her) is the Youth Programs Manager at the Walker Art Center. In her work she designs and facilitates informal learning opportunities for youth. She collaborates with curatorial staff to bring a learning lens to museum public engagement and a social practice bent on programmatic strategy. Before this, she was the director of WFNU Frogtown, a low-power radio station in Saint Paul. Simona holds a BA with honors from Macalester College and a master of education from the University of Minnesota. Simona sits on the Saint Paul Neighborhood Network board and volunteers at Planned Parenthood as an abortion doula.

Introduction

After several years of colleagueship, conversations, and collaboration on this publication, Dr. Kendall Crabbe and Simona Zappas came together to reflect on the impact and headroom created for both educators and youth when collaborative and creative pedagogies are employed in museum teen programs. The pair discuss the importance of critically reflecting on one's positionality and how this affects pedagogical and curricular decisions, flows of power in learning spaces, and the experiences of youth within and relating to arts institutions.

As mentioned in the introduction of this book, this is a call to action in teen programs. This piece hopes to encourage educators to recognize white supremacy within museums as institutions[1] and to reflect on our roles as educators and facilitators. Ultimately, this piece asks museum teen programmers to consider engaging Youth Participatory Action Research (YPAR) to reimagine teen programs in art museums.

---

1. See Mike Murawski, "Interrupting White Dominant Culture in Museums," in *Museums as Agents of Change: A Guide to Becoming a Changemaker* (Lanham, MD: Rowman and Littlefield, 2021); Priya Frank and Theresa Sotto, eds., *From Small Wins to Sweeping Change: Working Together to Foster Equity, Inclusion, and Antiracism in Museums* (Lanham, MD: American Alliance of Museums, 2022).

Conversation
Kendall Crabbe

My name is Kendall Crabbe. I use she/her pronouns. I currently work at the School of the Art Institute of Chicago. I recently finished my PhD at the University of Arizona. My dissertation focused on the intersection of Youth Participatory Action Research and Teen Council programs in art museums. I'm excited to be in conversation with Simona.

Simona Zappas

I am Simona Zappas. I use she/her pronouns, and I work at the Walker Art Center managing our youth and programs. I found an absolute shared excitement with Kendall over the need in museum teen programs to bring in supportive structures that both allow for an emergent design and serve as a guiding base for facilitators to stand on. This is to ensure satisfaction for youth because we want structures that allow youth to complete projects with an established and realistic scope. We're interested in something that facilitators can lean back on when they're (a) frustrated with how the institution is responding or directing youth or (b) when they're struggling with their own personal politics, identity, or positionality when working with young people in the museum. Moreover, a lot of our discussions over the years have been about what it means to use pedagogies that allow co-creation with teens and help facilitators navigate and recognize the internal power dynamics internally within the teen program and externally within the museum. We've been interested in how to reckon with everything that can seep into the program space—the galleries, the ex/internal politics of the museum teens' lives outside the programs...I could go on. We want to know how, as a facilitator, we have to wrap our arms around all of it.

Before we begin, I think it's also important at the onset of this conversation to recognize both of our identities. I'm a white cishet woman working with youth who primarily identify as BIPOC, queer, trans, or all of the above. I'm working and living in a city that I didn't grow up in, which is culturally very different from my hometown of Los Angeles. I'm navigating my own identity, while I'm also asking the teens to leverage and explore their own identities to connect and interpret the artworks in the museum. So, while we're talking about layers, they're adding up. It's getting pretty tall.

KC

Absolutely. Yes. I, too, will begin with my positionality. I am a white, middle-class, cishet woman in my midthirties from the Midwest. As my background differs racially, culturally, and geographically from the youth I work with, I believe it is important to observe the ways my positionality can and oftentimes does filter, skew, shape, block, transform, construe, and misconstrue the ways I collaborate with young people.

In my dissertation research on teen programs in art museums, and work on a Teen Council at the Art Institute of Chicago back in 2012, I noticed that historically there has been a focus on youth-driven and youth-led work, but not enough of an emphasis on educators and supports for adult practitioners doing this work in art museums. This book is meant to be an educator-to-educator resource and it is full of great suggestions and options for practitioners.

In our work together, Simona and I have come to understand YPAR as a powerful approach to doing intergenerational work in art museums.

SZ

Yes! Lots of YPAR love here. Kendall, what is your understanding of Youth Participatory Action Research and how have you engaged in YPAR?

KC   Sure! I understand YPAR as a collective form of inquiry in which topics of investigation are grounded in the lived experiences and concerns of young people. YPAR is also participatory in that youth work with adult educators to develop research questions, collect, and analyze data. It seeks to be transformative, changing knowledge and practices to improve the lives of youth and their communities. Finally, it is an intergenerational process in which youth and adults work to share space and power.[2]

I began working on teen programs in 2012 at the Art Institute of Chicago. We started a Teen Council program and I fell in love with this work.[3] My interest in youth agency within art museums led me to pursue a PhD at the University of Arizona. I was really interested in nonhierarchical curriculum, emergent strategies, and what it might look like to shift from a traditional co-created model to engaging YPAR in art museum teen programs. My dissertation drew on a three-year longitudinal qualitative case study of a YPAR collective that worked inside and outside a southwestern art museum.[4] The study centered the intergenerational desires and perceptions of youth and adult co-researchers in a teen-centric program. By investigating the counternarratives of teen and adult co-researchers, we sought to learn more about participation and creative agency from those at the center of these programs.

YPAR is not for the faint of heart. It can help

2. To learn more about YPAR, we recommend Julio Cammarota and Michelle Fine, eds., *Revolutionizing Education: Youth Participatory Action Research in Motion* (New York: Taylor & Francis, 2008).
3. Robin Schnur and Hillary Cook began the Teen Council. I, Kendall Crabbe, cofacilitated the program with Hillary.
4. Kendall Crabbe, "Intergenerational Counternarratives of Creative Agency: Reimagining Inclusive Practices through Youth Participatory Action Research" (PhD diss., University of Arizona, 2022), ProQuest (19891).

you, as the adult educator, and youth understand how young people experience the art museum: Who has agency? Who is fully able to participate? Who sets the norms? YPAR opens spaces, which can be both generative and challenging. YPAR is a way to critically engage young people in every aspect of the program so they can tell you what's working and what's not working for them. So again, I think YPAR is a very empowering process, both for youth and adult educators, but it can and will raise important questions and tensions.

SZ

Bunch of stuff there! Beautifully said! I loved your point on YPAR not being for the faint of heart, because it's goal oriented inasmuch as it's process oriented; the process is going to inform the goal and the goal is going to inform the process. As you said, there are iterative steps, but it changes for each project and it's something that must be kind of shaped with the youth.

KC

Like a cyclical process.

SZ

Yeah. Like a circle or spiral. Accepting there's something about YPAR that I think requires a little bit of accepting nonclosure and accepting kind of like an in-the-momentness that also requires always looking a few steps ahead to be responsive that I think is really hard for the educators and the youth. Anyone who's been in conversation with me knows my constant thing I'm repeating—that it's, like, how are we focusing on building skills for inquiry and tools that can be applied throughout life. One of the points of YPAR is that it mirrors and responds to the real world a little bit. It expands the classroom, and I think that's why it's really great in museums, because museums aren't classrooms, they're a "real world" space that teens can occupy in different ways. Inquiry-based pedagogies build skills for responses rather than reactions and can help make space for identities without neutralizing space; there can be safe contrasts. YPAR only works from a foundation of trust in the group. This leads to our next question of how to cultivate spaces for YPAR. Maybe, Kendall, some of what we want to address, first and foremost, is to go back to the question of our identities and our positionality as people who take up quite a bit of space and influence within the programs.

KC Absolutely. So, how has your positionality influenced your relationship with the people you work with in YPAR? As you were mentioning, Simona, thinking about positionality is critical. Since the 1990s when teen programs began in art museums, white women like us have engaged in this work with BIPOC youth. I have always wrestled with this tension. What is my role? How can I be responsive and not take up too much space when I'm working with youth, specifically youth from diverse backgrounds in Chicago and Tucson.

 I think what's great about YPAR is that it opens up that dialogue and it asks you to really think about your positionality, how you enter the space, and how you collaborate on a project. It is critically important for the educator to think about that and to call it out. Specifically, how power dynamics play out in intergenerational work between young people and adults; between white and BIPOC identities; between teachers and students. There are these norms and expectations that we're used to inhabiting in these roles that we traditionally play.[5] But with YPAR, you're trying to break down barriers and those norms. And it takes a lot of time, patience,

5. See 1.1.3. It's Not Sexy, but It's Crazy Cool on page 89 and 2.1.4. Performer, Producer, and Conduit on page 256 for more on this topic.

respect, and trust. So, I would say my positionality, and how it's influenced my work with young people, is really in taking a step back, engaging in consistent reflection on how my lived experiences shape curricular choices and how I take up space. Ultimately, it is important to consider where power lies, and how power impacts the work of the collective.

In my praxis, I take a lot of notes when collaborating with young people. I write about the decisions I make and how I interact. After our group has established trust, I ask my collaborators to let me know if and when I overstep.

I would say over time, and thinking about the beginning of the year with a group of young people, the educator does take on a lot of structure, just because you're organizing a group and everybody's like, "I showed up and what do we do now?" And you can't just say, "Now we're going to work together." And they're like, "Well, how? I don't know how," so you do have to start with that teacher-student relationship, but then over time, there is this trust that builds and this mutual respect and this leveling of the hierarchy. There is a gradual shift toward youth-centered ways of working that can lead to creative agency. When, as Sarah Travis puts it, youth and adult co-researchers "engage in a collective or collaborative effort of acting on and impacting the world through creative work." This shift in ownership is when the magic happens.

I think we, as educators, can and should spend more time thinking about how we develop trust, respect, and strong relationships in these programs. What are the strategies or approaches that are effective?[6] So again, just like in any relationship, you must think about who you are, what you bring to the table, and how that interacts

6. See 1.2.4. Respect Is... by Simona Zappas on page 185 in this publication.

SZ with those who are also at the table.

I couldn't agree more. One of the benefits of these programs is that we have this extended time with youth, and we have the luxury of relationship building that isn't always afforded in other educational program areas in the museum, or other institutions offering youth programs, like libraries. For museums following the teen arts council model, the strength comes from their relational drive. Building trust and getting to know the youth takes time. You can't expect teens to come in the first day and trust you. Maybe there's some, like, inherent trust that they're like, "Okay, well, Simona's the grown-up in the room, so I have to listen." But I think that's authority versus trust and respect and something reciprocal. YPAR requires an authority from the educator that is built on reciprocal trust that is then lent to support the youth in a horizontal leadership process. And I think, like, regardless of the drive to have that kind of more collaborative structure, there are hierarchies that we must recognize. And I think that one of the ways to kind of approach that is trying to think about the role we can play as a model in this space. I have a lot of comfort and power in the museum—I've worked there a long time. But I also grew up going to museums a lot. It was something that my parents prioritized and was a huge privilege that I grew up with. I also have an identity that is not policed in museums or in public spaces. I'm pretty relaxed in this space—to put it bluntly. Some of that modeling is demonstrating ways of being in the museum, and some of that modeling is enacting behaviors to build trust. And they're simple—being friendly, open, and asking questions in a respectful way. Part of that modeling is showing your way of expressing comfort and safety and exploring identity; for me, that's a frankness about my identity, but it's going to mean something different to everyone. Working in Minneapolis, in the wake of the murder of George Floyd, we continued having WACTAC [Walker Art Center Teen Arts Council] meetings and the teens were telling me that in a lot of their classes at school (which at that point were virtual—this is still the first few months of COVID-19) they were feeling like teachers were, like, dedicating classroom time to talk about what was happening in the city in a way that felt like they were checking a box. Sometimes the teens would express feeling baited, or like there were no ground rules set, so other students would say harmful things. They were being pushed to talk about identity in a way that didn't feel safe and good. And I had to recognize that they were maybe having to do this in every single class in their school day. Then showing up for WACTAC and being asked to do it again. This was where I felt relieved to have the structures set from YPAR practices, because the youth felt comfortable determining their parameters saying what would be helpful in exploring issues of identity. Sometimes after the days they were having at school, they simply were too burnt-out, so they could say what they needed the space to be. WACTAC was their intergenerational shared space instead of another space where they felt like they were being administered a conversation.

KC

I loved that point about authenticity. You know, young people can feel when they're being baited or asked questions to engage in an uncomfortable conversation. And I think the beauty of YPAR is that it really anchors the conversation and the work in young people's lived experiences and that they're the experts on their own realities, their own understanding of power, race, class, and gender identities. And so, they can engage in the conversation as much as they want. We trust them and they trust themselves in these conversations and this is good for sharing the space intergenerationally. And the other point is just that in doing research together and in this kind of reflective and responsive practice of taking notes on the group's dialogue, that was something I defaulted to during our conversations; at the beginning of each session, I would share my notes and say this is what you were talking about last time and what you were planning to do next. Is this still true?

    Taking notes was a way to check myself, to share the space intergenerationally, to not be the person setting the agenda as the educator, but to be a mirror, to reflect teens' ideas back in the following session. I found that to be a good way to kind of level the playing field. What's the next thing, what do you want to do with this information and these ideas that you were working on last week? And so that's another strategy that I'd like to offer.

SZ
I love that! It's like using their words as kind of like the source material, as, like, the guiding stuff. Like, instead of, you know, like, if you refer to your book, whatever, like in class, it's saying, like, here's the guiding information from you!

KC
The content/guiding information is from them. It's their voice and their ideas that center our collective work.

    Moving on to another question we generated, what are the challenges for you as an educator in sharing the space with the youth or other staff members, the art—how have you responded to, and/or reflected on those challenges? How do you find focus with all the things you're sharing space with, environmental factors like pizza, parking, and the other teens?

    With that question, what comes to mind first for me is really about my positionality as

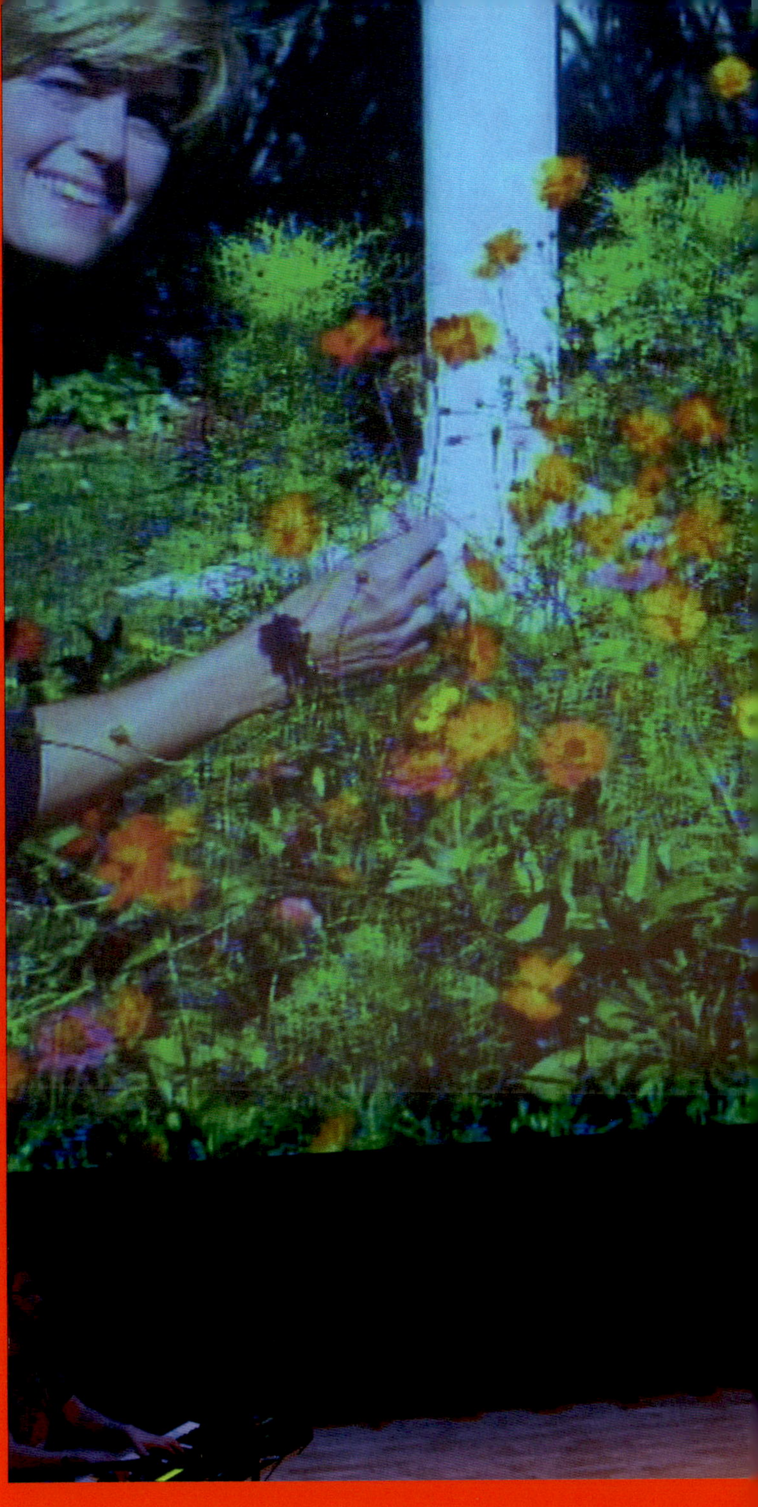

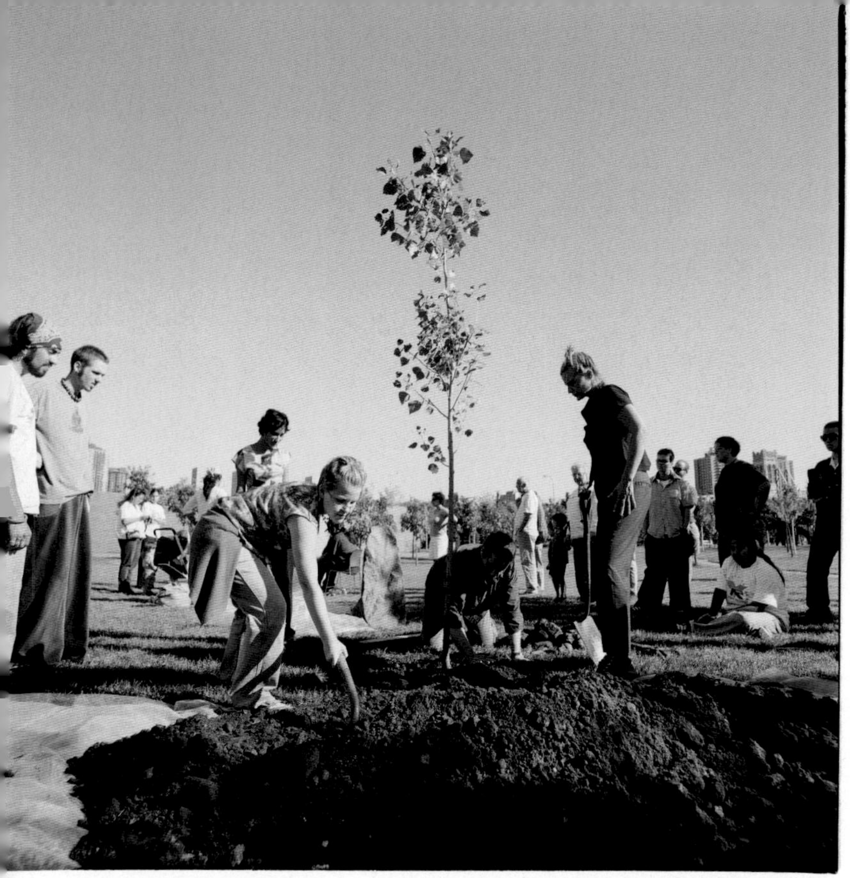

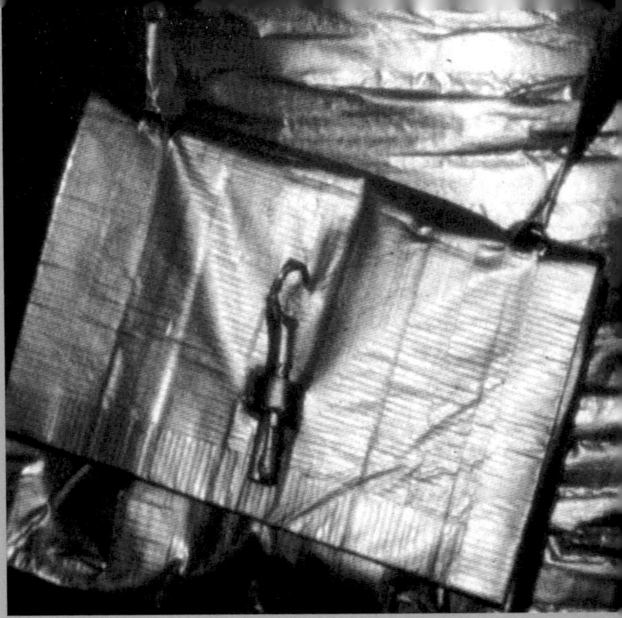

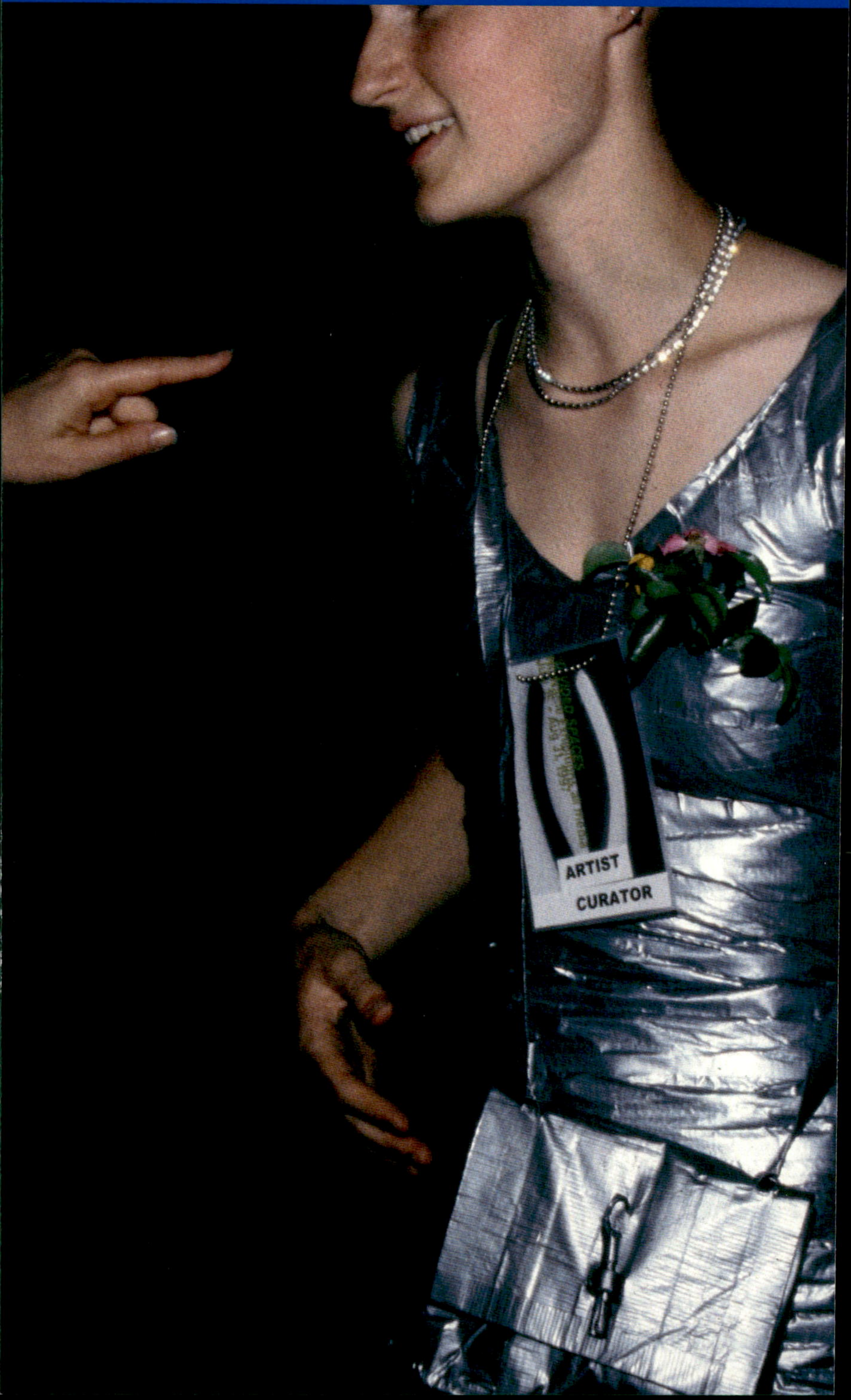
ARTIST
CURATOR

a white female heterosexual educator. And the fact that in Chicago and in Tucson I have worked with youth from very diverse backgrounds, both socioeconomically and racially. And so, while I was doing my dissertation research and engaging with critical race theory[7] [CRT] and critical whiteness,[8] I really reflected on the ways that those theories can and should shape our practice as educators. To really help us think critically about how we, again, share these spaces. Inherently, there are challenges with power when adults and young people work together. There is adultism. And there can be also me being a white person working with BIPOC youth. So again, there's an inherent asymmetry to the power dynamics between white and BIPOC individuals. And then there's a socioeconomic difference. Finally, we are working together in a whitestream art museum dominated by white-dominant cultural norms. So, there are several layers that I think are really important to consider. Centering CRT in this work and becoming familiar with it as an educator is necessary. CRT can help educators, specifically white female educators, be aware of and reflect on how race and power impact every aspect of our collective work, from curricular choices to the ways we engage young people.

And so, the main thing I wanted to talk about with critical race theory is that race is socially constructed and that racism is endemic to the United States of America. So if you start from that place and you situate the work with that

7. Richard Delgado and Jean Stefancic, eds., *Critical Race Theory: The Cutting Edge*, 2nd ed. (Philadelphia: Temple University Press, 2000).
8. Joni B. Acuff, "Smog in the Air: Passive Positions, Deracialization, and Erasure in Arts Education," in *The Palgrave Handbook of Race and the Arts in Education*, eds. Amelia M. Kraehe, Ruben Gaztambide-Fernández, and B. Stephen Carpenter II (Switzerland: Palgrave Macmillan), 515–35.

understanding, I think that it really helps you as the educator identify those challenges and recognize when and how race/power shape our work. Again, there are inherent asymmetries between young people and adults in this space, especially within whitestream art museums. So what does that look like and how can we be thoughtful about this work? And how do we center (even unconsciously) white-dominant norms and expectations when we're working with young people? How do we step back and not center those white-dominant narratives and norms? So, I think that I'll stop there, I want to let Simona speak to this question.

SZ

I was thinking through what I wanted to say to this question; I kept going back to thinking about how much time the youth participants are spending at the museums. I spend forty-plus hours a week working on, thinking about, talking about, and obsessing over my programs. And it's maybe two hours a week that we're with the youth. In those two hours we repeatedly ask teens to leverage their identities and use their identities to approach works and the museum. Everyone is living their identity every single day. And so, I'm thinking what does that mean in that two-hour window teens are at the museum for our programs? Just a snapshot of their week. I think that's kind of like the power of using YPAR. You're giving teens a chance to have control over how they want to engage with their identity in an institutional space. I think it's like a really interesting way to bring in artworks because it's a chance to engage with other perspectives in a way that's kind of open-ended and to kind of have a chance to understand them in conversation with your own and having these big gallery conversations that I think it can kind of like break open that snapshot a lot but it can also bring people together. I'm thinking a lot about this piece, that we have at the Walker, that's a series of Catherine Opie photographs that are these stark landscapes of ice-fishing huts on a frozen lake in Minnesota. There's no other way to describe the photo than cold. Like [laughter], it's a frozen lake, it's an overcast sky. The whole thing is almost just white except for these little dots of colorful ice houses. And we talk about the piece in WACTAC a lot, because it's a piece featuring Minnesota and has proven to lead to interesting conversations where teens can decide if they want to talk about themselves or the object. The piece elicits a lot of different reactions. Some teens see it and they're like, "Oh, my grandpa always took me ice fishing," or "It reminds me of my cabin." And then some teens are like, "I've never done that," or "I have never left the Twin Cities." And I'm coming in as a Californian horrified that people would even stand on a frozen lake or be outside when it's below seventy degrees. For this piece, in particular, a lot of aspects of socioeconomic class and access can be laid out. Cabins are a big part of the culture in Minnesota. So, I think we have to really think about what we're asking the teens to do, and what the potential impact can be of having a vulnerable conversation like this. What's the end goal for these two hours a week? How are we going to give them the option and control over discussing their identities in a way that can be validating for them and they can grow and learn from each other?

 I just always go back to building that trust in the group. Games, icebreakers, and other playful, low-stakes connection points are essential. However, I think artworks do really offer this absolute range of experience and representations that can show multiple perspectives and give teens control over how much they want to share. With object-based learning, we can shift focus onto the thing and let the teens decide how much they want to bring themselves in. At the Walker, we have the advantage of a contemporary collection with some pretty far-out stuff that can serve as an easier jumping-off point at times because teens can enter through abstraction so maybe it doesn't always feel so acute.

KC Yeah, Simona, that was beautiful. I think that's the perfect way to think about not having teens feel baited or be baited to have these conversations but centering an artwork and just allowing that conversation to unfold. And, over time, you know, in the program, teens start to feel a lot closer to each other. They come from very different backgrounds like you're just mentioning. So, you know, some teens have a second home, and some don't, and some just don't have experiences with ice fishing, you know, all these different things, but the artwork allows them to kind of sit in that space and know each other in their different identities in really authentic and thoughtful ways. And especially to think about identity and race in authentic ways. And I think that is the power of art and that is why doing YPAR in an art museum can be really special and really powerful, I think.

And then the other point that you made—about, you know, that we work on, we think about all this stuff for forty hours a week and then teens are in the space for two hours a week—I think is interesting because, again, we're asking them to talk about and think about their identities and how they show up in a white art museum basically. But then I think it's equally important for us as educators to critically reflect on our own positionality and how we are, again, making those choices in terms of, like, resources and who we're connecting youth to, and how we're facilitating conversations with staff and how we're that intermediary between teens and the museum.

And so, I tend to think of myself as an...I try to be an ally and very responsive—again, like we said earlier in this conversation, just thinking about, you know, transcribing conversations so that we're leveling the playing field and not being the controller or dictator of the conversation or the work. And so, what are the strategies and ways in which we can, you know, step back and decenter ourselves and be more of an ally or a support and a facilitator rather than—or a cofacilitator with youth—rather than someone driving the conversation or the work. I think that is—that's a really important tension that needs to be made transparent at all times—is something that I think is really important.

SZ

What I love about that point of allyship is that it requires a self-awareness that runs in a distinct parallel with the teens. The whole kind of, like, underlying question of adolescence is "Who am I?" so identity exploration is always sort of top of mind for teens. And I think that there's no way that that isn't a little contagious. As educators we have this advantage of being around that big energy. I think it's important when going into the space as an educator to think what are you bringing with you and what you're leaving at the door. Knowing your role as the facilitator going in makes a big difference because you want to guide, not steer. Ask yourself, realistically, what am I trying to get out of this session? Regularly revisit the learning outcomes, or if you're doing a YPAR project, like thinking about how you can help the teens get to the goal that they've identified. Check these things without erasing yourself. We're powerful in the group. We're the adult in the room. We represent the institution. And these can all be recognized without a heavy hand.

KC

Yeah. And teens will call you on that right away.

They'll say, what are you driving at? Or the museum wants us to do what, you know? I think they're very good at being transparent and identifying when things are authentic and true. And when they don't feel like they have the agency that they were told that they might have. Yeah. So, I think that's a really good point.

With my dissertation, one of the biggest findings was really honing in and learning from youth. How they want to collaborate and how they want to work together because they have organic inclinations to not take up too much space and to really listen to each other; they try to paraphrase other peoples' ideas correctly. And so, I think there's a lot we—like you were saying about learning from youth or kind of gaining that energy from them about their identity exploration and that rubbing off on educators. I think it's also true that we should allow their thoughtfulness about collaboration to inspire us as educators, to redefine research and collaborative practices.

And then the last thing is just really reflecting. So, thinking about critical race and critical whiteness theory, wherever you are on that journey. But again, I think as white female educators, and traditionally people in this position have been white female educators, just being honest with yourself about where you are in that journey. What is your role within the art museum? And I guess what I'm trying to say is that I'm not perfect and I don't have all the answers about race and equity work in art museums and with young people or even within YPAR. But that it is an evolving practice and it's a lifelong journey of learning about yourself, your positionality, and how that impacts your work with young people as you are an adult and as they are youth and how you can constantly negotiate and be responsive in that space with young people.

I think that commitment is really important.

To never stop learning and reflecting on how that's happening or not happening in collective practices. It is a delicate balance, but when it works, it works really well. Hopefully the group as a collective feels that each person is heard and is contributing. Because that's when the greatest work happens.

Dr. Yolanda J. Majors 3.1.2.

The Potential Impact of Walker Teen Programs for Youth

Bio

Yolanda J. Majors, PhD, is the founder and CEO of the Hurston Institute for Learning and Development. Dr. Majors's scholarship has focused on child, youth, and community learning development. She is the author of the book *Shoptalk: Lessons in Teaching from an African American Hair Salon* and over two dozen articles and book chapters on social contexts for learning. After Dr. Majors became a tenured professor (at the University of Illinois at Chicago), her focus shifted to designing and supporting out-of-school learning spaces for youth and adults. Her award-winning work has led to numerous corporate and organizational partnerships and, in 2019, the establishment of the Hurston Institute for Learning and Development (HILD). Through HILD, Dr. Majors provides instructional design support, research, evaluation, design-based research, and workshops worldwide for classroom and community educators. Dr. Majors writes a weekly advice column and facilitates online seminars and discussion forums for educators, administrators, and graduate students at hurstoninstitute.com.

Essay

Addressing the challenge of documenting the types of learning that take place in youth-serving opportunity spaces like the Walker Art Center is essential, mainly if the goal is to provide youth with opportunities that connect them to the academic and professional domain of the visual arts within a setting that valorizes "its innovative presentations...of contemporary art across the spectrum of the visual, performing, and media arts."[1] From 2018 to 2019, I worked with the Walker Art Center to engineer particular forms of learning and to study the supports educators offered while documenting how particular practices within the opportunity space of the Walker positioned youth as knowledge producers, meaning makers, and creators of their learning.

We found a connection between teens' reasonings about art and particular modes of literary problem-solving strategies, namely argumentation, and persuasion. From that, we hypothesized that some aspects of the program's participation structure and use of gallery works as mediational tools allowed teens to engage in academically sophisticated, enjoyable reasoning supporting their academic growth. In my 2015 book *Shoptalk: Lessons in Teaching from an African American Hair Salon*, I documented the kinds of robust learning opportunities that occur in informal, everyday community spaces, like barbershops and hair salons. Part of what doing this work taught me was that the local Black hair salon is a participatory space where youth and adults voluntarily come together to organize around communal problem-posing and problem-solving; sit together to create through cutting and styling; pass news about one another through oral and written networks; and use

1. Walker Art Center, "About," accessed January 9, 2023, https://walkerart.org/about/.

humor to communicate with one another. And, as decades of scientific research would have it, the Black beauty parlor is also an opportunity space. As such a space of learning, oral and communal patterns of dialogue contribute to participants' literate engagement in a practice I call "readings of Text of the Every Day."

Texts of the Every Day are printed, oral, art-visual, or musical texts with which youth are very familiar because they engage with these texts in their homes and communities as a part of everyday practices.

Features of Texts of the Every Day include, but are not limited to, the following:

> They place interpretative demands on the reader.
> They speak to a particular issue of genuine concern to the lives of youth as members of communities.
> The issue must be rooted in a conflict between an institutional perspective and values and youths' lived cultural perspectives and values.
> They must create a rupture between reader expectation and reader experience.

Additionally, such texts must construct two learning landscapes simultaneously. One is the "landscape of action," where the reader is implicated in the rupture of the action. The other is the "landscape of consciousness—what those others involved in the actions know, think, feel or do not know, think or feel."[2]

To read a Text of the Every Day, in the sense of understanding it, youth and adults must go beyond basic, individually siloed interpretations of that text. Rather, they collectively and collaboratively reconstruct that text in action and consciousness, imitate it in some way, to produce something around it that is new but bears some clear relationship to the original text. Understanding is manifested in restating that text and in making those restatements public. Texts of

---

2. Jerome Bruner, *Acts of Meaning* (Cambridge, MA: Harvard University Press, 1990), 16.

the Every Day transform into social texts when such readings are shared and made public to become a part of a complex social landscape of action and consciousness, often in narrative story form. Social texts, therefore, are multivoiced, multiscripted texts that, like stories, are models for the redescription of the world in that they convey, guide, inform, and generate meanings for learners, who simultaneously re-create old understandings into the new.

The social reading of texts, either orally, art-visually, or in writing, provides a way for us to organize our experiences; it is the primary activity of the mind. "We tell stories to think, and we think about stories we tell. But the story is not the model of the world as we see it," suggests Bruner. Rather, "the story is an instantiation, or artifact, of the models of meaning we carry in our minds. One rereads a story in the ways as one rereads art—in endlessly changing ways, ways that may nest on top of one another, marry one another, and or mock one another in the reader's mind."[3]

Social reading skills—revising, improvising, recounting, inferencing, and fathoming the moral and social meanings of events—are likely to be displayed only in context-appropriate ways. Therefore, undergirding these skills is one's ability to frame situations in domain-specific ways that fit well within the context in both form and function. Really smart educators consider such an ability to be a literacy skill that youth and adults rehearse and develop through their participation within and movement across different kinds of discourse communities.

As youth and adults routinely engage in life, they learn to voluntarily and involuntarily take part in multiple traditions (such as school, work, and play), with sometimes distinct, sometimes complementary structures for participation. In doing so, they draw from various norms, tools, values, participation structures, and literacies with which they are familiar.[4] Literacy, in and of itself, is an act. It is a way of thinking, not a set

3. Bruner, *Acts of Meaning*, 21.

of skills. And it is a purposeful activity—people interpret, decode, read, talk, create, and think about real ideas and information to ponder and extend what they know, communicate with others, present their points of view, and understand and be understood. The kinds of literate skills that teens and facilitators display in service to art engagement are not neutral, cognitive skills but a kind of appropriated tool kit that includes systems of values, language, discourse, and modes of reasoning or meaning-making and constructing individual and shared identities in the public, social world.[5]

To be literate, some suggest, is to display skill in decoding written, spoken, and or art-creative texts—texts that are intimately bound to the particular details and nuances of people's everyday lives and the varied cultural ways they make sense of those details.[6] Such skill, like that involved in making sense of works of art and text, comprises institutional and cultural technologies—the hammers and nails of social, ideological, and goal-directed practice.[7] As a kind of practice, one that involves repeated, goal-directed sequencing of activities using a particular set of tools and system of knowledge, the act of literacy is not simply knowing how to decode particular images and texts, "but applying this knowledge to specific purposes in specific contexts of use."[8] Literacy skills, it follows then,

4. Kris D. Gutiérrez and Barbara Rogoff, "Cultural Ways of Learning: Individual Traits or Repertoires of Practice," *Educational Researcher* 32, no. 5 (June/July 2003): 19–25.
5. Seth Chaiklin and Jean Lave, eds., *Understanding Practice: Perspectives on Activity and Context* (Cambridge: Cambridge University Press, 1996); Yolanda J. Majors, *Shoptalk: Lessons in Teaching from an African American Hair Salon* (New York: Teachers College Press, 2015).
6. Sylvia Scribner and Michael Cole, "Unpackaging Literacy," in *Variation in Writing: Functional and Linguistic-Cultural Differences*, ed. Marcia Farr Whiteman, vol. 1 of *Writing: The Nature, Development, and Teaching of Written Communication* (Mahwah, NJ: Lawrence Erlbaum Associates, 1981).
7. Carol D. Lee, "The Centrality of Culture to the Scientific Study of Learning and Development: How an Ecological Framework in Educational Research Facilitates Civic Responsibility," *Educational Researcher* 37, no. 5 (2008): 267–79.
8. Scribner and Cole, "Unpackaging Literacy," 236.

are cultivated in particular social, cultural, and discourse contexts, within and across space and time, art museums being one such space.[9]

As the dominant culture shifts, previously undervalued learning processes related to intercultural literacies will likely grow in importance: working across previously impermeable linguistic, cultural, socioeconomic, and political divides; participating in collaborative, distributive, transdisciplinary problem-solving; critically evaluating multiple and multimodal information sources.[10] These literacies require engaged, versatile, and interculturally competent citizenry and are not typically supported in US public schools. As a society, then, we face an immediate as well as long-term challenge: to take up the diversity of human experience, at the level of individuals, communities, and institutions, not as a problem to be solved but as a generative resource for learning and development across the life span.

Educational researchers have documented the extent to which voluntary nondirected learning co-occurs with high attentional focus on chosen models or situations and keen observation and awareness of environmental resources relevant to learning goals. The potential impact of Walker Teen Programs for youth is demonstrated through several studies, including *Room to Rise*, which notes, "Our findings revealed five significant areas of long-term influence: a growth in confidence and the emergence of personal identity and self-knowledge; deep, lifelong relationships to museums and culture; a self-assured, intellectually curious pursuit of expanded career horizons and life skills; a lasting worldview grounded in art; and a commitment to community engagement and influence."[11]

Furthermore, APA's innovations in *how* the Walker scaffolds its curriculum utilize the galleries to help youth understand different perspectives on topics

9. Majors, *Shoptalk*.
10. Bill Cope and Mary Kalantzis, eds., *Multiliteracies: Literacy Learning and the Design of Social Futures* (Psychology Press, 2000).

and acknowledge and speak to institutional power relations that undergird systemic racism and social inequality have proven these results with teens from diverse racial and socioeconomic backgrounds. This is a direct response to Minnesota's achievement gap and the national need for more specific tools to empower teens with diverse perspectives. More specifically, one aspect of APA is that it equips teens to understand better the machinations of power and privilege, including when and where they have it and how to speak back to power when they do not. This extension of empowerment theory considers the specific lived experiences of teens of color, LGBTQIA youth, and other marginalized identities. The APA project thus works to accommodate the needs of increasing ethnic, racial, and socioeconomic diversity of youth in the Twin Cities and their recognition of the issue of community dissonance and incivility. It supports the Walker Art Center Teen Arts Council's (WACTAC) self-expressed desire for more action-based work within their cohort that responds to issues identified by the teens. The mainstreaming component of the project also intends to address the lack of theory-based praxis in art museum youth education by developing and sustaining pedagogical knowledge and experience through a professional learning community and project research dissemination.

    The challenge of connecting museum-based teen learning, art-specific skill acquisition, and the diversity of youth identities is exacerbated by public perceptions of art museums as so-called white spaces, spaces in which only the white population feels comfortable, connected, and supported. These spaces have earned their reputations by failing to support racial and cultural diversity in and outside their organization, maintaining resource-based barriers to entry, or implicitly or explicitly preserving racist policies. They form political, financial, cultural, and educational institutions. Like many other large cultural institutions, Minnesota's Walker Art Center is working to shed its reputation for catering to a majority white population.

By disrupting the stratified social order that museums have historically symbolized, maintained, and mediated within and across society, those attending an art museum can, should they choose to in their commute, look around them and observe the disparate conditions of the surrounding urban landscape. Thus, for many, the geographical significance of museum life is a subtle social commentary on the political and social economy of the city, surrounded by a complex, interwoven maze of social inequality, privilege, and cultural interaction. Patrons and staff, for their part, have the opportunity to read and interrogate the experience of attending the museum through a kind of cultural and social border crossing, where people actively move across the socially, culturally, and politically constructed divides that separate cultural groups and communities.[12]

Second, explorations of art forms explore complicated and nuanced issues of culture, class, and racialized identities. Some scholars and patrons have recently called for museums as institutions to recognize that it is not enough to make equity claims if underlying color-blind, nonracist discourses and practices remain at the foundation of the curriculum. Canadian scholar Srivastava coined the term "nonracist" to refer to a *discourse of equality*. Such a discourse positions spaces like the museum as not connecting existent racist structures to the everyday language and sociomaterial acts that support and reify them. Hence, equity is a step, but it is not enough. This imperative becomes increasingly apparent as the racial divide continues to grow between

11. Danielle Linzer and Mary Ellen Munley, *Room to Rise: The Lasting Impact of Intensive Teen Programs in Art Museums* (New York: Whitney Museum of American Art, 2015), 24.
12. Gloria Anzaldúa, *Borderlands / La Frontera: The New Mestiza* (San Francisco: Spinsters / Aunt Lute, 1987); Yolanda J. Majors, "Joy and the 'Smart Kids': Competing Ways of Being and Believing," *Journal of Adolescent & Adult Literacy* 57, no. 8 (2014): 633–41; Yolanda Majors and M. Orellana, "Envisioning Texts or Reading the Other," paper presented at the annual conference of the American Educational Research Association, Chicago, IL, April 2003.

white educators and BIPOC youth in urban spaces. First and foremost, color-blind, nonracist discourse serves to calcify white-dominant ideals, privileging their normalized cultural and intellectual practices. For this reason, an attempt to achieve educational equity through arts-based practices must move beyond the discourse of nonracism and enact anti-racist action, a philosophy and practice committed to challenging racism as systemic in institutions and everyday life.

As a transformative equity-based framework, APA goes beyond the status quo nonracist discourse to draw on anti-racist and healing action. APA aims to help teens think critically and develop the skills to formulate, document, and justify their works by challenging dominant assumptions and illuminating collisions of ideas—the nondominant and dominant throughout the curriculum. Such an approach has afforded Walker teens opportunities to engage in critical thinking and to develop more reflective perspectives about what they are learning. APA pushes teens and educators to look with their heads, hearts, and hands as they critically examine issues inside and outside the museum space.

Finally, Walker's creation and implementation of the APA model is an investment in rethinking what it means to know and to teach. As a transformative equity-based framework, APA resists public discourses of sameness and conformity and addresses issues of identity that affect teaching and learning concerning teens who are members of cultural groups; APA invites an awareness of a kind of learning and engagement that constitutes a hybrid space where teens are allowed to reject prescribed formats for determining what gets interpreted or read, in art and who can be the reader, in favor of improvisational and culturally relevant ways of speaking back, redefining, and confronting what it means to be considered human.

An attempt to achieve educational equity through teen programming via a transformative equity-based framework contains an activist dimension. It not only tries to understand the museum context of teaching

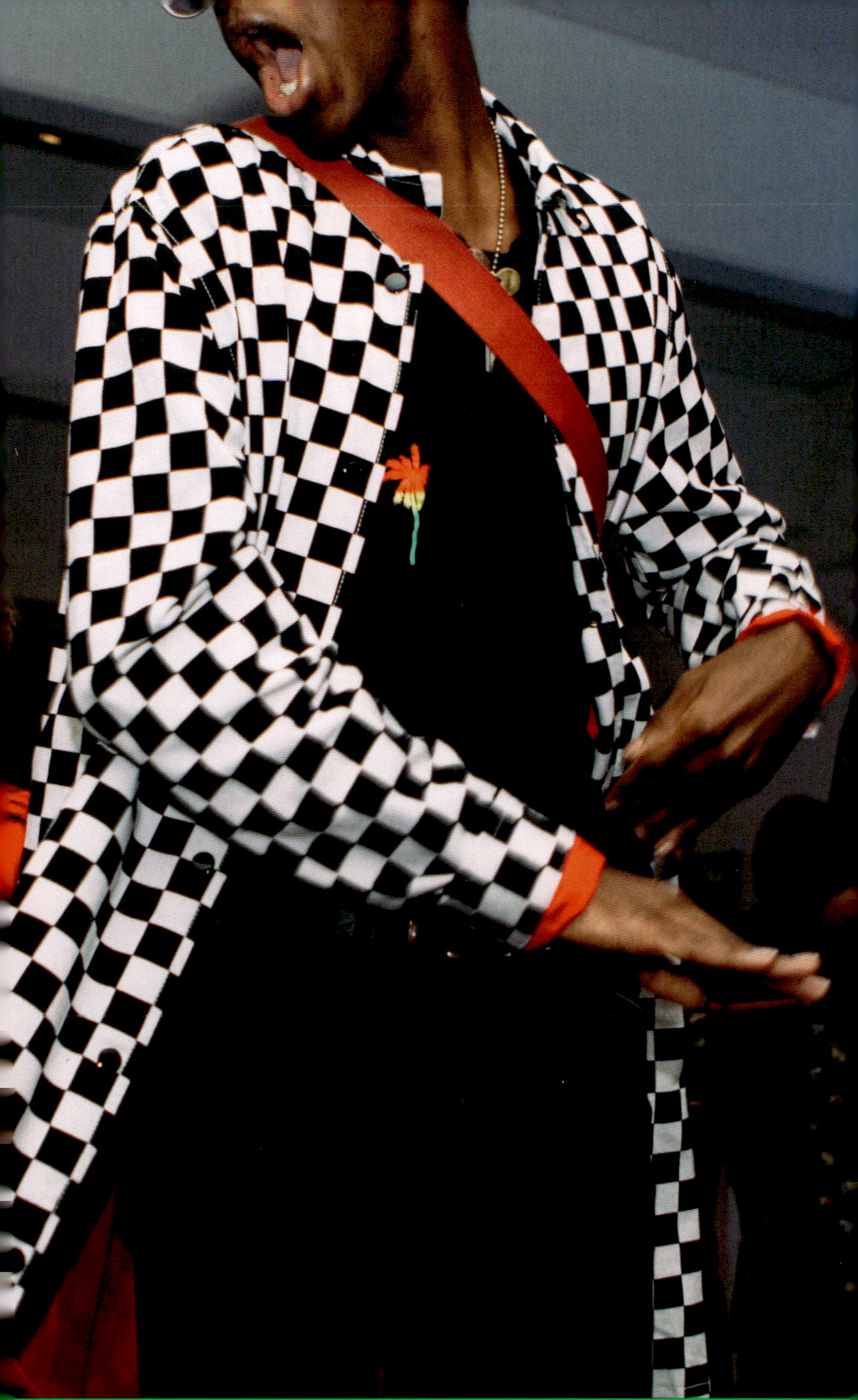

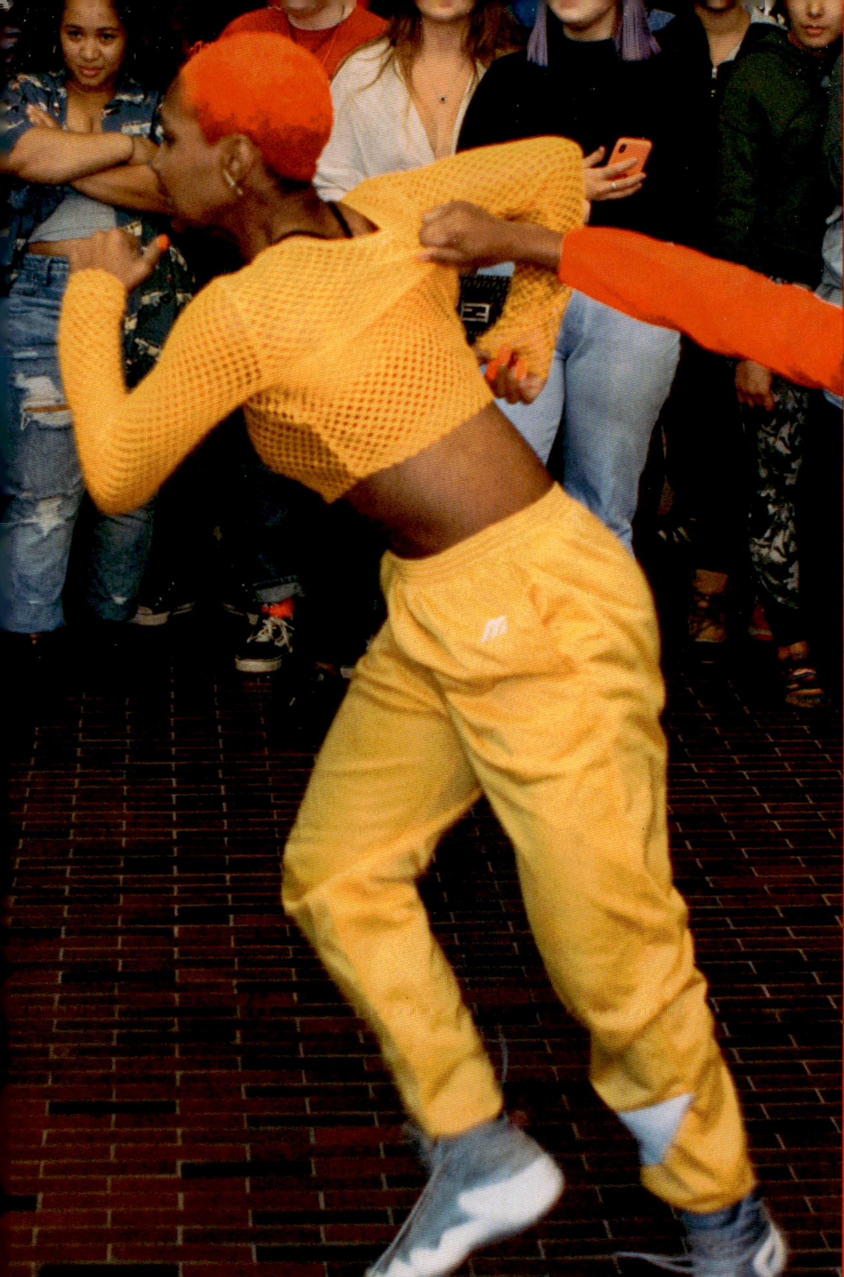

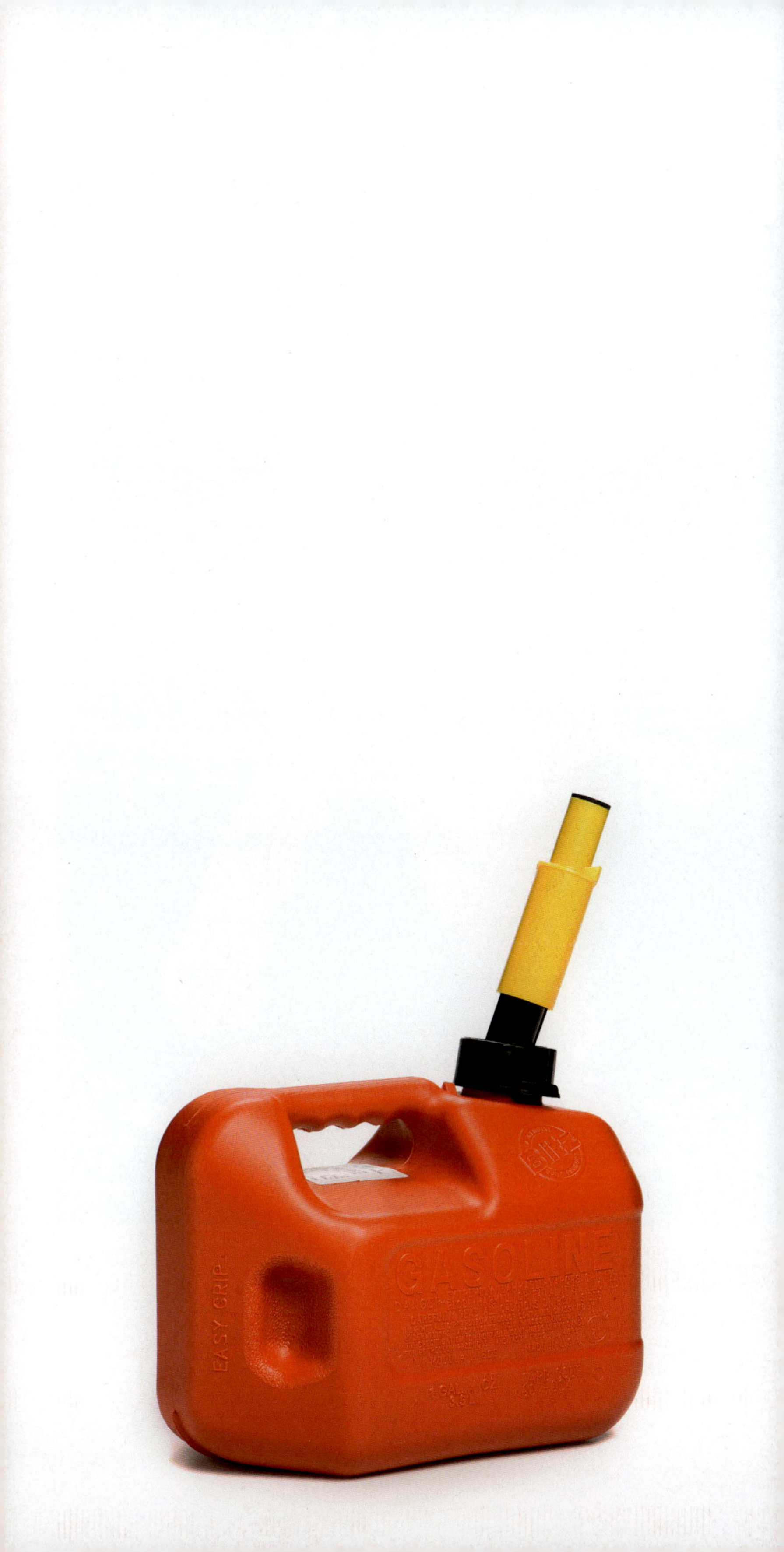
GASOLINE
EASY GRIP

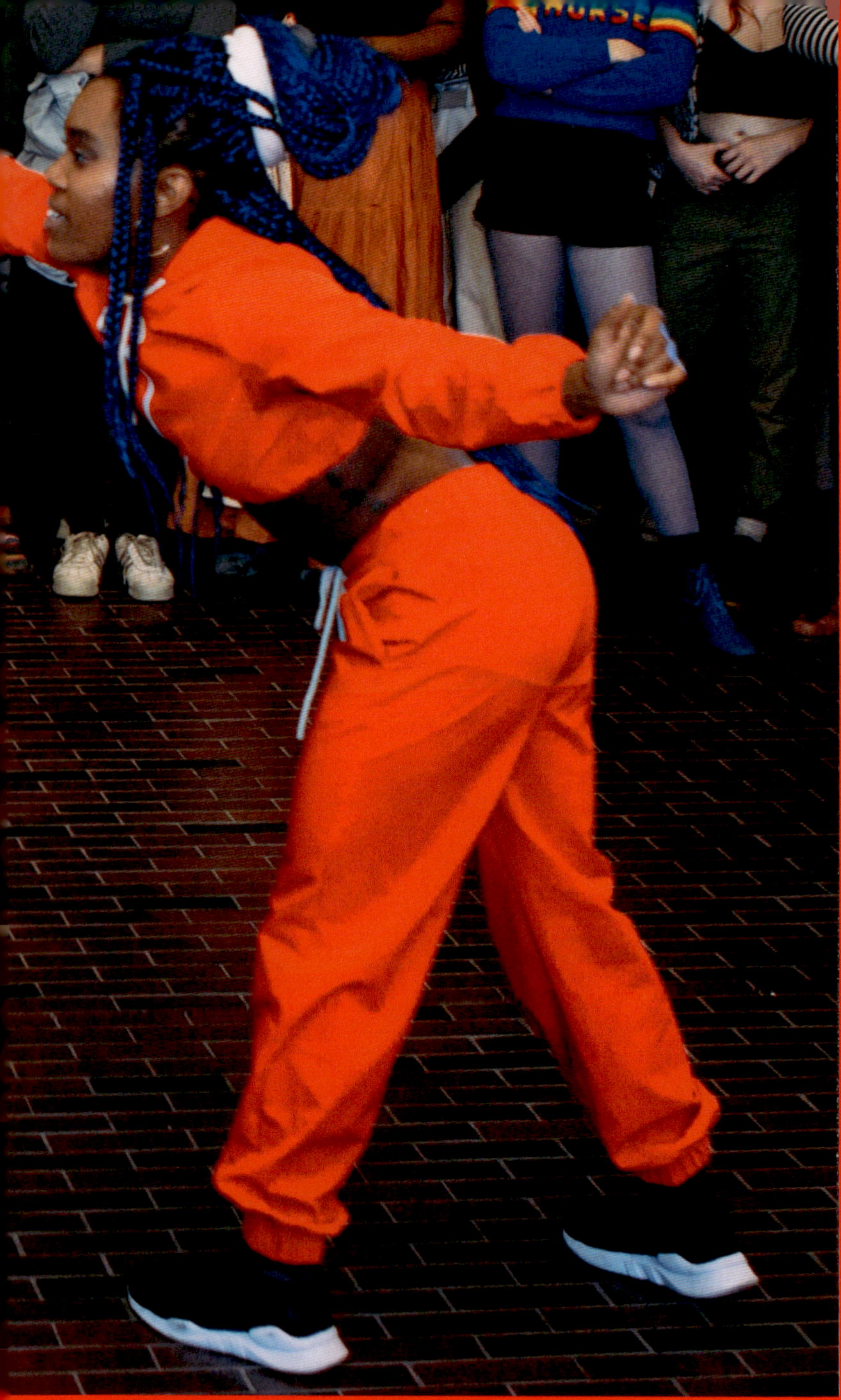

and learning as unequal in access and persistently "fun, folks, and festivals" oriented, but to change it. It sets out to ascertain how museum teen programming organizes itself along social and racial lines and hierarchies and to transform it for the better.[13] An important and determining factor in activating this goal is to create a curriculum for educators that allows youth to interrogate the inherencies and difficulties of an inequitable educational system and, further, to recognize institutional and cultural privileges that sustain their power. Moreover, understanding color-blind and safe-space discourses as integral aspects of white spaces denormalized the cultural practices and epistemologies that have become the standard in educational curriculum and pedagogy. The danger of not naming race (including whiteness) only serves to maintain institutional power and privilege.

As a form of oppositional work, an equity-based framework actively challenges the universality of the status quo museum experience and judgment as the authoritative standard that binds people and normatively measures, directs, controls, and regulates the terms of proper thought and expression, presentment, and behavior. The task of this approach is to identify values and norms that have been disguised and subordinated in our practices. To advance the goals of art educators who move beyond the image of caring, we need to develop a body of pedagogically aware educators. In its complexity, the intersection where our teens and our own experiences meet serves as a microcosm of society where ideological and historical factors hit the fan. Hence, it is a space where this framework can be productive, creating conversation, generating tools, and extending voice.

ⓒ

13. Richard Delgado and Jean Stefancic, eds., *Critical Race Theory: The Cutting Edge*, 2nd ed. (Philadelphia: Temple University Press, 2000).

Simona Zappas 3.1.3.

Setting Boundaries and Making Pivots

Bio
Simona Zappas (she/her) is the Youth Programs Manager at the Walker Art Center. In her work she designs and facilitates informal learning opportunities for youth. She collaborates with curatorial staff to bring a learning lens to museum public engagement and a social practice bent on programmatic strategy. Before this, she was the director of WFNU Frogtown, a low-power radio station in Saint Paul. Simona holds a BA with honors from Macalester College and a master of education from the University of Minnesota. Simona sits on the Saint Paul Neighborhood Network board and volunteers at Planned Parenthood as an abortion doula.

Essay
Boundaries
One of the most critical and challenging aspects of being a museum teen program practitioner is acknowledging and enforcing safe relational boundaries with the youth. Undeniably, we care about the

young people we work with, and we often see both fixable and devastating challenges in their lives firsthand. One of the driving tenets of our programs is fostering relationships with youth that build genuine care and trust, but for the safety and well-being of the youth and ourselves, we must occupy an appropriate role in their lives. This means accepting the limitations of our care—we are not trained counselors, social workers, therapists, peers, parents, or caregivers. This is not meant to reduce our work—we are mentors, educators, and trusted adults working to provide safer, accepting, and fun spaces for them. By recognizing and ethically enforcing safe boundaries of our relationships with transparency and clarity, we can best leverage the resources and care we *can* provide and ultimately provide the best support for the youth that matter so much to us.

To build boundaries, we should start by considering the context of where youth are coming from both developmentally and broadly in their lives. Teens are teens. They are in their adolescent phase of cognitive development—BIG feelings—every song is the BEST song, their BEST friend, the FUNNIEST joke, the STRICTEST teacher, the WORST day. At the risk of sounding like health class, teens are going through puberty—chemicals are firing, and their frontal cortex has not closed. Teens' reactionary, rebellious, and emotional assumptions are grounded in their literal neurological development. Teens are cognitively transitioning into adulthood but are still very much children. I do not say this dismissively but rather to elicit care. Teens confront real-world issues, traumas, and responsibilities. Some young people, sadly, are navigating these with life experience and skills honed through past triumphs or traumas, some are navigating them for the first time, and they are navigating them with varied support networks. Some real-world challenges are exciting parts that come with growing up—like friendships or dating—and others are deeply challenging, like increased family responsibilities. Youth are all navigating these challenges through the lens of their cognitive development—which is emotional, green, and raw.

It is hard to consider the vulnerability of teens confronting significant life challenges and not immediately want to protect, care, or weep. But that vulnerability is vulnerable, and even our best intentions can go awry. Youth are impressionable and actionable. What we say to them can have an impact, so we need to be thoughtful about our interactions. Boundaries do not mean not protecting or being there to provide care for teens; they are about finding the "right size" for your skills, scope, and relationship. Youth dealing with significant life challenges should consult with licensed professionals.

While I have worked with the Walker Art Center Teen Arts Council (WACTAC), youth have spoken to me about conflict with parents over gender identity, suicide, abortion, rape, and drugs. In all of these situations, I have considered the context; I recognize that I get only a snapshot of this young person's life. I may be working with them for an extended period, but I am with them for a highly facilitated group engagement for two hours a week. That said, WACTAC is a third space. Third space theory comes up in postcolonial theory, urban studies, and psychology. It describes the hybrid enjambment that forms personal identities from the spaces we occupy. For many, home might be a first space defined by family and ancestral cultures. Second space examples are where individuals come together in a group with dominant norms, like school or a place of worship. Third spaces can be broad—a dance club, a mall, a museum teen program. They are spaces where individuals can show up as the sum of their many sides and engage in exploratory transgressive acts because of the sense of ease and freedom created by acting from that expanded self.

On top of providing a third space for teens within WACTAC, I also recognize that I am an adult that they interact with differently than others. WACTAC is a relaxed, silly space built on the idea of listening to young people. My facilitation style is candid, and I am in my twenties. I build a rapport with the youth by learning about their interests and making jokes with them. This might be a more relaxed relationship than with other adults like teachers or family members, because there are no stakes like grades or tests or familial expectations. Much effort goes into building a safer space in WACTAC to ensure youth feel comfortable discussing art, including considering how I model nonjudgmental behaviors and aim to be warm and welcoming. The last thing I want to do is break that trust, invalidate their feelings, or put youth in harm's way. Because of this, I fully recognize the limitations of what I can safely offer them. I am someone with years of experience working with youth, but my experience is in arts-based skill learning. My degrees are in the humanities and education, and my background is in community media production. I do not have certifications or specific training in counseling youth or navigating mental health crises. My advice or help could negatively affect the youth despite my best intentions. Additionally, from an entirely practical and ethical standpoint, we have to consider our liability as youth workers—museums are museums, not schools, not institutions entirely set up around supporting youth. Our liabilities and child protection policies can be limited at best. We do not have nurses on hand, social workers employed, or staff with specific expertise in these areas. Our spaces are built for viewing art. We need to be realistic about the care we *can* provide. For example, during the height of the pandemic, many of my colleagues were excited to explore how we could provide community triage, like offering space for a food shelf—which is a great idea, but none of us knows how to run a food shelf. We know how to support folks in finding respite, inspiration, and connection with works of art. Acts of care should not be competitive in value. Yes, some have greater need and impact, but it goes back to the right sizedness of what we *can* do. The iterative acts build headroom and capacity for folks and have their own impact.

At the beginning of the program year, communicate this to the youth. It is not shutting them out to communicate clear boundaries of your role but instead giving them structure and direction. For example, in your initial meetings, you could include something short in your role description when you communicate the expectations for their roles. You could say, "I would like to offer myself as a resource for big questions—whether you are looking for advice on career or school, art, or something going on in your life. Please know that I will only speak from my experience and perspective. There are some areas where I can only be a compassionate listener, and I might help you identify supports in your life to help you move through the challenge."

If sensitive information is shared:

1. Remind the youth of your boundaries right away in the conversation. You can say, "I am here to listen. I am not a counselor or a social worker, so I will refrain from giving advice, but I can help by listening and maybe identifying other folks who can help."
2. Tell your supervisor and follow up with an email. This is not to sound alarm bells, but youth are vulnerable, and it is important to leave an administrative trail because it is a way to keep records to show you did your due diligence to be safe and accountable. Having another person aware of the situation is essential because their perspective could be helpful, and you might need help processing it. Consider where and how you share this—remember, it is the youth's information, not yours. Be private and consider how you share it could cause disruption or upset some of your colleagues.
3. Follow up with the youth to let them know you are checking on them. Reiterate the boundary.

4. Consider the redirection resources you have available. At the Walker, we have found success in connecting with the school counselors or social workers at the schools the youth attend; encouraging them to connect with other caring adults in their lives and asking if they have talked to friends or siblings about what they are facing can be a great redirection too. If they have talked to other people, you can ask, "Did you find that helpful?" or "What did you think of their advice?"

To be prepared for such an occasion, discuss the possible action plans with your supervisor. Does your museum have a child protection policy? Are you a mandated reporter in your state? What are your city's or county's policies or resources that are helpful to have? When you onboard youth, do you connect with parents or collect their information?

Consider, too, that even when sensitive information is not being shared, you should continue to enforce safe boundaries with youth across the program year.

Some things to consider:

1. If you have given your cell number to youth, consider enforcing a boundary that you will reply only during work hours or are available only for program-related information, like teens sharing that they are running late.
2. Do not be in a room with a closed door alone with a young person, and do not give them rides alone.
3. While the art we discuss in programs may call for a wide range of sensitive topics, that does not mean they are always on the table in programs for general conversation. Consider what is appropriate for your candor with your youth. We may show artworks with a sexual engagement, but that is not appropriate to talk about generally with the youth. Consider, too,

giving content warnings to youth before viewing challenging works. Some pieces that show violence best fit with an explicit content warning, or those that show or engage with racism or homophobia benefit from a trigger warning. Other pieces that may be dense, indirect, or less explicit in their engagement with challenging themes benefit from open-ended promptings, like "You may see things that leave you with questions or conflicting feelings. Some tools we have are to discuss it, ask more questions, journal about our thoughts, or step out of the gallery."

Remember, even if you are not the person to solve a complex problem for youth or save them from a desperate situation, you are making a significant impact in their lives. The power of a space where youth are recognized, respected, and listened to cannot be underestimated. Having time where they can be creative, ask questions, laugh, and be enmeshed in their interests is incredibly special. Safe spaces build the padding that allows for resiliency, and fun and laughter are just plain fantastic. For some youth, this may be the one space where they get to go by their preferred name, totally geek out on art, or learn at a pace that works for them. The work we do is essential. Art is a powerful escape.

Pivots

Sometimes in meetings you will need a change of direction when things go south, get intense, or fall flat. Pivoting is an essential skill for anyone working in museum teen programs. As facilitators, we must be aware of multiple factors simultaneously—the youth, the content, the goals, the exchanges between the youth, to name a few. If one of those goes up in flames, I encourage you to feel empowered to make the choice to change the direction, or pivot. Sometimes pivots are small, and we do not always even notice when we do them—like rephrasing a question that we asked that is received with crickets, making a joke, or breaking to play a quick game when energy is low. Maybe they become bigger actions on days when the energy from the youth is particularly low, so you respond by walking into another room or bringing in a backup plan to spend more time in the galleries instead of whatever else you had planned that day.

A lot of these responsive acts feel like reads of the room that can be picked up through experience as an educator and can be made easily, as long as you accept that sometimes what you design will not go as planned—accept that sometimes your work will fall flat. Prepare backup plans, and loosen your grip. Great things can happen with the unexpected. This is definitely with a rosy tint. All of these feel like pleasant pivots—galleries, change of scenery, jokes—but sometimes pivots are a matter of safety or a necessary means to deescalate a situation. To offer support in those situations, here is a short list of examples and tactics for making those bigger pivots to support youth.

You might need to make a more significant pivot when someone's mental health or identity is under duress or your group values are broken. Pivoting from these moments requires an acknowledgment that does not escalate the situation. Here are some examples:

> 1. Pivots are commonly needed when there is a microaggression in the group, like an offhand comment that un/intentionally causes harm to someone's racial, gender, sexual, religious, or physical identity. This has shown up in WACTAC as the youth misgendering their peers. I will fully admit that the first time this happened, I did not know what to do and did not handle it well. I let it happen and followed up with the two teens involved afterward. What I learned from that situation is that if/when it happens, correct it right away publicly. This can be very simple and done without fanfare. Jump in to

say, "[Youth's name] uses [he/him] pronouns." After that, follow up with the two teens. For the one who made a mistake, tell them you were not trying to put them on blast and only trying to remind them. Ask them how they feel. They are likely a little embarrassed so remind them that we are all learning. For the youth that was misgendered, ask how they feel and if that was an okay response. See if they have a way they would prefer it to be handled if it happens again. An excellent way to prepare, and hopefully prevent, this exchange is to have the youth share their pronouns regularly. Regular practice is also helpful in case someone's pronouns change. Always share them with names at the beginning of the program year and whenever a guest is present. Ask youth to include them on name tags, or buy some with a line built in so you do not need to prompt the addition. Additionally, if youth receive employee badges, ask if you can have pronouns added there. As a final reminder on this topic, some youth may be new to sharing pronouns, ask before assuming them, or to pronouns that expand beyond the gender binary. Model open information with this—for example, at the beginning of the program year, you could say, "Let us all go around and share our names and pronouns. Our pronouns are how we would like others to refer to us; these might be he/him, she/her, they/them, your name, or something else that makes you feel respected. I will go first—my name is Simona, and I use she/her pronouns." Let youth know it is okay to ask each other their pronouns if they forget, but I encourage you to ask the group what a respectful way to do that looks like.

2. Another time where a pivot might be needed is when you have to head off a potential conflict that could be caused by a comment made by a young person. The youth we work with are brilliant and great but sometimes say unkind or igno-

rant things. When you hear these things, as the facilitator it is your job to stop them from taking over. For example, in WACTAC (at the time of writing this), we are working on a zine with tips for discussing artworks in our galleries and are planning on having it printed in multiple languages and available as an audio description for blind and partially sighted visitors. While working on this project, one young person said, "What is the point of showing visual pieces to someone who cannot see them?" Before this could gain traction or become more problematic, I stepped in to say, "That is an interesting point—how can we highlight nonvisual ways to enjoy artworks or come up with descriptions that can support all visitors?" Pivot by turning ignorance into a chance to learn.

3. When pivoting is needed, it is less about inflammatory content and more about the youth's mental health. At the Walker, we had an exhibition that featured several works that depicted women in nonconsensual sexual situations. I had planned a conversation around the exhibition, specifically around questions on values and works on view, and before entering the exhibition, I gave the youth a trigger warning and encouraged them to self-select if they would like to go in or exit the show and/or the conversation at any time. This is a big part of the "rules" that I lay out at the beginning of the WACTAC year, and I remind the youth regularly that they are empowered to step away, put their head down, take a walk, or use the restroom at any time. WACTAC is a voluntary space, and we respect their knowledge of their needs. If they are gone for more than ten minutes, my cofacilitator or I will check in on them. Back to the story—while walking through the exhibition, a member of WACTAC was triggered and began to shut down. When we returned to our meeting space, this young person put their head

down and quietly cried. In this situation, I had two immediate needs to respond to: the teen in distress and the WACTAC group, which was highly concerned and focused on their fellow member who did not want to talk. In a situation where one teen may be triggered, exacerbated, or piqued, you must balance their needs without putting them on blast or derailing the rest of the group. It will always be a little messy because the other teens will want to help, but the best thing you can do in a scenario like that is to separate that young person from the group and follow their needs. I am fortunate that I have a cofacilitator to whom I can easily hand things off or, through a glance, communicate that I need their help. If you are also fortunate in that way, either rely on your cofacilitators or take action yourself: gently and without making it super public, ask that young person if they would like to talk or step out. If they would like to talk, bring them to a quiet public place, like another gallery or your lobby or office, and listen to them. If they would like to process independently, provide them with some coping tools—pen and paper, clay to mold, or an iPad. Give options. Continue to check on them. For the rest of the group, acknowledge it and say, "We all have different reactions to things, and this show was particularly hard for X; let us respect their privacy and move on from this as best we can. Since that content was challenging, if anyone else needs a minute or wants to step out or ask questions, we can take that time now; otherwise, let us try to move on with what we have planned for the day." If you do not have the luxury of cofacilitators, a situation like this could be handled on the way back to your space from the galleries. While walking, ask the young person in distress if they would like some time to themselves, or when returning to the room, deploy another pivoting tactic. Buy yourself time by coming back into the room and asking the teens to do a drawing or writing reflection. During that time, ask the youth in distress if they would like some time to themselves. In a case like this, there is no way to stop their reaction from being public, and there is likely little chance you will resolve how they are feeling. In this situation, your role is to deescalate the situation before the energy or distress takes over. Know that you are providing active care by offering a safe container for a young person to be acutely upset and calm down.

4. Often, the source of a need to pivot comes from an exchange between the youth that becomes heated or tense. In situations like this, begin by tracking the conversation. It might start in small groups with the youth or a full group discussion. As a facilitator, you should follow what happens in group conversations and check in on small groups. Disagreement does not mean conflict, and it can be fruitful, and a good thing for young people to learn how to work out with each other, or you can help prompt it into a positive space by repeating back what the youth say with the leading line, "From X's perspective...," and remind everyone that they all have different experiences and perspectives. Sometimes this does not work; arguments start, people team up, and chaos ensues. First off, it is okay to stop a conversation. If you see that there is no resolution, step in. Say, "Everyone is pretty worked up here and is really passionate about the two sides. Remember our group norms for how we want to treat each other. Since everyone is pretty focused on this, why don't we pause and take some time to breathe? We can draw in here, or if folks want to go into the galleries, you can spend ten minutes there, and then we can reconvene." I would warn that a risk in going into the galleries or having the youth unsupervised is that they could use that time to gossip about each other or continue to dig into their sides. I

think breaking the argument and pushing them to move on is crucial. If you are giving them options, try not to present too many because it can be challenging to decide. Follow up the following week with silly games and icebreakers to inject positivity into the group. Sometimes, the exchange might come from the youth and a visiting staff member or work presented by your museum that might be racially charged or insensitive. These are moments when you need to look at the immediate and long term. In the immediate, make sure the youth are safe. If the comment came from a staff person, regardless of the power hierarchy in your museum, step in and redirect, rephrase, or challenge what they shared. It is your program space; you can wrap up the conversation early. If it comes from a work of art, this can be an opportunity to begin the inquiry with your youth to encourage them to look for the why behind the choices that lead to its installation and create an argument for their response. Let the youth direct if it will become an inquiry project. It can cause more harm than good to have them revisit a triggering or traumatic piece continually, or it can be healing to take action against it. Follow their lead on that.[1]

One of the most challenging things to accept with times when you need to pivot is just knowing that much of this work is learning on the job. Sometimes a day might fall flat, you might not achieve what you wanted, or there was tension with the youth. It is okay. Since a program is the sum of its parts, a single day does not define the whole program, and problems can be remedied. Pivoting and moving through challenges is a way to model resiliency and problem-solving for youth. By being attentive,

1. See 3.1.4. Heartbreakers & Troublemakers by Jo Higgins; 3.1.2. The Potential Impact of Walker Teen Programs for Youth by Dr. Yolanda Majors; and 1.1.6. Planning for a Year of Programming by Simona Zappas.

proactive, and transparent with youth and bringing them along in the pivot, you are giving them skills for life. Honor your ability to do it, think on your feet, and be kind to yourself because no two problems will look the same. Rather than thinking about our progress as a group as linear with some bumps or turns, I encourage you to think of it as a series of connected circles on a meandering path. Some circles are bigger, some are smaller. Bear with me and imagine each circle is a challenge; our hope is for the circles to get progressively smaller so that we can cycle through each challenge faster, looping back on lessons learned from past challenges. As we resource ourselves, the process can expedite and shrink the circle. The end target is a moving one.

☺

Jo Higgins 3.1.4.

Heartbreakers & Troublemakers: How to Navigate, Embrace, and Ultimately Survive Disruption

Bio

Jo Higgins is an educator, writer, and public programmer living and working on unceded Gadigal Country in Sydney, Australia. Her work on informal, peer-led learning programs, arts partnerships, and research is underpinned by values of collaboration, generosity, creative risk-taking, transparency, and lifelong learning. Jo is a 2018 Churchill Fellow, and from 2017 to 2021 she was the Young Creatives Coordinator at the Museum of Contemporary Art Australia, Sydney. Over the last decade, she has worked across Australia, New Zealand, and the United Kingdom for organizations including the South London Gallery, Te Tuhi, Kaldor Public Art Projects, and the National Gallery of Australia.

Essay

I promise this is not a story about pivoting (or working through pandemics). It is, though, about the inevitability of disruption and some thoughts on adjusting your sails so the boat does not sink when it hits. And

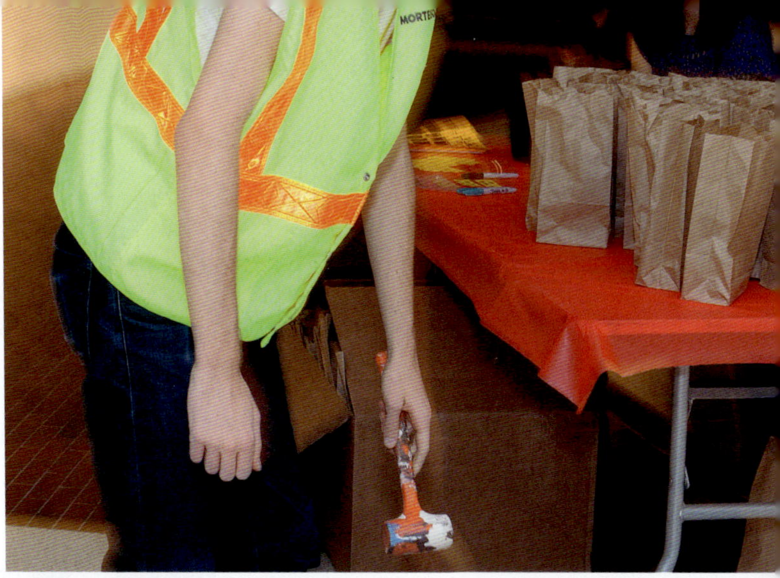

GLOBAL FIN@NCE

411 Fifth Avenue
New York, NY 10016

JOSEPH D. GIARRAPUTO
PRESIDENT AND PUBLISHER

November 2, 2001

Mr. Ken Lay
Chief Executive Officer
Enron
1400 Smith Street
Houston, TX 77002-7369

Dear Mr. Lay:

On October 4th, *Global Finance* conducted an Award Ceremony for the winners of its World's Best Company selections. A report on these selections was included in our September issue which is enclosed.

Also enclosed is a trophy commemorating Enron's selection. The attachment to this letter describes how you can obtain additional copies of this trophy.

Once again, congratulations to you and your colleagues at Enron on your selection as a World's Best Company.

Sincerely,

TELEPHONE: 646•742•2000 • FAX: 212•447•7750 • jdg@gfmag.com
NEW YORK • LONDON • MILAN • MEXICO CITY • RIO DE JANEIRO

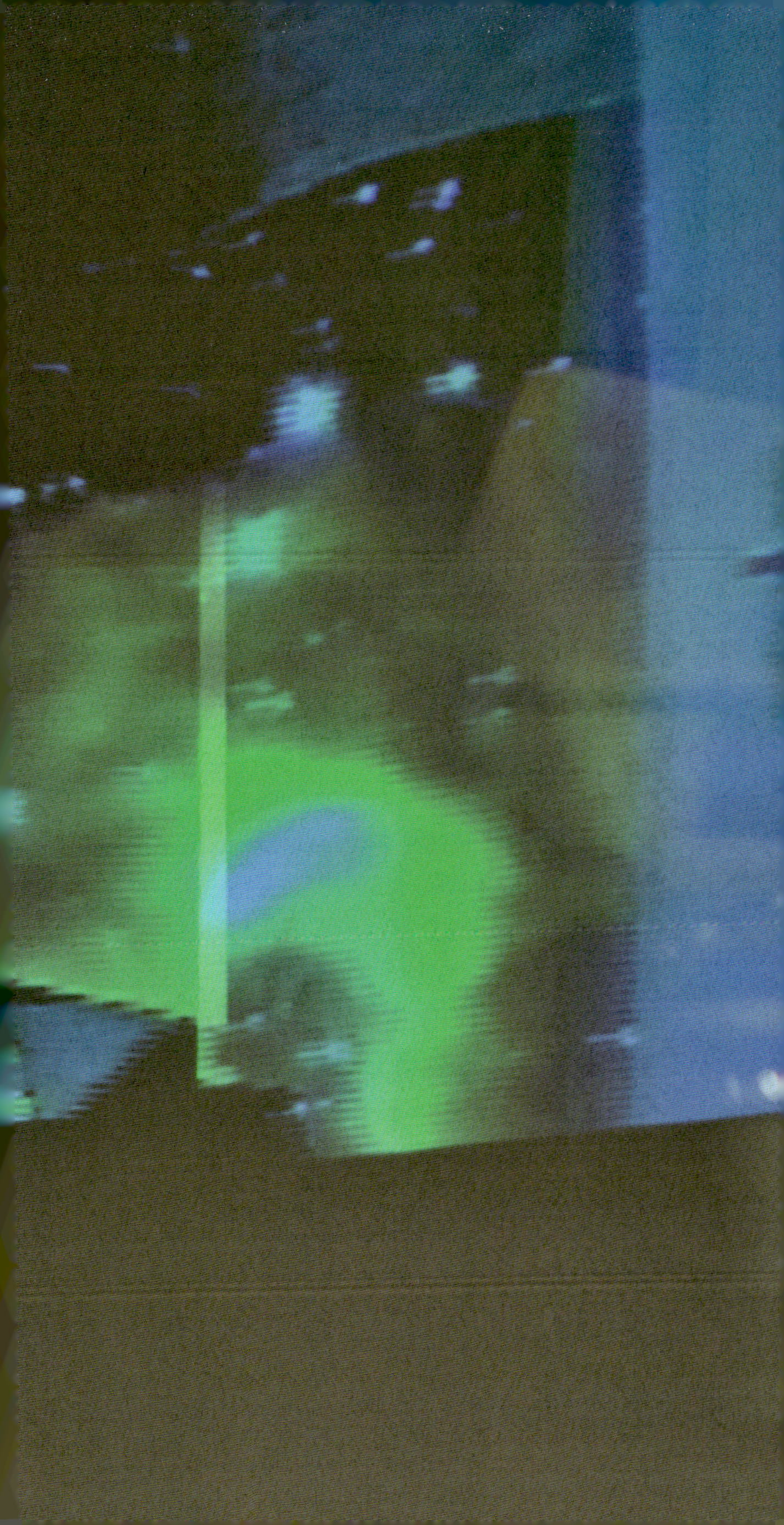

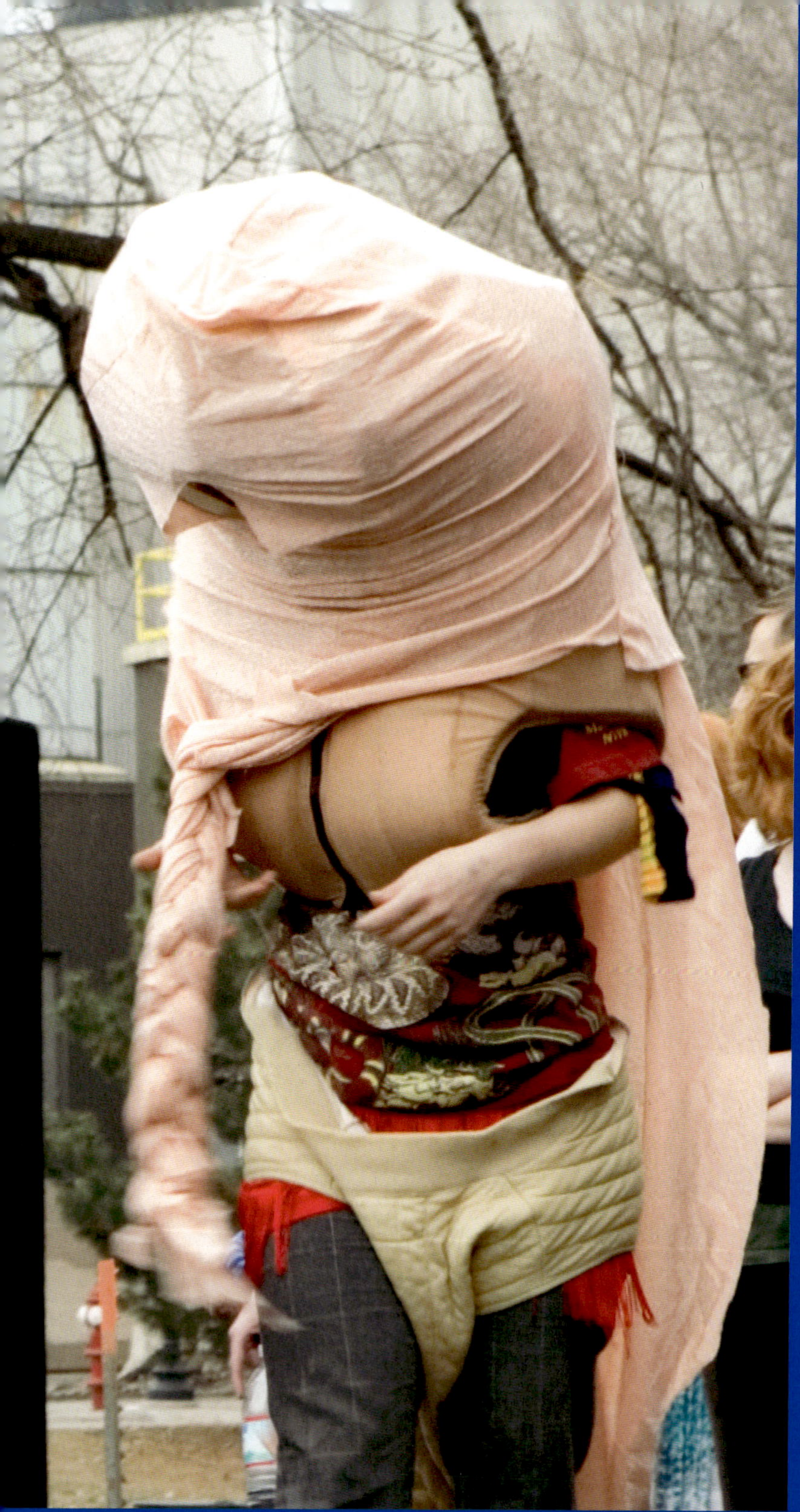

by boat, I mean your teen program. And you.

Welcome aboard, friends...

Let Me Introduce Trouble
Is it pessimistic to prophesize that if you are working in any kind of cultural organization today, at some stage, trouble is going to find you? *Probably.* But that does not mean I am wrong. (I am sorry.)

But what is this trouble? It could be a global pandemic that accelerates a social justice movement. But it could also be the acquisition or curation of a work with troubling content or provenance, a new museum policy, or a tone-deaf tweet; a staff petition or a problematic donor; or an article by a former staff member about their experiences at your institution; or the racialized experience of a front-of-house staff member by a member of the public; or, or, or...

Put simply: it is the kind of trouble you *did not* anticipate when planning your program for the year. It is the trouble that will affect considerations of everything taking place across your museum, from cultural safety strategies to access, equity, and diversity planning, to marketing and PR and public programs.

So, what does this trouble mean for the group of bright, curious, invested young people you have invited to be a part of your museum's community?

Trouble, Meet Good Trouble[1]
If your trouble has any kind of public ramifications (media coverage, strikes, petitions, social media campaigns, canceled events, hirings or firings), if your teens are going to hear about it, and if it is going to affect the way you program, then it is probably going to raise some questions or frustrations from the group.

How your teens respond to the situation, as well

1. Joshua Bote, "'Get in Good Trouble, Necessary Trouble': Rep. John Lewis in His Own Words," *USA Today*, July 18, 2020, https://www.usatoday.com/story/news/politics/2020/07/18/rep-john-lewis-most-memorable-quotes-get-good-trouble/5464148002/.

as their sense of agency or ability *to* respond, will depend on so many factors—how far into the year you are; how their participation at the museum has been introduced to them; how visible their platform is within your institution; how represented or affected (or *not*) they feel by the issue...to name just a few.

However, the gift of working with teens is that if something is not right and there is a disconnect between what they expect of the museum and what they experience, they will be sure to let you know. Furthermore, if your teens are anything like the teens I have worked with, they will want and need to talk about it, and they will almost certainly want to do something about it too. This is the *good* trouble.

Suppose you recognize your young people as experts in their own lives and as real arbiters of contemporary culture on any regular day. In that case, this good trouble might *only* be wild ideas or strong opinions.

Nevertheless, in the face of your (other) trouble, or as part of a broader moment of cultural or political reckoning, it is critical to recognize your teens' challenging questions and criticisms not as rebellion or disrespect but as a form of generosity; a collective, strategic call to action for the greater good.

Let's call it good trouble in the service of moving from something messy to something generative— which really is the work of young people. *Your* role is to create space in these feelings and responses to embed learning into this process.

However you have been running your program, whatever the intended outcomes and content are, you will have been developing and nurturing skills for teens to navigate trouble and steer it in the good trouble direction. Critical thinking. Accountability. Compassion. Collective action. Empowerment.

If I can offer some advice that an experienced, very generous peer once gave me: in the midst of any disruption, ask yourself, *What are the opportunities here?* So, I would encourage *you* to take this advice too. Center this provocation. (Consider it the anchor in our aforementioned boat metaphor, if you will...)

But First, a Check-In: How Are *You* Feeling? Whatever comes next—for your teens and the program—there is usually a hard truth to acknowledge.

Whatever it is that is happening at your institution, it is going to have an impact on you too. (I am sorry.) Even if you are not directly affected, the chances are you will feel disillusioned, frustrated, anxious...tired. Maybe a little heartbroken. And finding a way to process these feelings is *not the same work* as supporting your teens.

Truthfully, juggling your own very valid feelings with your duty of care to your teens, as well as the positionality of your museum on whatever the issue at hand is, well, it could be one of the hardest things you will have to do in your role. But it is good, meaningful work, so do not lose faith (but if you do lose a little faith, that is ok too).

One of the rich challenges of being a teen educator is striking the right care balance. Keeping our hearts full and our resilience bucket topped up is critical (trouble or no trouble), so whatever nourishes you, hold space for that. (Mine is year-round ocean swimming. No relation to the boat metaphor, I promise...)

Allyship, Allegiance, and the Importance of Transparency

A huge part of your role is advocating for the voice and contribution of your young people to the museum. They might be programming for their peers or engaging with your collection through zines, memes, audio guides, or tours. So, how do you situate your allyship without co-opting identities and advocate for their criticisms without compromising their sense of security or cultural safety—and your own?

So much of the richness and satisfaction we get from working with teens comes from the day-to-day emotional labor and joy of supporting their growth and learning, but when trouble or disruption occurs, navigating your allegiance to your teens is going to be challenging. We hold their trust, but we also represent the museum in their space, and we have an implicit power as a consequence.

Your positionality—how you feel personally about whatever is going on—should not be something else that your teens need to navigate. A lot of our power comes from what we choose to communicate and how we choose to do that. Transparency is essential (what useful information or insights can you share, for example?), but so is holding neutral space so that wherever your teens want or need to go, they are setting the direction.

Transparency (and boundaries) will be critical as you ensure your teens' safety and ongoing trust in you while also negotiating and communicating the limits of all your roles, the museum's positionality, and what capacity, if any, there is to affect change. (It is not straightforward, I know.)

So How Do You Scaffold and Hold Space for a Good, Troubling Conversation?

Every institution will have its own learning frameworks, own points of cultural reference, own needs and styles. The following approach is not definitive, but it did help me move meaningfully, productively, and respectfully through some very important, very difficult conversations with a group of teens talking about racism, equity, representation, and cultural safety. So, I hope there is something in this approach that could help you too.

Step 1: Prepare to Talk

Make sure everyone is starting from the same page. Do not assume everyone knows what has happened. Be proactive—send an email and stick to the facts. My advice: do not overexplain. Acknowledge what response there has been from the teens so far (if any) and invite questions or comments via an optionally anonymous feedback form. Explain your next steps—collecting feedback or questions and offering a space to come together to talk.

There might be other communication strategies you can use here, but the aim is to reassure trust and acknowledge that they have been heard.

Planning

In preparing your discussion, there are a few things you will need to think through logistically, emotionally, and intellectually to help shape your approach.

- How do you want your young people to feel in the space?
- Where will you meet them? Consider the implications of this space.
- What tools or language will they need to feel comfortable talking?
- How are you going to situate yourself as a museum representative but also as their ally?
- How will you answer their questions about your own personal feelings on the issue? Is there research, context, or background that you will need to provide?
- How do you want to frame the conversation so that it feels productive?
- What next steps or outcomes might you anticipate?
- Who else do you need in this space with you—your manager? Another educator? Who is going to do what?
- How will you document or make a record of the conversation? Will any information from the record need to be shared with external stakeholders from the group of teens? Your supervisor? Department head? Other colleagues? Will you need permission from the teens to share it?
- And that is just for the conversation with your teens.

You will also probably need to support your directors to understand why this conversation needs to happen—even if, or especially if, they are resistant to the idea of you meeting with your teens about this to begin with. What can you share from your teens and their programs to give them some insight? A zine they have made or a manifesto they have written? Your manager could also champion this process and be a great sounding board for how to facilitate the conversation and next steps for the teens.

However you frame it for them—as safety and care or containment or opportunity—transparency will be critical here too. Ask for your manager's support and input to help tell leadership what you will do and how. Take them with you and invite their input into this planning process as much as possible. Put it to them: What is the opportunity here *for us*?

Step 2: Facilitating the Talking
Acknowledgment of country
An acknowledgement of country or something similar is not only culturally significant; it can also be an opportunity to establish a space for reflection, respect, learning, and grounding. It can and should be so much more than a formality. If a cultural acknowledgment is not part of your museum's practice, consider other ways to welcome and ground your teens in a collective moment before starting.

Acknowledging today's space
Thank your teens for joining you. Acknowledge their care and generosity in being there and whatever anxieties or feelings they may bring to the space. Explain how the session will run; you would like to talk and facilitate the first half of your time together before opening up the conversation. Explain what will happen next—will this be the first and last conversation? How are you planning to give feedback to the museum? How will you continue to consult with and update them?

Safer spaces agreement
A safer spaces agreement (group norms, community agreement, accountability guidelines) can be valuable

for supporting participation in a difficult conversation. I recommend writing one at the beginning of the program year with your teens—embed the practice early and often. If your teens are not familiar with what a safer spaces agreement is, there are plenty of fantastic resources[2] out there you can share. However, at its core, it is about recognizing that different people need different things to feel safe and empowered—and that these things may also change from meeting to meeting.

Helping your teens coauthor a safer spaces agreement will help them to recognize each other's needs and manage their expectations of behavior. If you need to offer some examples to get them started, here are some helpful principles that some of my teens identified:

> Using nongendered language
> Acknowledging different types of participation—silence does not mean disinterest
> Active listening and not interrupting
> Having different opinions shared and listened to respectfully

Icebreaker
Time for a tempo shift. You know your group, so trust your instincts about what activity and communication style will work best. But think about how you can use this activity to gently embed some of the values or ideas you will discuss. Is there a playful or low-stakes get-to-know-you activity that invites positive peer-to-peer feedback or can demonstrate everyday experiences or values? Bear in mind whatever has come out of the previous activity.

Identity Iceberg
This is a simple exercise to help illustrate how we move through and experience the world—how we

2. The Anti-Opression Network, "Resources," accessed February 13, 2023, https://theantioppressionnetwork.com/resources/saferspacepolicy/.

respond to events and disruptions—is shaped by so many different elements. Some of them—the tip of the iceberg—are very visible (the color of our skin, the way we dress, our physical abilities). In contrast, others exist invisibly under the waterline (our sexuality, politics, home lives, values, education, experiences of travel, etc.). And some might sit right on the waterline (our religion, our cultural customs, even our diets).

As a group, brainstorm verbally or visually some of the visible and invisible aspects of identity before inviting the group to fill out their own iceberg worksheets. Sharing is entirely optional, but it can be nice to put the invitation out there.

Brainstorm: Talking about power
As I mentioned earlier, how empowered (or not) your teens feel within the museum depends on many different factors. So, it can be helpful to unpack with your teens how they might understand their own identities and experiences as a form of power and to reframe this as a form of expertise, particularly in spaces where they are advocating for change.[3]

As a group, brainstorm a list of different forms of power. How many of these do your teens have experience with or access to? What other powers do they have, and in what contexts? If we consider our lived experiences and identities, is there anything else we can reframe as a form of power or expertise to effect change in this space they hold within your museum?

Roundtable: Inviting questions or reflections about what's happened
If you have received questions from the group through your previous survey, these can be an excellent place to start your conversation. Go through the questions and answer them as honestly as you can, acknowledging the limits of your knowledge and explaining if there is something you cannot share. It is okay to say

3. Tara J. Yosso, "Whose Culture Has Capital? A Critical Race Theory Discussion of Community Cultural Wealth," *Race, Ethnicity, and Education* 8, no. 1 (2005): 69–91.

you do not know if you do not know. Transparency also means acknowledging your position and the power you hold in this space, situating your advocacy for them within the broader ecology of the institution. These sorts of limits can be helpful. It is important to remember that it is not your responsibility (or theirs!) to change the way your institution runs.

With that in mind, the next step is to invite the group to ask any other questions or share other thoughts or experiences. As part of this process, ask them to consider and articulate, if possible: What would they like in sharing this—to be heard? To discuss? For something to be actioned? *What is this an opportunity for?*

Wherever they take the conversation, just manage their expectations and be transparent about the parameters.

Next steps: What do you need to see happen?
How you wrap things up and what comes next will be shaped by the conversations that you just had. Again, managing expectations (of you, the museum, the program) is critical—you can all only do collectively as much as you can—so consider what is realistic and what feels productive.

Suppose they do have ideas for the next steps. In that case, it can be good to recap what you will do next, whether organizing a follow-up meeting to articulate goals and plans or connecting them with other resources or museum stakeholders.

Step 3: Wrapping Up
Check out
A final temperature check. *At the start of the session, I was feeling… At the end of the session, I am feeling…*

Ask the group to write their responses on a Post-it Note and pin it to the wall on their way out.

Follow up
Suppose you plan to share insights from your con-

versations with other museum stakeholders. In that case, I would recommend writing up your discussion notes and sharing them with the group for their edits and approval before circulating. Is there something you have missed or misconstrued or that the group wants left out?

This is a really effective way to co-create a record of these complex conversations and to demonstrate your trust and respect for them, whatever comes next.

So, What *Does* Happen Next?

Well, it might be a meeting with museum leadership. Some further conversations. It might be some training for your teens or a public program. Or, or, or… (This is the wind returning to your sails.)

Honestly, though? It is hard to say what may come of this trouble. In the short term, probably not much at an institutional level. (I am sorry.) However, it is still an opportunity. Your program may get to recalibrate or shift focus. Your teens might find new communities to collaborate with. You will keep having conversations, refining ideas, and identifying opportunities and new goals. Accept nonclosure.

If your teens feel validated, invigorated, and, most importantly, still welcome in your museum, well then, you have done your job.

(Now go fill your resilience bucket.)

☺

Nisa Mackie & Simona Zappas 3.1.5.

Museum as Home Base: Creating a Stable Foundation for Youth Changemakers

Bio
Nisa Mackie is currently the deputy director of learning and engagement at MoMA. She was the Head of Public Engagement, Learning, and Impact at the Walker Art Center (2015–2021). She developed strategies to expand inclusion and access, stimulate curiosity and critical thinking within museum audiences, and strengthen the museum's civic role. Mackie also worked at the Biennale of Sydney in Sydney from 2008 to 2010 and 2013 to 2016, creating learning programs, residencies, and public programs across the exhibition's five museum and nonmuseum venues. Born and raised in Sydney, Australia, Mackie earned her BA in creative arts administration from Macquarie University and her MA in art theory and sculpture performance and installation from the University of New South Wales. She holds a diploma in project management for government.

Bio
Simona Zappas (she / her) is the Youth Programs

Manager at the Walker Art Center. In her work she designs and facilitates informal learning opportunities for youth. She collaborates with curatorial staff to bring a learning lens to museum public engagement and a social practice bent on programmatic strategy. Before this, she was the director of WFNU Frogtown, a low-power radio station in Saint Paul. Simona holds a BA with honors from Macalester College and a master of education from the University of Minnesota. Simona sits on the Saint Paul Neighborhood Network board and volunteers at Planned Parenthood as an abortion doula.

Introduction

In June of 2022, former Head of Public Engagement, Learning, and Impact at the Walker Art Center and current deputy director for learning and engagement at the Museum of Modern Art spoke with Simona Zappas, the Youth Programs Manager at the Walker Art Center, on the genesis of a new curriculum for the Walker Art Center Teen Arts Council (WACTAC). This curriculum aimed to support teens in transforming blanket criticism into critical inquiry by developing textual literacy, information gathering, and negotiation, and by teaching teens to balance multiple and often conflicting perspectives. This new approach to WACTAC also supports developmental milestones for teens as they formulate their identity against and through their interactions with communities, social groups, and institutions. This conversation analyzes the dual responsibility that museum educators have of helping teens understand the machinations of the museum while simultaneously representing and advocating for young people within the institution. This often requires educators to curtail their positionality in order to platform teens' developing and expressing their own opinions and perspectives in ways that can be heard (and potentially actioned on) by the museum. This shared work between Simona, Nisa, and contracted evaluator Dr. Yolanda Majors is contextualized by and in response to heightened political division across the country, the rise of new identity politics among teens, youth politicization earlier in life through social media, and a heightened public awareness of the power structures within museum organizations.

Conversation
Nisa Mackie

To kick off, my name is Nisa Mackie. I currently work as the deputy director for learning and engagement at MoMA. Previous to my role at MoMA, I was the Head of Public Engagement, Learning, and Impact at the Walker Art Center. I joined the Walker in 2015, and one of the programs I was really excited about was the Walker Art Center's Teen Arts Council. I always referred to it as the jewel in the crown of the Walker's education programming, mainly because the Walker was one of the first museums to start a teen program.

One of the projects underway when I first entered the institution was a Guerrilla Girls Twin Cities Takeover that brought together curatorial staff, the teen programs coordinator, and WACTAC. The museum worked with several colleges and cultural institutions—including the Minneapolis Institute of Art (Mia), Saint Catherine University (St. Kate's), the Minneapolis College of Art and Design (MCAD), and several other smaller organizations. Each was to stage a component of the citywide project. The components took the form of outdoor billboards, exhibitions, and workshops, talks by the Guerrilla Girls; the Walker was also planning its own installation in the museum by the artists. Part of the project was to engage the Guerrilla Girls with youth-led and youth-serving entities across the city. The Minneapolis Institute of Art's teen group was involved, WACTAC was involved, and smaller nonprofits such as Native Youth Arts Collective and Juxtaposition Arts. Over the course of these interactions, a really interesting political friction emerged wherein the young people who met with the Guerrilla Girls began to question the way their lived identities intersected with their practice. First and foremost, it is important to note that the Guerrilla Girls are understood within an art historical context to be a critical second-wave feminist collective. However, one component of their history was that the group had primarily consisted of white women, many of whom took pseudonyms of female artists of color. This was one issue identified by local youth. There was also a critique being waged at the Guerrilla Girls on social media that their work was transphobic as it primarily focused on researching and addressing gender equity through a cisgender lens. This is part of the challenge of contextualizing certain historically rooted activist practices within a shifting political landscape, particularly one very focused on identity. WACTAC became very involved in raising awareness around these issues as they became more familiar with the Guerrilla Girls. They staged a large-scale community meeting that brought several teens and young-adult groups together to talk about and respond to the takeover, discussing potentially even boycotting the project. And so, it became a very polemical situation within the institution. On the one hand, we had the museum that wanted to mount this exhibition by these very well-respected artists, and on the other hand we had our group of teens who felt that the museum should not present these artists because they did not represent the politics of, at least, WACTAC. Looking back, I always refer to this as a moment of accidental YPAR (Youth Participatory Action Research).[1] That is, the teens identified an issue expressed through textual means, they conducted research, gathered information, assessed different viewpoints, and ultimately mounted a response that aimed to broaden the conversation (as opposed to opting out or protesting). I am proud of the teens' work, the coordinator, and Olga Viso, the director, who brought the youth and the artists together to have a challenging conversation about where they were coming from. As a result of our teen's consciousness-raising, the Guerrilla Girls changed the poster they were to install in the museum. In addition, the teens ran their own parallel public program where they lifted up the voices of gender-expansive and BIPOC youth and artists living and working in the Twin Cities. This ran at the same time as the opening of the Guerrilla Girls project, not in protest, but I would say as an extension of the activist politics of that artist group. Even though I think the outcome was positive, I would not lie in saying that it was not a stressful situation to navigate. In particular, contemporary art institutions, I think, are known for placing the needs and desires of the artists that they are working with really at the center of everything that they do. So, when that comes into tension with another constituent group, sometimes it can be very challenging to navigate those conversations.

 Educators often focus on platforming the agency and self-determination of the youth they are working with because they want to build those leadership and collaboration skills, and they want youth to be empowered through their work and engagement with the museum. On the other hand, curatorial and other departments are very focused on mounting a successful artist project. These types of agonisms involve a lot of conversation and negotiation. Now,

1. Julio Cammarota and Michelle Fine, "Youth Participatory Action Research: A Pedagogy for Transformational Resistance," in *Revolutionizing Education: Youth Participatory Action Research in Motion*, eds. Julio Cammarota and Michelle Fine (New York: Taylor & Francis, 2008), 1–11.

Simona, you came into the organization as our Youth Programs Coordinator after this project. However, by then, I think I had realized something about the structure of our teen programming. When I say "our programming," I am referring to our curriculum and instructional design—that it was not set up to support these challenging interactions or truly empower youth within institutional parameters of what was possible. And so maybe with that I will hand it over to you, Simona, to talk about your entry into the program.

Simona Zappas
 Thanks for the intro, Nisa! So, I am Simona Zappas, I use she/her pronouns, and I am the Youth Programs Manager at the Walker Art Center. I came into my role in March of 2018, maybe a year after this project happened. It was an exciting moment to step into because there was a lot of raw material to work with in the youth program, just from the memory of the Guerrilla Girls Takeover and Nisa's drive to turn the lessons learned into learning strategies. As Nisa said, the Walker is a museum that's been supporting youth programs for a long time. So, a lot of support and resources, like institutional buy-in, money, and a legacy, were waiting to be activated. Before joining the Walker team, I only had experience working in one youth program, and my background had actually been focused on digital media and media literacy learning for adults and elders. I had worked at a public access TV station and an independent radio station and had also worked with youth in a homework help center. I repeatedly saw a lack of emotional boundaries between the adults and the youth in those social services organizations. My team oversaw homework help and general enrichment activities. However, the youth we worked with came from high-need situations, where they were often in precarious situations

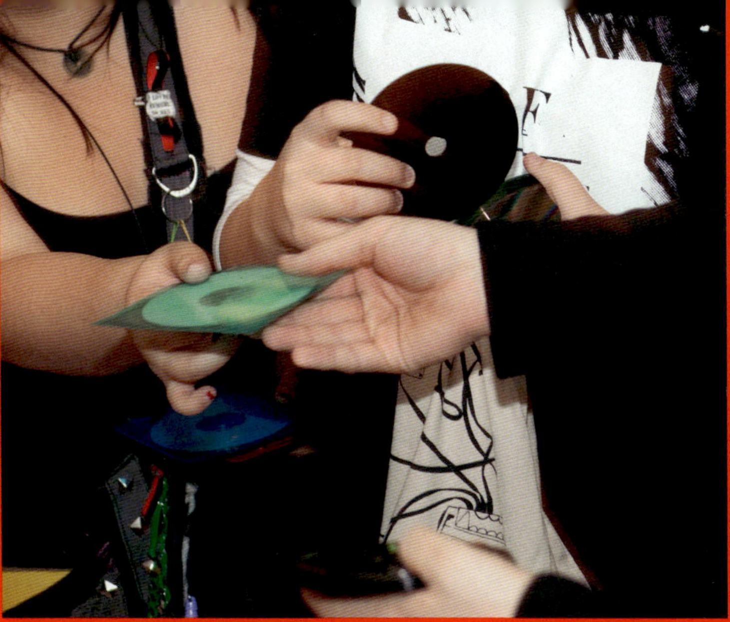

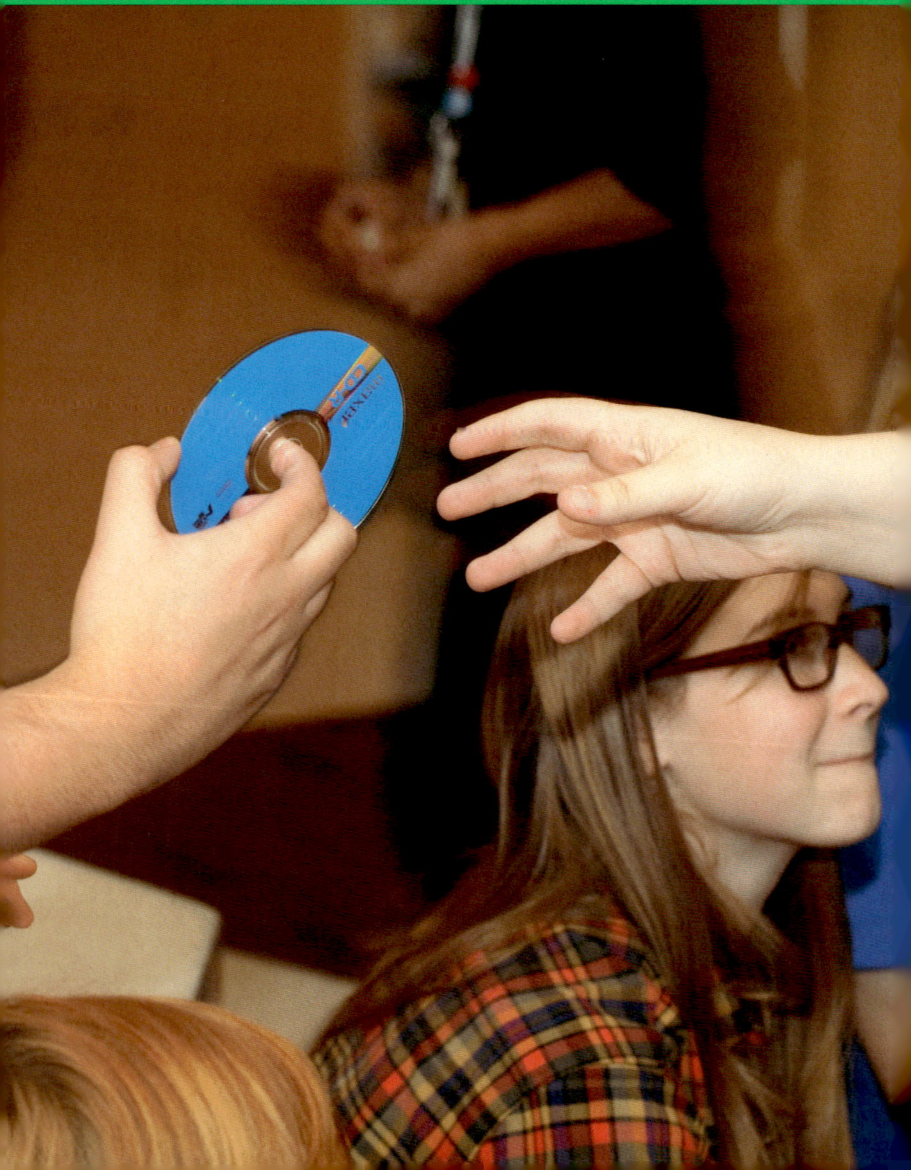

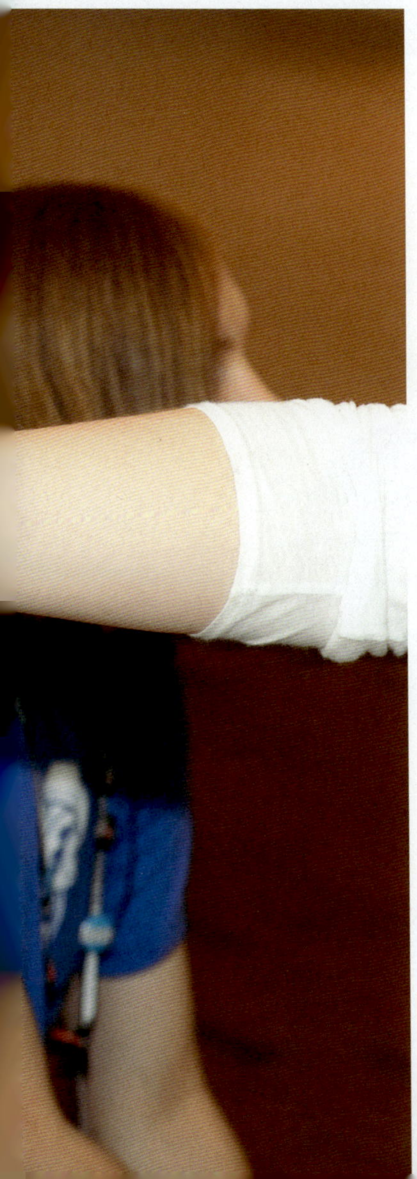

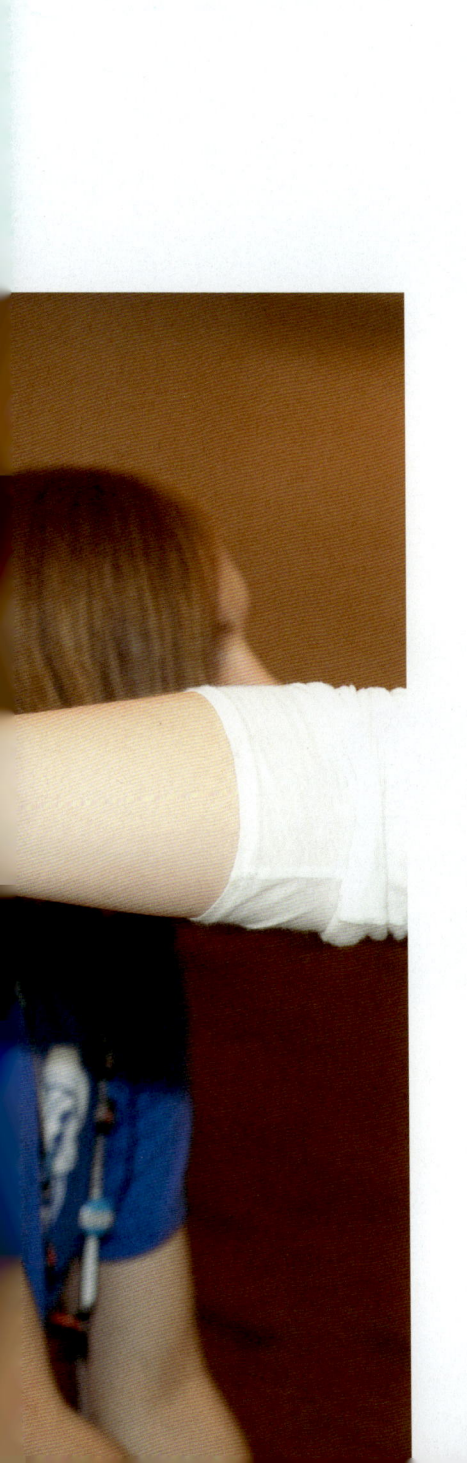

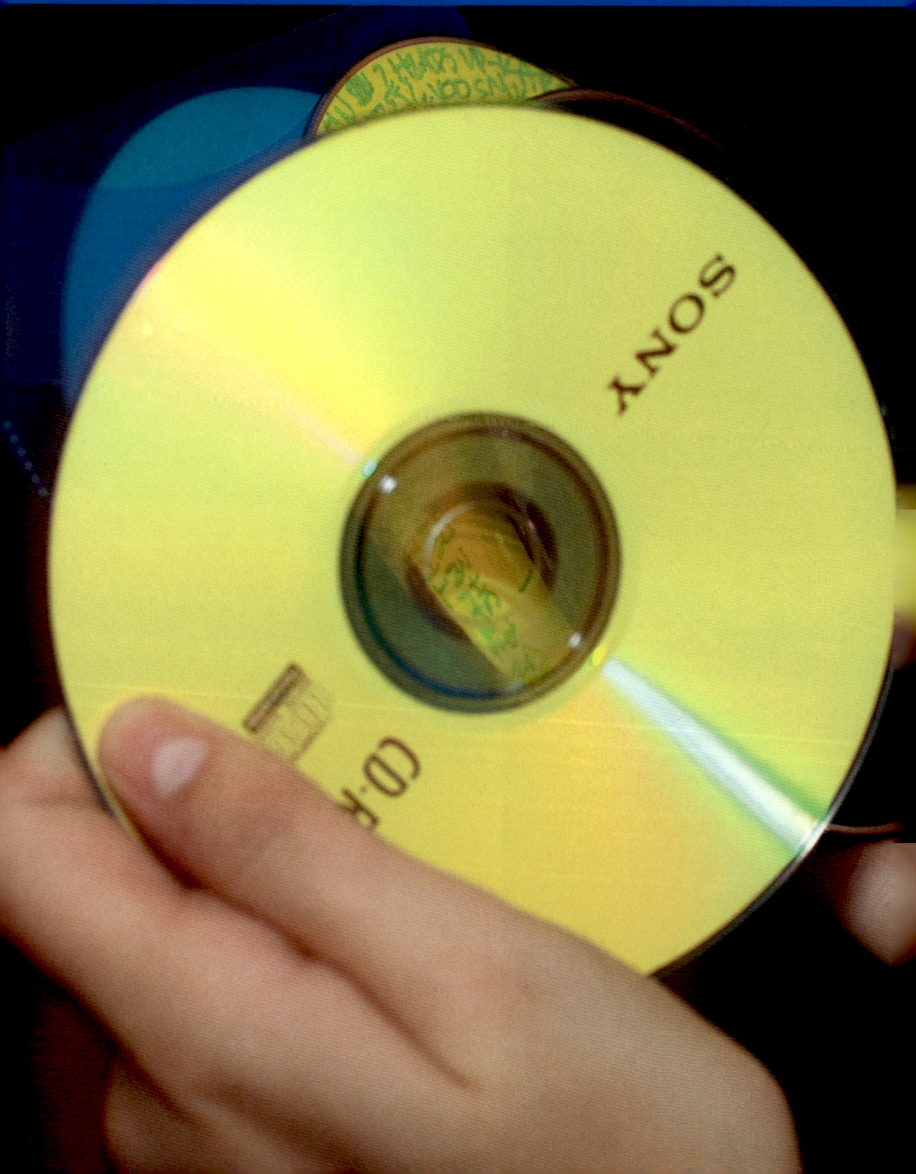
SONY

or had immediate, urgent needs. My team was not resourced, in terms of skills or materials, to support them, so a constant emotional overwhelm took over and shaped our plan for the programs to those that were actually in our purview and realism for our work. This is not to say we should not have cared or tried to help, but that we focused energy in areas where we could make a little impact rather than in areas where we could make some significant impact. So, it was exhilarating to come to an organization that focused on its approach and understanding of where we could help youth.

NM
I want to chip in and say that you touched on something essential that we identified as we met with various teen program coordinators and educators across the country,[2] which is that there is this kind of primacy of the idea of empowerment. It comes from a very good place, but we should dig into the question "What does it mean to empower teens?" Perhaps falsely, what many have felt is necessary in order for that to happen is to remove any constraint put in front of young people, especially by the institution, be it funding, political constraints, mission-based constraints, or constraints related to the specificity of people's roles and/or what they are and are not allowed to do. Organizations and societies function on rules, be they legal, social, or community based. Moreover, we live in a world where power exists in varied forms at macro and micro levels. That is something that museums have been grappling with quite significantly over the past five to ten years. Particularly within the teen program space, young people today are incredibly savvy and attuned to how power

2. From February to August of 2021, Nisa Mackie, Simona Zappas, and Dr. Yolanda J. Majors led a virtual peer learning community for museum teen programs staff to discuss the challenges and best practices of the work.

and inequity manifest. Some types of power are much more visible to our teens than others, and more often than not our youth committees want to engage with and challenge those power structures... Do you want to talk more about managing that in the unique space of the teen meeting?

SZ

It is funny that you brought up the idea of an accidental YPAR because the work of running a teen program is kind of like participating in a YPAR project. Each year when you have a new cohort, it is many firsts—learning who the youth are, how to support them, how to get them engaging with each other and the museum, focusing their ideas on the project at hand, etc. One of the skill sets that are required for running a teen program is being able to manage how adolescence can be kind of contagious. I mean, teens come in with energy, humor, high emotionality, and urgency they can easily fall into. Working with teens requires meeting them where they are at and genuineness so you can engage with those very teenage sensibilities while being able to not get caught up in those big feelings. We can have them, but we must model moving from the big feelings into that inquiry and then action in the program space. As staff, we have the power to facilitate youth in practicing how to respond or react to challenges they are confronted with or issues they disagree with. We can do this by modeling and equipping them with methods and tools to practice using in projects or discussions in our programs. It is not asking teens not to be teens but rather to equip them to take advantage of their big feelings to fuel the next steps. So, instead of becoming overwhelmed when confronted with something that feels unfair or inequitable, teens can be confident in their skills to interrogate, understand all of the competing perspectives and priorities, and think deeply about where their energies are best placed and what they want the outcome to be. Ultimately, it is breaking down those significant issues into something digestible that supports teen empowerment. These actions do not have to be big, but the ability to identify tools to take action can have significant results. Knowing that teens enter programs with preconceived notions, misunderstandings, and different perspectives, it is exciting to leverage the fact that adolescence is defined by feeling big things and forming new opinions, so to be able to cement or challenge them in low-stakes areas like gallery discussions can provide the tools for the more significant, thornier issues or conflicts—as well as how to navigate their identity and sense of self in and among various and competing discourses. When done correctly, or, rather, when done effectively, we have an ability to kind of use the museum itself as a gameboard to explore how to cross borders, how to broker connections, and how to translate inquiry skills into long-term confidence to speak back and to seek out how to understand the reasons behind things and form opinions from there to back up that initial question. It should not be a goal of teen programs for teens to leave with criticisms of institutions, but they should be critical. I think the big feelings can often go toward a place of criticism—and most of the time, it is valid! Most institutions are complex and have histories of bad behavior. But, building literacies around being critical does not mean having criticisms; it is about inquiry, not flat-out disagreement. We should aim for teens to have the tools to understand how society works and to ask the why behind the way things—the policies, attitudes, systems, and structures—inform them. Honestly, starting in my role, it was a lot of having to kind of do that myself. We can balance our own opinions with nuance and not neutrality. It is tough having just the two hours a week that I was with the youth, versus, you know, the other thirty-eight hours a week that I was a Walker staff member and then my life outside of work.

NM Why don't you give an example? I think you touched on something really interesting: one of your primary roles is to support teens in taking a huge problem and breaking it down into something manageable. We often have teens that come in wanting to discuss the big-isms that govern our lives. As educators and facilitators, how do we use the institution's texts to build literacies to talk about these issues effectively, and how do managers help guide staff in supporting that development in scalable ways?

SZ Do you remember the video the 2018–2019 WACTAC cohort made of *Five Ways In*?[3] The teens hated the piece *Great American Nude #32* by Tom Wesselmann. They found it to be such a direct example of the male gaze that they were shocked to see it in a contemporary institution because it felt so dated. They researched it and came up with thoughtful questions to encourage formal analysis that added a time context that ultimately backed up their initial analysis. However, it was a great way to test moving from that initial reaction to making a supported argument. I am thinking, too, about that question of big feelings. My reactions and remembering during a different program where a teen had shared some particularly upsetting information with me, and I came into the office crying—a completely valid reaction. However, in that moment, the best place to put my empathy and

3. In 2019, the WACTAC cohort produced a video tour of the Walker permanent collection exhibition *Five Ways In: Themes From the Collection*. The guiding concept of the video was to explore how knowing about an artist's identity can affect how a viewer interprets an artwork. The video can be viewed on the Walker Art Center's YouTube page.

concern was to connect her to the appropriate support resources. I see that as a big moment of you modeling action over reaction to me and making sure her needs came before my reaction. To go back to WACTAC, though, we have the advantage of working with a captive group of teens for nine months, so we can watch their perspectives across that time change, grow, or solidify. In WACTAC, we do an evaluative exercise in the middle of the year where we place a big sheet of butcher paper on the wall, and the teens can draw or write out responses. I think the questions were "What did we learn so far?" "How did we get there?" "What did you think at the beginning of the year?" "What do you think now?" One teen drew out a comic at each point that was something like "I love the Walker / I don't love the Walker / I accept the Walker." It showed me a developing comfort with sitting in a gray area.

NM

I love that idea of building comfort in the gray; what you described is kind of a timeline that's evidence of growth. The teen in that last example moved from a space of, as you say, black or white or polemical thinking or understanding of a situation to an acceptance that things that seem in opposition to one another can live side by side and exist simultaneously. A huge challenge for museums, particularly teen programs, is how they grapple with their complicity in systems like structural racism or structural inequity, or the nonprofit industrial complex while simultaneously being places of respite, inspiration, education, growth, positive platforming, and civic vitality. I think that, as museum practitioners, we struggle with that. We struggle with the coexistence of those two exigencies or those two aspects of what it is to be an institution in today's society. Many of the projects that WACTAC has gone through over the past few years have been about using the museum to understand the many institutions that are a part of our lives, be it the education system, policing, marriage, etc. I want to go back to the examples you just described regarding being in the galleries and viewing artworks. In the peer learning community we ran with museums across the country, all the programs took slightly different forms, but we tried to focus on longitudinal and intimate engagements. I wanted to talk a little bit about curriculum design because one of the reasons why I think teen programs are one of the most exciting spaces in the museum learning department is that because you are meeting with the same group regularly, you have the opportunity to sequence activities and engagements in ways that build literacy and learning and self-development over time. As teaching artists or educators, we often identify and anchor our work in either visual thinking strategies, art-making, or giving teens access to artists—but the committee space is incredibly powerful. We should not underestimate that this space is where many of these things come together simultaneously. While those other powerful literacies are being developed, it is all in the context of other learning forms like HOMAGO,[4] peer-to-peer learning, etc.—teens are hanging out, they are building community, they are problem-solving together, and they are doing it in a relaxed setting at their own pace. This space provides these first building blocks of textual literacy, self-regulation, planning, scaling, and communicating in creative and legible ways.

4. HOMAGO stands for hanging out, messing around, and geeking out. The term comes from Mizuko Ito, whose academic research explores informal and networked learning for youth. HOMAGO describes the discovery and experimental learning practices youth conduct when using new media like video games, social media, or media produced on their own. See Mizuko Ito et al., *Hanging Out, Messing Around, and Geeking Out: Kids Living and Learning with New Media* (Cambridge, MA: MIT Press, 2009).

SZ

Yes! And it is all in the context of the museum! One of my favorite moments in WACTAC was when a teen told me how much he loved that we were eating Domino's Pizza at the Walker—that contrast was special to him and made him feel comfortable, revealing his sociocultural literacy. But to go back to the museum space more broadly, we cannot hide museums' historic economic and racial politics. One of the things that is complicated about museums is that we are showing works in the galleries, especially contemporary museums, where politics expressed by a lot of the works and the artists might be at odds with the past and present policies of some museums, or are engaging in subjectivities of identities the museum has repressed. It is visible and very implicit. And the teens see this, and many are personally affected by it and will not hold back when they engage. That engagement and visibility of power in those conversations should not be lost. As a museum practitioner about your work in those conversations, it is easy to feel conflicted to sit there and have that dual vision. However, the fact that the conversation is happening should not be lost. Those conversations are the work of change and impact. We should not lose sight of the impact of our programs that might get lost in big feelings. I have gotten feedback from many teens that the teen program is one of the few places they get to go by their preferred name or their preferred pronouns. And that that should not be lost that the power of an institution with complicated past or future politics could overshadow the fact that a teen feels that comfort and safety. And I think it's about, like, as staff, like, not kind of like losing the forest for the trees, or however you say that.

NM

As museum practitioners, we are in this really challenging moment. Many museum professionals seem to be living their own version of the Enlightenment; we have lost faith in the institution, in the religion of the museum. We must not conscript young people to be the soldiers of our own existential conundrums as staff. Despite the partial loss of faith that we might feel about museums not showing up in the world in the ways that we would like or doing things that disappoint us, or our communities, I think it is important to remember that teens are not yet adults. They still require support and scaffolding. It does not empower them to lay out all the problems without structuring and building skills toward how they might create solutions—potentially even systemic solutions.

☺

Lyra Hill

Ritual within Teen Creative Agency: A Brief Overview

Bio

Lyra Hill is an artist, educator, and master of ceremonies. They host and organize the ritual variety show Multi Cult and teach across disciplines including drawing, writing, filmmaking, performance, magic, group facilitation, conflict resolution, and martial arts. Lyra brings play, meditation, visualization, and deep emotional presence to their work with all kinds of audiences in service of authentic connection and healing transformation.

Introduction

Hello, Lyra here. I wrote this document in preparation for leaving my role as lead artist of the Teen Creative Agency (TCA) program at the Museum of Contemporary Art Chicago (MCA), a position I held for three years in partnership with my co-teacher Grace Needlman. In bringing ritual to TCA, I drew on my roots in neopagan and Earth-based spiritual practice. Intended as a quick guide for the incredible teachers who would replace us in this sacred role, this document is a product of robust collaboration and experimentation by me, Grace, and all the members of TCA who embodied our ritual practices on a weekly, monthly, and yearly basis.

Ritual is a beautiful technology for maintaining robust group spirit and core values while encouraging adaptability and evolution. After I departed from TCA, my successor, lead artist Jeremy Kreusch, dove deeper into the value of this practice in the essay that follows.

Essay

What do we mean when we talk about "ritual"? Rituals within TCA take many forms and serve many purposes. We use the word "ritual" to describe moments of intentionally crafted significance, where the meaning in our actions is elevated to have a greater impact on personal or group dynamics. Ritual within TCA is focused internally, in contrast to our public programs, which are created for museum audiences.

Rituals within TCA can be divided into two categories:

1. Activities that repeat reliably every week and potentially every month, semester, or year. These might be icebreakers, roles within the group, or types of visitors the teens come to expect, like artists or staff members.
2. Big and beautiful moments of intentional significance or transformation. These might be moments like events, behind-the-scenes experiences, or special events to mark the beginning or end of the program.

Ritual types 1 and 2 provide templates for creating other rituals as the need arises. Type 1 example: In 2016, we put youth in charge of the weekly rituals to strengthen our social media presence. Type 2 examples: In 2014, we added a motivational ritual soon after winter break to refocus and galvanize

TCA for the work of spring. In 2015, we held a spring ritual to motivate commitment to our projects and reveal the news that I would be moving. In 2016, we held a ritual to say goodbye to the MCA studios for the last time.

What is ritual good for? Why do we do it?
Type 1
    Establishing habits; Remembering small tasks
Type 2
    Bonding; Imparting purpose; Processing difficult emotions
How do they relate to our vision?
    Another way to build community; Self-reflection; Confidence of purpose; Empowerment

What does ritual within TCA look like?
Type 1 rituals do not require the same atmosphere as Type 2 rituals. Because they are regular and necessary for the functioning of any session, they must be flexible and able to be performed anywhere that members can gather, see, and hear one another. Type 1 rituals can easily be amended, added, and subtracted from the session. Type 1 rituals mark the beginning and end of each session. Without these rituals, a session feels "off," and gathering focus and attention throughout the day is much more difficult.
    Type 2 rituals are scripted, participatory activities with a beginning, middle, and end. They require a sizable chunk of one session to establish an atmosphere, heighten awareness, and allow time for the intended transformation.

Ritual Checklist
Intention
    A simple statement (usually one sentence) in the present tense describing the desired outcome of the ritual; Something that can be written down, repeated aloud, and revisited in the future
Grounding
    Any exercise to bring participants into their body,

into the space, and into the present moment
"Casting," or creating the container
> A gesture performed (often in a circle and by each participant in turn) to mark the beginning and end of the ritual; A way to mark the boundaries of the experience, both in time and space

Common exercises to do inside the container once it is created
> Guided meditation (dark space with cool lights, pillows, etc.); Spell making (altering some small object in a meaningful way; doing something with that object); Performance; Group noise; Group motion (milling, dancing, shaking it out); Passing an action around the circle; Recognizing each individual in turn

> Ritual is making meaning: seriousness & history in TCA

Ritual is making meaning. Words are even more powerful within ritual because this is the space where what we say or dream becomes our reality. For this reason, words should be used carefully in rituals—on this note, it is essential to remember that the word *ritual* itself ascribes significance to any activity to which it is applied. In this way, the word is a tool that can be used to concretize regular efforts. Be careful not to apply this word to too many different things because it will lose potency if stretched too far.

Establish the seriousness and deliberateness of the moment.

Rituals historically are gifts between lead artists and members.

Rituals imbue physical objects and actions with great significance. These objects and actions can become quick ways to recall significant feelings or commitments.

Remember that the small tools and atmosphere of ritual can be invoked at any time to pull focus.

How do you maintain the intensity and deep focus outside ritual space?

Too much noise, scattered energy? Make sound together.
Too little energy, reticence, negativity? Meditate or ground. No one needs to interact during these activities.
Lack of focus? Identify or revisit intentions.
Sadness and pain? Desire for support and care? Aura cleanse or other partner-care game.

Recommendations
Inject rituals into facilitation routines
Ritualize evaluation
Continue to encourage TCA to practice and lead these skills and exercises
Unpack what ritual means to TCA; potentially, what magic means to TCA

☺

Rituals and Belonging, Values, and Care: Some Thoughts on Agency and Collaboration

Bio
Jeremy Kreusch is associate director of learning at the Museum of Contemporary Art Chicago, where he develops interpretation strategies for exhibitions and performances. Jeremy received his bachelor of fine arts in media studies at the Columbus College of Art and Design and his master of arts in art history at Louisiana State University.

Introduction
Agency is the power to act. It is the goal of confidence, self-awareness, and empathy. Agency is the ability to engage those traits with a purpose. Collaboration is the process of sharing initiative and responsibility with others. These two foundational skills are connected—one necessitates the other symbiotically. Without a collaboration built on shared initiatives, responsibility, and values, agency is unstable. Collaboration is a fragile exercise without individuals who feel empowered to practice confidence, vulnerability, and empathy. An approach to

empowering young people and building community should likewise be connected.

Ritual is an instrument that connects community building, meaning-making, and empowerment. It has various roots in groups—cultural, religious, familial, and so on. For our purposes, though, ritual is a structural practice separate from the historical rites of any particular group. It is our strategy for building a strong community full of empowered members. It is the practice with which we cultivate and maintain it.

In a concise guide, Lyra Hill, my predecessor as the lead artist facilitating the Teen Creative Agency (TCA) program at the Museum of Contemporary Art Chicago, described the use of ritual in the context of youth programs, which clarifies a distinction in what we mean when we say ritual. First, there is what we will call ritualization: the routine daily activities that are transformed by their intentional repetition into meaningful rites. Second, there is a ritual, a special set of acts and actions designed to create particular social effects and linked to the interplay of various social activities: creating community, marking transformations, and discovering inner power. Both types of rituals are important to nurturing agency and collaboration.

Essay

In his in-depth study of interaction rituals, Randal Collins outlines their key ingredients:

1. Two or more people are physically assembled... so they affect each other by their bodily presence.
2. There are boundaries to outsiders.
3. People focus their attention on a common object or activity, and by communicating this focus to each other become mutually aware of each other's focus of attention.
4. They share a common mood or emotional experience.[1]

On the surface, this list could be read as a simple description of a collaborative environment. However, there are a few places where the ingredients step beyond the ordinary, easy collaborative practices common to working and learning environments. These are the areas of critical importance, in that they pull an entirely practical experience into the bodily, the emotional, and the moral. Collaboration is not just about physical assembly; it is recognizing that we affect one another on fundamental, even corporeal levels. "Boundaries to outsiders" can sound negative but are necessary to establishing belonging. It is not enough to pay attention; we will share a common emotional experience.

Collins's ingredients, when successfully combined, build "high levels of mutually focused and emotionally shared attention." Participants experience:

1. Group solidarity, a feeling of membership.
2. Emotional energy in the individual: a feeling of confidence, elation, strength, enthusiasm, and initiative in taking collective action.
3. Symbols that represent the group. Persons pumped up with feelings of group solidarity treat symbols with great respect and defend them against the disrespect of outsiders, and even more, of renegade insiders.
4. Feelings of morality: the sense of rightness in adhering to the group, respecting its symbols.[2]

Supporting one another in bodily, emotional, and moral communion leads not only to "group solidarity" but also is a gateway to agency, "confidence, elation, strength, enthusiasm, and initiative."

Of course, there is a huge responsibility in wielding this power; a strong sense of solidarity, respect for symbols, and a feeling of rightness can lead

1. Randall Collins, *Interaction Ritual Chains* (Princeton: Princeton University Press, 2004), 48.
2. Collins, 49.

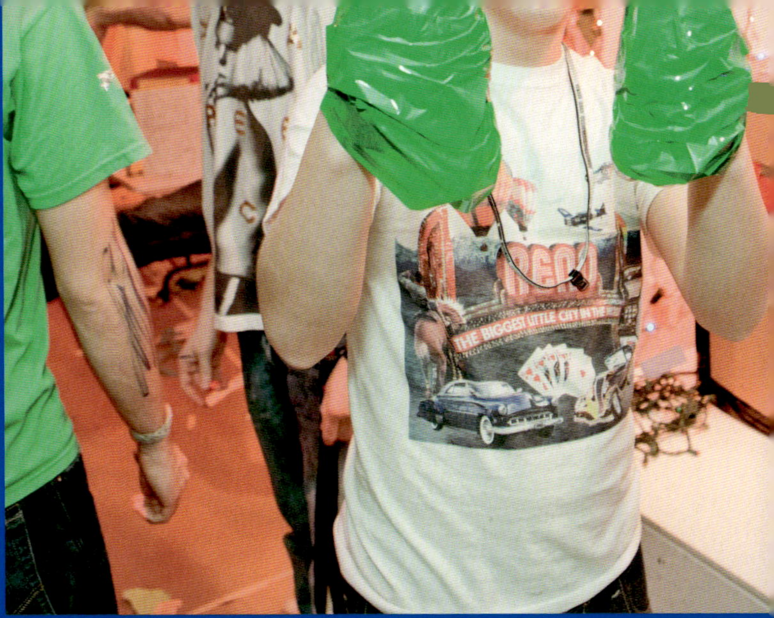
RENO
THE BIGGEST LITTLE CITY IN THE

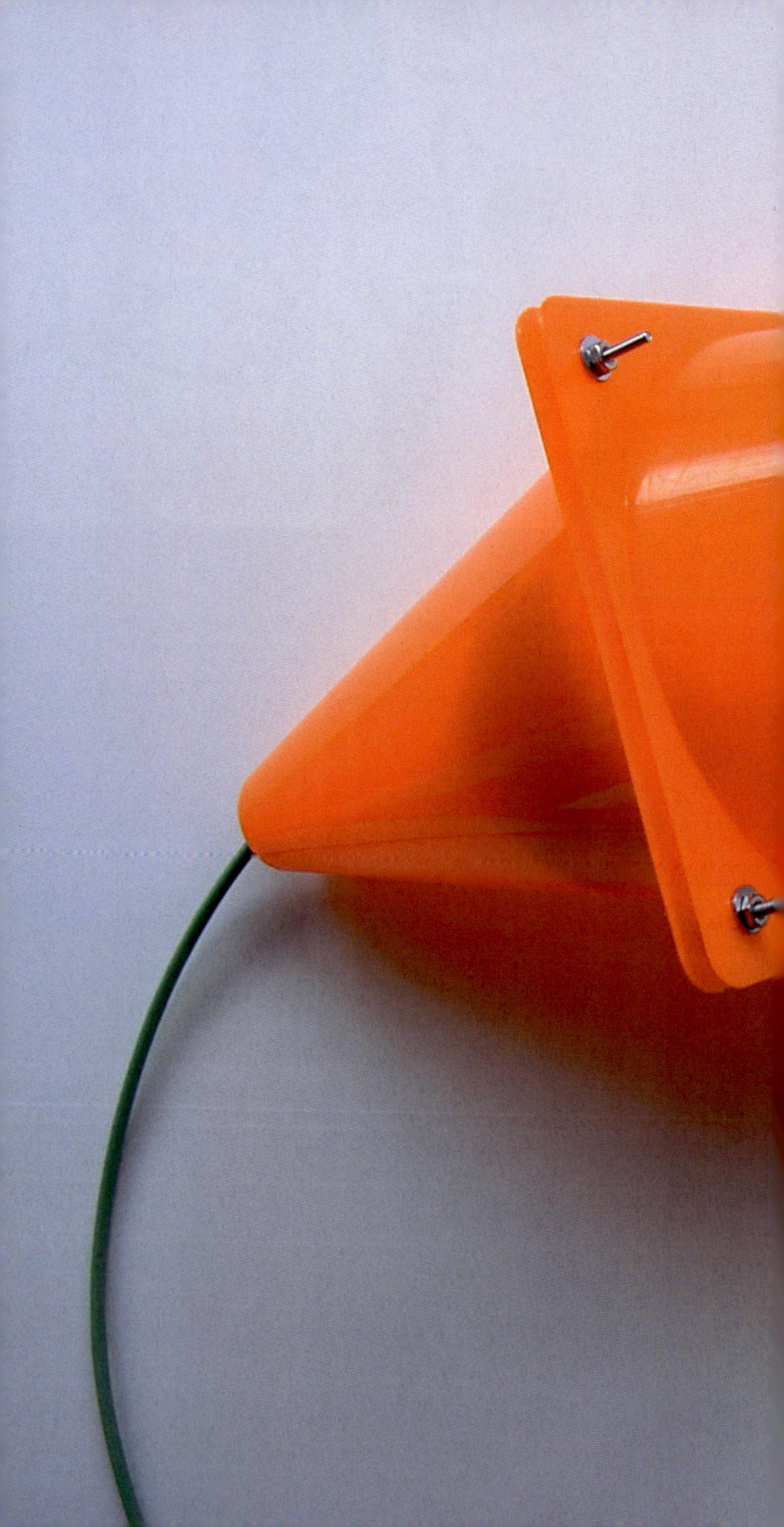

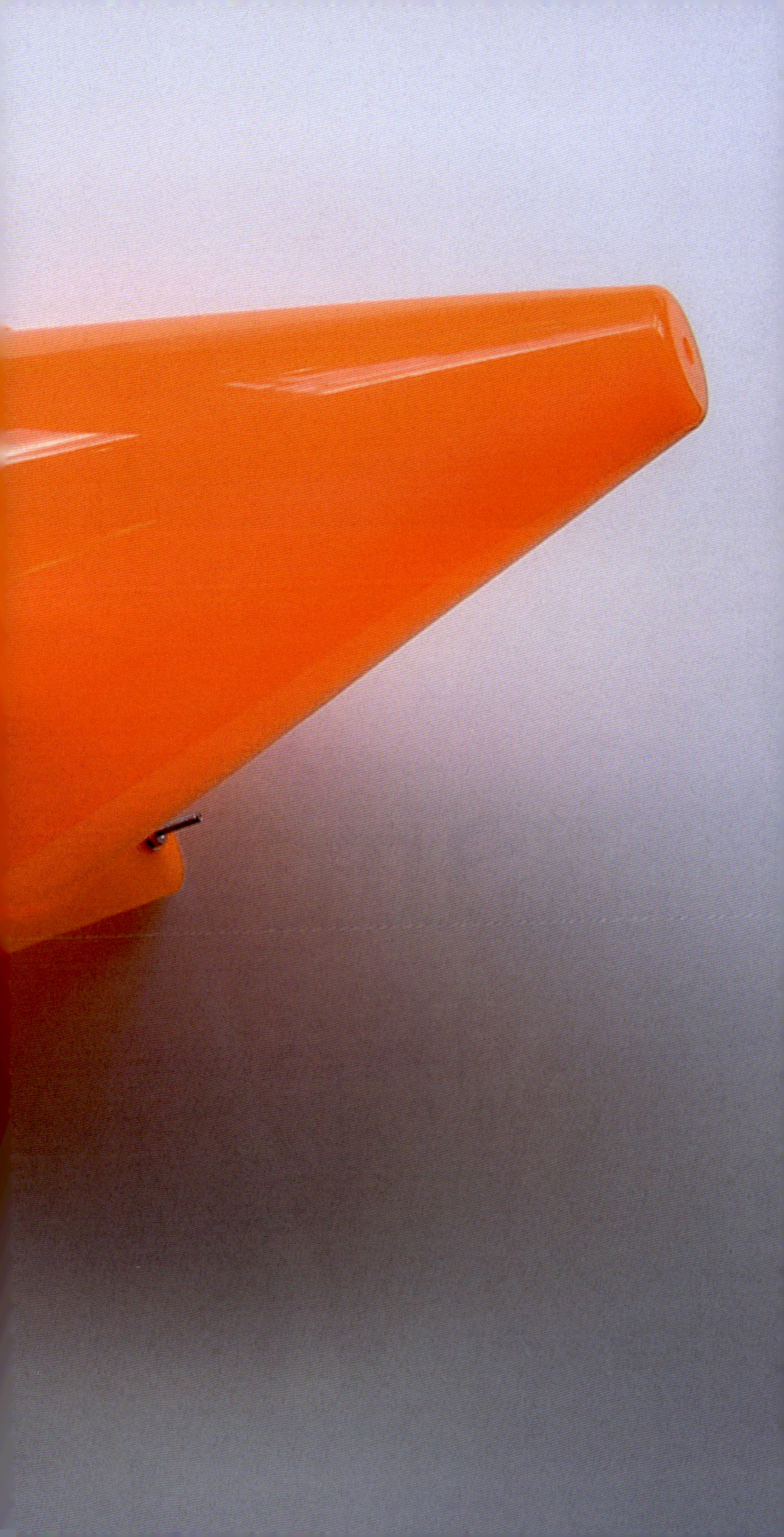

Slug vibe

down problematic paths. But without stakes, without urgency, without the absolute necessity to establish a safe and brave culture, at a high cost, with high risk, the ideas of empowerment and community lose their potency. This is why, hand in hand with ritual practice, we must build a culture of visible values and a practice of care for ourselves and one another. If our symbols are our values, and our values build human connection, dismantle oppression, and practice care, we are doing work worthy of great respect and rigid defense.

☺

Amanda Hunt & Simona Zappas

Strategies for Engaging Colleagues

Bio
Amanda Hunt joined the Walker as the Head of Public Engagement, Learning, and Impact (PELI) from the Lucas Museum of Narrative Art in Los Angeles. She served as director of public programs and creative practice. Previously, Hunt was the director of education and public programs at the Museum of Contemporary Art, Los Angeles, co-curator of the 2019 Desert X Biennial, associate curator at the Studio Museum in Harlem, and curator at the Los Angeles-based nonprofit LAXART.

Bio
Simona Zappas (she/her) is the Youth Programs Manager at the Walker Art Center. In her work she designs and facilitates informal learning opportunities for youth. She collaborates with curatorial staff to bring a learning lens to museum public engagement and a social practice bent on programmatic strategy. Before this, she was the director of WFNU Frogtown, a low-power radio station in

Saint Paul. Simona holds a BA with honors from Macalester College and a master of education from the University of Minnesota. Simona sits on the Saint Paul Neighborhood Network board and volunteers at Planned Parenthood as an abortion doula.

Introduction

In this piece, Simona Zappas, Youth Programs Manager at the Walker Art Center, reflects on her experience navigating personal anxieties that got in the way of promoting both her own work and that of the teen participants in Walker teen programming. Amanda Hunt, Head of Public Engagement, Learning, and Impact at the Walker Art Center, builds off Simona's reflections with expanded strategies for a youth-centered, cross-departmental museum engagement.

Essay

Simona

One way we entice teens to apply for the Walker Art Center Teen Arts Council (WACTAC) is the promise of meeting and forming connections with museum staff. As practitioners, we rely on our colleagues to help connect teens and artists, behind-the-scenes tours, help in promoting our programs, and overall providing a holistic look at museum work. A major challenge is that not all staff have experience working with youth and might need some support in understanding the hows and whys of our work. Sometimes gaps in understanding of teen programs can lead to scheduling challenges, visits from staff that result in misaligned language or content, and well-intentioned but inaccurate views of our work. As a young teen programs practitioner starting off in the museum, working in a large institution was intimidating. For better or worse, museums are hierarchical institutions that have historically prioritized resources for and equated scholarship and rigor with more traditional curatorial roles. This context influenced me, and so did the insecurity of being in my early twenties and learning the ropes of working at a large institution for the first time. For me, this started to manifest as downplaying my work—I would make jokes that reduced my work to Hot Cheetos and doing dabs (even though those both have distinct instructional purposes!). If I reached out to colleagues asking them to speak in meetings or help connect me with an artist for a visit, I would be self-deprecating or overly saccharine in emails to the point of almost prostrating myself (yes—*that* many exclamation points). I would be so focused on saying thank-you (still a very important thing to do!) that I would not take the time to communicate crucial programmatic information like what the teens were interested in, working on, and the existing knowledge that was creating their learning context, and how the staff member's visit fits into our learning goals and outcomes.

While I am always grateful for staff to come and speak in meetings (and still use an excessive amount of exclamation points), as I stayed in my role longer, I realized I was not doing myself or my colleagues any favors. I was doing rigorous work. I designed complex curricula, conducted research, and facilitated programs. My work had significant academic and curatorial prowess. By reducing my work, I was not preparing my colleagues for visits and missing out on opportunities to build more meaningful exchanges and collaborations between them and the youth, affecting the teens' experiences.

Through great mentorship, experiencing the impact of working with the teens, and time, I developed more confidence and increased my ability to name and communicate the hows, whys, and ways of my work and its impact. To both empower myself and create broader staff understanding of the distinct skill set going into the program and that youth develop through participation, I held an optional meeting open to all staff where I presented an overview of the WACTAC curriculum, learning goals, and outcomes, and explained when is a good time to approach me with projects, and what a meaningful collaboration with the teens would look like. Included here is the presentation I provided to all staff. I felt the meeting created a significant change in the understanding, inclusion, and treatment of my work. I believe that impact came from the conversation being an invitation and an explanation. I assumed positive intent and aimed to resource them with information on how and why to work with the teens, and I promoted myself at the same time. Soon after the presentation, I got emails to plan projects significantly further in advance. I sat on more working groups for cross-institutional projects and offers to include the teens in multiple new projects. Staff across the institution now see my work as an applied ability to facilitate skill growth and turn experiences into opportunities for learning. I help with exhibitions, programs, designing residencies and outreach campaigns.

I realize this arc sounds pompous—a sort of "I did it and so can you" narrative, and frankly, it kind of is. Everyone's experience is very different, and the supports we get for our programs vary from institution to institution. I have been fortunate to work at an institution with cultural and financial buy-in and dedication to teen programs, and that advantage is not universal. However, what I think carries over is that carving out our place in our institutions, both culturally and professionally, is not always easy. Working in cultural institutions means fast pace, juggling projects, and engaging with multiple power and value structures. It is only human to have a mental or emotional impact from that stew. Taking action to promote an understanding of our work is part of the necessary steps toward building collaborative and supportive engagements and opportunities for the youth in our programs to feel like enmeshed contributors to the museum.

Amanda
Thinking about the Walker, its history, and its lead-

ership, our teen programs are uniquely positioned because we are considered leaders in that area. We were one of the first museums in the country to create a program model specifically for teens to experience museums in a way that is both a privilege for the staff and about valuing teens' learning at different stages all in one place. The program pays attention to a person's development as a young adult, recognizing that this is a critical time in one's life and that it is pivotal, vulnerable, and special.

Adolescence is a moment in which you define yourself by referencing examples of how to be or resisting ones you have known for a long time. Teens are primed for possibility, so WACTAC creates opportunities for teens to try new ways of defining themselves in a safe space for learning. I do not use "safe space" lightly—it is a space of care, accountability, and ownership. At the Walker, we have had the luxury of time to cultivate that safe space within the program directly but also across the institutional culture of the museum. We have a thirty-plus-year history serving as a foundation of socialization, connection, collaboration, cross-pollination, and stakeholder sharing, all of which have created an implicit understanding of the value of the voice of teens here. We understand that it is a distinct privilege for staff to work with young people in the museum and recognize that it is during this transformational developmental time. This gives Walker staff a definite advantage to be more nimble or from the ground up, but that does not mean it is always easy to bring people into the process.

Moreover, this is why you make a case for your work as a teen programmer. For me, it goes back to an idea, not of labeling our work or the departments we are housed in broadly as "education," but as "learning" or "lifelong learning," because it is a continuum, right? If our work traditionally as education departments is to promote the understanding that there is value in creating entry points for children to engage with museums, that ethos applies and is expanded under the label of lifelong learning across an individual's life. So, that language builds a fundamental understanding between colleagues of why we are all here and the value of what cultural organizations and institutions offer to the public. Teens are a natural part of that. It is just a different stage of life and thinking and empowering oneself to connect with art and culture.

For some of our colleagues, engaging with teens is a transactional model. They package some content, present, and deliver it—end of the transaction. What I want us to represent is that it is a porous exchange. That exchange can continue and take different shapes and forms that do not need to be a super-formalized interaction. However, what I realized in my exchange with teen programs in a previous role at MOCA (they started that program in '92; so we can duke it out, Walker or MOCA, over the first teen program!) is that, for staff, there is an intimidation factor when meeting with teens. We identify it in other areas where we hear feedback. Whether from a stranger or a survey or whatever, there is always some intimidation—a not knowing how to act or interact, I think, for colleagues coming into a teen space; and I can own some of that feeling myself, and being met with that tenderness and seriousness teens present because of where they are in that critical time of trying on and defining identities. There is no hiding from them; they make it clear when you bomb! They ask the tough questions.

I can remember very fondly, at MOCA, bringing in a colleague to share their work with the teens; they would be floored by the questions they would ask. The level of insight that was shared by, you know, people sixteen to eighteen, and these are colleagues maybe without children or maybe with children. Nevertheless, there is always a rich reward in the interaction because it connects you to your work and a part of yourself that you feel good about and want to share. And I think for all parties to remember that the possibilities are endless in the spirit of sharing and opening up. You do not know what will come of it. And that is the fun.

I have had to check myself when I enter a space of teen programming because it is not about a presentation; it is really just showing up and sharing yourself. I read the room, offer what I can from my experiences that feel most relevant to their questions and the things they are questioning, and that is simply what I can bring to that table. And that is what you can ask of your colleagues: come from your place of knowledge, understanding, and expertise, even if it is in a different department, field, or arena, and bring that to this space. Be open, be open to the questions, the experience, and the observations. There is a sweet parallel between some staff working with teens for the first time and someone coming to a museum for the first time. I think it is a level of unfamiliarity sometimes and not knowing how to operate or function. Moreover, you just have to bring colleagues into that and let them know you are supporting them in it, which will pay dividends.

☺

3.2. RESOURCES

3.2.1. THE WACTAC GUIDE TO TOUGH CONVERSATIONS

Simona Zappas, Walker Art Center

> **Bio.** Simona Zappas (she/her) is the Youth Programs Manager at the Walker Art Center. In her work she designs and facilitates informal learning opportunities for youth. She collaborates with curatorial staff to bring a learning lens to museum public engagement and a social practice bent on programmatic strategy. Before this, she was the director of WFNU Frogtown, a low-power radio station in Saint Paul. Simona holds a BA with honors from Macalester College and a master of education from the University of Minnesota. Simona sits on the Saint Paul Neighborhood Network board and volunteers at Planned Parenthood as an abortion doula.

Introduction

This guide was created for the Walker Art Center Teen Arts Council (WACTAC) members in the summer of 2020. The teens were planning an event called Unmuted Mic. It was a COVID-19 modification of our annual Teen Takeover event. Rather than keeping the museum open late and for teens only for an evening of live music, open galleries, and lots of free food, we were hosting a virtual party on Zoom with games and an open mic, and the teens wanted to build space for open exchange for attendees to reflect on supportive mental health practices. However, the teens expressed concerns over initiating open conversations just a few weeks after the protests following the murder of George Floyd and the general mental fatigue of the initial months of the COVID-19 pandemic; the teens were unsure if they would be met with combativeness, contrasting opinions, or a group that would not want to talk. I created this facilitation to encourage the teens to think about how to actively take on their role as facilitators and understand the responsibility and gravity of how they can hold space. We used it to guide a discussion in a WACTAC meeting ahead of the event. The open sections are where the teens were asked to fill in their responses initially by writing them in, then in conversation. This facilitation was designed to be used on Google Docs over Zoom but can be easily reimagined for in-person programming. Either way, I encourage you to vary the conversation styles to include time for personal reflection (perhaps through writing), small group discussion (either with a partner or in groups of three to four), and whole group discussion.

This section is to be shared with the group by the facilitator.

We want Unmuted Mic to be a space where people with different perspectives and experiences can come together in an open conversation to process, feel connected, and learn. To do this, everyone in WACTAC will need to rely on their facilitation skills to model how we hope people will show up (vulnerable, open-minded, willing to share), create ground rules for safer exchanges, and offer helpful information to encourage participation. This activity explores helpful tips and things to keep in mind and offers some sentence stems for how to respond when someone says something racist, ignorant, or hateful. It is just a sampling of ideas and will always be a work in progress.

Activity

Title. What makes a good facilitator?
Written by. Simona Zappas

Instructions

Let's start with a reflection (ask the teens to reflect on these solo, in small groups, or all together):

- When were you part of a group that was facilitated well? Who was facilitating?
- What did it feel like? What did it look like? What did you notice?
- What are practices that encourage you to share your thoughts? What can a facilitator do to make it feel safe?
- Bad facilitation practices?

Background

Ask the teens to share as a whole group, offer some of

your suggestions as you connect, and validate their contributions. This is a chance to be transparent about your working style and expertise. You will learn a lot from the youth too!

Here are some of the things I (Simona) think makes a good facilitator.

Context. Good facilitators know that everyone in the group has different levels of experience and knowledge, so they do what they can to provide information to get everyone on the same page so that the different perspectives can be in conversation rather than creating tension. This might mean:

- Explaining terms
- Being transparent about what will be done in the session together
- Asking people follow-up questions so they can describe terms or feelings so the group can better understand them
- Letting people know it's okay to have differing opinions or not to have an opinion

Facilitators do not need to be experts on everything, but it is good when they have background knowledge on the subject being discussed to answer questions. They must be honest when they do not know the answer to a question.

Modeling. A good facilitator demonstrates the behaviors they want to see from the group. We are all human, so we slip up sometimes, but do what you can to *show and tell* folks ways to participate in the group. If you are being silly, it signals to the group that they can be silly; if you are being serious, it signals to the group to do the same. Even in groups where you are hoping to share power, facilitators are guideposts to set norms for the others in the space.

Listening. Be aware of how much you talk to make time for others, encourage others to speak by asking questions, and validate teens/participants for sharing. Listen to your group to understand where they are and what they are interested in. Sometimes it is helpful to repeat back what folks say in your own words to make sure you understand their contribution or to help make connections between the different ideas shared by the group. Writing stuff down where everyone can see it is a great listening tool!

Not passing judgment but knowing when to step in. No one is or can be neutral, and everything we think and say is informed by our beliefs, experiences, and biases. This can all be invisible to us! It is okay to have opinions as a facilitator, but actively judging the beliefs of others can shut down open exchanges. Asking questions is a great antidote. Sometimes people might say things that are a bit off from what they are trying to say. Give them a chance to answer follow-up questions to clarify. However, in any group, there is always a chance of people saying something harmful or disagreements. *It is okay for people to disagree; disagreements do not mean conflict. Be watchful to see how the disagreement evolves.* If someone says something harmful, you can step in and stop that right away without allowing it to escalate. You can say simple statements like "Let us stop there," "This is not the right conversation for that," and "That statement might be hurtful to folks here. I will ask that we stop that here, and we can check in after the conversation."

Guide, don't steer. Always go into the conversation with questions or statements to encourage the type of conversation you want, but do not go into it married to a set outcome. People are always coming from different places and will get a lot of value from organic exchanges. Step in with questions when the conversation slows.

Knowing how to effectively respond when someone says something problematic, ignorant, racist, or hateful can be challenging, especially in the moment. There are many ways to respond; try to use it as an opportunity to ask questions; sometimes, the best way to facilitate is to take the position of the learner.

Tips for Practice

Here are some ways that I (Simona) suggest responding directly and opening up space for learning. Can you add more? Do you disagree with any or have examples of something that has worked for you or on you in the past?

Step 1. Make it clear that you are redirecting the conversation and letting the person know that you want to engage with them. Model that you are open and want to engage. Here are some phrases you could start with:

- I want to challenge what you shared.
- I disagree.
- Can we unpack/spend some more time with that statement?

Sometimes asking questions is an excellent way to open it up:

- Why do you think that?
- Where did you learn that?

Step 2. Offer new information. Be direct in sharing information, and make sure you explain any terms that they might not know. Here are some ways to open that up.

Make sure you share information that is yours to share. Try citing articles or facts you have learned rather than personal experiences that are not yours.

Here are some ways to start sharing:

- I have experienced that differently (then share an experience you are comfortable sharing).
- I have learned that…

Here are some other things to keep in mind:

- If you are a white ally, do not expect the BIPOC people in the conversation to take care of problematic speech for you.
- Accept that not everyone's mind can be changed by one conversation.
- It is frustrating that the emotional labor of calling people into growth is not put onto the person who said something harmful.
- We all can and should grow more. Always be an open

and active listener.

Some things need to be corrected directly instead of through conversation. For example, if someone is misgendered or there is another microaggression, address it directly. It can be quick, like stepping in and saying the correct pronouns. Follow up with everyone involved after one-on-one.

Have some open time to brainstorm more tactics and concerns with the group.

Let us talk about our responses in the group.

General Tips

- Remember that your intent might not match its impact.
- Listen to hear, not to respond.
- It is okay to change your mind, and for others to change their minds—it is good! Our opinions should grow, change, and be nuanced.
- No one knows everything.
- Disagree with an opinion, not a person.
- Remember, with the stress of COVID-19, everyone's capacity is limited—be gentle.
- Never assume opinions, someone's experiences, or identity.
- Vulnerability takes work. Acknowledge and appreciate it, and do not expect it off the bat—lay the groundwork of trust.
- If you are an ally—if you are white and supporting BIPOC friends, or cisgendered and supporting trans friends, or straight and supporting queer friends—it is your job to educate yourself, no one else's.
- Be proactive, not reactive. Defensiveness never helps. Soften.
- If you have a different opinion, try to hear people out before going on the defensive—it is hard and okay to have a different opinion.
- Everyone is at a different place with the work they need to do, and that is okay.
- Use *I* statements and speak from your own experience.
- Your safety always comes first—if anyone is mak-

ing you feel unsafe, you do not need to continue a conversation.
- This is lifetime work.

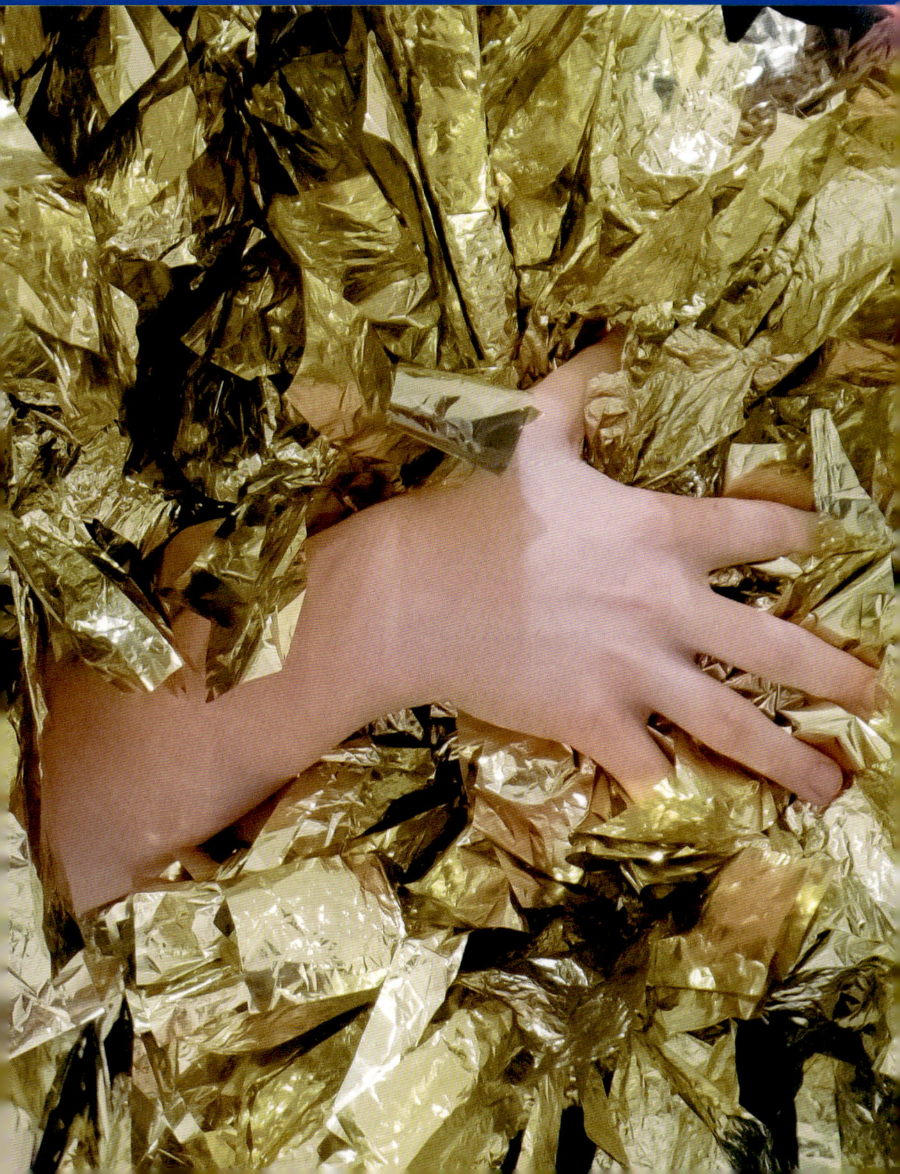

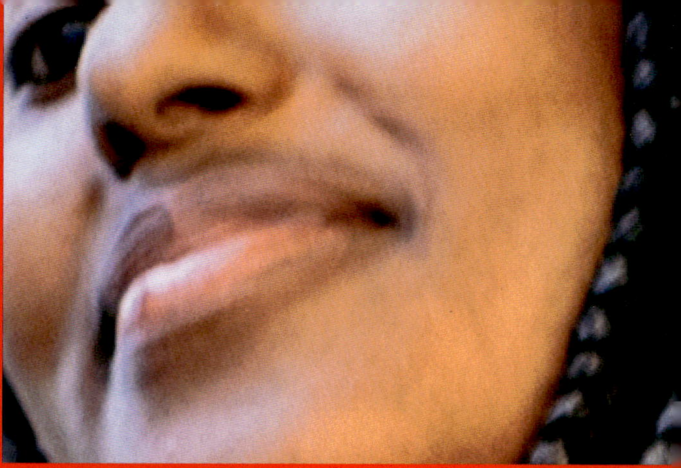
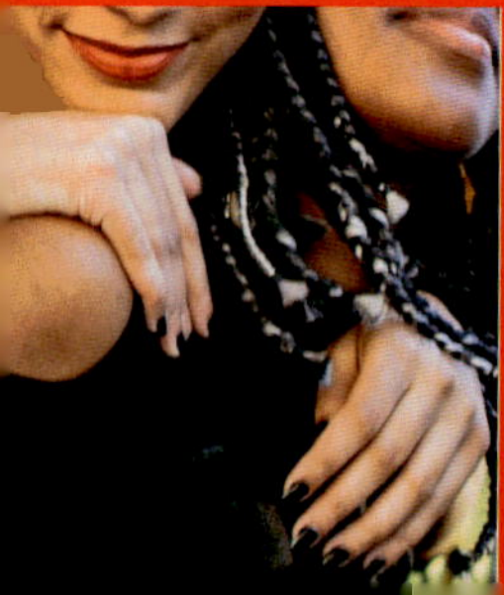

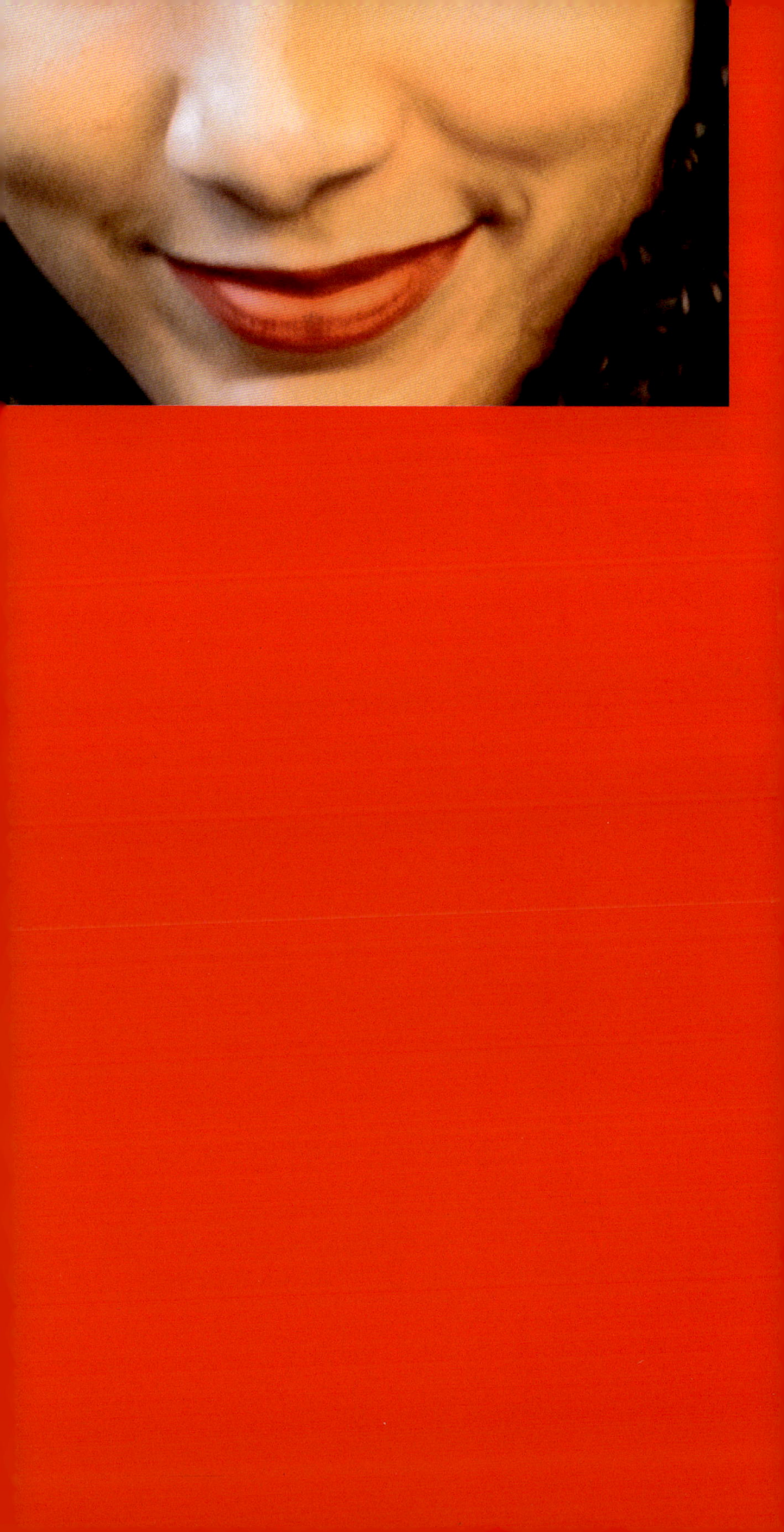

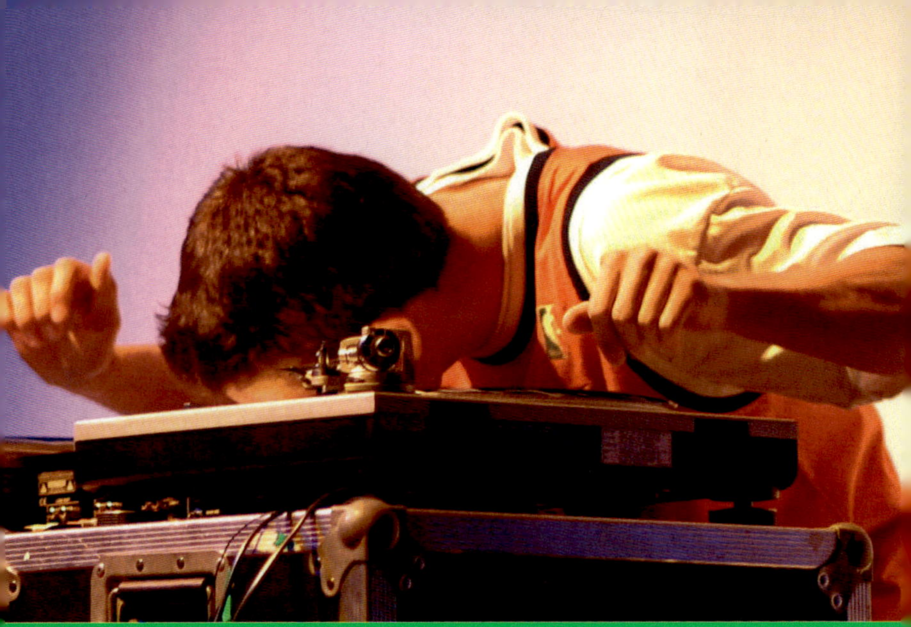

3.2.2. INTERGENERATIONAL TOOLS FOR CONSTRUCTIVE CONVERSATION

Nancy Nowacek

> **Bio.** Nancy Nowacek is a research-based and socially engaged artist. Her current research includes urban waterways and climate change, and intergenerational mental health. She cofounded the art collective Works on Water (worksonwater.org) to support and grow the community of artists committed to advocacy for urban ecologies. She is also one-half of Always Working Group (notworkinggroup.art), a social practice collective that explores contemporary political issues through social forms. Nowacek holds an MFA in social practice from California College of the Arts, an MFA in visual communication from Virginia Commonwealth University, and a BFA in photography and design from the University of Michigan.

Introduction

Tools for Constructive Communication was developed to help people from different backgrounds and ages find common language and concepts for respectful and caring exchange. Owing to the fact that both language and cultural values are dynamic, this chart is a snapshot of the current vocabulary and definitions pertaining to age, race, gender, sexuality, and physical and neurological differences. *This contribution was researched and compiled by Zoé Hamblett with Nancy Nowacek.*

> **Speaking**
>
> *For Younger Adults.*
>
> "I" statements identify problems in the first person: "I feel unheard."
>
> "We" statements identify problems as a group: "We all

want to feel heard."

"You" statements assume the receiver's intentions, thoughts, and experiences: "You're not listening."

To learn more and see more examples, go to "I, You, and We statements."

For Older Adults.

"I" statements convey feelings and ideas clearly. "You" statements can lead more easily to miscommunication.

"I" statements identify problems in the first person: "I feel unheard."

"We" statements identify problems as a group: "We all want to feel heard."

"You" statements assume the receiver's intentions, thoughts, and experiences: "You're not listening."

To learn more and see more examples, go to "I, You, and We statements."

Listening

For Younger Adults.

Listening can be more beneficial to constructive communication than speaking. Feeling unheard can create a feeling of isolation and lead to withdrawal from the group.

To learn more about the importance of listening, go to "Understanding Listening."

Signs of good listening:

- Responses that demonstrate attention to, and understanding of, what's been said.

- Questions that explore the speaker's point of view without the intent of convincing or correcting.
- Research shows that when strangers ask questions of one another, they feel more connected.
- Body language such as eye contact and parallel body position physically demonstrates attention and presence.

Thinking Prompt: Can you recall a time that you felt heard and how it made you feel?

Ways to build listening skills:

- Focus on the sound of the speaker's words instead of a typical meditation mantra.
- Bring attention to body language and sensations.
- Notice moments of distraction. Make a conscious choice to return to the present moment.
- Ask open-ended questions that invite a sharing of viewpoints, or that seek clarification.

Try to avoid:

- Focusing on moments of distraction, which can lead to even more distraction.
- Deciding or rehearsing what you want to say next.
- Interrogating questions that don't convey genuine interest in the speaker, like "What's your job?" or "Where do you live?" These indicate the intent of ranking someone in a social hierarchy.

To learn more skills and strategies for good listening, go to "How to Listen."

For Older Adults.

Listening can be more beneficial to constructive communication than speaking. Feeling unheard can create a feeling of isolation and lead to withdrawal from the group.

To learn more about the importance of listening, go to "Understanding Listening."

Signs of good listening:

- Responses that demonstrate attention to, and understanding of, what's been said.
- Questions that explore the speaker's point of view without the intent of convincing or correcting.
- Research shows that when strangers ask questions of one another, they feel more connected.
- Body Language such as eye contact and parallel body position physically demonstrates attention and presence.

Thinking Prompt: Can you recall a time that you felt heard and how it made you feel?

Ways to build listening skills:

- Focus on the sound of the speaker's words instead of a typical meditation mantra.
- Bring attention to body language and sensations.
- Notice moments of distraction. Make a conscious choice to return to the present moment.
- Ask open-ended questions that invite a sharing of viewpoints, or that seek clarification.

Try to avoid:

- Focusing on moments of distraction, which can lead to even more distraction.
- Deciding or rehearsing what you want to say next.
- Interrogating questions that don't convey genuine interest in the speaker, like "What's your job?" or "Where do you live?" These indicate the intent of ranking someone in a social hierarchy.

To learn more skills and strategies for good listening, go to "How to Listen."

Age

For Younger Adults.

Ageism. Like many aspects of identity, age exists on a

spectrum. Every person changes throughout their life. Life experience cannot be simplified to the binary of "young" to "old." Every person's growth is multidimensional (physical, cognitive, psychological, etc.) and defies universal division of age, such as being "middle-aged."

Separating stages of growth by chronological age creates in-groups and out-groups in a way that inherently values and treats people differently based on their age.

Treatment of another based on the perception of age has the potential to perpetuate ageism.

Internalized ageism is the internalization of negative views of one's life stage received from social and environmental messages. Internalized ageism begins at a young age and contributes to anxiety around the experience of different life stages.

Individual positive attitudes about aging and the aging process are essential first steps in challenging societal ageism.

Thinking Prompt: What expectations and assumptions do you have of older adults? Why?

Inclusive Language/Communication.

Try:

- Using relative language, such as "younger/older adults"
- "Person(s) aged (age or age range)"
- "Elders" only in a cultural context
- Using the term "grandfriends"
- Using person-first language if an older adult has legitimate impairment to their physical ability or health (refer to Physical Diversity section)
- Thinking about what you're really trying to convey when describing someone—"She looks happy," "He has exciting energy"

For Younger Adults.

The Harm of Internalizing Ageism. The internalization of negative views about aging perpetuated by society is detrimental to the mental and physical health of older adults. This is especially true for older BIPOC adults.

Older adults' internalized ageism can lead to reinforcing language and behavior, creating a cycle that harms physical and mental health.

Additionally, unspoken assumptions about younger adults' behavior and motivations can cause miscommunication between generations.

Intergenerational (IG) communication has been shown to improve ageist beliefs and lessen the use of stereotypes by younger adults.

In order to promote productive intergenerational communication, it's important to understand some common communication barriers:

Over-accommodating speech based on age stereotypes includes:

- Taking on a "teaching" role without indication that there is a lack of understanding based on the assumption that younger adults are less knowledgeable
- Using condescending language that indicates an assumption of lack of experience or intelligence

Underaccommodating communication fails to meet the needs of those in conversation with you.

- Using vocabulary or terms of a certain time period most likely unfamiliar to younger adults
- Not using proper pronouns or identity-based language, even when asked to do so
- Unclear expectations of roles in the relationship

To learn more about the negative patterns that arise in IG communication, go to "How Ageism Affects Intergenerational Communication."

Thinking Prompt: What expectations and assumptions do you have of younger adults? Why?

Inclusive Language / Communication.

Instead of:

- Age absolutes, such as "old," "young," "youth"
- Older terms commonly used to address young adults (not young children), like "gal," "young/little lady," "girl," "boy," "missy," "youngster," "you kids"
- Generalizations or stereotypes that younger people are "overly sensitive," "entitled," "lazy"
- Age-based descriptions (even if a compliment) such as "You're so young and beautiful," "You're mature for your age," "You have an old soul"

Try:

- Using relational language, such as "younger/older adults"
- "Person(s) aged (age or age range)"
- Using "I" or "we" statements to describe what you're feeling in relation to the behavior of a specific younger adult
- Thinking about what you're really trying to describe— "You look very nice," "You seem grounded," "You have calm energy"

Race

For Younger Adults.

Microaggressions. Acts of "subtle" racism that reinforce racial stereotypes and inequitable social norms, and are not dependent on intent or perception. The unconscious or conscious justification of microaggressions comes from the acceptance of widely shared racial stereotypes that contribute to inequality and oppression. They are context based and not defined by specific actions.

Examples:

- Negative statements. "Asians are bad drivers."

- Seemingly positive statements. "Black people are good at basketball."
- Assumptions that someone is not a true American. "Where are you really from?"
- Statements that convey color blindness or deny the importance of race. "All lives matter" or "I don't see race."

For more examples and explanation, go to "Examples of Racial Microaggressions."

Microaggressions are harmful to BIPOC (Black, Indigenous, people of color) persons' physical and mental health. Research shows that microaggressions cause more harm than blatant racism. The detriments include but are not limited to increased rates of anxiety, depression, and suicide.

To learn more, go to "The Effects of Microaggressions."

Experiences of Older Brown and Black Folks.

- Older BIPOC adults' experiences with the combination of ageism and racism contribute to higher rates of major depression, poor physical health, and function limitations. Due to a history of discrimination in health care and cultural norms within BIPOC communities, BIPOC older adults are also less likely to access mental health resources.
- This makes intergenerational connection all the more important for those who identify with the BIPOC communities. Research shows that older BIPOC adults having involvement with other BIPOC groups and specifically older LGBTQ BIPOC adults feeling bonded with other members of the LGBTQ community improves self-reported happiness and health.
- Try to keep these factors in mind when communicating with older BIPOC adults, because mental health influences how we communicate.

To learn more, go to "Race, Ethnicity, and Age as Contributors to Mental Health."

Communication Strategies and Language.

Try using contemporary racial and ethnic group terms:

- "Asian," "American Asian and Pacific Islander (AAPI)," "Black," "African American," "white"
- Hispanic/Latinx/Latino/Latina
- "People who identify with more than one race" or "people of more than one race"
- If possible, identify a person or group by their specific tribal affiliation (Navajo, Lenape, etc.); if not possible, you could say, "American Indian, Native American, or Alaska Native persons/communities/populations"
- If a group or person is affiliated with multiple tribes, you could use the terms "tribal communities/populations" or "Indigenous communities/populations"

There is some uncertainty and discourse around using the term "American Indian" vs "Native American," and there is no one "correct" term. It depends on preference, and, if appropriate, you can respectfully ask someone what term they use.

For Older Adults.

Microaggressions. Acts of "subtle" racism that reinforce racial stereotypes and inequitable social norms, and are not dependent on intent or perception. The unconscious or conscious justification of microaggressions comes from the acceptance of widely shared racial stereotypes that contribute to inequality and oppression. They are context based and not defined by specific actions.

Examples:

- Negative statements. "Asians are bad drivers."
- Seemingly positive statements. "Black people are good at basketball."
- Assumptions that someone is not a true American. "Where are you really from?"
- Statements that convey color blindness or deny the importance of race. "All lives matter" or "I don't see race."

For more examples and explanation, go to "Examples of Racial Microaggressions."

Microaggressions are harmful to BIPOC (Black, Indigenous, people of color) persons' physical and mental health. Research shows that microaggressions cause more harm than blatant racism. The detriments include but are not limited to increased rates of anxiety, depression, and suicide.

To learn more, go to "The Effects of Microaggressions."

Try to avoid generalizations about any racial, ethnic, or cultural population. Before you say or do something, check yourself and see if what you're doing is from a place of bias and could be a microaggression.

Race and Mental Health. Younger generations experience higher rates of mental health issues. BIPOC young adults face more difficulties with mental health and are less likely to use professional psychological or mental health services. They are more likely to seek support from their community, making intergenerational connections all the more important.

To learn more, go to "Race, Ethnicity, and Age as Contributors to Mental Health."

Communication Strategies and Language.

Instead of:

- Referring to people by a race/ethnicity in the plural.
- Referring to Indigenous people of North America as "Native Americans," "American Indians," or "Indians"
- Referring to BIPOC persons as "people/communities of color"
- Using historically racist, generalizing, or harmful ethnicity/racial group terms
- "The (racial/ethnic) community" ("the Black community," "the mixed community")
- Generalizations rooted in racial bias and stereotypes

Try using contemporary racial and ethnic group terms:

- "Asian," "American Asian and Pacific Islander (AAPI)," "Black," "African American," "white"
- Hispanic/Latinx/Latino/Latina
- "People who identify with more than one race" or "people of more than one race"

If possible, identify a person or group by their specific tribal affiliation (Navajo, Lenape, etc.); if not possible, you could say, "American Indian, Native American, or Alaska Native persons/communities/populations"

///

Gender

For Younger Adults.

Pronouns. If you are unfamiliar with ideas around gender and how to use pronouns, you can refer to the adjacent column. There is absolutely nothing wrong with wanting/needing to understand gender information as a younger adult; this referral is in an effort to save space.

Sharing your pronouns when introducing yourself (or making a name tag) is a great way to prompt others to share pronouns and become comfortable around sharing and using pronouns.

Patience is the best way to help everyone feel welcomed and respected.

Gender-Related Ageism. Many older people have experienced life with more traditional gender norms and been treated as such by others. It's important to respect the views and experiences of anyone around their gender. Internalized ageism works in combination with gender stereotypes for older people. Rates of some of the key detrimental effects of ageism are higher for different genders.

- More older women live alone

- Older men have higher rates of suicide and substance abuse

Communication Strategies and Language.

Instead of:

- Using gendered ageist terms, such as "grandma" or "grandpa" (if they are not your grandparents), "old man" or "old lady," "hag," "crone"
- Assuming older adults don't understand contemporary ideas of gender
- Assuming older adults don't experience gender in a more complex way than the binary

Try:

- Referring to older adults by name and pronouns
- Remembering that every individual regardless of age has a unique experience with gender
- Considering the possibility that there may be more similarities between the two of you and your experiences with gender than you realize
- Using questions to seek understanding

Questions:

- "What does it mean to you to be a man/woman?"
- "What does your gender identity mean to you?"
- "Do you feel like you've been accepted by others for who you are as a person based on your gender?"
- "How has gender dictated your life decisions and views?"

For Younger Adults.

Contemporary ideas about gender are changing. *Sex* is a label assigned at birth based on genitals and chromosomes. *Gender* refers to the characteristics of women, men, girls, and boys that are socially constructed. This includes norms, behaviors, and roles associated with being a woman, man, girl, or boy, as well as relationships with each other. As a social construct, gender varies from society to society and can change over time.

It is now widely accepted that gender is a spectrum, not a binary. Gender is a unique experience for every individual. Gender identity is one's internal perception, experience, and label of their own gender. Gender expression refers to how a person presents their gender, including their pronouns.

Thinking Prompt: What does your gender identity mean to you? How do you express that?

Pronouns. A person's pronouns are a facet of their gender expression and are affirming to their gender identity. A person's pronouns do not always align with their gender identity, especially if they are not in a position to freely express their gender identity. You should use whatever pronouns someone has told you to use and never assume. Using the correct pronouns is a way to show respect, and studies have shown that using correct pronouns and names reduces depression and the risk of suicide.

How to use nonbinary (instead of he/she) pronouns:

- They/them. "They are a writer and wrote that book themself (or themselves)." "Those ideas are theirs." "I like both them and their ideas."
- No pronouns. "Lan is a writer and wrote that book." "Those ideas are Lan's." "I like both Lan and Lan's ideas."

Communication Strategies and Language.

Instead of:

- Asking someone's pronouns directly
- Using gendered binary language, such as he/she pronouns, "miss," "boyfriend/girlfriend," "ladies and gentlemen"
- Using generalizing and harmful gender terms, such as "transgendered/transsexual/transvestite," "biologically male/female," "genderless"
- Using gender-specific scientific labels that reduce people to their sexual reproductive organs when referring to cis people

Try:

- Sharing your own pronouns when introducing yourself
- Using gender-neutral language whenever possible, such as they/them pronouns, the person's name, "partner," "everyone," "server"
- Using accepted gender and identity terms, such as "transgender," "assigned male/female at birth (AFAB/AMAB)," "nonbinary," "gender nonconforming," "gender-fluid"

///

Sexuality

For Younger Adults.

Sexuality and Older Adults. Sexuality is a natural part of the human experience regardless of age. A component of ageism is the attitude that older adults are nonsexual and the sexuality of older adults being deemed grotesque. This is detrimental to the esteem of older adults and their relationships with their own sexualities. Older adults want their sexuality to be acknowledged and normalized; doing so could help improve mental and physical health.

Thinking Prompt: How have you viewed or talked about the sexuality of older adults in the past?

LGBTQ+ Older Adults. Conversations around queer sexuality tend to be centered around "the youth," which aligns with the ageist belief of older adults being nonsexual.

Along with other minority older adults, LGBTQ+ older adults experience higher rates of serious illness and disabilities. Many older LGBTQ+ adults have untreated mental illness and lack of professional emotional support. Older LGBTQ+ adults report getting their emotional support from friends and community.

Connecting generations of the LGBTQ+ community provides support to all queer people who feel isolated and misunderstood.

Communication Strategies and Language.

Instead of:

- Using terms that describe any "nonstraight" person as "homosexual," "MSM (men who have sex with men)," "homo"
- Using umbrella terms such as "gay," "gay community," "homos/homosexuals"
- Saying "sexual preference" (which implies someone's sexual orientation is a choice)
- Asking, "What's your sexuality?" "What's your percentage?" (i.e., to what extent they are attracted to certain genders), or "Are you gay?"

Try:

- To use specific terms of sexual identity
- To describe multiple sexual orientations with terms such as "LGBTQ, LGBTQIA, LGBTQ+, or LGBTQIA2"; "LGBTQ+ community" (to describe queer people as a population or community), "queer"
- To use "sexual orientation" or "sexuality"
- To not ask—unless it's required, relevant to the conversation, or for official purposes, you don't need to know people's sexual orientation. Sexuality is an individual and private piece of identity. Questions about sexuality may make those around you feel unsafe.

Note about the term "queer": "Queer" is a historically derogatory term. Some older adults might be uncomfortable with using the word "queer." If someone expresses concern, try to open a dialogue to seek understanding, or ask if you are unsure.

For Older Adults.

The Spectrum of Sexuality. A person's "sexual orientation" is defined as an emotional, romantic, or sexual attraction to other people. Similar to age and gender, sexuality exists on a spectrum and is unique to every individual. Sexuality is fluid. It can look different for every person and is not a stagnant part of a person's identity.

Different Sexual Identities. The range in experiences and beliefs around sexuality makes defining identities complex, but the most common term associated with referencing people who do not identify as heterosexual or cisgender is the acronym LGBTQ, which can most traditionally be defined as lesbian (women attracted to women), gay (men attracted to men), bisexual (being attracted to both men and women), transgender (this is not a sexuality and is defined in "Understanding Gender"), or queer, an umbrella term describing any gender or sexuality that is not the societal norm of being cisgender or heterosexual.

Communication Strategies and Language.

Instead of:

- Using terms that describe any "nonstraight" person as "homosexual," "MSM (men who have sex with men)," "homo"
- Using umbrella terms such as "gay," "gay community," "homos/homosexuals"
- Saying "sexual preference" (which implies someone's sexual orientation is a choice)
- Asking, "What's your sexuality?" "What's your percentage?" (i.e., to what extent they are attracted to certain genders), or "Are you gay?"

Try:

- To use specific terms of sexual identity
- To describe multiple sexual orientations with terms such as "LGBTQ, LGBTQIA, LGBTQ+, or LGBTQIA2"; "LGBTQ+ community" (to describe queer people as a population or community), "queer"
- To use "sexual orientation" or "sexuality"
- To not ask—unless it's required, relevant to the conversation, or for official purposes, you don't need to know people's sexual orientation. Sexuality is an indi-

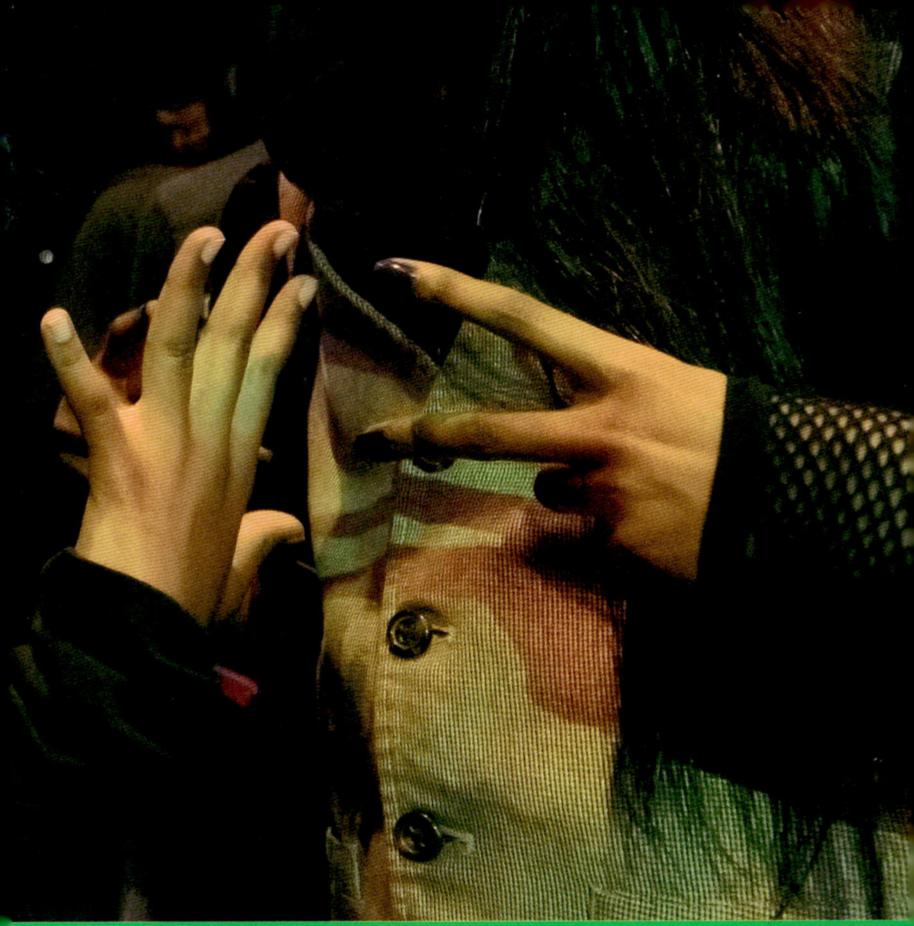

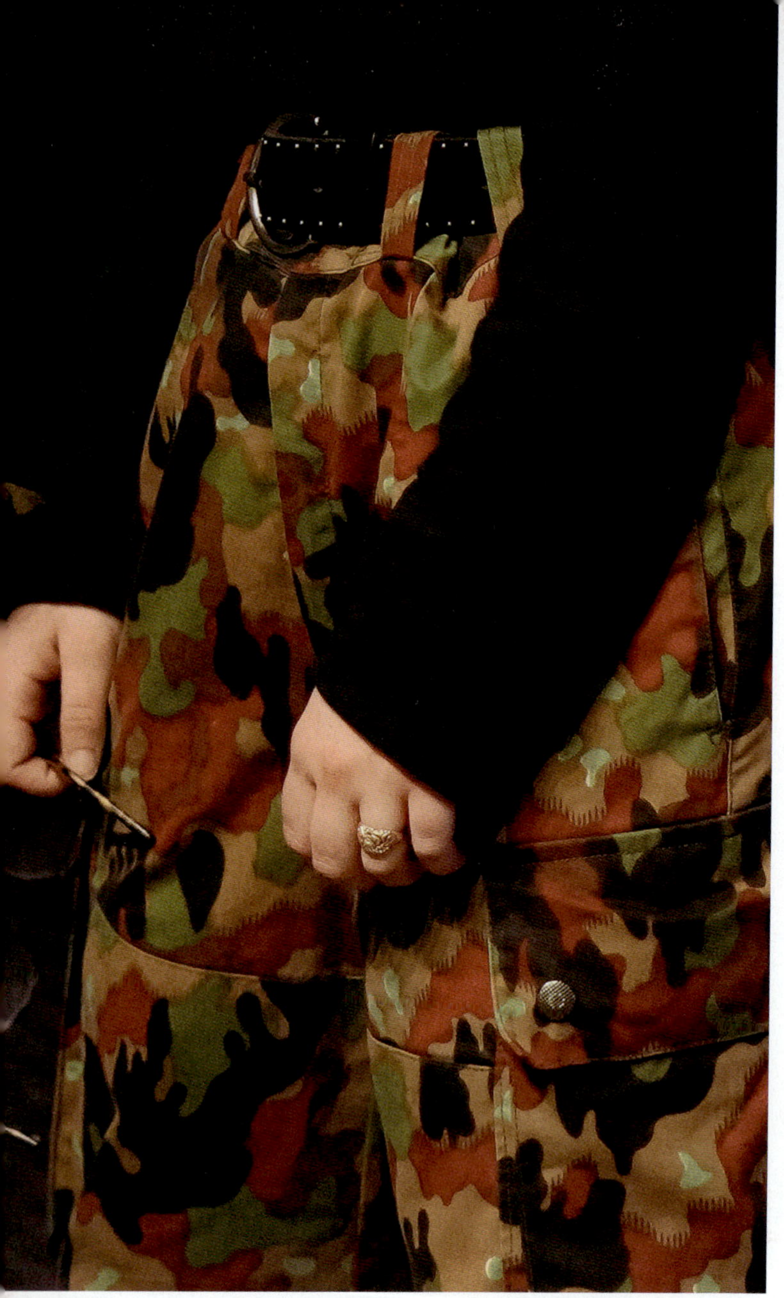

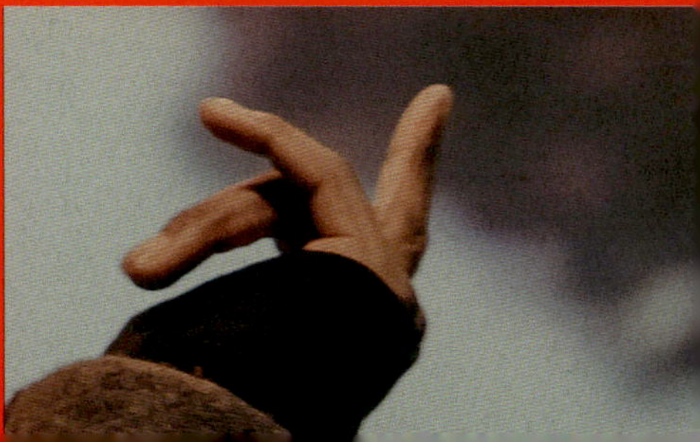

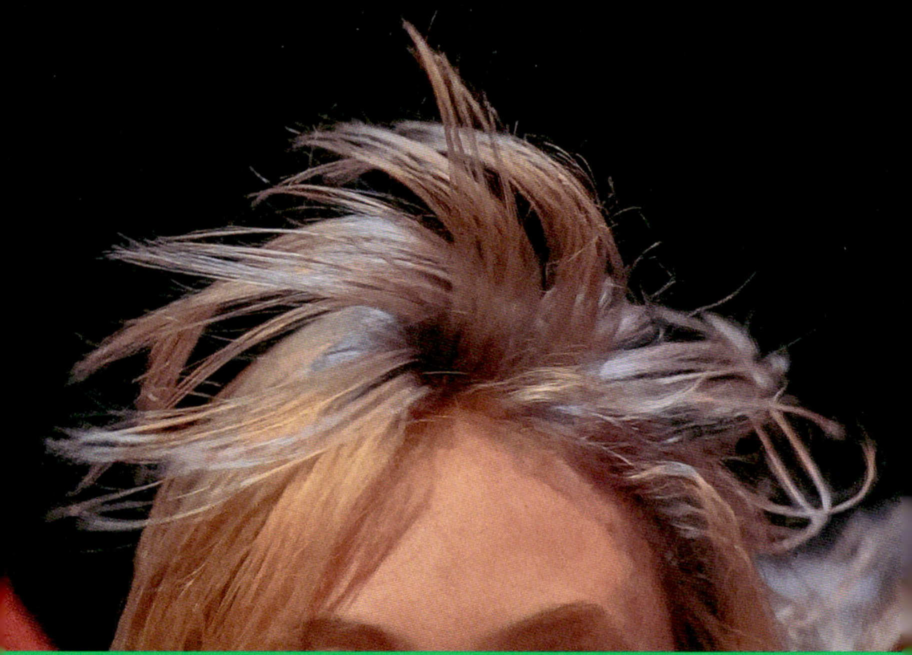

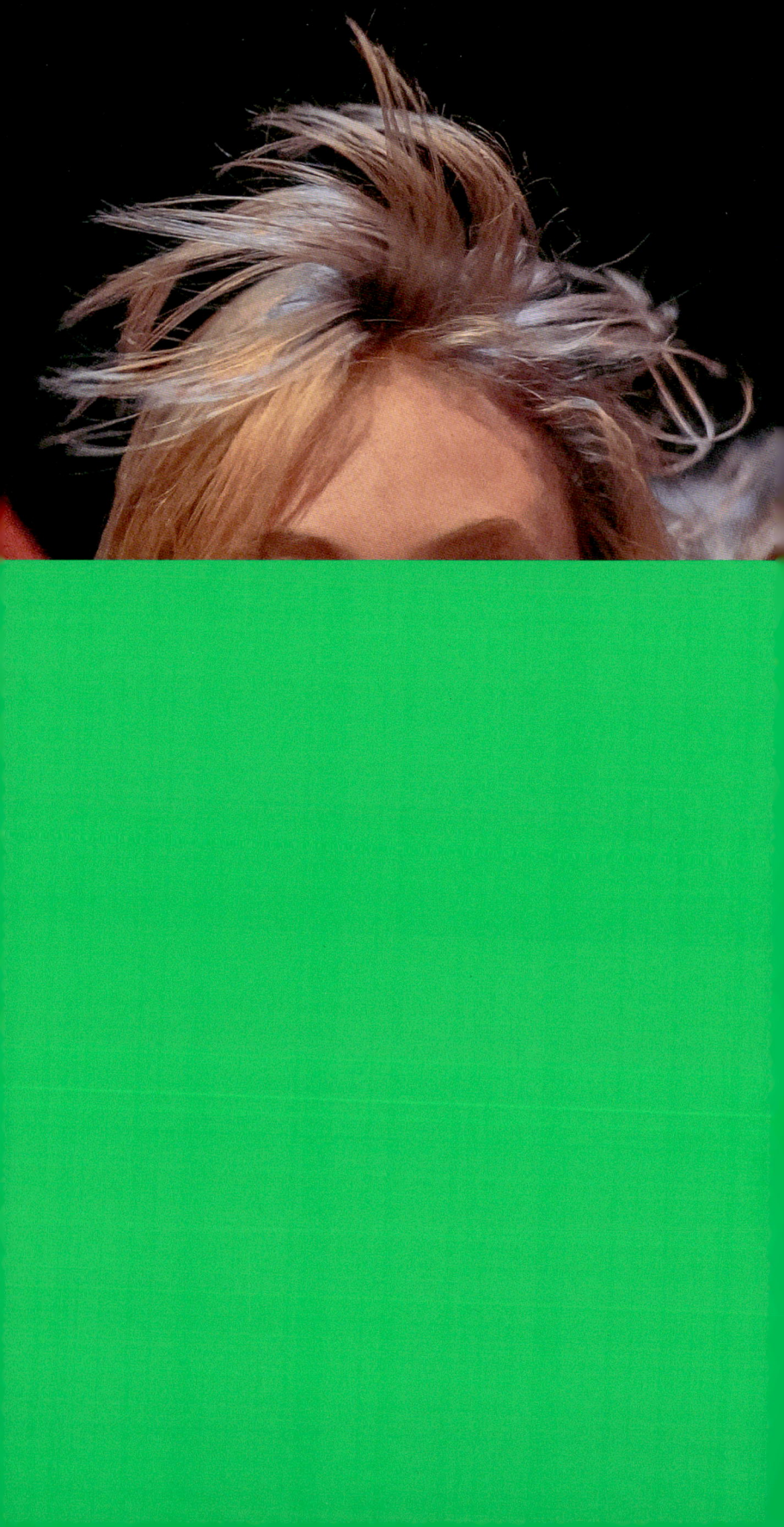

vidual and private piece of identity. Questions about sexuality may make those around you feel unsafe.

Note about the term "queer": "Queer" is a historically derogatory term. If you are uncomfortable with the use of that term, please express your concerns and open a dialogue to seek understanding.

Physical Diversity

For Younger Adults.

Physical Disabilities.

- Very generally, disability is another binary construct: abled verses disabled.
- The concept of disability is imposed upon people by an oppressive social and institutional structure. The difficulties faced by those of physical diversity are a result of these structures, not of the actual physical differences or "disabilities."
- Consider the possibility that a person is not disabled but that the world around them has not been designed to include them.

Physical Diversity in Older Adults.

Avoid:

- Patronizing language or talking down
- Binary language such as "normal," "able-bodied"
- Overcompensatory language such as "So strong for your age," "Still so lively"
- Referencing "impairment" as a constant, which implies that something is objectively wrong with a person's body, in relation to a person's disability or not
- Using the terms "disabled," "differently abled" "afflicted," "handicapped," "confined to a wheelchair" or "wheelchair bound," or "special needs"

- Using gendered and perceived beauty standard terms such as "pretty" or "handsome," "skinny," "thin," "slender," "fit," "curvy," "heavy," "fat," "larger"
- Phrases like "suffers from," which suggest a sense of hopelessness

Try:

- Using a normal tone and volume of voice
- Person-first language, such as "person with a disability"
- Assuming someone is capable unless shown or told otherwise
- Asking questions if you are unsure about someone's capabilities, such as "I notice you're wearing a hearing aid—is there anything I can do to make sure that you catch everything I say?"

For Older Adults.

Body Image in Younger Adults. The same societal ageism that deems aging as nonbeautiful or grotesque also fetishizes young age, which harms the body image of youth and fuels sexual harassment of younger people. This is harmful to all genders and ages. Older adults can do their part in disrupting societal age beauty standards by not commenting on young adults' physical appearance in any relation to age. Research has shown sexualization to be correlated with eating disorders, low self-esteem, and depression, the three most common mental health issues faced by younger and older women.

Physical Disabilities. "Disability" is defined by ideas of "normal" and what it means to be able-bodied in the world. It is another form of structural discrimination and exclusion. The difficulties faced by those with disabilities are a result of a narrow definition of "capable" human bodies, and the failure of a world designed for this narrow range.

Avoid:

- Patronizing or talking down to someone because of their physical differences

- Assuming an understanding of any body's lived experience
- Assuming that physical differences correlate to mental incapacity
- Referring to differences as "impairments"
- Using the terms "disabled," "differently abled" "afflicted," "handicapped," "confined to a wheelchair" or "wheelchair bound," or "special needs"
- Phrases like "suffers from," which suggest a sense of hopelessness
- Commenting on any part of a person's body or physical appearance if unnecessary
- Using gendered and perceived beauty standard terms such as "pretty" or "handsome," "skinny," "thin," "slender," "fit," "curvy," "heavy," "fat," "larger"

Try:

- Person-first language, such as "person with a disability"
- Assuming full autonomy of every body unless otherwise expressed
- Asking questions if you are unsure about someone's capabilities, such as "I notice you're wearing a hearing aid—is there anything I can do to make sure that you catch everything I say?"
- Speaking in a regular tone of voice

Mental Health

For Younger Adults.

Anxiety, Depression, Isolation, and Loneliness. As people age, they lose loved ones, and their social networks can naturally shrink. About a third of people over the age of seventy-five live alone, and half of women over seventy-five live alone.

Poor mental health in older adults is often undiagnosed. Loneliness and isolation contribute to mental health and have been shown to increase rates of anxiety and depression as well as other physical health issues. Research has shown that older adults who engage in their community have lower risks of dementia and depression.

Communication Language.

Instead of:

- Using the terms "crazy," "insane," "psycho," "looney," "screw loose," "nuts," "freak"
- Referring to someone with a known mental illness as "mentally ill" or "having a mental defect"
- Referring to health-center-based resources as "insane asylum" or "psych ward"
- Using mental illness/health terminology to describe emotions not associated to a disorder, such as "depressed," "OMG I'm so manic," "I'm so OCD about these things," "I'm so bipolar," "That's so ADD of me"
- Labeling/diagnosing other's emotions or behaviors, as in "That person is a sociopath/a narcissist/anorexic/bipolar/ADD/OCD"

Try:

- Describing someone's behavior with the emotions/characteristics they seem to be displaying, such as "eccentric," "angry," "upset," "confused," "energetic"
- Using person-first language, such as "people with a mental illness," "a person with depression," "someone who has an anxiety disorder"
- Referring to health center resources as "treatment centers," "a psychiatric hospital/facility"
- Using terminology not associated with a mental illness or behavioral disorder that accurately describes what you're feeling, such as "energetic," "sad," "detail oriented," "nervous," "stressed"

A note on "crazy" and "insane" to describe contexts: These terms are often used in a derogatory manner and imply there to be a version of reality or emotional state that is "normal." Instead of "crazy," an unexpected moment or experience can be "surprising," "unexpected," "thrilling," "out of the ordinary," "bananas," "unique," "exciting," "overwhelming," "scary."

For Older Adults.

Anxiety, Depression, Isolation, and Loneliness. Younger adults (ages eighteen to twenty-four) have the highest rates of loneliness. Loneliness and isolation have been shown to increase rates of anxiety and depression, as well as other physical health issues.

Speaking to Younger Adults with Mental Health Issues. In younger adults, signs of serious and concerning mental or emotional distress are often dismissed as "hormones" or the "dramatic emotions of young age." Many young people are also often in familial or financial situations that constrain their access to mental health resources.

Mental health can affect how younger people interpret social cues and interpret the words spoken to them. Often without conscious intent, younger adults with mental health struggles can feel attacked or interpret communication from older adults as confrontational or threatening, especially those with trauma.

Instead of confronting a younger adult about a problem in front of a group, try speaking to them one-on-one.

Communication Language.

Instead of:

- Using the terms "crazy," "insane," "psycho," "looney," "screw loose," "nuts," "freak"
- Referring to someone with a known mental illness as "mentally ill" or "having a mental defect"
- Referring to health-center-based resources as "insane asylum" or "psych ward"
- Using mental illness/health terminology to describe emotions not associated to a disorder, such as "depressed," "OMG I'm so manic," "I'm so OCD

about these things," "I'm so bipolar," "That's so ADD of me"
- Labeling/diagnosing other's emotions or behaviors, as in "That person is a sociopath/a narcissist/anorexic/bipolar/ADD/OCD"

Try:

- Describing someone's behavior with the emotions/characteristics they seem to be displaying, such as "eccentric," "angry," "upset," "confused," "energetic"
- Using person-first language, such as "people with a mental illness," "a person with depression," "someone who has an anxiety disorder"
- Referring to health center resources as "treatment centers," "a psychiatric hospital/facility"
- Using terminology not associated with a mental illness or behavioral disorder that accurately describes what you're feeling, such as "energetic," "sad," "detail-oriented," "nervous," "stressed"

Walker Art Center
Board of Trustees
2022–2023

Executive Director
Mary Ceruti

President
Seena Hodges

Vice Presidents
Karen Heithoff
D. Ellen Wilson

Treasurer
Sarah Lynn Oquist

Secretary
Pilar Oppedisano

Public Members
Mark Addicks
Simone Ahuja
Carlo Bronzini Vender
John Christakos
Patrick J. Denzer
Andrew S. Duff
Dayna Frank
Mark Greene
Daniel Grossman, MD
Lili Hall
Chris Haqq
Anne Labovitz
Valerie Lemaine, MD
Muffy MacMillan
David Moore Jr.
Vikesh Nemani
Joan Nolan
Michael Peterman
Brian Pietsch
Charlie Pohlad
Teresa Rasmussen
Peter Remes
Brian A. Rice
Keith Rivers
Joel Ronning
Wim Stocks
Jeffrey Swinton
Christine Walker
John P. Whaley
Houston White
Susan White
Robin M. Wright

Walker Family Members
Ann W. Cadwalader
Ann Hatch
Jean K. Walker Lowell
Adrian Walker

Honorary Trustees
H. B. Atwater Jr.
Ralph Burnet
Roger Hale
Erwin Kelen
Lawrence Perlman
Steve Shank

National Advisory Board
John Dayton
Martha Gabbert
Jeanne Levitt
John Pappajohn
Donna Pohlad
Mary and Dick Payne
Robert and Rebecca Pohlad
Lois and John Rogers
Judy and Steve Shank
Marge and Irv Weiser
Audrey Wilf
Margaret Wurtele

Walker Art Center Staff
February 2023

A

Rahma Ajaraam, Gallery Assistant
Matthew Allen, Gallery Assistant
Savior Allen-Knight, Sales Associate
Asli Altay, Head of Content and Communications
Alycia Anderson, Associate Director, Annual Fund and Membership
Kristen Andring, Visitor Experience Box Office and Admissions Manager
Kate Arford, Design Studio Manager
Justin Ayd, Projectionist/Film Specialist

B

Ian Babineau, Graphic Designer
Mikile Baker, Youth Programs Coordinator
Alyssa Banks, Visitor Experience Manager
Nicholas Barker, Overnight Guard
David Bartley, Senior Registration Technician
Beryl Belmonte, Gallery Assistant
Doug Benidt, Associate Curator, Performing Arts
Mark Berg, Prospect Research and Management Associate
Carol Bessler, Gallery Assistant
Kerstin Beyer Lajuzan, Director of Annual Giving and Donor Stewardship

Philip Bither, Senior Curator, Performing Arts
Ella Bjork, Gallery Assistant
Andrew Bogard, Design Fellow
Heather Bradley, Annual Fund Coordinator
Scott Browning, Gallery Assistant
Roman Buck, Gallery Assistant
Savannah Bustillo, Lead Educator
Caroline Byrd, Donor Relations Associate

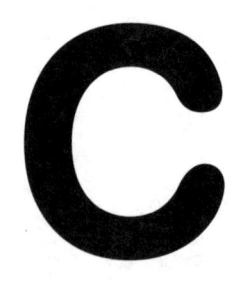

C

Alexandra Callais, Chief Guard
Mary Ceruti, Executive Director
Naomi Crocker, Manager of Director's Office and Strategic Initiatives
Kevin Curran, Gift Officer
Doc Czypinski, Associate Director, Exhibition Installation

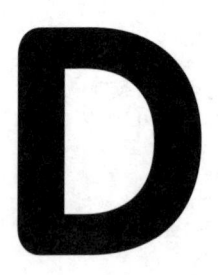

D

Ava DeShazer, Gallery Assistant
David Dick, Exhibition Carpentry Specialist
Mikha Dominguez, Educator
Jhoselin Dominguez, Gallery Assistant
Hanna Dougherty, Gallery Assistant
Donna Dralle, Gallery Assistant
Lilly Drew, Gallery Assistant
Megan Dunn, Gift Officer
Randolph Durbin, Overnight Supervisor

E

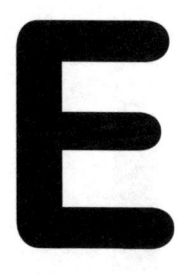

Judy Earl, Gallery Assistant
Barbara Economon, Visual Resources Specialist
Emily Eicher, Gallery Assistant
Ryan Ellingson, Event Tech Coordinator
Siri Engberg, Senior Curator and Director of Visual Arts
Darren Erickson, Desktop Administrator

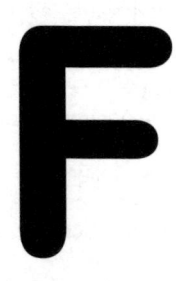

F

Claudius Faciana-Smith, Gallery Assistant
David Fallon, Gallery Assistant
Catt Fear, Gallery Assistant
Roman Feldhahn, Educator
Makenzie Flom, Department Coordinator, Moving Image
Paris Fobbe, Gallery Assistant
William Franklin, Educator
Ana Freeberg, Visitor Experience Associate

G

Richard Gangelhoff, Gallery Assistant
Sidney Gasner, Gallery Assistant
Nia-Symonne Gayle, Visitor Experience Associate
Deborah Girdwood, Program Manager, Moving Image
Matthew Goldencrown, Server Administrator
Hannah Goldfarb, PR and Marketing Coordinator
Nathan Gould, Director of Marketing and Public Relations
Ricky Graham, Lead Sales Associate
John Greenwald, Gallery Assistant
Jon Grippen, Chief Guard
Atigula Gul, Gallery Assistant

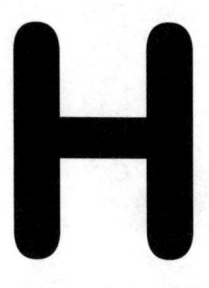

H

Anna Haglin, Lead Educator
Jessica Hakala, Department Coordinator, PELI
Peter Hannah, Lead Preparator and Minneapolis Sculpture Garden Project Manager
Molly Hanse, Department Administrator and Curatorial Assistant, Performing Arts
Michael Hansen, Visitor Experience Lead Associate
Christopher Harrison, Gallery Assistant
Wyatt Heatherington Tilka, Production Manager
Carolyn Hernandez, Gallery Assistant
William Hernández Luege, Curatorial Assistant, Visual Arts
Kameron Herndon, Image Specialist
Ellie Hohulin, Digital Content Creator
Kim Hollingsworth Taylor, Chief Financial Officer
Brian Huddleston, Graphic Designer
Daniel Hughes, Lead Gallery Assistant
Henriette Huldisch, Chief Curator and Director of Curatorial Affairs

Amanda Hunt, Head of Public Engagement, Learning and Impact

I

J

Hussein Jama, Control Guard
Ji Jang, Gallery Assistant
Taylor Jasper, Assistant Curator, Visual Arts
Pamela Johnson, Senior Editor
Chris Joiner, Chief Guard
Rachel Joyce, Associate Director of Public Relations
Leif Jurgensen, Tessitura Administrator

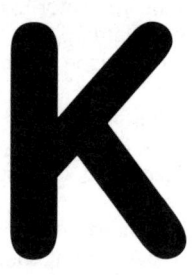

K

Jonathan Karen, Lead Preparator
Morgan Kavanagh, Educator
Alex Kermes, Installation Support Technician
Joe King, Director of Collections and Exhibitions Management
Jon Kirchhofer, Lighting Supervisor
Flora Klein, Gallery Assistant
Lilly Knopf, Lead Educator

Courtney Kowalke, Overnight Guard
Ashley Kronebusch, Gallery Assistant

L

Charles LaBerge, Chief Guard
Sarah Lampen, Manager of Lifelong Learning and Accessibility
Steve Landmesser, Manager of Security
Samuel Larom, Visitor Experience Lead Associate
Megan Leafblad, Manager of Public Engagement
Morgan Lee, Education Programs Coordinator
Rahsaan Lee, Visitor Experience Associate
Michael Lind, Collections Management Coordinator
John Lindell, Manager, Operations Administration
Douglas Livesay, Audio Engineer
Lanka Liyanapathiranage, Lead Educator
John Lyon, Cataloging Librarian

M

Carly Madigan, Gallery Assistant
Jaidyn Martin, Director of Human Resources
Michelle Maser, Visitor Experience Specialist Volunteer Coordinator
Dita Masters, Gallery Assistant
Serena Mauro-Brown, Gallery Assistant
Becca Mayo, Member Relations Coordinator

Kirk McCall, Exhibition Installation and Drafting Specialist
Rammy McKee, Visitor Experience Associate
Erin McNeil, Program Manager, Curatorial Affairs
Lena Menefee-Cook, Department Coordinator, Visual Arts
Deborah Meyer, Visitor Experience Associate
Matthew Villar Miranda, Curatorial Fellow, Visual Arts
Laura Moran, Marketing Manager
Jeff Morrison, Control Guard
Chelsea Moskal, Gift Officer
Michael Muenchow, Engineering Manager
Diane Mullen, Gallery Assistant
Peter Murphy, Exhibition Media Specialist

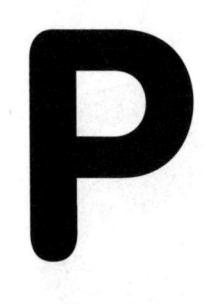

N

Myrto Neamonitaki, Lead Gallery Assistant
Cherith Nelson, Sales Associate
Kayla Nordlund, Associate Registrar
Nastja Nykaza, Installation Support Technician

O

Felicia O'Brien, Director of Business Development
Pablo de Ocampo, Director and Curator of Moving Image
Amy Oeth, Gallery Assistant
Mark Owens, Design Director and Curator

P

Jennifer Riestenberg Pepin, Assistant Librarian
Keith Parker, Director of Operations
Brielle Pizzala, Sales Associate
Michelle Poss, Gift Officer
Matthew Prediger, Development Events Associate
Angela Prictoe, Visitor Experience Specialist, Membership
Pavel Pyś, Curator, Visual Arts

Q

R

Rosa Raarup, Visitor Experience Specialist, Performing Arts
Laurel Rand-Lewis, Curatorial Fellow (Collections), Visual Arts
Tom Reed, Audience Analytics and Insights
Evan Reiter, Registration Technician
Wallace Rice, Gallery Assistant
Janie Ritter, Educator
Aaron Robinson, Stage Supervisor
Tara Robinson, Lead Gallery Assistant
Jessica Rolland, Registrar

Mark Rusch, Accounting Associate

S

Hadi Saleh, Gallery Assistant
Hanna Schindlbeck, Gallery Assistant
Tracy Shultz, Associate Director of Hospitality
Joel Schwarz, Frame Shop Supervisor
Kei Scully, Gallery Assistant
Jeffrey Sherman, Media Installation Technician
Damon Smith, Building Maintenance Assistant
Tammy Smith-Foyt, Visitor Experience Associate
Diana Soderholm, Control Guard
Lucky Sok, Retail and Sales Operations Manager
Robert Somers, Assistant Building Engineer
Tonette Sowell, Payroll and Benefits Administrator
Marla Stack, Director, Director of Special Projects Fundraising
Christopher Stevens, Chief of Advancement
Glen Straight, Gallery Assistant
Garett Strickland, Gallery Assistant
Victoria Sung, Associate Curator, Visual Arts

T

Corra Thompson, Lead Gallery Assistant

Elizabeth del Toro, Human Resources Generalist
Samantha Travis, Sales Associate

U

V

Samuel Van Fleet, Gallery Assistant
Patricia Ledesma Villon, Bentson Archivist and Assistant Curator
Julie Voigt, Senior Program Officer, Performing Arts
Krista Vosper, Gallery Assistant
Jill Vuchetich, Archivist, Head of Archives and Library

W

Kova Walker-Lecic, Assistant Registrar
Leia Wambach, Family and Access Programs Coordinator
Pierre Ware, Project Photographer
Deborah Weaver, Accountant
Cameron Wittig, Senior Project Photographer

X

Y

Jake Yuzna, Managing Content Producer

Z

Simona Zappas, Youth Programs Manager

Museum Teen Programs How-To Kit is published by the Walker Art Center, Minneapolis.

This publication is made possible with generous support from the Institute of Museum and Library Services.

INSTITUTE of Museum and Library SERVICES

First Edition
©2023 Walker Art Center

All rights reserved under pan-American copyright conventions. No part of this publication may be reproduced or utilized in any form or by any means without permission in writing from the publisher. Inquiries should be addressed to: Publications Director, Walker Art Center, 725 Vineland Place, Minneapolis, MN 55403.

Every reasonable attempt has been made to identify owners of copyright. Errors or omissions will be corrected in subsequent editions.

A Cataloguing-in-Publication record for this book is available from the Library of Congress.

Head of Content and Communications: Asli Altay
Design Director: Mark Owens
Designer: Ian Babineau
Editors: Vanessa Christensen and Dr. Kendall Crabbe
Publications Manager: Jake Yuzna
Design Studio Manager: Kate Arford
Proofreader: Annemarie Eayrs

Printed by Musumeci Spa, Italy

Typefaces: Saguaro Sans, DeVinne, Bodoni

Typeface note: Saguaro Sans was designed by Brian Huddleston. It is a loose revival of Sonoran Sans, an early version of Arial as it existed in 1984.

Papers: Munken Lynx Rough, Refutura, Magno Gloss

17

18

19

20

37

38, 39

40

57

58

59

60

C.1.

497

77

78

79

80

97

98

99

100

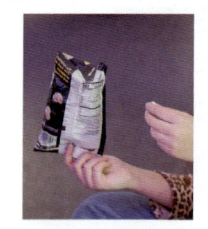

117

118

119

120

498 C.1.

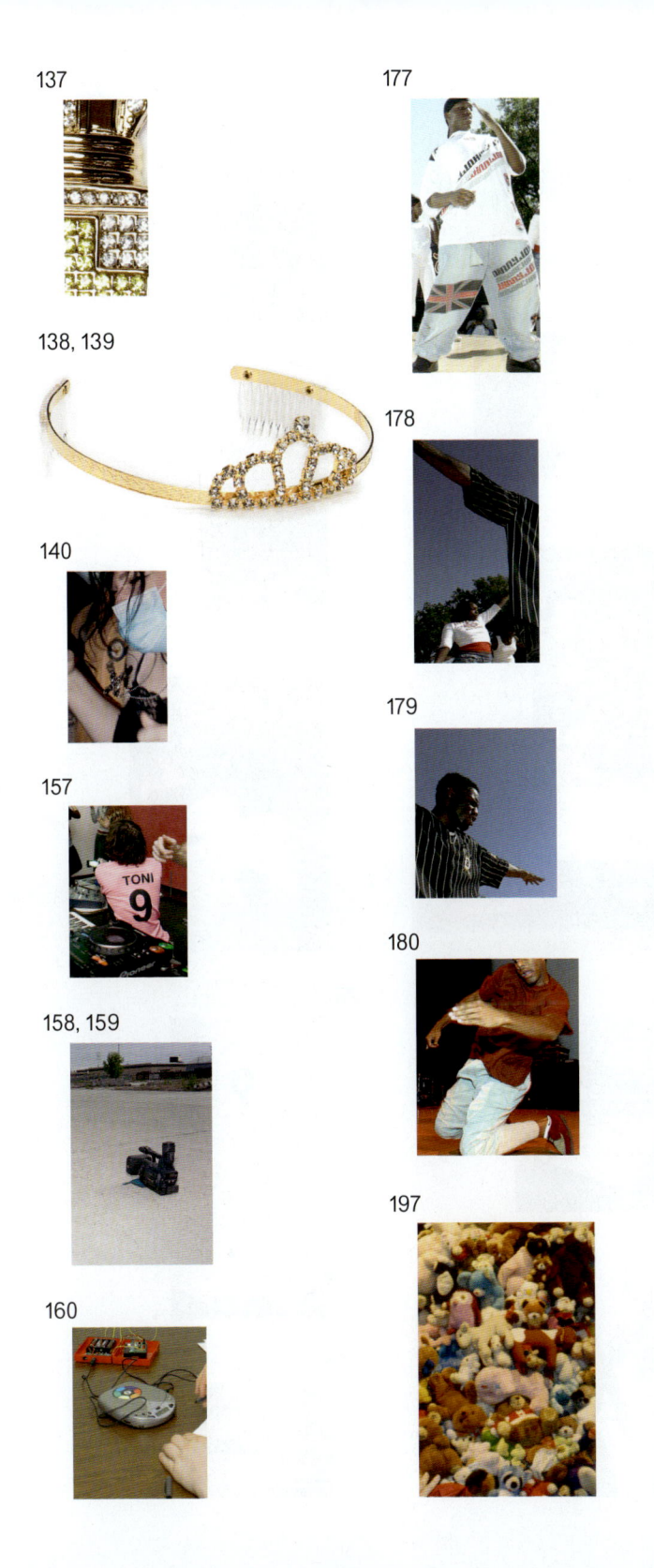

137

177

138, 139

178

140

179

157

158, 159

180

160

197

C.1. **499**

198, 199

200

217

218, 219

220

237

238

239

240

257

258

500   **C.1.**

259

260

277

278

279

280

297

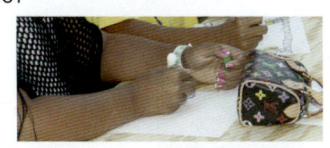

298, 299

300

317

C.1. 501

318, 319

320

337

338

339

340

357

358

359

360

377

378

502 C.1.

379

380

397

398

399

400

417

418, 419

420

437

438, 439

440

C.1.

457

458

458, 459

460

477

478

479

480

504   **C.1.**

The photo essay that appears throughout this publication contains a selection of archival images from over 30 years of Walker Art Center teen programs. A heartfelt thank-you to Jill Vuchetich, Walker Art Center archivist and head of archives and library, for generously assisting in the process of finding and contextualizing these images.

17
Materials at *Don't Sleep on It: 24-hour Art-making Marathon*, a free event co-presented by the Walker Art Center Teen Arts Council and MnArtists during the Art-A-Whirl festival, presented at the California Building in Northeast Minneapolis, 2009. Photo: Gene Pittman for Walker Art Center.

18, 19
Teens lounging in the Walker galleries at Teen Takeover, 2021. Photo: Awa Mally for Walker Art Center.

20
WACTAC member, Walker staff member at work in a Radio ReVolt workshop with artists Allora & Calzadilla, 2004. Photo: Walker staff member for Walker Art Center.

37
Portrait of the 2009 Walker Art Center Teen Arts Council, 2009. Photo: Cameron Wittig for Walker Art Center.

38, 39
Portrait of the 2013 Walker Art Center Teen Arts Council, 2013. Photo: Gene Pittman for Walker Art Center.

40
Group portrait of the 2001 Walker Art Center Teen Arts Council, 2001. Photo: Dan Dennehy for Walker Art Center.

57
Teen friends in a dancing embrace at the Teen Takeover, 2021. Photo: Awa Mally for Walker Art Center.

58, 59
Teens posing in the Walker galleries at Teen Takeover, 2021. Photo: Awa Mally for Walker Art Center.

60
Dance performance by Al Taw'am and We're Muslim Don't Panic at Teen Takeover: Where Art Thou? Presented by the Walker Art Center Teen Arts Council, 2013. Photo: Gene

77
 Exchanging mix CDs at School of Rock: The Annual Student Open House event presented by the Walker Art Center Teen Arts Council, 2009. Photo: Gene Pittman for Walker Art Center.

78, 79, 80
 Participants at Below the Belt: Battle of the Underage, a poetry battle with graffiti, beatboxing, written and slam poetry, spoken word, and video works, part of The Squared Circle: Boxing in Contemporary Art, 2003. Photo: Cameron Wittig for Walker Art Center.

97
 Members of the Walker Art Center Teen Arts Council hanging out and snacking in a meeting space, 2003. Photo: Cameron Wittig for Walker Art Center.

98, 99
 Members of the Guerrilla Girls giving a talk onstage at the Walker Art Center, 1998. Photo: Dan Dennehy for Walker Art Center.

100
 Snacks at Teen Takeover, 2019. Photo: Awa Mally for Walker Art Center.

117
 Participant at a Target Free Thursday Nights event titled Warhol Remix: Teen Multimedia Battle, 2006. Photo: Gene Pittman for Walker Art Center.

118, 119
 Crowd enjoying a video game at a Target Free Thursday Night Student Open House planned by the Walker Art Center Teen Arts Council, 2006. Photo: Gene Pittman for Walker Art Center.

120
 Participants at a Target Free Thursday Nights event titled Warhol Remix: Teen Multimedia Battle, 2006. Photo: Gene Pittman for Walker Art Center.

137
 Detail of a gold cross pendant, one of the objects from Collecting Corruption installation created and curated by the Walker Art Center Teen Arts Council, David Bartley and Matt Bakkom, 2008. Photo: Gene Pittman for Walker Art Center.

138, 139
 A gold diamond studded tiara crown, one of the objects from Collecting Corruption installation created and curated by the Walker Art Center Teen Arts Council, David Bartley and Matt Bakkom, 2008. Photo: Gene Pittman for Walker Art Center.

140
 Teens moshing to local band Kids Ski Free at Teen Takeover, 2021. Photo: Awa Mally for Walker Art Center.

157
 Teens at Student Open House: The Big Dance presented by the Walker Art Center Teen Arts Council featuring Miami-based artists Sam Borkson and Arturo Sandoval III, and DJ Talk Radio, 2007. Photo: Gene Pittman for Walker Art Center.

158, 159
 Filming at a skate video workshop from Ty Evans for teens, 2009. Photo: Gene Pittman for Walker Art Center.

160
 Work in progress at a Radio ReVolt workshop with artists Allora & Calzadilla, 2004. Photo: Gene Pittman for Walker Art Center

177, 178, 179
 Performers at the Third Annual Twin Cities Hip-Hop Festival presented by the Walker Art Center Teen Arts Council and Yo! The Movement held at a park off-site from the Walker campus, 2004. Photo: Cameron Wittig for Walker Art Center.

180
 Performer at an event for Below the Belt: Battle of the Underage, a poetry battle with graffiti, beatboxing, written and slam poetry,

spoken word, and video works, part of *The Squared Circle: Boxing in Contemporary Art*, 2003. Photo: Cameron Wittig for Walker Art Center.

197
Stuffed animal sculpture at the 1997 *Hot Art Injection (Hold Still)* exhibition, showcasing artwork, performances, and spoken word curated by WACTAC, 1997. Photo: Photographer Dan Dennehy for Walker Art Center.

198, 199
Radio made out of a Care Bear, batteries, and a chip by a Walker Art Center Teen Arts Council member in a Radio ReVolt workshop with artists Allora & Calzadilla, 2004. Photo: Walker staff member for Walker Art Center.

200
Teen-made stuffed animal created at Student Open House: It's Complicated presented by the Walker Art Center Teen Arts Council featuring artist Cali Mastny and Radio K, 2014. Photo: Courtney Perry for Walker Art Center.

217
Performers at the Third Annual Twin Cities Hip-Hop Festival presented by the Walker Art Center Teen Arts Council and Yo! The Movement held at a park off-site from the Walker campus, 2004. Photo: Cameron Wittig for Walker Art Center.

218, 219
A performer stretching onstage with some friends at the Third Annual Twin Cities Hip-Hop Festival presented by the Walker Art Center Teen Arts Council and Yo! The Movement held at a park off-site from the Walker campus, 2004. Photo: Cameron Wittig for Walker Art Center.

220
Performers and audience members at the Third Annual Twin Cities Hip-Hop Festival presented by the Walker Art Center Teen Arts Council and Yo! The Movement held at a park off-site from the Walker campus, 2004. Photo: Cameron Wittig for Walker Art Center.

237
Graffiti artist at the Third Annual Twin Cities Hip-Hop Festival presented by the Walker Art Center Teen Arts Council and Yo! The Movement held at a park off-site from the Walker campus, 2004. Photo: Cameron Wittig for Walker Art Center.

238, 239
Members of the Guerrilla Girls giving an artist talk on *Bitches, Bimbos and Ballbreakers: The Guerrilla Girls' Illustrated Guide to Female Stereotypes*, as part of the Walker Art Center Teen Arts Council presented Picture Day: Student Open House, 2003. Photo: Cameron Wittig for Walker Art Center.

240
Denim fashion at the Teen Programs Alumni Holiday Party, December 19, 1997. Photo: Dan Dennehy.

257
Teens posing and participating in a free pop-up photo studio and gallery workshop led by local photographer Galen Fletcher, 2019. Photo: Galen Fletcher for Walker Art Center.

258, 259
Teens in a dance party in the Walker's freight elevator as part of the Student Open House: Happenings, a collaboration with artist Andy DuCett, inspired by Walker Art Center exhibition *Claes Oldenburg: The Sixties*, 2013. Photo: Gene Pittman for Walker Art Center.

260
A playset from *The Little Mermaid*, 1989, part of the *Collecting Corruption* installation created and curated by the Walker Art Center Teen Arts Council, David Bartley and Matt Bakkom, 2008. Photo: Gene

Pittman for Walker Art Center.

277
Models posing at the Walker Un-Prom: Not Yo Mama's Formal, 2006. Photo: Gene Pittman for Walker Art Center.

278
Makeup being applied to a model at the Walker Un-Prom: Not Yo Mama's Formal, 2006. Photo: Gene Pittman for Walker Art Center.

279, 280
Model posing at the Walker Un-Prom: Not Yo Mama's Formal, 2006. Photo: Gene Pittman for Walker Art Center.

297
Attendees making art at the Third Annual Twin Cities Hip-Hop Festival presented by the Walker Art Center Teen Arts Council and Yo! The Movement held at a park off-site from the Walker campus, 2004. Photo: Cameron Wittig for Walker Art Center.

298, 299
Dance group New Black City, taking a bow at the Fall 2018 Teen Takeover event presented by the Walker Art Center Teen Arts Council, 2018. Photo: Carina Lofgren for Walker Art Center.

300
A pose in the elevator at Teen Takeover, 2019. Photo: Awa Mally for Walker Art Center.

317
Teens moshing to local band Bugsy, at Teen Takeover, 2019. Photo: Awa Mally for Walker Art Center.

318, 319, 320
Teens moshing and crowd surfing to local band Bugsy, at Teen Takeover, 2019. Photo: Awa Mally for Walker Art Center.

337
A teen catching a breath between songs in the mosh pit at Teen Takeover, 2019. Photo: Awa Mally for Walker Art Center.

338
Smiling friends at Teen Takeover, 2019. Photo: Awa Mally for Walker Art Center.

339
In the pit at Teen Takeover, 2019. Photo: Awa Mally for Walker Art Center.

340
Screaming with joy at the the Fall 2019 Teen Takeover event presented by the Walker Art Center Teen Arts Council, 2018. Photo: Awa Mally for Walker Art Center.

357
Performers onstage at the Youth Showcase, a Target Free Thursday Night event put on by the Walker's Performing Arts, Education and Community Programs, and Teen Programs teams, featuring young local spoken-word and video artists created during the residencies of Marc Bamuthi Joseph and Eli Jacobs Fantauzzi, 2008. Photo: Gene Pittman for Walker Art Center.

358
Walker Art Center Teen Arts Council members planting a cottonwood tree in the Minneapolis Sculpture Garden as part of independent curator Todd Bockley's *7,000 Oaks Minneapolis project*, 1997. Photo: Dan Dennehy for Walker Art Center.

359, 360
DIY Duct Tape designs at the 1997 *Hot Art Injection (Hold Still)* exhibition, showcasing artwork, performances, and spoken word curated by WACTAC, 1997. Photo: Photographer unknown for Walker Art Center.

377
The center of the dance floor at the Fall 2018 Teen Takeover event presented by the Walker Art Center Teen Arts Council, 2018. Photo: Carina Lofgren for Walker Art Center.

378
Dance group New Black City performing at the Fall 2018 Teen

Takeover event presented by the Walker Art Center Teen Arts Council, 2018. Photo: Carina Lofgren for Walker Art Center.

379
A gas can, part of the *Collecting Corruption* installation created and curated by the Walker Art Center Teen Arts Council, David Bartley and Matt Bakkom, 2008. Photo: Gene Pittman for Walker Art Center.

380
Dance group New Black City performing at the Fall 2018 Teen Takeover event presented by the Walker Art Center Teen Arts Council, 2018. Photo: Carina Lofgren for Walker Art Center.

397
Teens in construction gear as part of the Student Open House: Happenings, a collaboration with artist Andy DuCett, inspired by Walker Art Center exhibition *Claes Oldenburg: The Sixties*, 2013. Photo: Gene Pittman for Walker Art Center.

398
A 2001 World's Best Company award for Enron, part of the *Collecting Corruption* installation created and curated by the Walker Art Center Teen Arts Council, David Bartley and Matt Bakkom, 2008. Photo: Gene Pittman for Walker Art Center.

399
Participants and projections at WAC ATTACK: Imagine Lands, an experimental art-making event presented by the Walker Art Center Teen Arts Council and Jenny Schmid, 2011. Photo: Cameron Wittig for Walker Art Center.

400
Costumed performer at March of Madness: Bands on the Run! A part parade, part progressive party, part rock festival, city-wide scavenger hunt by the Walker Art Center Teen Arts Council and Michael Gaughan, 2007. Photo: Cameron Wittig for Walker Art Center.

417, 418, 419, 420
Teens trading CDs at School of Rock: The Annual Student Open House event presented by the Walker Art Center Teen Arts Council, 2009. Photo: Gene Pittman for Walker Art Center.

437
Teen in the midst of an important task at the Walker Art Center Teen Arts Council TASK Party, a project designed by New-York based artist Oliver Herring, 2011. Photo: Cameron Wittig for Walker Art Center.

438, 439
Radio made out of traffic cones, batteries, and a chip by a Walker Art Center Teen Arts Council member in a Radio ReVolt workshop with artists Allora & Calzadilla, 2004. Photo: Walker staff member for Walker Art Center.

440
It's a slug vibe. Meme produced by 2021–2022 WACTAC member Patrick Burns for the @walkerteens Instagram account, 2022. Photo: Patrick Burns for Walker Art Center.

457
Teen Takeover attendee with their arms full of decorations, 2021. Photo: Awa Mally for Walker Art Center.

458, 459
Friends at the Spring 2018 Teen Takeover event presented by the Walker Art Center Teen Arts Council, 2018. Photo: Bobby Rogers for Walker Art Center.

460
DJ at Below the Belt: Battle of the Underage, a poetry battle with graffiti, beatboxing, written and slam poetry, spoken word, and video works, part of *The Squared Circle: Boxing in Contemporary Art*, 2003. Photo: Cameron Wittig for Walker Art Center.

477
Teens showing off their nails at

Teen Takeover, 2021. Photo: Awa Mally for Walker Art Center.

478 Teen fashion at Teen Takeover, 2019. Photo: Awa Mally for Walker Art Center.

479 Performer onstage at Teen Takeover, 2019. Photo: Awa Mally for Walker Art Center.

480 Teen hair at Teen Takeover, 2019. Photo: Awa Mally for Walker Art Center.

©2023 Walker Art Center

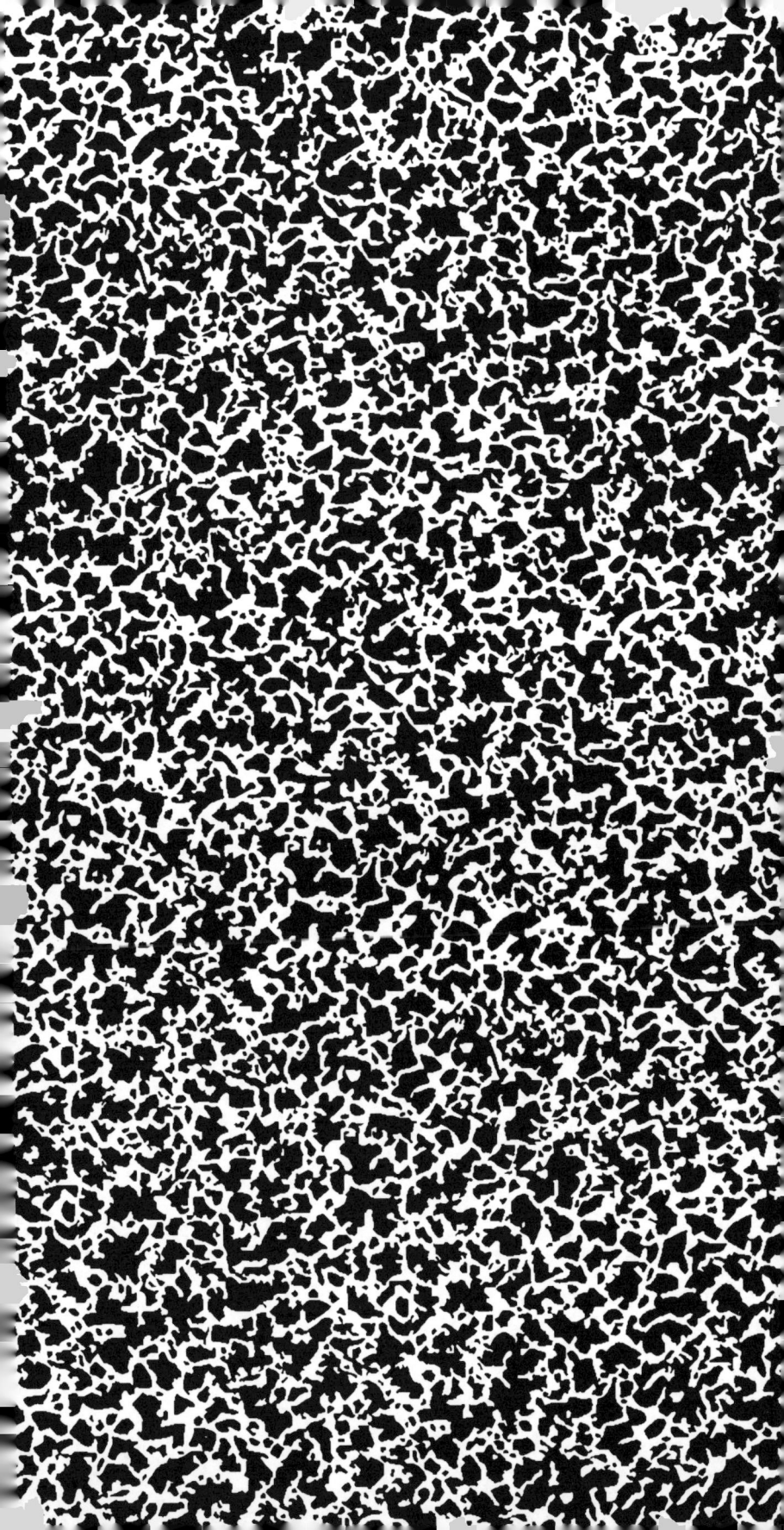